THE COMPLETE ILLUSTRATED GUIDE TO
EVERYTHING SOLD IN GARDEN CENTERS
(EXCEPT THE PLANTS)

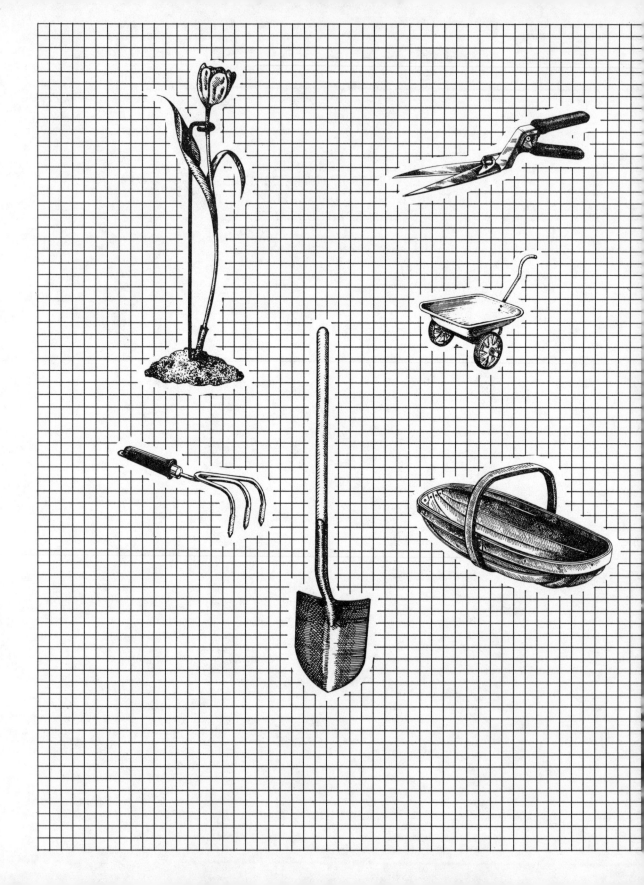

The Complete
Illustrated Guide to
EVERYTHING SOLD IN
GARDEN CENTERS
(Except the Plants)

by Steve Ettlinger

RESEARCH BY Robert S. Coleman, Brooklyn Botanic Garden

ILLUSTRATIONS BY Robert Strimban

conceived and edited by Stephen R. Ettlinger Editorial Projects

Macmillan Publishing Company   NEW YORK
Collier Macmillan Canada   TORONTO
Maxwell Macmillan International   NEW YORK OXFORD SINGAPORE SYDNEY

This book is intended only to orient the consumer to the various categories of products available. It is by no means intended to be a buying guide to specific products, and neither the author nor the publisher recommends the purchase or avoidance of any items listed here, nor do they recommend avoiding any products *not* listed here. Sample brand names appear from time to time but do not imply any endorsement of any kind.

Furthermore, neither the author nor the publisher can be held responsible for the use of any items noted within. Use tips are by their very nature incomplete and not intended to be fully instructive.

The authors or publisher cannot be responsible for any accidents caused by the tools or products described herein.

Macmillan Publishing Company
866 Third Avenue, New York, NY 10022

Collier Macmillan Canada, Inc.
1200 Eglinton Avenue East, Suite 200
Don Mills, Ontario M3C 3N1

Library of Congress Cataloging-in-Publication Data
Ettlinger, Steve.
The complete illustrated guide to everything sold in garden centers (except the plants)/ by Steve Ettlinger; research by Robert S. Coleman; illustrations by Robert Strimban; conceived and edited by Stephen R. Ettlinger Editorial Projects.
    p. cm.
ISBN 0-02-536301-8
1. Gardening—Equipment and supplies. 2. Garden tools. 3. Garden centers (Retail trade) I. Coleman, Robert S. II. Stephen R. Ettlinger Editorial Projects. III. Title.
SB454.8.E87 1990
631.3—dc20   90-5611
                                                                                      CIP

Macmillan books are available at special discounts for bulk purchases for sales promotions, premiums, fund-raising, or educational use. For details, contact:
Special Sales Director
Macmillan Publishing Company
866 Third Avenue
New York, NY 10022

10 9 8 7 6 5 4 3 2 1

PRINTED IN THE UNITED STATES OF AMERICA

This book is dedicated to all of us who appreciate knowing the difference between potting soil and topsoil, as well as between a dibble and a widger.

Acknowledgments

The principal research for this book was done by Robert S. Coleman, of the Brooklyn Botanic Garden, Brooklyn, New York. He proved to be ideally qualified for this work by his background as a professional gardener and research librarian as well as that of a dedicated and enthusiastic teacher. He also conceived the sections on garden ornaments (chapter 11) and appendix D ("Mail-Order Catalog Guide"). I gratefully acknowledge his hard work and long hours, which helped make this book happen. I am also grateful for the helpful comments made by other members of the staff of the Brooklyn Botanic Garden who reviewed the manuscript for accuracy and otherwise encouraged and helped me.

· · ·

The following organizations, individuals, and garden center personnel are among the many who were open and generous with their time and expertise, granting interviews, reviewing parts of the manuscript, providing leads for further research, or giving me run of their garden centers, without which this book would not have been possible:
Longacre's Nursery Center, Lebanon, New Hampshire; Agway Farm, Home and Garden Supplies, Holden, Massachusetts; Silver Fox Nursery, Worcester, Massachusetts; Jay Dubrofski of Midtown Garden Center, Brooklyn, New York; Fred Hicks and Vinnie Drzewucki of Hicks Garden Center, Westbury, New York; Tom Durkin of Cedar Grove Garden Center, Cedar Grove, New Jersey; Russell Ireland, Bill Simmeral, Elizabeth Stout, and Wayne Bourdette of Martin Viette Nurseries, East Norwich, New York; Bruce Butterfield of the National Gardening Association; P. Whitney Yelverton of the Fertilizer Institute; Beverly C. and Dr. Eliot C. Roberts of the Lawn Institute; the American Association of Nurserymen; the Garden Council; the Office of Pesticides and Toxic Substances, Environmental Protection Agency, Washington, D.C.; the National Pesticides Hotline; Susan Cooper of the National Coalition Against the Misuse of Pesticides (NCAMP); Melba Davis of the California Association of Nurserymen; Wally Patterson of Frank's Nursery and Crafts, Inc.; Anne W. Markle, gardener; Henry Handler, gardener; Edward Ettlinger, gardener; Alex L. Dommerich, Jr., gardener; Ann Marie Thigpen, garden ornament expert; Professor James B. Beard, Texas A & M University; and John Ameroso.

A note of thanks is due to the many garden

centers around the country which I visited anonymously, poking around the aisles while surreptitiously taking notes. I made a point to buy at least one thing on each of these visits, in case you wondered.

Thanks are due to the many different manufacturers who so kindly sent their catalogs, and a special thanks to those who also answered detailed queries for technical information over the phone. Some individuals employed by these companies provided invaluable expertise by reviewing certain parts of the manuscript. This effort went well beyond the normal range of their work, and I appreciate the time they took for this book.

The general support and enthusiasm of my colleagues at Macmillan is gratefully acknowledged, especially that of Pam Hoenig (my editor), Susan Richman, Barry Lippman, and Bill Rosen. For all those who supported my work on *The Complete Illustrated Guide to Everything Sold in Hardware Stores,* especially David Wolff, a second round of thanks. The success of that book encouraged me to work even harder on this one.

Debbie Steele and Whitney Hanscom assisted me on the error-free preparation of the final manuscript and illustrations with unflagging enthusiasm and energy.

Though this is not the kind of book that usually has strong personal roots, it should be noted that I was lucky enough to have my mother, an avid gardener (and orchidist) who was on the staff of the Chicago Botanic Garden, assist in the research and editing. Her perceptive thoughts and razor-sharp opinions helped shape the book in numerous essential ways. I was helped on my earlier book on hardware by my father, who has a wonderful affinity for the stuff. I am delighted to have their extensive contributions. More importantly, and more relevant to the journalistic approach to research required by this kind of book, my father taught me to question experts to the third degree while my mother taught me to be observant. They have both given me the urge to try to figure everything out, for which I am ever thankful and because of which I am, of course, still unsatisfied. Stand by for more books.

This book is also dedicated in part to my son, Dylan Alexander, born as this went to press, who will certainly show me a thing or two about growing. I would also like to thank and further dedicate this book to my wife, Gusty Lange, who has always supported my need to work long hours, who has amazingly accurate editorial judgment, and who inspires me in so many different ways.

Steve Ettlinger

Contents

Preface

WHY THIS BOOK

You could say that this book is the sequel to *The Complete Illustrated Guide to Everything Sold in Hardware Stores,* but that would be too simple.

However, there is no doubt that the reasons for this book are the same as for that one: All of us, at one time or another, have gone into a hardware store or garden center slightly unsure of what it is that we need and have found ourselves intimidated by the vast array of similar-looking items on the shelves. They all turn into whatchamacallits and thingamajigs. The clerks are often just not available to explain comparative points well (especially in the large self-service stores), or if they are, they may use terms that are unfamiliar. That leaves much of the decision making to you.

Most of us want to know what the difference is between the various choices we are confronted with so that we can make our own intelligent decisions, but it is all complicated by the bold claims made in the advertisements and on labels and compounded by the assertion that certain products replace all others, do everything, and do it perfectly, no less. On top of that, labeling is often inconsistent.

Furthermore, to the uninitiated, differences may not seem important. Probably the most common request a garden center clerk hears is, "I'd like some fertilizer, please." Now one thing you will learn from this book is that there is no such thing as "just plain fertilizer." Nor is there *just* a trowel—there are long and short, narrow and wide, curved and straight ones, each designed for specific uses. And when you ask for a hoe, for example, you'll most likely be offered the choice between a solid-socket or tang-and-ferrule model. Terms have to be understood and decisions made. This book will help you make those choices.

Despite all the books on gardening, there is no one book that lists all the stuff you have to buy—there are plenty of books explaining *how to,* but none saying *what with,* across the whole spectrum of products. This book was conceived to address that problem. I hope it helps you get what you need without fear of being intimidated by the daunting displays at your garden center.

—Steve Ettlinger

Introduction

ABOUT THIS BOOK

The chapters of this book correspond roughly to the areas of the front "store" sections of a typical large garden center, though there are plenty more items listed here than you would normally find there.

The chapters themselves fall into two basic groups, just like the items in the garden center: Part 1 is supplies, or *packaged goods,* and part 2 is tools, equipment, and accessories, or *hard goods.* Unfortunately, it isn't possible to make this an absolutely clean division and you will find some overlap. For example, you'll find fencing that is used as a pest barrier in the chapter on pest control products in part 1 and fencing that is used for other purposes in the chapter on growing products in part 2.

Items are grouped by association, and alphabetically within each chapter. Make good use of the index—it lists much more than you might expect, including all cross-referenced and associated items, as well as, and perhaps more importantly, the various names by which things are called from the "Also Known As" sections.

Please note that some of the names listed in the "Also Known As" sections may be incorrect. Listing doesn't assure correctness: Certain aka's are just plain wrong, corruptions that have found their way into print or the mouth of a professional by any of a number of ways. As a matter of fact, many of them are taken from the distributors' and manufacturers' catalogs, where the use of poetic license is in widespread practice, sometimes fueled by quite imaginative translations of descriptions of imported items. Furthermore, right or wrong, a number of different tools are called by the same name—it is up to you to fully describe what you want when you go to the garden center. The illustrations should help you get what you want. In any case, aka's have been included so you can find something in the index even if you have been given an incorrect or colloquial name.

No reference book would be complete without a disclaimer, so here is ours:

Brand and trade names are used here as an aid to the consumer, and are in no way meant as an endorsement of any product or manufacturer; likewise their omission is in no way meant to be a negative comment. In some cases, brand names are used by the public in a generic way, and we have made every effort to note when this is so. Trade names and trademarks are noted to the best of our ability; we will be glad to make any corrections necessary if a manufacturer should find us in error. All in all, the items listed in this book are simply meant to be representative of what you might be able to buy in a garden center. Nothing is implied to be essential or even beneficial by its inclusion.

WHAT IS NOT INCLUDED IN THIS BOOK

First of all, as per the title, no plants or flowers (the "green goods") are listed here, although appendix A has some general advice about shopping for them. This book lists only the supplies, tools, equipment, and accessories (the "packaged goods" and the "hard goods") that an average home gardener might find in a well-stocked garden center; you should not expect every garden center to have everything listed here.

Furthermore, items that fall in the broad "outdoor living" category—such as furniture and recreation equipment—are not included. Nor will you find pet supplies or farming equipment or landscaping materials or general home improvement items that are found at some garden centers. The line had to be drawn somewhere. Regular home gardening, with a slight nod to decoration, is the limit.

Some of the items listed (or some you might find in catalogs) are intended for professionals. Most garden centers will be glad to special-order these items for you, and in fact they probably already sell to a small group of local professionals (landscapers, tree surgeons, or groundskeepers) on a special-order basis. This is especially true of garden centers that also have their own nurseries, which is quite common (and a good sign), because their own growers need these professional products. So don't be shy about asking for products that you don't see on the shelves.

You may find that we don't list certain chemical products that you know of, especially pesticides. There are so many, including some that are mixtures, that it is impossible to be complete. Also, some chemical products, even well-known commercial ones, are sometimes abruptly removed from the market as tests determine that they are much more dangerous than previously thought. Legislation that was pending for many years may have suddenly become effective, or regulations that vary from state to state may lead you to search out something that is unavailable where you live. Another reason some chemical pesticides go off the market is that the pests become resistant to them, rendering them ineffective. As in all related matters, checking with your local Cooperative Extension agent (see appendix B) is the best way to go.

A PERSONAL NOTE TO READERS

I am always glad to hear from readers who have found items or "Also Known As" aliases that were not included in this edition. Suggestions for use tips and buying tips are always welcome, too. Please write me c/o Macmillan Publishing Company, 866 Third Avenue, New York, NY 10022.

Supplies

Growing Media and Soil Conditioners

ABOUT SOIL

Dirt is what you track into the house. *Soil* is a complex growing medium that holds moisture and nutrients for plants. It is composed of microorganisms and bacteria—organic, or living, matter—and mineral particles—nonliving matter. It has structure and chemical balance. Some soils are better than others for growing plants, and some types are better than others for particular plants. For a variety of reasons, your soil may need help. You can improve the soil in your garden, both in terms of chemical makeup and in terms of structure, if need be, with *garden soils, soilless mixes, pro-mixes, topsoil, soil amendments,* or *conditioners,* all sold at garden centers. To better understand what these products are and how to use them, it is important to understand the three primary soil types, *clay, sand,* and *silt,* each of which has differently sized mineral particles and different texture.

TYPES OF SOIL

• *Clay soil* is composed of the smallest particles found in soils. It also is referred to as a *heavy* soil. When wet, the particles in clay stick to each other, making it impervious to water and, for that matter, plants. When dry, it becomes hard and often cracks. Clay soil contains little air, and water does not drain easily through it: It needs to be loosened or opened

3

up. Humus (decayed organic matter), peat moss, or other organic matter or gypsum can be added to clay soil to make it lighter, counteract its tendency to stick together and pack down, and allow water to drain through it.

• *Sandy soil* is composed of the largest particles found in soil. It is referred to as a *light* soil. When wet, the particles do not stick to each other and water, along with fertilizers and other nutrients, flows easily. Because it has such good drainage, sandy soil may not retain enough moisture to aid good plant growth. Sandy soil can be improved by adding peat moss or humus or organic matter that will become humus to help it retain more moisture. This humus needs to be replenished every few years, as it has a tendency to wash away.

• *Silt soils* are composed of particles in sizes between those of sand and clay.

• *Loam* refers to soils that are composed of a desirably balanced mixture of the particles found in clay and sand along with organic matter. Loam is good for plant growth because it is open, retains moisture well, and has a crumbly structure, or good *tilth*. Loam is what every gardener wants. Surprisingly, loam consists of about 50 percent open pore space that can be filled with air and water.

A NOTE ABOUT SOIL TESTS: A *soil test,* in which a few tablespoons of soil in solution are chemically analyzed, determines the composition of your soil: the exact type of soil, the percentages of various nutrients in the soil, and the pH of the soil.

The *pH* (potential hydrogen) is the term used to express relative acidity (low pH, or "sour") or alkalinity (high pH, or "sweet") of soil on a scale of 0 to 14, with 7 being neutral. Each level of pH represents ten times the concentration; a pH of 5.0 is ten times as acid as a level of 6.0. This is probably the most important test you'll take in your garden. The range for the average garden is 6.0 to 7.5, and experts disagree as to what is the absolute best range, though most nutrients are available to the plants in a range between 6.0 to 6.8. Essentially, pH level affects the solubility of the nutrients, which allows them to travel through the soil and into the plant roots. An extreme pH on either end of the scale prevents the plants from getting the nutrients they need.

Soil tests can be done with a variety of meters or kits (see pages 237–38) for free or at a nominal fee by your local Cooperative Extension (see appendix B), or by a private laboratory (often listed in the Yellow Pages under "Laboratories—Testing"). Lab tests are more accurate than kit tests, of course.

If you have not had your soil tested, you might want to do so before adding any fertilizers or additives to your garden. A soil test is one of the few ways of determining the amount of phosphorus, potash, and nitrogen in your soil, as well as its acidity. This is important information when choosing fertilizers as they will raise or lower the pH, depending on their ingredients. Consider tests a one-time effort, or at most something to be done every three or four years, usually in the autumn or spring, as a search for the basis of specific problems.

If you know your soil pH and the level that is optimum for the plants you are growing, you can then choose fertilizers (see chapter 3) that will maintain a good pH level for your plants. For example, plants like azaleas, rhododendrons, heaths, and heathers prefer a more acidic soil (with a lower pH) so you will want to buy fertilizers that will keep the pH lower. Without a soil test, though you may be able to judge the soil's needs from the appearance of your lawn or plants, you could be paying a lot for special fertilizers that contain trace elements or nutrients that are already present in your soil, or worse yet, not buying the fertilizers that could provide the nutrients lacking in your soil.

The most typical choice for *raising* the pH of soil is to add lime, and to *lower* it, to add a soil acidifier like sulfur in one of its various forms, such as aluminum sulfate. The amount you need to add is noted on the package of whatever kind of product you are using. For example, to raise the pH of sandy soil by one pH level, you need to add 7½ ounces of ground limestone per square yard, but for clayey soil, you need to add 15 ounces. To lower it by one pH level, that is, to increase the acidity, approximately 2¾ ounces of aluminum sulfate are needed per square yard (1 pound of sulfur per 100 square feet), or 6 pounds of manure. There are many other products and measures that you can use; these examples are provided just to give some perspective. All these additives will take different lengths of time to achieve their effects, from a few days to a few months. Check the labels and general gardening reference books.

ABOUT PACKAGED SOILS

Few gardeners have soil in their gardens that is suitable for houseplants or seed starting. Indoor gardening, with its intensive watering, puts a strain on soil, necessitating various requirements that are met by the specialized soils listed here. Some are mere refinements of a suitable all-purpose blend, so choice becomes just a matter of personal preference. Mixing your own can be fun also and sometimes better. Growing media, soils, and conditioners are sold in packages ranging from a few ounces to 100 pounds. Buy larger packages; smaller ones always cost much more per pound. They are also sold by the quart and by the cubic foot, depending on the manufacturer.

Growing media are literally anything you can grow a plant in, and are generally used to refer to those media that do not contain soil.

General Use Growing Media

HUMUS

ALSO KNOWN AS: Compost (incorrect), composted topsoil, peat muck

DESCRIPTION: Humus is a general term for decomposed and decayed organic matter and is an ideal, stable part of rich soil with little nutrient content. It looks like soil and is sold in bags (typically 40 pounds) just like topsoil (see page 8). Some gardeners consider compost and leaf mold (see page 14) forms of humus.

TYPES: *Peat humus* (also known as *organic peat):* Humus derived primarily from decomposed reed-sedge peat (see page 16) and other decomposed organic matter. Mined from bogs in Michigan, New England, Pennsylvania, and a few other states.

   Pine bark humus (also known as *pine bark conditioner):* Humus derived from decayed pine bark, i.e., mined from the forest floor. Consists of "woods matter" and leaves and can be either gathered in the wild or produced commercially (composted).

USE: Building up soil in containers, lawns, or flower beds, or replacing topsoil that has been removed in building construction. Can also be used as a conditioner to enrich soils and improve their drainage and friability, but it is essentially a growing medium.

USE TIP: Doesn't hold water or nutrients as well as topsoil. Mix with soils or use straight; often used as a growing medium for potted plants and in greenhouses.

POTTING SOIL

ALSO KNOWN AS: Houseplant soil

DESCRIPTION: Ready-to-use soil that is a mixture of organic and inorganic ingredients such as peat moss, compost, sand, and vermiculite. Sold in packages that range in size from 9 to 40 quarts or 2 to 40 pounds. Some contain small amounts of slow-release fertilizer and trace elements and some are sold in bags that are meant to be used as planters. *Sterile* potting soils have been heated to over 180° F to kill bacteria and weed seed.

USE: Good for houseplants and for starting seeds because of increased drainage and the decreased chance of rot and a variety of fungal problems, especially damping-off, soil-borne fungal diseases that kill seedlings. Gardens need the bacteria and microorganisms found in nonsterile or partially pasteurized soils.

USE TIP: Good potting soil rewets better than plain soil. If it dries out, it won't pull away so much from the sides of the pot.

BUYING TIPS: Soils intended for interior use can be sterilized, but it is not necessary for general exterior use for mature plants. Also, if you are using organic fertilizers, you must *not* use sterilized soil, as it lacks the microorganisms needed for the fertilizer to work.

SOILLESS MIXES

ALSO KNOWN AS: Light potting mix, peat-lite mix, seed starting mix, soil-less mix (see chapter 9)

POPULAR BRAND NAMES: Pro-Mix®, Peat-Bark Mix

DESCRIPTION: Growing medium for potting mixes formulated from all organic material that contain no grit soil (mineral particles). These mixes are extremely water and nutrient retentive. They have been sterilized so they contain no bacteria or weed seed. Available in sizes that range from bags of 8 quarts to compressed bales of 5½ cubic feet.

The most common types sold contain peat moss, perlite, vermiculite, and gypsum, along with nutrients and trace elements. Some are specifically formulated for container gardening, and include good-quality sphagnum moss and composted softwood bark, which increase water retention—loss of water being a major problem in container gardening.

USE: Seed-starting growing medium, for both potted plants (indoors and out) and gardens. They can also be mixed with soil. Because some are sterilized, they prevent damping-off, soil-borne fungal diseases that kill seedlings. (See also seed starting products, chapter 9.)

USE TIP: If soilless mixes are used in containers or tubs on terrace gardens, mix in sand or soil to make the mix heavier. This is particularly important if you are growing trees or shrubs in a container as soilless mixes alone do not hold up the heavier plants very well.

BUYING TIP: This is a convenient packaged item to buy, but you can mix your own very easily if you want, which might also be less expensive. Typical mixes include peat moss (2 parts), vermiculite (1 part), perlite (1 part), fertilizers, a small amount of ground limestone, and a wetting agent, all of which are sold individually and all of which are described later in this book.

TOPSOIL

ALSO KNOWN AS: Loam, garden loam, top soil

DESCRIPTION: A rich, dark soil with a high quantity of organic matter. Topsoil is the rich top layer of soil created naturally when leaves and organic matter weather and decompose completely. Most often sold in natural form, with microorganisms, or sterile, with none.

USE: Topsoil is an excellent additive when building up the quality of the soil in a garden. It can be used when creating your own soil mixes, and as part of a soil mix for use in containers and tubs. Often during the construction of new homes the topsoil is removed by bulldozers during the grading process. If this rich soil is not replaced by the contractor, the new homeowner has to replace it in order to have a garden.

USE TIP: Sterile topsoil is preferable for potting soils used for starting seeds and rooting cuttings, as there is less likelihood of rot or damping-off, a soil-borne fungal disease that kills seedlings. Once the seedlings have grown this is no longer necessary.

BUYING TIP: Look for soils with a lot of organic matter.

Specially Formulated Growing Media

AFRICAN VIOLET SOIL

DESCRIPTION: A prepackaged soil mix composed of sterile organic ingredients that holds moisture extremely well but still has excellent drainage. Sold in sizes from 2 to 8 quarts. Typically contains peat moss, ground limestone, vermiculite, and perlite.

USE: Specifically prepared to be used for African violets.

BUYING TIP: Though regular potting soil should be adequate for African violets, the special African violet soil mixes are usually the same price and formulated to be better for the plants, containing slightly more perlite or vermiculite for increased drainage and aeration. African violets seem to attract a good number of specialized products, which actually may have more to do with their popularity as houseplants and the vast market that creates than with their horticultural needs.

CACTUS SOIL

DESCRIPTION: Porous blend of sterile sand, organic matter, and sometimes nutrients. Products may vary in color from white to reddish brown, depending upon what types of sand are used. Most often cactus soil is sold in 4-quart sizes. Has more perlite and less peat moss than other potting soils.

USE: For cactus and other succulent plants.

ORCHID BARK

DESCRIPTION: Chips of redwood bark or a mixture of chips of redwood and pine barks. Despite its name, it is not made from gigantic orchid plants.

USE: Growing medium for orchids.

OSMUNDA FIBER

DESCRIPTION: A coarse, reddish brown fiber that is made from the roots of the *Osmunda* fern. *Tree fern fiber* is similar, but darker.

USE: As an anchoring medium for some epiphitic orchids and other plants that get their moisture and nutrients from the air, collectively known as *air plants.*

USE TIP: Moisten, squeeze out excess moisture, and attach to wood, bark, or cork block with wire.

BUYING TIP: Tends to be sold as an expensive specialty item, so shop around for the best price.

SHEET AND SPANISH MOSSES

ALSO KNOWN AS: Decorator moss

DESCRIPTION: Either of two types of long, fibrous moss in its natural state: *Sheet moss,* which is harvested from South Carolina forests in sheets and is very green, or *Spanish moss,* which is lighter and more bulky, and light gray.

USE: Sheet moss is used primarily for lining wire hanging baskets, and both are used in a variety of decorative arrangements and wreaths.

USE TIP: Birds may nest in a well-watered sheet moss basket.

TERRARIUM SOIL

DESCRIPTION: Special mixes of organic and inorganic ingredients. Often these soil mixes contain some ground charcoal to absorb salts and other chemicals that tend to build up in an enclosed environment.

USE: Terrarium soils can be used as a medium for growing plants in terrariums, jars, and other closed containers and pots with no drainage.

USE TIP: If you have a decorative pot without drainage that you wish to grow plants in, this would be a good choice of soil, though it is always better to provide drainage.

Soil Conditioners and Additives

ABOUT SOIL CONDITIONERS

Most gardens are planted where the gardener likes them to be, rather than because of a perfect soil. Gardeners usually find that their soil is lacking in some character of structure, as well as in nutrients, either because of inadequate soil care in the past or because of the special requirements of the plants you intend to grow. Fertilizers can add nutrients, but soil conditioners, often called *soil amendments,* improve the ability of the soil to hold water and to deliver nutrients to the roots, as well as improve aeration, drainage, and structure. Some conditioners are more often found as components of fertilizers, but are also sold separately. Others merely raise or lower the pH, depending on whether they are soil sweeteners or soil acidifiers, respectively.

ALUMINUM SULFATE

ALSO KNOWN AS: Aluminum sulphate, sulfate of aluminum

DESCRIPTION: Powdered bauxite that has been treated with sulfuric acid. Sold in bags from 5 to 100 pounds.

USE: Soil acidifier for acid-loving plants. Brings out the color, especially the blue, in hydrangeas. Can also be used as a coagulant for home swimming pools.

COW MANURE

DESCRIPTION: Dried and ground-up cow manure that has been aged in such a way that it has rotted, losing its smell and increasing its concentration of nutrients. More often considered a fertilizer (see its more extensive entry in chapter 3).

USE: Makes the soil friable, adds organic elements, and generally improves all soils. Also contains nutrients. Mixed into any soil, but routinely mixed into soil that is being put into tree holes or new gardens.

EARTHWORM CASTINGS

ALSO KNOWN AS: Worm castings

DESCRIPTION: Coarse brown powder sold in small, convenient bags (2-pound size is typical). Consists of ground-up earthworm castings, an imaginative euphemism for worm manure. Odorless. A similar product is *cricket castings*.

USE: A general soil amendment that increases the friability of soil, acting as a soil builder that increases water retention.

USE TIP: Ideal for potted plants.

GARDEN CHARCOAL

ALSO KNOWN AS: Soil freshener

DESCRIPTION: Chunks of charcoal that range in size from $\frac{1}{16}$ inch to $\frac{1}{2}$ inch. It is usually sold in 2-quart bags.

USE: When added to soil mixes, charcoal helps absorb odors, acids, salts, and other impurities. It also eliminates odors in terrariums and containers having no drainage and holds moisture. Especially good to have at the bottom of a container. Helpful as well in the water of vases containing cut flowers.

USE TIP: When planting in a terrarium or in a container without drainage, place a layer of gravel on the bottom, followed by a layer of charcoal, and then the soil or growing medium.

BUYING TIP: If you cannot find garden charcoal in your garden center, try pet stores, where it is sold as aquarium filter material.

GYPSUM

ALSO KNOWN AS: Land plaster, sulfate of lime

DESCRIPTION: Light-colored, finely powdered rocks or pellets containing calcium sulfate. Similar products that are blends of calcium and sulfur are *gypsite* (crystalline form of gypsum) and *lime sulfur* (which is sold as *calcium polysulfide*). The latter may have a wetting agent that makes for deeper soil penetration.

USE: Improves packed-down and clayey soils for water penetration (drainage) and aeration by making the fine particles of clay stick together and neutralizing the salt in salty (high-sodium) soils, without raising the pH as lime (see page 14) does. The process is a chemical one, whereby sodium ions are exchanged for calcium ions, which separates the clay particles enough to create "pore space" for air and water. Because it is a mild soil acidifier, gypsum may be used where the use of lime would pose a problem to acid-loving plants. Also supplies calcium and sulfur, both secondary nutrients (see pages 46–47).

USE TIP: Can be used in great quantities if warranted. Has been used since the days of the early Greeks.

BUYING TIP: The pelleted form is easier to use than the powder form.

HORTICULTURAL SAND

DESCRIPTION: Pure sterilized sand often sold in 2-quart bags. May vary in color, depending upon what type of sand is used. Contains no salt or other impurities that might bother plants.

USE: Mixed with potting soil to aerate and help with drainage. It can be used for rooting succulents and cacti, and as the primary base in a cactus soil mix.

BUYING TIPS: Regular *builder's sand,* which can be purchased at hardware stores or construction sites, is cheaper and works just as well as horticultural sand. Do not use ocean beach sand for plants, as it contains salt. Look for sharp and relatively coarse particles. Avoid fine, rounded ones.

IRON SULFATE

ALSO KNOWN AS: Iron sulphate, copperas, ferrous sulfate

DESCRIPTION: Granular product commonly sold in 5-pound bags or as small containers of liquid. Often sold as *iron chelate*.

USE: Contains 20 percent iron and 11.5 percent sulfur. Provides iron and acidifies the soil. Assists in the production of chlorophyll and corrects iron deficiencies (yellowing, or chlorosis, and green veins). Aids in blooming.

USE TIP: Make sure that your plant is definitely deficient in iron before applying, and if you do, apply carefully and strictly according to the directions. Too much iron can damage a plant. Yellow leaves are the usual sign of an iron deficiency, but the problem might lie elsewhere as well. Check your books or with experts.

BUYING TIPS: The standard granular product is for application to the soil and takes awhile to affect the plant. The liquid form, used as a foliar spray, tends to give quicker results (2 or 3 days).

LEAF MOLD

ALSO KNOWN AS: Woods soil, compost (when sold commercially)

DESCRIPTION: Shredded flakes of partially decomposed leaves and forest litter, usually an attractive dark brown. When a local nursery sells its own leaf mold as compost, it is usually sold by the cubic yard or small truckload. Often considered a mulch (see chapter 2), it also has fertilizing characteristics; some gardeners consider it a form of humus (see page 6).

USE: A particularly good source of humus and a general organic soil conditioner for vegetable gardens, as it opens up the soil, making it friable. Encourages development of fibrous roots. Also a good mulch for any area of the garden, because as it breaks down and turns into compost, it can be mixed into the soil to become a soil conditioner.

USE TIPS: Enriches and fertilizes the soil where it is used. It can be worked into soil to help build up the humus. Not effective if it is powdery. Lightens clayey soils. Can be turned into the soil after use as a one-season mulch to go to work as a soil conditioner.

BUYING TIP: Leaf mold is a bargain at about $1.50 a cubic foot, considering what it does for the garden. Very difficult to find for sale, though.

LIME

ALSO KNOWN AS: Ground limestone, limestone, liming material, pulverized limestone, agricultural lime, garden lime

CHEMICAL NAME: Calcium carbonate ($CaCO_3$) in a number of forms; commonly mixed with magnesium carbonate ($MgCO_3$)

DESCRIPTION: A fine, white powder, pellets, or granules of ground limestone. When mixed with magnesium (which is quite common), it may be called *dolomitic, dolomite,* or *magnesium limestone.* Lime is often incorrectly considered a fertilizer, probably because calcium is a secondary nutrient and magnesium is a micronutrient that all plants need. *Marl,* a natural mixture of weathered shells containing clay and calcium carbonate, is another source of lime.

USE: Primarily to raise the pH of soils—to make them more alkaline, or sweeter, which means essentially to neutralize soil acidity—so that microorganisms can help break down organic matter into the all-important humus. However, it is helpful in many other ways as well. Though it is not a fertilizer, lime is a catalyst for the release of nutrients and improves the structure of clayey soils by increasing moisture retention and drainage. Lime is also helpful in the control of club root, a disease found in plants of the cabbage family Cruciferae. Also prevents moss growth, disinfects, and can be used for both whitewashing and pickling vegetables.

USE TIPS: Most lawns require annual liming, especially in areas of the country with acid rain, such as the Northeast. Fall or spring is the best time to do this, depending on where you live, although fall is usually better. Be sure to water it in well. In acid soils (those with a low pH), liming is necessary to grow many perennials and vegetables. Do not apply at the same time as manure, or else they will combine and release ammonia gas, wasting valuable nitrogen and killing plants. Refer to your soil test to determine how much to apply (that is your *lime requirement),* and be patient: Trying to raise the pH of your soil by more than one point a year can be harmful to your plants, as it ties up the nutrients. Hydrated lime acts faster, but it can burn the plants—measure carefully and apply lightly.

BUYING TIPS: Though there are several forms of lime sold, be sure that you are buying a *dolomitic* or *ground* limestone (dolomitic is better because of the magnesium it contains); the general term used from time to time is *agricultural lime.* This type minimizes the risk of "burning" the foliage of plants, particularly grass. Most soils can use the magnesium and are not harmed by a slight excess. *Hydrated,* or *slaked, lime* is a third choice, though it must be applied carefully because it is very caustic and therefore dangerous to handle, and leaches out quickly. Other types of lime, such as *builder's lime,* are designed to be used in construction materials such as mortar and plaster. They are much more concentrated and will burn plants. Do not use *quicklime* in your garden—it will damage the soil. Pelletized limestone has less dust than fine ground limestone.

OYSTER SHELLS

DESCRIPTION: White material consisting of coarsely ground oyster shells, which are full of calcium carbonate ($CaCO_3$).

USE: As a liming material to raise the pH of soils (to make them more alkaline), although sometimes used as a fertilizer to add calcium, a secondary nutrient (see page 46).

USE TIP: Better used as a way to raise the pH of soil than as a fertilizer.

PEANUT HULL MEAL

DESCRIPTION: A tan to brown meal obtained from ground peanut hulls.

USE: In the South, often used as a soil conditioner to help open up packed soil. Also used as an additive or filler in fertilizers.

BUYING TIP: Generally less expensive and more commonly found in areas where peanuts are grown.

PEAT

ALSO KNOWN AS: Peat moss, peat muck, peat mulch, sphagnum peat moss, sphagnum peat, sphagnum moss

DESCRIPTION: Dried and partially to fully decomposed roots, leaves, stems, moss, and other plant debris that have been harvested from wetlands. Light brown to black. Compressed up to half the normal volume and roughly ground up for commercial packaging, peat is light, loose, and fluffy when unpacked, though some types are granular. Peat moss is much more commonly available than peat muck, which contains more mineral and fully decomposed plant matter.

TYPES: *Reed-sedge peat* (also known as *reed, fibrous,* or *sedge peat):* The product of partly decomposed plant residues (reeds, rushes, cattails, grasses, and the like) that grew in a water-saturated environment. *Michigan peat* is reed-sedge peat from Michigan, and is a bit darker and denser than the regular Canadian peat moss, having decomposed slightly. Sometimes sold as *humus.*
   Sphagnum peat moss (milled and unmilled): Partially decomposed sphagnum moss and other bog plants that

grow well in parts of Maine, Minnesota, and Canada. Most packages from Canada—the source of 90 percent of sphagnum peat moss sold in the United States—are also labeled in French, *Tourbe de spaigne.* It is the most common type of peat moss available.

Milled peat is dark to light brown in color and is simply sphagnum peat harvested by a mechanical milling process. May be sold as *organic seed starter.* Sold compressed to half its normal volume and packaged in heavy-gauge plastic bags. Usually not labeled as "milled." The most common form of peat, sold in large plastic packages of 1 to 6 cubic feet. Also available in super-compressed plates that expand when wet.

Unmilled peat (also known as *floral sphagnum moss)* is a greenish light brown material that looks more like you would expect dried moss to look: fibrous, with small branches and leaves visible. Usually sold in small plastic bags. Not readily available as it is harvested by hand.

Note the difference between two confusing uses: Sphagnum *moss* is gray and stringy, harvested before it has decomposed. Sphagnum *peat moss* is brown and is made of partially decomposed plants.

USE: As a soil additive, particularly when the pH needs to be lowered (mix it with lime if you don't want to lower your pH). Its main characteristic is its great water-holding capacity: Peat absorbs between five and fifteen times its weight in water (good-quality air-dried sphagnum will absorb up to twenty times its weight). It aids in opening up clay soil for better aeration and supplies organic matter to poor soil. Besides these special qualities, it improves all soils in terms of water retention and porosity. Though it is not recommended (see Use Tips, below), sphagnum peat is commonly used as a mulch (see chapter 2) for acid-loving plants, breaking down after about three years. Unmilled peat is used as a growing medium for orchids and other epiphytic plants and bromeliads, as well as a lining for wire baskets to hold soil. Milled peat is used not only as a conditioner but as a seed starting medium, and mixes well with perlite and vermiculite for container gardening.

USE TIPS: Moisten and work the peat into the soil well; if it gets packed down it might block water from reaching the plant. Use wet as a soil amendment. Peat does not make good mulch because if it is allowed to dry out, it will block water like a thatched roof. Also, remember that peat tends to lower the pH of soil as it breaks down.

BUYING TIPS: Peat moss is sold in cubic foot bales. Usually, the larger the bale, the lower the cost per cubic foot, so don't hesitate to buy more than you might need right away. It keeps well. Buy in the fall, slash the packaging, and allow to absorb water over the winter. Try to buy name brands of peat from reputable dealers, as good peat is over 95 percent organic fiber.

PERLITE

ALSO KNOWN AS: Horticultural perlite

DESCRIPTION: White, light, hard, porous, gritty material similar to vermiculite (see page 19) in appearance. Formed when lava (volcanic rock) is heated, which causes it to expand. Nontoxic, sterile, and odorless. *Construction grade perlite* is made of smaller, lighter particles.

USE: Increases drainage (loosens heavy soils), improves aeration (gets oxygen to the plant roots), and decreases the weight of potting soils, an important consideration for planters on decks. Also helps retain water, which attaches to the particles' surface. Can be used as a rooting medium on its own. Construction grade perlite is used as loose fill insulation and as a light aggregate with concrete where weight is a factor, such as on roof decks.

USE TIP: Use the finest ground forms of perlite for seed starting mixes; if it is not finely ground, it tends to go to the top of a mixture. Coarser grades combine well with peat moss for lightweight container mixtures.

SOIL SULFUR

DESCRIPTION: Granular or powder form of the basic garden chemical, sold in 5- to 80-pound bags.

USE: Acidifying and breaking up (or *flocculating*) the soil, as does gypsum (see page 12–13). It causes clay soil to form small particles, allowing air and water to accumulate and making the soil friable, or better for growing things. The sulfur actually breaks down into sulfuric acid, which reacts with the natural calcium carbonate in the soil to make calcium sulfate, the basic stuff of gypsum.

USE TIP: Use carefully—follow all precautions on the label. It is caustic, and most people are sensitive to sulfur. Its use is the fastest way to lower your pH, but can be toxic if overdone—apply no more than 1 pound per 100 square feet in any one application, and no more often than every eight weeks. Work into the soil and water in thoroughly to avoid burning leaves in the sun.

VERMICULITE

ALSO KNOWN AS: Horticultural vermiculite

DESCRIPTION: A gray or white, extremely lightweight granular substance, with grains about 1/16 inch in diameter (known as no. 3 grade). It is formed when mica chips are heated and expanded to many times their original size. Contains some potassium, magnesium, and calcium, which are slowly released in soil. *Construction grade vermiculite* is larger, and is used for loose fill insulation.

USE: Used in soil mixes to increase the water and fertilizer retention of the mixture, as well as to lighten and open it up. Considered a soil amendment and a rooting medium as well as a mulch (see chapter 2).

USE TIP: It is a very light material, lighter than sand, and is an important additive to container soil mixes. Avoid adding to clayey soils as the clay bonds with the vermiculite, instead of the vermiculite breaking up the clay.

WATER RETENTION CRYSTALS

ALSO KNOWN AS: Water release crystals, root-watering crystals, water retention granules, water-retaining soil additive, hydrogel crystals, super absorbant

POPULAR BRAND NAMES: Agrosoke™, Water Gels, P-4, Water-Grabber®, Aquagel

DESCRIPTION: Fine, translucent white granules that absorb many times their own weight of water (some brands claim five hundred times) in about thirty minutes. They swell up to form moist, sticky beads of gel that then release almost all the absorbed water evenly over a long period, increasing the time between waterings, depending on the brand. A nontoxic, nonbiodegradable, and pH-neutral polymer. Lasts about five years. Sold in packets as small as 2 ounces.

USE: Reduces the frequency of plant watering. Mixed with soil in lawns but especially in containers to maintain an even distribution of moisture; sort of a moisture reservoir that acts like a sponge. Plant roots actually attach themselves to the water-swollen crystals, stimulating the production of feeder roots. The increase in the size of the crystals aerates the soil, too. Minimizes transplant shock and reduces the need for watering by up to 50 percent, according to some manufacturers—one good soaking may last three weeks, for example. Can be mixed into small containers, placed around specific plants, or spread over entire gardens. Helpful if you find it hard to water regularly.

USE TIPS: Add the crystals to the soil after they have absorbed water (or been hydrated) so you can mix in the right amount. A 6:1 ratio of soil to hydrated crystals is typical. Most brands are compatible with fertilizers, but check the label to be sure. Helps prevent overwatering, the scourge of houseplants, to a certain extent. Don't overload a container with this, though, or you will end up holding so much water that you'll create a swamplike condition and rot your plant roots. Test before using regularly—some critics claim these don't work.

BUYING TIP: The amount of water that crystals soak up varies tremendously by brand. Be sure to compare labels. Avoid starch-based versions, which do not last long. Popularity greatly the result of the interest shown in container gardening by otherwise capable young urban professionals who can't seem to take responsibility for even the simplest domestic chores.

WETTING AGENT

DESCRIPTION: Granules or liquid sold in 10- and 50-pound or quart and gallon containers. Larger containers are available to professionals.

USE: Granules are mixed into soil and soilless mixtures (see pages 7–8) used for potting plants. Reduces watering needs and speeds up delivery of fertilizers by improving water penetration and drainage of growing media, especially hard soils. Liquid is more often used by professionals on lawns and flower beds.

CHAPTER 2

Mulches and Grass Seed

ABOUT MULCHES

Mulches are organic and inorganic substances that are placed in planting beds and around plants because they are not only decorative (they are often called *decorative ground cover),* but more importantly because they retain moisture in the bed by shielding it from the drying effects of the sun, help cool the bed during the warm seasons, help insulate it during winter (the general term is *temperature fluctuation protection),* attract earthworms, and above all, help keep down weeds. They also act as an erosion control. Mulches are sold in a wide range of package sizes, measured by weight or volume. Mulching is one of the essential gardening practices in low-maintenance gardening.

Organic Mulches

ABOUT ORGANIC MULCHES

Organic mulches are simply those derived from natural material, meaning that they are able to break down and decompose over a period of time, improving soil structure and enriching it. Many gardeners find organic mulches more attractive and natural-looking (naturally!) than inorganic mulches. They are not permanent, though a breakdown over several years is certainly not hard to deal with. You merely need to add some new mulch annually. Their decomposition slowly adds nitrogen to the soil; however, most organic mulches initially deplete some of the nitrogen in the bed because as organic matter breaks down, the microorganisms that aid in decomposition utilize nitrogen in the initial stages of the process. It is therefore necessary to add extra nitrogen to beds where you are using organic mulches that decompose rapidly, that is, over a year or two. Apply most to a depth of 3 to 4 inches.

Listed here are the most common organic mulches sold nationally; some very good mulches may not be listed here because of their general unavailability. For example, the by-products of regional agricultural crops, such as various nut shells or rice hulls, are often sources of unusual and excellent mulches. These are often available only from local food-processing plants. There are also some good homemade mulches, such as shredded newspaper, which are not sold commercially and of course are not listed here either.

BARK CHIPS AND SHREDDED BARK

ALSO KNOWN AS: Bark nuggets (bark chips)

DESCRIPTION: Pieces of chipped or shredded tree bark. Both items are a pleasant brown color, and texture varies from medium to coarse. Generally three types are available: *hardwood bark, cedar* or *cypress bark,* and *pine bark nuggets* or *mulch,* which may come from any kind of pine. In all cases, these mulches should contain no more than 15 percent wood (as opposed to bark). *Shredded bark* is made of thin, light pieces less than 1½ inches long. *Nuggets* are larger, as big as 3½ inches in diameter, and more decorative. *Mini-nuggets* are ¼ to 1½ inches in diameter. *Pine bark mulch* is made of particles ⅛ to ¼ inch long, though all these terms and sizes vary considerably from manufacturer to manufacturer. In the West, bark is sold as *West Coast large* (or *Western*) and *West Coast medium nuggets;* the fine stuff that is left over from the chopping and screening is called *West Coast pathway,* but in the rest of the country it is called *fines.* Western red cedar, redwood, and driftwood barks are also popular. Domestic cedar bark is reddish brown and has a distinct cedar aroma. Canadian cedar is lighter in color and does not have as much aroma. Cypress mulch has similar characteristics and is light gray. A popular alternative found in the Northeast is *root mulch,* often made of shredded licorice root.

Oddly, *orchid bark* (see page 9) is not made from extremely large orchids but is a mixture of pine and redwood barks, and is used for growing orchids.

USE: Bark is an excellent natural-looking mulch that, depending on the size of the chips, takes about three to four years to break down, longer than most organic mulches. It can be used for flower beds, around trees and shrubs, and even in the vegetable garden. Shredded bark is more efficient as a mulch, but nuggets are more decorative. Root mulch may be used as a soil conditioner to provide humus.

USE TIPS: Use as you would any mulch. A depth of about 3 inches is sufficient to ensure weed control and moisture retention. Hardwood bark lasts longer and is usually heavier, so it doesn't blow away; pine bark nuggets might float away in a heavy rain if the garden is on a slope. Thirteen bags of 2 cubic feet cover about 100 square feet to a depth of 3 inches. Barks are often placed over a layer of plastic sheeting, called *bark base mulch,* to keep it from decomposing into the soil.

BUYING TIPS: Bark is usually easy to find at most garden centers, selling for around $2 per cubic foot. Your local parks department may also offer shredded bark as a public service, though you must check with them as to whether any diseased trees of the same species as yours were shredded into the mulch, in which case, avoid their mulch like the plague. Of course, you can get bark directly from sawmills if you live near a cooperative one. Cedar bark is more expensive but lasts longer (it resists both insects and rot) and is better for the garden, though it tends to acidify the soil. Shredded cypress bark lasts the longest, as it is basically inert. Root mulch is usually expensive.

BUCKWHEAT HULLS

DESCRIPTION: A fine-textured, dark brown mulch that comes from the hulls of buckwheat. Resembles cocoa shells (see next entry) in appearance, but is much lighter.

USE: An attractive, natural-looking mulch well suited for any area of the garden or on houseplant pots. It is particularly pleasing in a perennial border.

USE TIP: Because they are so light, buckwheat hulls will blow away if placed in exposed, windy areas. They will stay in place after aging a bit and if they are kept well wet down. Put down about 2 inches and add new mulch after two or three years, when it begins to break down.

BUYING TIP: Buckwheat hulls, like many organic mulches, are cheaper where buckwheat grows. They are more expensive than cocoa bean hulls and tend to blow away more, but if you like the look, they are well worth the extra cost.

COCOA SHELLS

ALSO KNOWN AS: Cocoa bean hulls, cocoa hulls, cocoa mulch, cocoa shell mulch

DESCRIPTION: Crushed dark brown hulls of the cocoa bean. They have a pleasant texture composed of particles sized ¼ to ½ inch. If they are fresh, they smell like chocolate when they are first put down, but unfortunately soon lose this delightful fragrance. Usually sold in large, 3– or 4–cubic foot bags.

USE: An attractive mulch for almost any area of the garden. The dark brown color is a natural complement to most plant material. Breaks down after a couple years, adding nutrients at the grade of about 2.5-1-3 (see page 48 for an explanation of *grade).*

USE TIPS: When first put down it may be necessary to add extra nitrogen to the soil to compensate for the nitrogen taken out in the initial stages of decomposition. Very good for rose beds. Don't expect it to stay put in windy areas—it is too light. Rinse off any mold that appears in the process of decomposition. Apply to a depth of 3 to 4 inches for best results.

BUYING TIPS: In areas of the country where there are chocolate factories cocoa hulls are less expensive and readily available, sometimes for free directly from a candy factory. In other areas they may be more expensive, if available at all, costing as much as $3.50 a cubic foot, which makes them one of the more expensive organic mulches.

PEAT MOSS

Though this is often used as a mulch, it is more commonly and more effectively used as a soil conditioner. See its entry on pages 16–18.

SALT HAY

DESCRIPTION: Dried salt marsh grasses, light brown or tan in color and thin textured. Available in bale form in the coastal parts of the country, though it is sometimes sold in other areas at a higher cost.

USE: An all-purpose organic mulch. Like straw (see next entry), it is popular as a winter mulch for protecting tender perennials and bulbs.

USE TIP: Salt hay is particularly good for winter protection of vegetable and flower gardens because, unlike straw, if properly stored, it does not contain any seed (that is, any that would germinate in your garden—they need salt water to germinate). Salt hay breaks down during one growing season and needs to be replaced each year, although if it is in good shape, it can be stored for a season. Put it down to a thickness of about 4 inches for good weed control. Watch out for wind and fire, both of which are enemies of this mulch.

BUYING TIP: Prices fluctuate from year to year, but it is usually more expensive than plain straw. The fact that it is seed-free makes it a better buy than straw.

STRAW

DESCRIPTION: Straw, a long, dry grass, is tan to yellow in color and differs from hay in that it is composed of the stems of grain crops, whereas hay contains both stems and leaves. Much of the straw sold for mulches comes in rectangular cubic bales weighing from 30 to 50 pounds a bale.

USE: Straw is an attractive and useful mulch for most areas of the garden, but it is commonly used in the vegetable garden or even on garden paths to keep down weeds. Most popular as a winter mulch for its insulation quality.

USE TIP: Straw tends to blow around a lot and is very flammable when dry. Don't use it or store it where a careless smoker might drop a cigarette or you might see your garden go up in flames. As straw comes from the stems of grain crops, grain seed is often present. These can germinate and become weeds; oat straw is particularly notorious for its seed content. Because of this, straw is not a highly recommended mulch for repeated use, but will do in a pinch, or when price is the biggest problem.

Breaks down in one season. Depth of application varies from a light scattering over newly seeded lawns or construction sites to 6 inches on walks (it packs down nicely).

BUYING TIP: Straw is one of the least expensive organic mulches. It sells for under fifty cents a cubic foot. Make sure it is *weed-free.*

WOOD CHIPS

DESCRIPTION: Small, odd-shaped pieces of wood created when tree limbs are chipped and shredded. They form a coarse-textured mulch that is white, yellow, and brown, darkening to gray and brown as it ages. It may be colored and sold in small bags for indoor use; it is bagged or sold in bulk for outdoor use.

USE: Wood chips are a good mulch for weed control on path areas of a garden. They can be used around plants, but their texture is often too coarse for the flower bed or the vegetable garden. They are better suited for trees and shrubs than for regular plants. Wood chips break down after about three to six years, making them one of the longest-lasting mulches.

USE TIPS: Be sure that you are getting wood chips that have aged at least a few months. Fresh wood chips that are compacted may actually absorb nitrogen and heat up as they oxidize, damaging your plants. You can mix them with fertilizer in storage to avoid this. Additional chips can be added every few years. Try to verify that no diseased trees were included in the chipping. Apply at least 3 inches deep. Your garden will require additional nitrogen as this mulch decomposes.

BUYING TIPS: Wood chips can be purchased for as little as fifty cents a cubic foot. They can also be purchased or had for free from many municipal parks throughout the country that shred tree limbs as part of a normal pruning and maintenance program. They are often given free to community gardening programs and projects in large cities.

Inorganic Mulches

ABOUT INORGANIC MULCHES

Inorganic mulches are those that are not derived from living organisms. Being inorganic, they do not break down or decompose. This can be an advantage because they do not have to be replaced: They are as long-lasting as any landscape accessory. They do not, however, have the more natural appearance of organic mulches, and they add no nitrogen to the soil as organic ones eventually do. They also get "dirty" over time, if that is a concern from a decorative point of view.

FIBERGLASS BATTING OR MAT

ALSO KNOWN AS: Weed control mat, erosion preventer, erosion cloth, geotextile

DESCRIPTION: Woven fiberglass matting the color of which varies from manufacturer to manufacturer. Sold in sheets or rolls.

USE: Placed in a bed or on a border. Holes for plants can be cut in them. Great for insulation and temperature control, if that is an important concern.

USE TIP: It is easy to cover a fiberglass mat with an attractive organic mulch like bark or straw. If it is not porous, use a soaker hose underneath it to irrigate your plants.

BUYING TIP: Fiberglass mats sell for around $1.25 to $1.50 a square yard.

LANDSCAPE FABRIC

ALSO KNOWN AS: Weed-blocking fabric, weed mat, ground cover

POPULAR BRAND NAME: Typar®

DESCRIPTION: A number of porous woven or nonwoven, spun-bonded permeable sheet products made from plastics and natural, and inorganic fibers that come in colors including white, off-white, redwood, brown, and black, and range in size from 3 to 6 feet wide by 15 to 50 feet long. Larger sizes are available to professionals. Biodegradable versions are available, too, made of cloth or peat paper. Available with various degrees of porosity.

USE: Landscape fabrics allow moisture and water to penetrate through to the plants, but prevent weeds from growing. Not considered suitable for landscaped gardens (unless covered with a thin layer of organic or decorative stone mulches as they are very unnatural looking, but quite useful in a vegetable garden, where they also warm up the soil for early-season planting. Cut holes for plants to grow through. Open-weave fabric is also useful for covering newly seeded lawns to keep the seed from washing or blowing away, and to encourage germination, if not treated with weed preventative chemicals.

USE TIP: Some fabric is made from fibers (such as peat moss and recycled paper) that break down—a good product for annual use in a vegetable garden, as it does not have to be removed but can be plowed into the field at the end of the season.

BUYING TIP: This is usually an expensive product: A roll 3 by 100 feet might sell for around $60.

POLYETHYLENE SHEETING

ALSO KNOWN AS: Black polyethylene, black plastic mulch, black poly sheeting weed shield, weed barrier

DESCRIPTION: Rolls of black plastic, usually 3 or 6 feet wide and 25 to 100 feet long, although it can be found in sheets 40 feet wide by 100 feet long; commercial growers use rolls 3 and 4 feet wide by 1,000 feet long. Comes in thickness ranging from 1.5 to 6 mil; for comparison, a sturdy garbage bag is about 3 mil thick (a mil is one-thousandth of an inch); 4 mil is considered average strong sheeting, while 6 mil is used under stone mulches. Some brands have millions of microscopic holes that allow water to penetrate while still preventing weeds from growing.

USE: A good mulch for vegetable gardens, but not suited for landscape mulching, though it is often placed under sand and brick patios to prevent weeds from growing. Also used under decks and concrete for the same reason. Because of its color, it absorbs the sun and helps warm up a vegetable bed and speeds up seed germination. This is particularly useful for plants that need warm soil when they begin growth. Cut holes in the plastic for the plants to grow through.

USE TIP: If you are using solid plastic sheet, water cannot penetrate, so you must get water underneath by using a soaker hose (see chapter 8) or other means of irrigation. Although it can be placed under a decorative mulch, it may eventually show through.

BUYING TIP: Black plastic is a good vegetable crop mulch and is not very expensive at twenty-nine cents a square yard.

STONE MULCHES

ALSO KNOWN AS: Landscape chips, landscape stone, garden stone, decorative stone mulch

DESCRIPTION: Pebbled, chipped, or crushed rock of varying sizes, shapes, and colors. Pebbles may be sorted into colors as different as pink, yellow, and brown.

TYPES: *Brick nuggets:* Deep red pieces of brick in three sizes, ¼ to 1½ inches across.

Granite chips: Chips of granite, red or black in color. As with all stone mulches, the texture varies according to "grind."

Limestone chips: White stone chips of varying size and texture.

Marble chips: Usually white, sometimes red or black chips varying in size from pea-sized to 3 to 4 inches in diameter. Texture varies, depending on how the stone is chipped.

River gravel (also known as *river pebbles):* White or off-white rounded pebbles available in different textures.

Volcanic rock (also known as *lava rock* or *volcanic stone):* A red or black rock mulch created when volcanic rock is chipped into different-sized particles. One-third the weight of regular stone products.

USE: Low-maintenance mulch. Often seen in commercial landscaping around fast-food places, industrial buildings, and shopping malls, but generally not around homes where gardeners are not willing to make the trade-off of convenience versus aesthetics: This type of mulch does not rot, decompose, harbor termites or other insects, burn, fade, or erode—but it is not natural. Some people find the starkness of white stone mulch pleasing in contrast to the colors of their plants, even though it is an unnatural pairing.

USE TIPS: Use as you would any mulch, applying to a depth of about 1 to 3 inches. For extra weed control, chips can be placed over landscape fabric or a polyethylene sheeting mulch (see pages 27–29). Marble chip mulch raises the pH slightly, and therefore should be avoided with shallow-rooted, acid-loving plants such as azaleas. Lightweight volcanic rock is likely to float off slopes in rainstorms.

BUYING TIPS:

Granite chips: Like other stone mulches, this is more available in areas of the country where the stone is found naturally. Prices vary according to availability. Granite chips are generally among the more expensive mulches, going for around $4 per cubic foot.

Limestone chips: Considerably cheaper than marble chips. Selling for around $1.50 per cubic foot, it is one of the less expensive inorganic mulches, especially in areas of the country where it is mined.

Marble chips: One of the most expensive mulches, retailing at around $7 a cubic foot.

River gravel: A moderately priced inorganic mulch selling for around $2 per cubic foot.

Volcanic rock: Where it can be found, volcanic rock is a moderately priced inorganic mulch, retailing for about $2 per cubic foot. Easier to handle in quantity, due to its lighter weight.

Grass Seed and Sod

ABOUT GRASS SEED

Purchasing the right seed for your site is one of the most important steps in seeding and reseeding lawns. To help you make an informed decision about which grass seed to buy, a number of factors have to be considered, but they are not too complicated. Typical among them are

• How sunny or how shady is your site?

• How much time do you have to spend maintaining your lawn? Some grasses and combinations of grasses demand more care and maintenance than others.

• How much traffic will your lawn encounter? Will children be playing on it?

- How much water is available and how often will you be able to water the lawn?
- How quick-growing does the grass need to be? Is it being planted on a slope?
- What climatic zone you are in—do you need a *Southern, (warm-season)* or *Northern (cool-season)* grass?

There is a strong tradition in America of having a beautifully maintained lawn, and that tradition is not about to die; a "perfect," uniformly green lawn remains a basic element of suburban life. It is, however, likely to evolve somewhat as its high costs—environmental, monetary, and labor—become unacceptable. In some parts of the country, water alone is a major cost. More and more homeowners are choosing to conserve water by using less water-intensive landscaping than lawns, such as a plan that emphasizes trees and shrubs.

Most people cannot afford to be so picky about lawns resembling perfectly manicured outdoor carpets as professional "turf managers" who care for golf courses and the like. After all, the model for perfect lawns is British, and few places in this country have the ideal growing conditions that the British do (indeed, grass is native to few of our settled areas), let alone the years it took for them to get their lawns going right. Just pouring chemicals and other products onto the ground every weekend does not make a perfect lawn. A little thought and planning can solve problems better than lots of money and products, and a beautiful lawn can be had if the idea that it must be absolutely perfect is put aside.

Today's sensible approach to lawns includes such notions as:
- A well-prepared and maintained site will produce a healthy lawn more able to resist diseases, pests, and weeds without the need for reliance on natural or synthetic chemicals.
- Chemical herbicides are not the only way to a weed-free lawn (and the possible threat to the environment of herbicide abuse makes a few weeds seem quite tolerable). Ninety percent of all weeds can be controlled through proper mowing and fertilization, according to some experts.
- Fertilizing twice a season will produce an acceptable turf cover, though some synthetic fertilizer manufacturers still recommend four or more feedings a year.
- The choice of the right grass seed and mixtures to fit the site has as much to do with how well the lawn will grow as anything else.
- We should break the typical American habit of overdependence on chemicals, especially new "convenience" blends that may duplicate others or include unnecessary products.

Synthetic chemicals should be used for what they do best: curing specific problems. Nontoxic methods should be explored and adopted wherever possible.

The best time to reseed or seed a lawn of cool-season grasses in the North is the early fall. This allows the grass to establish a good root system before winter. In the South, late spring is best. Look for the grass seed mixtures long before you are ready to plant to assure yourself that you will be able to get just what you want. Settling for whatever is available after the prime planting season will result in a poorer lawn that needs much more work.

You can't just throw the seed onto the ground and expect it to grow well. Soil preparation for a new or renovated lawn involves a fair amount of work. The soil should be tilled to a depth of 3 to 6 inches. All rocks, weeds, and old grass clumps should be removed. Hard soil should be opened up by incorporating peat moss, humus, and fertilizers as needed. Finally, the area should be leveled, rolled, and raked. After seeding according to directions, the lawn should be kept moist for the first few weeks and covered with a light, biodegradable lawn netting (see pages 283–84) or a thin layer of salt hay to protect the seeds a bit from birds, wind, rain, and excessive sun.

ABOUT SEED TYPES AND MIXTURES

In the North, many manufacturers offer premixed seed specifically developed for certain types of lawns, or the garden center may have its own mixture, or you can mix your own from the single types available. It is always important to know the types and amounts of seed in the mix to determine if you are really getting what you need. To do this, you need to know a little about the types of grass you can grow and what situations they are suited for, which is what this chapter is about.

Usually the *Northern,* or *cool-season,* mixes contain the ever-popular, hard-wearing Kentucky bluegrass, some turf-type fast-germinating, narrowleaf perennial ryegrasses (as opposed to the common broadleaf type), and some fine fescue. The actual mix depends entirely on the part of the country where it is sold and, of course, on your taste, budget, and needs. *Southern,* or *warm-season,* grasses are generally not mixtures but rather one single type of grass, most of which are sold as sod, plugs, or sprigs (individual plants) instead of seed.

Some mixtures are described in general terms, such as *play* (for high traffic), *sun* (for more than four hours of sun daily), *shade* (for less sun), and *sun/shade* (for the typical mix of areas). The local garden center quality mixture is sometimes a good bet, if the ingredients are listed so you can judge for yourself.

Should you go with one variety of grass or a mixture of several? Particularly in the North, if you use just one variety of seed for your lawn (monoculture), you may be courting disaster. Lawns of a single variety may be badly injured by diseases that affect that variety, whereas lawns that contain a blend of types of grasses are more likely to have only some affected by the disease while the others survive. Nothing is sadder than a completely browned-off and dead lawn of a single type of grass, while surrounding lawns of mixed types survive! A mixture of grasses also produces a lawn with a more interesting texture than the single-variety lawns. Southern grasses are unfortunately not usually seeded (sod is laid down), nor are they compatible aesthetically in mixes.

As already mentioned, it's important to know what you're getting when you buy grass seed. The label on a mixture lists the types of *grass seed, crop seed, inert matter,* and *weed seed.* You want the lowest levels of the latter three items, of course, no more than 1 percent of each (in fact, there should be no crop seed or, at most, a few tenths of a percent). Note the percentages of grass seed types and see if that meshes with your needs and desires. This chapter should help you decide what's best, or check with your local Cooperative Extension for help (appendix C). The *percentage of seed germination* should be 80 to 90 percent and the seed should have been tested *during the year of purchase.* The state of origin should not affect its growth. All of this information should be on the label.

The listing of the types of grass seed can be a little confusing, though the following pages should help explain this. *Cultivars* (or *cultivated varieties* or *named varieties* or *proprietary types)* and *hybrids* (types that are the result of crossing or breeding plants of different species or varieties to respond to needs, ranging from pure aesthetics to better disease and insect resistance) are specific types of grass that tend to perform well; most are new and improved types, and new ones are constantly being added to the market. Look for these when buying grass seed. There are over three hundred of them now, biologically different (they are even patented or registered by the developers—the symbol is *PVP,* for Plant Variety Protection), but only some of the essentially similar and more commonly found ones are listed in this chapter as an example. There are many more that are perfectly fine but that are not listed.

Manufacturers may swear by one or another variety, but the differences are subtle and the ultimate performance of all grass seed is influenced by weather, fertilizer, watering, and soil to a great extent. No miracles should be claimed by the manufacturers. Be leery of any that do. Price generally reflects quality, and national brands are dependable.

Most of the grass seed in a mix should be of the fine-textured type, and should be cultivars rather than "unnamed" or "common" types. For example, "Adelphi Kentucky bluegrass" is better than "Kentucky bluegrass." Much like wine, the generic types are not as good nor as expensive as the ones with more specifics on the labels—region, year, etc. The common, unnamed variety is often listed as "variety not stated." This is the kind of seed labeled "red fescue" or "perennial ryegrass." Try to find named seed for a more vigorous, disease-resistant, and longer-lasting quality lawn. Unnamed varieties are better for a special use such as a quick cover crop to prevent erosion or mud or to solve a particular overwintering problem. The more named seed in the mixture, the better the buy.

As to which specific cultivar is best for you, get all the advice you can, experiment, and keep in mind that almost any of the new ones are bound to do better. The fact that they are named is sufficient to set them a cut above the unnamed kind and to make them worth a little bit more in price.

State land grant universities and the U.S. Department of Agriculture evaluate turf grass types by characteristic and by overall performance on a state-by-state basis, providing yet another way to decide which type is best for you. Check with your Cooperative Extension (see appendix C) for more information. With gene transplants entering the picture, we may yet find the "perfect" grass seed—but don't hold your breath.

SOD

DESCRIPTION: Grass sheets, like pieces of a grass rug, typically 2 by 4 feet and 2 to 4 inches thick (including the grass), that have formed a thick root mass. Type of grass depends on where grown and is the choice of the supplier.

USE: Provides an instant lawn on well-prepared sites. Sod is particularly useful on sloping sites as erosion control, where the time that grass takes to grow from seed is a problem.

USE TIPS: Best installed in the spring through early fall, provided there is ample water. Sod should not be laid if the ground is too wet to be prepared correctly, but it must be moist soil. Soil preparation for sodding is similar to that for seeding. Sod is laid down in a pattern that looks like brickwork; this staggering ensures that horizontal seams do not meet. The strips are laid perpendicular to a slope. If installed properly, seams do not show and the sod appears to be one continuous lawn.

Most sod contains grasses that do well in the sun and not so well in shade. A few sod growers do provide a shade-tolerant type, but it will probably have to be specially ordered by your garden center.

BUYING TIPS: Sodding is initially more expensive than seeding, but offers the possibility of instant gratification for those who can pay for it or need it for erosion control. After all, it is essentially an instant lawn. Most sod sold in garden centers does not have a label that tells you what grasses are in it. *Ask!* If your garden center cannot provide this information, it is best to go somewhere else. Much of the sod sold in the North today contains Kentucky bluegrass or blends, which are better than those that contain only one type. Using a sod that contains a blend is wise as each variety has its own strengths, with some able to resist diseases and pests better than others. On the other hand, Southern grasses are sold in the South unmixed, such as Bermudagrass or St. Augustinegrass. In either case look for thin-cut sod, which roots faster. Roots and soil should be ½ inch thick. Three- to 4-inch thick-cut sod can tear easily because of the weight and is harder to handle.

Northern Grasses

ABOUT NORTHERN GRASSES

The following cool-season grasses grow well in the Northern climates and at higher altitudes in the South. Wherever there is a winter snow, they should thrive, growing especially vigorously in the spring and fall.

COLONIAL BENTGRASS

BOTANICAL NAME: *Agrostis tenuis*

SAMPLE AVAILABLE CULTIVARS: 'Exeter,' 'Highland'

DESCRIPTION: Bentgrasses are finer in texture than Kentucky bluegrasses and require more care; they are therefore more likely to succumb to disease. These grasses usually spread by rhizomes (a below-ground-level spreading branch) and have thin, erect blades.

USE: A grass that does well in shade and sun and in acid soils that won't support other grasses; mixes well with fine fescues. Bentgrass helps produce a thick, rich lawn in areas of the country that are seasonally moist, such as the Northwest and Northeast coastal regions, and some areas around the Great Lakes. Fares well in inland New England, too. Avoid using in hotter, drier areas.

USE TIP: Colonial bentgrass needs frequent mowing to a height of ¾ to 1 inch, which often means mowing twice a week in areas where it grows rapidly.

CREEPING BENTGRASS

BOTANICAL NAME: *Agrostis palustris*

SAMPLE AVAILABLE CULTIVARS: 'Emerald,' 'Penncross,' 'Prominent'

DESCRIPTION: Creeping bentgrass is a beautiful fine grass that spreads naturally by lateral stolons to produce a thick, green carpet. *Creeping* is a term used interchangeably with *spreading*.

USE: This is the incredible stuff you find on putting and bowling greens, mowed to as short as ¼ inch—or even less.

USE TIP: These grasses need lots of moisture, fertile soils, and much attention. Not recommended for homeowners, unless your home is a country club and you have (or are) a full-time groundskeeper.

BUYING TIP: Avoid any mix containing this seed for the reasons stated earlier, though this is unlikely to be found in a typical seed mixture.

FINE FESCUE

SAMPLE AVAILABLE CULTIVARS:
Red type: 'Boreal,' 'Dawson Red,' 'Flyer,' 'Fortress,' 'Pennlawn,' 'Ruby'
Chewings type: 'Agram,' 'Banner,' 'Cascade,' 'Highlight,' 'Jamestown,' 'Koket,' 'Shadow'

Hard type: 'Aurora,' 'Biljart,' 'C-26,' 'Reliant,' 'Scaldis,' 'SR 3000,' 'Waldina'

DESCRIPTION: Thin-leaved and olive to dark green in color, with a thinner and finer blade than that of bluegrass. Often found in mixtures with bluegrass because it is particularly suited to Northern areas of the country and faster to establish itself.

TYPES: *Red fescue (Festuca rubra*—also known as *spreading* or *creeping red fescue):* Though it spreads slowly (by rhizomes, a sort of swollen underground stem), it establishes itself quickly in the first season and is therefore often mixed with slow-to-establish bluegrass.
 Chewings fescue (Festuca rubra 'Commutata'): Tends to form dense clumps; named after the man who developed it, a Mr. Chewings of New Zealand. Can be cut shorter than red.
 Hard fescue (Festuca longifolia or var. *duriuscula):* Developed for an increased tolerance to heat and drought.
 Sheep fescue (Festuca ovina): Very clumpy. Better used as an ornamental border plant than for turf. Usually very blue. Not commonly available.

USE: Most often found in mixtures with other grass seed. Grows under drier and shadier conditions than many other grasses— hardier in general than bluegrasses. Fine fescues are tough grasses that wear well in traffic areas.

USE TIPS: Give this grass sun or dry shade and it does well even in poor soil. Does not require as much nitrogen as bluegrass and can be mown to a minimum height of 1½ inches, though 2 inches is better for the health of the grass in the heat of the summer.

BUYING TIPS: Buy in a mix with other grasses rather than alone. The best shade grass. The varieties 'Highlight' and 'Jamestown' are good Chewings types for thick lawns.

KENTUCKY BLUEGRASS

BOTANICAL NAME: *Poa pratensis*

SAMPLE AVAILABLE CULTIVARS: 'Abbey,' 'Adelphi,' 'America,' 'Arboretum,' 'Baron,' 'Bensun,' 'Birka,' 'Bonnieblue,' 'Bristol,' 'Chateau,' 'Classic,' 'Delta,' 'Derby,' 'Eclipse,' 'Enmundi,' 'Estate,' 'Flyking,' 'Freedom,' 'Glade,' 'Gnome,' 'Huntsville,' 'Liberty,' 'Majesti,' 'Merion' (developed from a single plant found on the course of the Merion Golf Club in Ardmore, Pa.), 'Merit,' 'Monopoly,' 'Nassau,' 'Nugget,' 'Plush,' 'Ram I,' 'Rugby,' 'Sydsport,' 'Touchdown,' 'Vantage,' 'Vieta,' 'Windsor'

DESCRIPTION: An attractive, fine-textured, dark green, perennial grass. It is often in sod because it spreads from rhizomes (underground stems) to form a thick carpet. Over eighty cultivars have been developed, making this one of the most common and popular grass seeds. Some are listed here; researchers continue to develop better ones constantly.

USE: Kentucky bluegrass seed produces a thick, good-looking lawn. It is your basic Northern grass. In order for it to be able to compete with weeds and withstand heavy traffic or play, and because it takes a while for bluegrass to establish itself, it is often mixed with *fine fescues* or *perennial ryegrasses* (see preceding and next entries, respectively), which establish themselves much faster and are a little hardier or shade-tolerant. Does best when mowed to a height of at least 1½ inches (higher in shady areas) and needs a fair amount of feeding, moisture, and light, though types vary in their needs. 'Glade,' 'Bensun,' and 'Eclipse' are excellent performers in shade. 'Adelphi' is one of the most popular types.

USE TIPS: Do not overwater during the hotter months. Mow grass often so that it does not grow more than 2 to 3 inches in height, but without cutting more than one-third of the length of the blades. Grows best in sun, but some varieties tolerate shade better than others.

BUYING TIPS: Select varieties and blends that include disease-resistant cultivars. Specialized publications will tell you which diseases each grass resists. Avoid mixes of bluegrass and turf-type tall fescues, as the fescues tend to overwhelm the bluegrass.

PERENNIAL RYEGRASS

ALSO KNOWN AS: Turf-type perennial ryegrass

BOTANICAL NAME: *Lolium perenne*

SAMPLE AVAILABLE CULTIVARS: 'All*Star,' 'Applause,' 'Blazer,' 'Citation,' 'Delray,' 'Derby,' 'Diplomat,' 'Fiesta,' 'Gator,' 'Loretta,' 'Manhattan II' (developed from a single plant found in New York City's Central Park), 'NK-200,' 'Omega,' 'Ovation,'

'Pennant,' 'Pennfine,' 'Prestige,' 'Regal,' 'SR4000,' 'Tara,' 'York-town II'

USE: Provides quick cover and is tough and clean-mowing during the summer (it will cut well only with a very sharp mower blade during the late spring). However, it often does not come back or does not do well the second year after it is planted in locations with severe winter cold and little snow cover. Found in mixtures because it provides coverage while the slower-germinating spreading grasses fill in, and it looks good, to boot.

USE TIPS: Ryegrass needs the same care as Kentucky bluegrass (see preceding entry) and should be mown as frequently. Grows best in full sun with plenty of water. Mow to 1 to 2 inches.

BUYING TIPS: When mixing or buying in a mix with bluegrass and fine fescue, make sure there is no more than about 20 percent ryegrass in the mixture. Used in higher percentages, the rye-grass crowds out the slower-growing grasses. Look for varieties that are new *turf-types* with endophytes (insect resistance). 'All*Star,' 'Manhattan,' and 'Pennfine' are good choices. Avoid annual or Italian ryegrasses.

REDTOP

BOTANICAL NAME: *Agrostis alba*

DESCRIPTION: A coarse grass that forms a thin turf.

USE: Primarily as an erosion control or cover grass along high-ways and open lands. Not a permanent grass, and too thin and unattractive for use as a lawn.

USE TIPS: Redtop requires minimum care and maintenance, and does well in wet, cool sites. Does not require much fertilizer and grows in poorly drained soils. Moisture is its primary require-ment.

BUYING TIP: Avoid mixes with redtop in them. It is not at all suited to use as a lawn grass, though it was once found in grass mixes.

ROUGH BLUEGRASS

BOTANICAL NAME: *Poa trivialis*

SAMPLE AVAILABLE CULTIVAR: 'Sabre'

DESCRIPTION: Prostrate (meaning it lies down) light green grass, similar to the bentgrasses. It spreads by surface stolons, but is not a very hardy grass.

USE: Does well in moist, cool shade but is not as drought-resistant as other grasses as it is shallow-rooted.

USE TIPS: Does not grow well in sun or under dry conditions. 'Sabre' is a cultivar that grows well in the North; in the South it is used as a winter grass to overseed lawns after Bermuda-grasses go dormant during the winter season. Mow to 1 to 2 inches.

BUYING TIP: Buy this grass seed in shade mixtures with fine fescues and other seed.

TALL FESCUE

BOTANICAL NAME: *Festuca arundinacea*

SAMPLE AVAILABLE CULTIVARS: 'Arid,' 'Bonanza,' 'Carefree,' 'Chesapeake,' 'Falcon,' 'Galway,' 'Houndog,' 'Kentucky,' 'Mustang,' 'Rebel II,' 'Tempo,' 'Titan,' 'Trident'

DESCRIPTION: A coarse-textured bunchgrass (one that does not spread), but once established, its deep roots allow it to be persistent. Relatively disease-, wear-, heat-, shade-, and drought-tolerant. Good winter recovery and spring green-up. New cultivars, known as *turf-type tall fescues,* have much finer texture owing to their thinner leaves.

USE: Particularly suited to difficult sites in the central United States between Northern and Southern regions—transition areas. It can be used in areas that get little attention, as it does well in poor soils without needing maintenance, and is often used wherever bluegrass or the fine fescues have failed. Often considered a weed in Northern areas where it is difficult to remove from bluegrass lawns. It does, however, prove useful in areas where nothing else grows well. If it is found in a mixture with Kentucky bluegrass, it should be the main component—over 90 percent. Developed for use in the transition zones that fall between the Northern and Southern areas of the United States.

USE TIPS: Tall fescue requires basic care, though it keeps its color better if fertilized in the spring and fall. Mow 2 to 3 inches high.

BUYING TIP: In a major exception to the rule, this is not good to have in a seed mix, especially if appearance is important to you. It doesn't spread, but it does persist. Use it alone, and use only improved varieties.

Southern Grasses

ABOUT SOUTHERN GRASSES

Most of the following warm-season grasses will grow only in the South, though some can be grown in the so-called transition areas at the lower altitudes. Therefore most will be found for sale only in the South. Also, unlike the Northern grasses, these are not aesthetically compatible and thus are used alone and not in mixtures. They are, however, more resistant to weeds, heat, and drought than Northern grasses. Generally only the common types are available as seed—all, except Bahiagrass,* are propagated vegetatively, so they must be planted as sod, plugs (small clumps of sod), or sprigs (individual grass plants).

BAHIAGRASS

ALSO KNOWN AS: Bahia grass

BOTANICAL NAME: *Paspalum notatum*

SAMPLE AVAILABLE CULTIVARS: 'Paraguay,' 'Pensacola,' 'Wilmington'

DESCRIPTION: An easy-care, coarse-textured grass. Considered a weed if mixed with other grasses. Has unattractive seed heads. Commonly available as seed.

USE: Bahiagrass is an inexpensive, low-density, coarse grass that grows well in the South, especially along the Gulf Coast. A few varieties can grow in cooler regions where the temperatures get as low as 5° F. Bahiagrass grows in poor conditions, such as sandy soils, where little else will grow. Drought-tolerant.

USE TIPS: This is a relatively low-maintenance grass. It tolerates some neglect and poor conditions, but of course looks better if

---

*Throughout the industry, on packages and in books and magazines, these grasses are written as one word, i.e. Bahiagrass. Unfortunately, the correct form according to Webster's is to use two words, i.e. Bahia Grass. Because this is a guide to what you find in stores, and because at least one Northern grass is written as one word in Webster's (Bluegrass), they are listed here as used, that is, one word. Both forms are acceptable.

at least some care is given. Mow high, between 2 and 3 inches. Needs frequent mowing.

BUYING TIP: Bahiagrass in a mix with fine fescue produces a quick cover, but the fine fescue dies out as the Bahiagrass fills in.

BERMUDAGRASS

ALSO KNOWN AS: Common Bermudagrass

BOTANICAL NAME: *Cynodon dactylon*

SAMPLE AVAILABLE CULTIVARS: 'Cheyenne,' 'Guymon,' 'Midiron,' 'Sahara,' 'Sunturf,' 'Tifton,' 'Tifgreen' ('Tifton 328'), 'Tiflawn' ('Tifton 57'), 'Tifway' ('Tifton 419'), 'Tufcote,' 'U-3,' 'Vamont'

DESCRIPTION: Medium- to fine-textured grass with dark green color. Some types are sterile hybrids that must be planted as sod, plugs, or sprigs—they do not come as seed. The first three listed above are the newest, improved seeded types.

USE: Easy-to-grow, wear-resistant grass that responds well to good care in areas where the temperature remains high. Common seeded types are found in mixtures for Southern or warmer areas of the country, intended for lawns as well as golf courses. The best sportsfield turf.

USE TIPS: Unlike Bahiagrass (see preceding entry), some Bermudagrasses demand much attention. They generally require much fertilizing to look good, though some varieties are hardier than others. They only stay green where the temperature is above 55° F. They turn brown at the first frost and remain so until the return of summer. Lawns in frost areas must be winterseeded or overseeded with cool-season grasses (such as perennial ryegrass) to keep weeds from invading. Mow to ⅔ to 1¼ inches.

BUYING TIP: Often included in mixes sold in hospitable areas. Because it is a high-maintenance grass, buy only mixtures with a lower percentage of Bermudagrass seed.

ST. AUGUSTINEGRASS

BOTANICAL NAME: *Stenotaphrum secundatum*

SAMPLE AVAILABLE CULTIVARS: 'Bitter Blue,' 'Floralawn,' 'Flora-tam,' 'Floratine,' 'Raleigh'

DESCRIPTION: Attractive, wide-leaved, rapid-spreading, shade-tolerant, medium green grass with flat-tipped leaves. The leaves are in bunches and give the lawn a thick appearance. Not available in seed form—it must be planted from sod, plugs, or sprigs.

USE: One of the most widely used Southern grasses. Grows well in shade and sun, and tolerates salty soils. It is often used in sod or sold in small clumps (plugs) to be set out in a grid pattern to fill in, as this grass spreads rapidly.

USE TIPS: Though normally it should be relatively easy to care for, St. Augustinegrass has been affected by several severe diseases and pests in the last few years. Unfortunately, these problems require high chemical maintenance, and if it were not for these plagues St. Augustinegrass would be easier to grow. Also needs lots of water. Does best in neutral to alkaline soils. Mow to 1½ to 2 inches.

BUYING TIP: A very good grass for Southern lawns, but given the problems recently with pests and diseases, try to buy more resistant varieties. Check with your local Cooperative Extension agent (see appendix C) for advice.

ZOYSIAGRASS

ALSO KNOWN AS: Japanese carpet grass

BOTANICAL NAMES: *Zoysia japonica, Z. matrella, Z. tenuifolia*

SAMPLE AVAILABLE CULTIVARS: 'Belair,' 'El Toro,' 'Flawn,' 'Meyer,' 'Midwestern' (all *Z. japonica)* and 'Emerald' (a cross between *Z. japonica* and *Z. tenuifolia)*

DESCRIPTION: The thickest and most attractive of the Southern turf grasses. Its most distinguishing characteristic, unfortunately, is that it turns brown during its long off-season. Certain varieties have been developed that will grow in the Midwest and other areas of the country. Similar in appearance to Bermudagrass. Very slow to establish—it may take up to four years to form a lawn. *Z. japonica,* also called *Meyer zoysia,* is the most common improved species, and has medium width leaves. *Z. matrella* has the widest leaves (and is very rarely available) and *Z. tenuifolia* has the finest. Common seed is available in limited quantity; most is sold as sod, plugs, or sprigs.

USE: Used in Southern lawn mixtures where density is desired, mixed in with a good companion cover grass such as turf-type tall fescues. It grows well in sun but not as well in shade. Thickest and most resilient cover of all grasses. Best used in transition zones.

USE TIPS: Though not as high-maintenance as Bermudagrass, zoysiagrass is slow to germinate and mature. It does not recover as well as Bermudagrass does against pests or damage by soil compaction. It should be mixed with other grasses to provide a quick cover and crowd out weeds. You may need a heavy-duty mower to cut this. Mow to a height of 1 to 2 inches. Avoid planting in poorly drained, moist areas. Remove thatch regularly.

BUYING TIP: Zoysiagrass seed is good in a turf mix in areas of the country where it will grow. It should, however, be mixed with grasses that mature more quickly. Unfortunately, seed is rare and costly—sprigs are more common.

CHAPTER 3

Fertilizers and Plant Care Products

ABOUT FERTILIZERS

Fertilizers may very well be the most common product purchased in garden centers—and the one that causes the most confusion. Here's an extended introduction to help orient the average beginning gardener who wants to know the background for the terms used on fertilizer labels and found in gardening advice. If you want to get right to the essential listings, just skip over the next few pages and start in with the first item, on page 55.

Though often referred to as *plant food,* fertilizers are just a part of the plant food creation process. Green plants actually make their own food through photosynthesis, the process whereby green plants use sunlight, water, and carbon dioxide to produce the carbohydrates that nourish the plant. Sixteen elements, or *nutrients,* are essential in order for green plants to do this. The first three elements needed are carbon, hydrogen, and oxygen, and they come from water and air. Whenever any of the thirteen other nutrients are lacking in the soil (or just need to be replenished as they are naturally used or leached out of the soil by water), they can be provided by fertilizers.

The most important basic nutrients, commonly known as *primary nutrients* (or *macronutrients,* or *essential,* or *major nutrients),* are *nitrogen* (chemical symbol N), *phosphorus*—also referred to as *phosphate, phosphoric acid,* or *phosphoric oxide* (chemical symbol P, also P_2O_5), and *potassium*—commonly referred to by its soluble name, *potash* (chemical symbol K, also K_2O).

Each of these elements affects plant growth differently (and each plant a bit differently) and must be chosen according to what you have determined the plant needs. In general, though, the primary nutrients work as follows:

- *Nitrogen* promotes the growth of green leaves and stems. (Grass is a big consumer of nitrogen.)
- *Phosphorus* aids in the production of roots, flowers, and fruit. (This is most desirable for ornamentals, vegetables, and especially bulbs.)
- *Potassium* aids in the flowering and fruiting, as well as the sturdiness, of the plant in terms of disease and stress resistance (like winter weather).

All plants and soils require these nutrients in a particular balance, and providing too much of one nutrient over another will cause stress and problems for the plant. For example, plants getting too much nitrogen will have plenty of green leaves, but they will be soft, the root system will be underdeveloped, and the blooms for flowers or fruit will be retarded. Read your detailed gardening guides carefully to determine what your plants really need.

The three primary nutrients described above work in conjunction with three *secondary nutrients* and at least seven *micronutrients,* which ultimately help the plant function, much as vitamins and minerals do for humans. Just as we need a balanced diet with different vitamins to turn our food into energy, plants cannot process the macronutrients without a proper amount of micronutrient minerals in the soil. Macronutrients also tend to balance out the pH of the soil, pH being the term used to describe the relative acidity or alkalinity of soil (see page 4 for a discussion of pH).

The secondary nutrients are *calcium, magnesium,* and *sulfur,* and are sometimes lumped with the macronutrients. Under normal circumstances, these occur naturally in soil in sufficient quantity but need to be added to correct a deficiency or to cure a particular problem—much as with humans and vitamin pills. And too much can be a bad thing. Here's what they're needed for:

- *Calcium* is needed for the cell-manufacturing process— particularly important for early root growth. It is usually supplied by lime or other soil conditioners.
- *Magnesium* is a prime element of seed development and development of chlorophyll. It is usually found with calcium.

• *Sulfur* is a primary element of plant proteins and helps give plants a dark green color. It is supplied by most fertilizers and nature (including rain from polluted skies!), often in some form of sulfate. (*Sulphur* and *sulphate* are alternative terms.)

Micronutrients include *iron, manganese, copper, boron, zinc, chlorine,* and *molybdenum.* As fertilizers, they are usually applied to specific plants to cure specific conditions of deficiency. They occur sufficiently in normal, pH-balanced soils, although houseplants, being in an unnatural environment, may need a boost sometimes via special products (see chelated micronutrients, page 68). They should be added only when you know your soil needs them, otherwise you may damage your plants—just as humans can overdo it with vitamin supplements. In most cases, though, it is easier to change the pH of your soil in order to get your micronutrient levels where they should be. They are needed in very small quantities, so small that the amount is called a *trace,* giving them the alternative name *trace elements;* iron is needed in larger quantities to promote chlorophyll production and the resulting green color.

One important thing to keep in mind when using fertilizers is that only the right amount will do. It helps only when the nutrients are needed; more is not better and may be quite harmful (in fact, overfertilizing is more harmful than underfertilizing), so do not overapply. With many plants, such as fruit trees, you can reduce the need for fertilizer by pruning and mulching, among other good gardening practices. Finally, no amount of fertilizing can make up for serious environmental problems, such as poor soil, rampant disease, extreme acidity or alkalinity, lack of moisture or sunlight, or (and this is the hardest to accept for so many of us) an inappropriate climate. Plants cannot be forced to grow where they really don't want to just by pouring on more fertilizer.

ABOUT FERTILIZER LABEL TERMS

Fertilizer packages are labeled with a host of confusing terms, the most common of which are defined here. Note that some items are mixed together to provide a balance of characteristics; the most important thing to understand is that certain ingredients make the fertilizer fast- or slow-acting. All nutrients are absorbed by the plants via osmosis when in solution, so you always need water with fertilizers. The details you find on product labels are required by laws that vary from state to state.

COMPLETE FERTILIZER: Fertilizers intended for general use which contain significant amounts of the three primary nutrients (N, P, and K). Hundreds of these formulations are marketed for use as "plant food," "vegetable food," or for specific plants, as explained later in this chapter. The percentages of these three elements contained in any mixture (and their sources) are required by law to appear on the package label. N, P, and K percentages are stated as three numbers separated by dashes—5-10-5, 8-6-4, 22-3-3, etc. This is called the *grade, ratio, rating, guaranteed analysis,* or *NPK number.* The first number is always the percentage of nitrogen, the second number is always the percentage of phosphorus, and the last is always the percentage of potash. The grade tells you how much of each nutrient is in the package, by weight, which is what you are ultimately concerned with—fertilizer is usually applied at a rate of so many pounds per 1,000 square feet. Obviously, these same numbers tell you the ratio, or proportion, of one nutrient to another as well.

Keep in mind when comparing prices that you pay for the nutrient concentration, not the weight per se. Once you have determined the square feet of the area you wish to fertilize (most helpful if rounded off to the nearest 1,000 square feet) and what your fertilizer needs are, purchase the fertilizer with the appropriate grade for the amount of nutrients you want, while taking into account the size of the bag. For example, a common lawn fertilizer, Scotts Turf Builder, is rated at 29-3-4. A 15.5-pound bag contains 29 percent nitrogen, or 4.5 pounds. If you bought a fertilizer rated 15-3-4 instead, you would need almost twice as much fertilizer—30 pounds—to obtain the same 4.5 pounds of nitrogen. And always note how much of it is going to be released quickly and how much released slowly, according to the information on the types of nitrogen noted later on in this chapter.

INCOMPLETE FERTILIZER: If a fertilizer contains only one or two of the primary nutrients, it is called *incomplete.* This is not to say that it is of lower quality, but simply to identify it as a fertilizer to be used in a specific way to treat a specific deficiency. An almost infinite variety of mixes are made for specific applications, which are explained later in this chapter. Keep in mind when shopping that the unit cost of each nutrient increases as the package size decreases.

ORGANIC FERTILIZER: Any fertilizer produced by natural, once-living or live sources—animals or plants—is *organic, natural organic, natural, bio-organic,* or *naturally derived.* These products all contain carbon compounds. (The opposite of natural organic is *synthetic,* or man-made, fertilizer—manufactured products made from nonliving sources—called *inorganic, chemical,* or *petrochemical fertilizers.)* If a natural product is mined and then treated in some chemical process, it is no longer considered purely organic. The nitrogen in organic fertilizers is the *water-insoluble,* slow-release type, meaning it lasts longer in the soil before leaching out and probably will not "burn" the plants. Some well-known organic fertilizers are manure, blood meal, and fish tankage, all expanded upon later on in this chapter. They nourish the plants as they decay naturally with the help of microorganisms.

However, and this is terribly important, a fertilizer may be labeled "organic" even if part of it is from manufactured sources, as long as a certain percentage of it is from water-insoluble materials (most synthetic chemical products are almost 100 percent soluble, which is why they work and then wash out of the soil so quickly). Standards for use of the word *organic* in fertilizer labeling are determined by each state and can vary quite a bit. *Natural organic* is the most precise term, and the one generally used in this book, though in labeling it is used interchangeably with just plain *organic.* The fact that a product may be labeled by its manufacturer as organic or partly organic when it contains man-made chemicals or is chemically treated is confusing at best and downright misleading at worst, especially in this day when there is a certain cachet attached to the word *organic* by many consumers. *Caveat emptor.*

WATER-INSOLUBLE NITROGEN (WIN): This is a slow-release form of nitrogen. A certain amount is desirable, especially when mixed with faster-acting nitrogen sources like those noted here. A higher percentage of this kind of nitrogen in relation to the fast-acting kind means that the plant does not receive much nitrogen right away, but it does eventually; this is usually desirable because the plant has time to get the nitrogen in a useful way. Check your gardening guides to determine how much to apply, as the size and frequency of the applications will be dictated by the percentage of insoluble nitrogen. More than 50 percent means fewer applications. The presence of water-insoluble nitrogen tends to make the fertilizer more expensive, but less likely to burn the plant or to leach out, like the fast-acting nitrogen sources. Organic fertilizers are high in this kind of nitrogen. Container plants that are watered frequently need this kind of nitrogen.

AMMONIACAL, UREA, AND NITRATE NITROGEN: Fast-acting

("quick-release"), inexpensive, synthetic, water-soluble sources of nitrogen, derived from the salt of an acid. These may lower the pH of the soil (acidify) various degrees, depending on the type of nitrate compound used. Various nitrates are usually mixed in complete fertilizers to lessen their effect on pH. They act quickly (they can even burn the plant) and are generally inexpensive, but also tend to leach quickly from the soil. Synthetic fertilizers are high in this kind of nitrogen, and because it is caustic, it should be handled very carefully. Too much too fast, and your plants may weaken, making them susceptible to fungi.

Included in this group are *ammonium nitrate, ammonium sulfate (sulfate of ammonia), calcium nitrate,* and *nitrate of soda* (though one brand of nitrate of soda is organic: Bulldog, from Chile). While these are usually components of complete fertilizers, most are also available separately—they have up to 46 percent nitrogen—if you want to mix your own fertilizer (not a great idea, by the way) or cure a particular major deficiency in extreme conditions, such as cool weather, when nutrients move slowly. Their labels indicate whether they acidify or alkalize the soil; most acidify the soil (lower the pH), as indicated in the *potential acidity equivalent,* explained below.

UREA-FORM, UF, OR UREAFORM, OR METHALINE UREA: Urea reacted with formaldehyde to make it partially water-insoluble, resulting in a slow-releasing, nonburning source of nitrogen, containing 35 to 40 percent nitrogen. Urea is a man-made form of nitrogen derived from natural gas products, and even though it is synthethized, because it contains carbon it is sometimes labeled "organic" or "synthetic organic." It is not organic, according to all but the broadest definition of the term. It competes with organic fertilizers in the marketplace, offering more slow-release nitrogen per pound, in general.

COATED SLOW-RELEASE UREA NITROGEN: This is the earlier-mentioned quick-release nitrogen coated with sulfur to delay its release, adding sulfur to the soil at the same time (which reduces the pH, meaning it acidifies the soil) and reducing the tendency of the chemical burn. Sometimes abbreviated SCU, for sulfur-coated urea. Each coated granule is called a *prill,* or *sprill.* Another form of synthetic, slow-release, treated nitrogen is IBDU, or isobutylidene diurea, which has about 30 percent nitrogen that releases at low temperatures over a long period of time.

POTENTIAL ACIDITY EQUIVALENT: This tells the degree to which a synthetic fertilizer will change the pH of a soil (natural organic fertilizers are not obliged to list this), expressed in terms of pounds of calcium carbonate per ton, that is, the amount of $CaCO_3$ needed to neutralize the acidifying effect of the fertilizer, and can range from 0 to over 2,200 pounds, with anything over about 400 being considered acidic, and a range up to about 1,000 being common. Most gardeners can ignore this—it is only important if a soil test indicates a pH problem or you are concerned about plants that are fussy about pH, such as hydrangeas. The actual degree of effect is not acute and really depends on many other factors. It's really more a question of building up acidity over time. Check your how-to books to find out if your plants need an acid or alkaline soil, and take soil tests to determine where you stand. Organic fertilizers do not create this problem as much as synthetic fertilizers, which tend to be acidic, especially the faster-acting, less expensive ones.

CHELATES OR CHELATED SECONDARY AND MICRONUTRIENTS: Water-soluble compounds of metals that are made readily available to the plants. Usually in the form of a foliar spray (one that is sprayed directly onto the leaves), they can also be applied to the soil like any other fertilizer. These nutrients would not be available to the plants unless they were chelated. Micronutrients may be aided in their becoming rapidly available by a chemical catalyst called a *chelating agent.* Iron, magnesium, manganese, copper, and zinc are the most common ones sold individually, although some products include more. Many gardeners consider these to be professional products only.

FORMS OF FERTILIZERS

LIQUID: Concentrations of either water-soluble powders or liquids that need to be diluted with water. Liquid fertilizers, also called *nutritional sprays,* may be used as a *foliar spray* (applied to the leaves—also called a *nutrient leaf spray)* or as a *ground spray* (applied to the ground to be absorbed through the roots). They are more easily applied (especially in small quantities) and usually more readily available to the plant than other forms, making them popular for houseplants. However, they are less practical for large areas and easy to overapply by mistake, which may burn the plant, and they are also easily leached from the soil. Most are meant to provide a special boost to plants in difficulty, and usually contain more micronutrients than the other forms of fertilizer.

SOLUBLE POWDERS: As the name suggests, these are plant nutrients in powder form that are dissolved in water before use. They offer quick sources of nutrients to plants suffering nutritional disorders, but are easily leached out of the soil. They may be blown away by the wind and can cake in storage, but generally cost less than other forms.

TIME-RELEASED OR CONTROLLED RELEASE: Fertilizers in capsule form (sometimes called a *prill* or *sprill),* covered with a resin membrane that dissolves slowly when the plant is watered and as the soil temperature rises, thus releasing the nutrients over a period of time. Often a sulfur coating, it lets water in through osmosis or just breaks down slowly. Some brands may last in the ground up to nine months, releasing fertilizer as the plant needs it. *Osmocote* is a well-known brand name of this sort.

PELLETIZED OR PELLETED: These are powders that have been compressed into pellets, in some cases containing uniform amounts of each nutrient. As it takes longer for the pellets to break down, the easily leached nutrients are released more slowly. They can be applied through spreaders, aren't affected by wind as powders are, and resist caking. Very large pellets may be called *tablets,* and are used mostly by professionals for planting shrubs and trees when they want the fertilizer to last up to two years.

SPIKES: Sticks or stakes, 2 to 3 inches long, made from a compacted fiber impregnated with fertilizer. These are often used for houseplants but are also available in larger sizes for trees and outdoor shrubs. The fertilizer is released slowly as the spike disintegrates in the soil. Some spikes also contain pesticides. This is the most convenient form for houseplants and small gardens, but expensive in terms of the amount of nitrogen.

GRANULAR OR GRANULATED: Granules, designed to be applied with spreaders, consisting of larger particles than found in powders but generally smaller than pellets. The granules break down over time with exposure to moisture, releasing the chemicals slowly. This is the most common form for *top-* or *side-dressing* (applying fertilizer directly to the soil surface).

TRIONIZED: Homogeneous granules, usually containing vermiculite or other lightweight material to which the three primary nutrients have been bonded, making for a very even distribution of nutrients. Each granule contains all three nutrients.

SIMPLE-MIX: Variously sized granules of nutrients which, though blended, may be unevenly distributed in the bag because of their different weights and textures; therefore fertilizer may be delivered unevenly to a lawn or plant.

POLYFORM: The lightest, most concentrated form of fertilizer. The nutrient granules have been screened, so they are all the same size.

GENERAL BUYING TIPS

Fertilizers are sold in packages ranging from a few ounces to 100 pounds. As with many products, the larger the package, the cheaper the fertilizer is per pound, often dramatically so. Keep in mind that the grade—the three numbers on the label—indicate the percentage of the package by weight of each major nutrient, and that therefore you need less of a fertilizer with a higher grade than of one with a lower grade to obtain the same results.

Most gardeners can get by with the general mixes of the 5-10-5, 10-6-4 (for lawns, evergreens, and trees), and 10-10-10 varieties. As for specialized fertilizers, these are for fine-tuning when you know precisely what kind of problem you are addressing, and for personal preference in brands, forms, price, and the like. One thing is sure: Gardening is far from an exact science. It is quite amusing to hear people (sellers and consumers alike) absolutely swear by or about one product or another—with totally opposite conclusions.

An alarming aspect of fertilizer merchandising which takes advantage of this manic search for the one perfect product is the common practice of manufacturers (particularly those among the best known and most widely distributed) to sell the exact same fertilizer labeled in different ways, for example, *flower* as well as *shrub, tree,* and *ground cover* fertilizer, or *lawn food* and *garden food.* This may help the gardener who needs to be told as a convenience or reassurance that a particular product is OK for his or her garden or lawn or flowers, but it also might encourage that same gardener to buy twice as much as needed, that is, two containers when one would do. It is not difficult to read the labels to see if they are any different from one another.

Natural Organic Fertilizers

ABOUT NATURAL ORGANIC FERTILIZERS

Technically known as *naturally derived fertilizers,* these are made from nutrients taken from plants or animals; they are not manufactured (see "About Fertilizer Label Terms," pages 47–51). Some manufacturers argue that any carbon-based or mined material is organic, but in gardening terms this definition is not narrow enough, as it allows the inclusion of synthesized or treated materials. However, for the sake of brevity here, the term *organic* is used to mean "natural organic."

Organic fertilizers help build up the soil, in terms of both structure and microorganisms. Over time, organic fertilizer use builds up the micronutrients and the earthworms in a soil. Some gardeners claim that after regular use of organic fertilizers, you may need to use less, a persuasive argument for their use; the opposite is considered true of synthetic fertilizers by these same gardeners. All soils need organic matter, if only to encourage earthworms and other organisms to do their work, and synthetic fertilizers add none. Organic fertilizers generally do not harm the environment in manufacture nor in use, and need only renewable sources of energy for their "production." While synthetic fertilizers may cost less per bag in the short run, they require huge factories and vast amounts of nonrenewable energy for their manufacture. The essential characteristic of organic fertilizers is that they act as soil conditioners (see chapter 1) as well as low-nutrient fertilizers. The basic idea of organic fertilizers is to build up the soil, as well as to fertilize the plant.

However, organic fertilizers have some drawbacks: They are usually not complete fertilizers, in that they do not contain a conveniently balanced mix of the primary nutrients (N, P, and K). Typically, each kind of organic fertilizer is a particularly good source of one or two of the primary nutrients, and other types of fertilizers must be used to provide the balance, meaning more work for the gardener. They also release their nutrients slowly, which may not be fast enough to solve an acute nutrient problem. They need warm temperatures for the microorganisms to do their work, while chemical fertilizers need only water. And some are hard to store, owing to their bulk. Finally, you may have to apply many pounds more than you would of a synthetic fertilizer in order to achieve the same effect, because they are less concentrated, making for more work. Synthetic fertilizers are usually more convenient, precise (that is, packaged for particular needs and plants), and easy to store.

Much has been written and argued about the value of using organic instead of synthetic fertilizers; your final decision will probably involve your perception of the merits of short-term versus long-term effects on the environment and your attitude toward chemicals in general. A balanced approach of mixed use is a typical solution, though promoters of the strictly organic approach to gardening make good sense, especially for the home gardener. After all, gardening is essentially a natural operation, and they suggest you keep it that way.

General Use Organic Fertilizers

COTTONSEED MEAL

DESCRIPTION: Cotton seeds ground or powdered after the oil has been extracted from them (the seeds are left over from cotton production). *Soybean meal,* rated at 6-2-2, is a similar product.

USE: Rated at 6-2-1 or 7-2-2, it also contains some trace elements and micronutrients. Good for acid-loving plants and shrubs. Nutrients more available to plants in warm soil.

USE TIP: Often used as cattle feed as well as a fertilizer.

BUYING TIP: A good grade of meal is deep yellow; fermented meal is red-brown; ground meal containing the hull of the cottonseed is dark brown.

GUANO

DESCRIPTION: Guano is the decomposed, aged manure of seabirds and bats. (The word *guano* is from the Quechua language of the Incas, and originally referred only to the droppings of seabirds.)

TYPES: *Peruvian guano:* The decomposed manure of cormorants and other fish-eating birds found on certain extremely dry desert islands, making it both concentrated and rare. Rated at around 12-11-2.

Phosphatic guano: A now rarely found bird manure that has been leached by rain and is rated at about 10 to 14–8 to 10–2. It was popular in the United States before the 1960s, at which time rock phosphate (see page 62), which provides a less expensive source for phosphate, started being processed commercially in South Carolina and Florida. Very strong and difficult to use.

Bat guano or *desert bat guano:* The dried, decomposed manure of bats, and a complete fertilizer rated from 2-8-.05 to 8-4-1 with the phosphorus and the potash immediately available to the plants; also contains most micronutrients, including iron, calcium, magnesium, boron, and sulfur. It is an odorless, fine, brown powder.

USE: A good source of phosphate and a generally balanced and complete fertilizer supplying both fast- and slow-release nutrients. Bat guano is one of the best organic fertilizers (and soil conditioners) around, particularly suited for flowering ornamental trees and shrubs.

USE TIP: Organic fertilizers such as these do not usually burn plants, so the amount used does not have to be exact, but the recommended quantities on the label should be used in any case.

BUYING TIP: Because the term *guano* has been loosely used to describe animal manures, fish scrap, or tankage containing feces, check to see that you are purchasing bat guano or Peruvian guano. If it is hard to find bat guano in garden centers near you, try a mail-order source. Not inexpensive.

MANURE

DESCRIPTION: A finely ground, dry, soillike material with a very slight or no manure (ammonia) odor. Sold in bags ranging from 5 to 100 pounds.

The term *green manure* refers to succulent crops, such as mustard, buckwheat, annual ryegrass, and winter rye, that are grown specifically to be plowed right back into the ground before they ripen, thus enriching the soil. *Fresh manure* comes straight from a local farmer, or more accurately, from the farmer's horse, cow, or other animal. This is usually not found for sale in garden centers; if you want to use it, beware of weeds: You should heat it up and decompose it for about one season in your compost heap in order to kill the weed seeds.

All manures fall into two general categories:

Hot manures: These are high in nitrogen and come from chickens, crickets (yes, crickets), horses, sheep, and rabbits. They range from 1 to 4 percent in nitrogen at the very most; chicken and cricket manures contain the most primary nutrients, up to 4-4-2. Some manufacturers label

mixtures of these manures as "supreme" or "super" manure. (The term *hot manure* is also used colloquially to mean any fresh manure that is decomposing.)
Cold manures: These are lower in nitrogen than the hot manures and come from cattle and hogs. They usually have no more than 1 or 2 percent nitrogen. Dehydrated and composted cow manures are rated as high as 5-5-5 and as low as .2-.1-.2; pH tends to the balanced range; dehydrated manures are more concentrated.

TYPES: *Composted* (also known as *decomposed, rotted,* or *aged):* Aged with compost and exposed to microorganisms over a period of time, which has caused it to break down.

   Dehydrated (also known as *dried):* Similar to composted manure, but pasteurized (heated up to 180° F) and reduced to about 17 to 30 percent moisture, killing all the weed seeds and plant pathogens, and ground into a fine, soillike texture. Some companies heat the manure naturally, in a giant compost pile, without the use of fossil fuels.

   Fresh-milled: Shredded, usually with straw or other "bedding litter." Fresh-milled manure is not treated in any way other than being chopped up ("milled") and it is drier than manure fresh from the animal.

USE: A source of nitrogen in a form that is not as concentrated and is less likely to burn than chemical fertilizers. Cow manure is also a very effective soil conditioner (see page 11), and many gardeners think of it as one, instead of as a fertilizer, because it is so low in nutrients (it may also be labeled as such, though because it is really a fertilizer, it has an NPK number). This makes it better for mixing in with soil when planting rather than as top-dressing fertilizer. Manures both add and stimulate essential microorganisms in the soil and build humus. All good-quality manures contain sufficient macro- and micronutrients to maintain healthy soil, though they are more concentrated in dehydrated manure. Composted cow manure is best for turning into the soil of an entire garden with the use of a power tiller, while dehydrated is better suited to mixing into bedding or container soil mixes with hand tools. A must for roses.

USE TIPS: Cattle manures are often low in nutrients, but when used in sufficient quantities do provide enough to make a difference. They also improve soil condition by adding organic material humus, which opens up the soil to air and water (improves the tilth). If too much manure is used, or if it is insufficiently decomposed, even it may burn plants; fresh cow manure may burn your plants and introduce weeds from the straw in it. Furthermore, the bacteria that breaks down fresh manure needs extra nitrogen to do so and competes for it with your plants. And besides, it smells! Chicken manure should be used with care and then only after it has been sufficiently rotted, or else it will burn your plants.

BUYING TIPS: Dehydrated cow manure is much more expensive than composted cow manure, as it is more concentrated per pound—so you use less. That lower price of composted manure includes a lot of water. Dehydrated cow manure is also easier to spread. Check with local stables or zoos for sources of different kinds of manure.

SEWAGE SLUDGE

ALSO KNOWN AS: Activated sewage sludge

POPULAR BRAND NAMES: Milorganite®, Electra

DESCRIPTION: Created from municipal sewage that has been treated with microorganisms, heat dried, and aerated in a special process. Looks like a rich soil mix. Depending on the source, it may vary from dark gray to black in color. Rated at about 5-2-5, with iron. *Does not smell of sewage.*

USE: As a fertilizer and a soil conditioner, usually on lawns and in ornamental gardens. Particularly well suited to houseplants. It is a good substitute for fish emulsion (see page 60) as it smells less, not only to humans, but to domestic cats.

USE TIPS: Sewage sludge may contain pesticides, industrial chemicals, and heavy metals that may be harmful to you or the environment, so it is not recommended for use in the vegetable garden. Even when it is used on a lawn or ornamental garden (it is commonly used on golf courses), you could possibly be adding harmful chemicals to the water table. Experts are quite divided on this question.

BUYING TIP: Avoid buying sludge that does not identify all the chemicals contained in it. With more and more municipal sewage contaminated by the often unlawful disposal of heavy metals and industrial chemicals, it is worth checking to see if any of these chemicals are present in sewage sludge before purchasing or using it.

TANKAGE

DESCRIPTION: The dried, ground, and rendered by-products of slaughtered animals—what's left over after the meat has been processed for commercial food consumption. Rated at 7-10-0. Some specialized forms are *hoof and horn meal,* with a grade of 14-2-0, and *leather meal* or *leather dust,* rated at 5-0-0. A more specialized, but similar product, bone meal (see below), is made from bones only.

USE: Tankage is a common fertilizer ingredient and is sometimes available in pure form to be used as a fertilizer. It was more available pure in the past, before it became popular as an additive to animal food.

Specialized Organic Fertilizers

ABOUT SPECIALIZED ORGANIC FERTILIZERS

Fertilizers can be blended, or simply occur naturally, in ways that are particularly well suited to specific purposes and plants. Organic fertilizers tend to occur with concentrations of one of the major nutrients, as you can see by the entries that follow.

BONE MEAL

ALSO KNOWN AS: Steamed bone meal

DESCRIPTION: As the name suggests, this product is obtained from the animal bones left over after processing for meat (renderings); they are steamed and ground. It is sold in powder form, has a mild smell, and is white in color. Slightly alkaline, a typical grade is 4-12-0. *Raw bone meal* is harder to find but is slower acting and longer lasting.

USE: A natural source of phosphorus, usually a minimum of 12 percent. Especially helpful for giving bulbs a boost.

USE TIP: Commonly placed in the bottom of the planting holes for bulbs, shrubs, and trees.

BUYING TIPS: The phosphorus level in bone meal today is lower than in the past, owing to more efficient slaughterhouses. Today, bone meal contains fewer additional animal parts (meat, marrow, or blood) than previously because they are being used as additives to pet food. Superphosphate (see pages 73–74) might be a better source of phosphorus, especially when it is used for the fall planting of spring bulbs, as might a commercial mix called something like *bulb booster.*

DRIED BLOOD

ALSO KNOWN AS: Blood meal

DESCRIPTION: Dried and ground blood from slaughtered animals, containing on the average about 12 percent nitrogen, and no other primary nutrient (12-0-0). May be red or black in color, and is kiln-dried or spray-dried.

USE: A good source of nitrogen sold as a powder, which may be applied as a diluted liquid as well. The nitrogen in dried blood is readily available to the plant.

USE TIPS: Has a strong smell that sometimes attracts rodents and some people find unpleasant. Capable of burning plants.

BUYING TIPS: Spray-dried blood meal is finer and faster acting. Blood meal is more expensive than many other organic fertilizers.

FISH EMULSION

DESCRIPTION: Sold in a concentrated liquid form, fish emulsion is a thick brown liquid with a decidedly fishy smell, though some brands are now deodorized. It is sold in plastic bottles ranging in size from a few ounces to a gallon. Usually 5-1-1 or 5-2-2.

USE: A popular organic form of nitrogen, as it is easy to use and widely distributed. The nitrogen in fish emulsion is released slowly to the plant roots. Can be used as a foliar fertilizer (applied to and absorbed by the leaves) when diluted and sprayed on.

USE TIPS: Neighborhood cats may be attracted to the garden when fish emulsion is used. Be sure to follow the dilution rates on the bottle, as there is no standard rate.

BUYING TIP: The nitrogen level of fish emulsion is often not listed on the label as it varies from manufacturer to manufacturer.

FISH SCRAP

ALSO KNOWN AS: Fish tankage, dry ground fish, fertilizer grade fish meal

DESCRIPTION: Dried and ground parts of rendered and unrendered fish, crab meal, and fish manure. (Rendered fish contains the parts that are left after the primary commercial food products have been processed.) Typically made from such fish as menhaden and dogfish and the leftovers from fish canneries. Usually contains the primary nutrients in percentages of 9-7-0. Fish scrap, especially the manure, is sometimes treated with sulfuric or phosphoric acid to break it down and called *acid fish* or *acidulated fish tankage;* its percentages of primary nutrients are 6-6-0.

USE: As an organic source of nitrogen and phosphate.

USE TIP: Acidulated or plain fish scrap can be used interchangably.

BUYING TIP: An excellent, easily procured source of nitrogen.

GREENSAND

ALSO KNOWN AS: Glauconite

DESCRIPTION: A *pulverized rock powder* of sandy clay material (iron-potassium silicate) with 6 to 7 percent potash (K) and up to thirty trace minerals, magnesium, and silica. Mined from natural marine deposits found near the New Jersey coast. *Granite dust,* or *granite meal,* which is just crushed granite, is a similar item with 3 to 5.5 percent potash. Its potash comes from the feldspar and mica in the granite.

USE: Adding a natural source of potash to vegetable garden soil as well as lawns and orchards. Retards soil compaction and holds moisture. Some people consider it and granite dust soil conditioners because of these qualities.

USE TIP: Often recommended for roses and greenhouse potting mixtures where moisture retention and drainage are issues.

LANGBEINITE

POPULAR BRAND NAMES: Sul-Po-Mag, K-Mag

DESCRIPTION: Mineral mined in the Southwestern United States, usually composed of 20 to 22 percent sulfur, 20 to 22 percent potassium oxide, and 10 to 18 percent magnesium oxide.

USE: Potassium source rich in secondary nutrients.

ROCK PHOSPHATE

ALSO KNOWN AS: Phosphate rock, rock powder, pulverized rock powder

DESCRIPTION: Pure mined phosphate rock, most likely from South Carolina or Florida, with 20 to 30 percent phosphoric acid. When treated with sulfuric acid, becomes superphosphate (see pages 73–74). *Colloidal phosphate,* or *soft rock phosphate,* is a similar product from Tennessee rated at about 18 to 20 percent phosphate and which contains calcium and trace minerals. Quicker acting than rock phosphate.

USE: An organic source of water-insoluble, very slow-release phosphorus, but also a general soil conditioner. Good source of many trace elements.

USE TIP: Because it is a natural mineral source it does not leach away as fast as superphosphate. However, it may have no effect at all on soils with a pH over 6.2, and is most effective on pea family plants and compost, rather than on lawns.

BUYING TIP: Must be exceedingly fine ground to be of use; superphosphate is much more effective, but not an organic product. Has largely replaced bat guano (see page 56).

SEAWEED EXTRACT

ALSO KNOWN AS: Kelp, kelp meal, liquid seaweed, liquefied seaweed

DESCRIPTION: Brown liquid in concentrate form made from ocean kelp, rated around 1-0-1.2, with up to 33 percent trace minerals.

USE: Good but expensive source of micronutrients and potash, which are necessary for root development and overall stress resistance, especially for seedlings, for which nitrogen is not so important.

BUYING TIP: The amount of nitrogen is often not given on the label as it varies.

Organic Plant Care Products

ABOUT ORGANIC PLANT CARE PRODUCTS

There are many products sold in garden centers alongside the fertilizers. These products promise to take care of your plants in more direct ways, such as maintaining a good moisture level.

ANTITRANSPIRANT

ALSO KNOWN AS: Antidesiccant

POPULAR BRAND NAMES: WILT-PRUF®, Vapor-Gard®, ForEver-Green®, Cloud Cover®

DESCRIPTION: Most are made of a natural pine oil emulsion or natural, latexlike, biodegradable polymer in ready-to-spray liquid, concentrate, or aerosol form, sold in a wide range of sizes. Nontoxic. Some contain chemicals that cover the stomata (tiny openings in the leaves) through which moisture escapes. Dries to a clear, glossy film and does not affect the natural breathing and growing processes of a plant.

USE: Sprayed on ornamental plants, especially evergreens such as pine trees, dormant tubers, bulbs, and bare root stock to prevent excessive moisture loss after transplanting, during shipment, over winter, and during storage. Small plants may be dipped in it. Also effective against windburn and drought, or any other condition that dries out plants. One spraying lasts for about three months. Also used as a fungal preventive on annuals.

USE TIPS: These products should be used only during periods when there is excessive evaporation of moisture—otherwise you can harm the plant by preventing some needed transpiration. Because some plants may be sensitive to an antitranspirant, test some first on a small part of the plant. Be sure to dilute it correctly if necessary.

BUYING TIP: Read the label on the product to see that it will do what you wish it to.

LEAF POLISH

ALSO KNOWN AS: Leaf gloss, leaf shine, shine and cleaner, leaf shiner and cleaner, leaf cleaner

POPULAR BRAND NAMES: Moonshine, Ortho Leaf Polish

DESCRIPTION: Liquid chemical mixture sold in small hand-pump spray containers or regular bottles. Normally does not contain any fertilizer. Usually organic, but not necessarily, so check the label. Most are made with mineral oil, but some are made of a surfactant that breaks up dirt without clogging the plant's pores.

USE: Shining and cleaning leaves of hard surface houseplants and decorative arrangements.

USE TIPS: The myth behind the desirability of polished foliage may very well be similar to the one about a fat baby being a healthy baby—hard to prove. Even if these products claim no harm to plants, some brands may leave residues on the foliage that clog pores and prevent or slow down the natural processes of the leaves, as did the buttermilk your grandma may have used to clean her plants.

BUYING TIPS: A clean leaf may be healthier than a polished leaf. Stick to tepid water to wash the foliage of houseplants as harmful dust does build up, or try to find those cleaners that really lift off the dirt or wash it away. You can use a lamb's wool ball made for this purpose, or put your plants in the shower (really!).

Synthetic Fertilizers

ABOUT SYNTHETIC FERTILIZERS

Please note that some manufactured brands of fertilizer contain organic matter as well, and in fact may be labeled in a way that leaves you confused as to whether this is a natural or manufactured product. For example, "rich in organic matter" means that it contains both natural and artificial ingredients. There is nothing wrong with this; on the contrary, it means that the mixture takes advantage of the qualities of both kinds of ingredients. However, products that contain anything artificial or that are chemically treated are included in this section rather than the preceding one. Most fertilizers label organic sources as such, but not chemical sources; anything in a fertilizer not noted as natural can be assumed to be synthetic.

Notation of the breakdown of sources and percentages of types of nitrogen is required on the labels of synthetic fertilizers but not on those of natural organic ones in most states. If you like to have a well-balanced mixture of nitrogen sources, look for more *water-insoluble nitrogen* than *fast-acting* sources (see "About Fertilizer Label Terms" on pages 47–51).

Synthetic fertilizers are man-made. Most are combinations of chemicals that form a complete fertilizer as defined in "About Fertilizers" (see pages 45–47). They are mixed to fit many needs, including some quite specialized ones. Convenience and price are their trademarks. However, there are definitely some trade-offs for that convenience. The end result of complete dependency on and overuse of synthetic fertilizers is that you may need more chemicals to counteract the first chemicals and their side effects, ultimately harming the environment through water pollution and soil depletion, which is added to the environmental cost of their industrial manufacturing. Pound for pound, organic fertilizers may be more expensive than synthetic ones, but over time, you will probably need to put more synthetic fertilizer in your garden than if you use organic fertilizer, and in any case more often, because the very characteristic that makes synthetics act so fast—water solubility—also makes some of their nutrients wash out of the soil with the rain. They add nothing to the soil permanently and may actually harm the soil's microorganisms and valued earthworms.

Many gardeners choose to use chemical fertilizers sparingly, in coordination with naturally derived (organic) fertilizers. More and more gardeners, in fact, are becoming organic gardeners. And now even the National Academy of Sciences has begun to recommend the use of biological interactions instead of agricultural chemicals for many tasks. This said, there are more chemical products than organic ones on the market, proving their popularity and wide acceptance.

Specialized Synthetic Fertilizers

ABOUT SPECIALIZED SYNTHETIC FERTILIZERS

To make life easier, special fertilizers are available for use on specific plants or types of plants. Fertilizers can be purchased for foliage (typical for houseplants), flowering and fruiting plants, acid-loving plants, container plants, African violets, roses, geraniums, tomatoes, cacti, lawns, vegetables, and so on. Also, certain formulations that have just about nothing other than one of the primary nutrients are available, such as potash (0-0-60) and urea (46-0-0). These latter items are used to solve specific plant problems, such as building up an aspect of disease resistance. They are sometimes called *simples*.

Using these products does raise the problem, however, that you may be giving the plant more than it needs of certain nutrients, particularly micronutrients. Some minor trace elements or micronutrients, such as water-soluble salts (borates and sulfated forms of copper), iron, manganese, and zinc, are helpful to plant growth in small quantities, while others, such as boron and molybdenum, can be harmful—even toxic—in excess. A garden plan and a complete soil test (see pages 237–38) should indicate how much and which trace elements and/or micronutrients are already present in your soil and which you need. Reading the fertilizer labels will tell you if it contains just what you need or whether you are paying more for extra, unwanted nutrients.

Many manufacturers make complete lines of fertilizers, creating a lot of duplication on the shelf. Some specialize in liquid fertilizers, others in granular, for example, making the choice more one of which form you find most convenient rather than of product performance. The plant doesn't care about the form of nutrients as much as you do. The choice is large and encourages experimentation—it is very much a question of personal preference or "feel" for a particular line of products that governs a final choice.

ACID-LOVING PLANT FERTILIZERS

POPULAR BRAND NAMES: Holly-tone®, Miracid®, Ortho Azalea, Camellia, and Rhododendron Food

DESCRIPTION: Granular or liquid fertilizer, often containing chelated iron and other micronutrients and soil acidifiers. Other ingredients that may be found include aluminum sulfate (bauxite that usually has been treated with sulfuric acid), ammonium sulfate (or sulfate of ammonia) that has 20.5 percent available nitrogen, and iron sulfate, which helps correct iron deficiencies. A grade of 4-6-4 is common, as is 5-10-10, 7-7-7, 10-7-7, and 4-12-12, depending on the plant it is intended for, and 30-10-10 is also available. Aluminum sulfate (see page 11) is packaged pure as well, as a soil acidifier. Sold in bags from 5 to 20 pounds.

USE: Fertilizing hollies, azaleas, rhododendrons, evergreens, and the like, all plants that crave acid soils, by promoting growth and good color. Aluminum sulfate imparts a blue color to hydrangeas.

USE TIPS: Spring and fall feedings, depending on the particular brand. Follow the directions on the bag for each type of plant.

BUYING TIP: Sulfate of ammonia is slow acting but long lasting.

AMMONIUM NITRATE

DESCRIPTION: Granular form of rapidly available nitrogen, usually in a 33-0-0 concentration.

USE: Fast-acting source of nitrogen for quick greening of turf grasses such as fescue, bluegrass, and Bermudagrass, especially during cool seasons.

USE TIP: Extremely concentrated; may burn. Most people are better off with traditional sources of nitrogen.

BUYING TIP: Considered a professional product—not necessarily available in small packages.

AMMONIUM PHOSPHATE

DESCRIPTION: Granular source of fast-acting nitrogen and phosphorus, usually rated at 16-20-0.

USE: For fast growth of lawns, especially in the South.

USE TIPS: Reapply every sixty days—this goes fast. Not recommended for dichondra, a grass substitute used in the Southwest. Difficult to use accurately.

BULB FOOD

ALSO KNOWN AS: Bulb booster

DESCRIPTION: A complete fertilizer that contains more phosphorus than nitrogen or potassium, typically in a 4-12-8 or similar grade. Often blended natural organic (bone meal, for instance) and synthetic materials. Sold in small bags or boxes for the home gardener.

USE: Encourages healthy root development so essential to bulbs.

USE TIP: Place in the bottom of each bulb's planting hole.

BUYING TIP: Cheaper than bone meal with a comparable phosphate rating, but just as effective.

CHELATED MICRONUTRIENTS

DESCRIPTION: Powdered, granular, or liquid form of water-soluble compounds of the metallic nutrients made with organic chelating agents that make these micronutrients available to the plants when they normally wouldn't be. Very similar to vitamin pills for humans—in fact, some are sold mixed with vitamin B-1. Micronutrients include iron, manganese, zinc, boron, copper, chlorine, and molybdenum.

USE: Treating certain deficiencies of micronutrients in soil.

USE TIPS: Use only as directed, and only when you are quite sure that you need them. Normally balanced and well-fertilized soils should not be lacking in micronutrients, and a major deficiency should be thoroughly analyzed. Iron is the most commonly deficient micronutrient, causing leaf yellowing (chlorosis). May be very fast-acting.

BUYING TIP: Professionals have more use for these items than amateurs. If you must absolutely buy them, and have trouble finding them in a garden center, try to find a professional source through a landscaper or botanic garden.

FLOWERING OR FRUITING PLANT FERTILIZER

DESCRIPTION: Complete fertilizer heavily weighted to supply nitrogen and potash or, most often, equal amounts of all three primary nutrients. Commonly rated at 12-12-12.

USE: Encouraging normal growth and fruiting of fruit-bearing woody plants.

USE TIPS: Sprays are not useful on fruit trees except when a superficial fix is desired; ground application in the fall or early spring is the best. Applications to large trees such as apple trees last longer when accompanied by hay or straw mulching and heavy pruning.

BUYING TIPS: Keep in mind when deciding on a particular grade that large fruit trees, such as apple and pear trees, may not require much phosphorus or calcium or micronutrients, which many of these fertilizers may contain. Pay special attention to the tips on the package label.

HOUSEPLANT FOOD

POPULAR BRAND NAMES: Liquid Miracle-Gro® House Plant Food, Stern's Therapy for House Plants, Schultz Instant Liquid Plant Food, Granny's Bloomers, Granny's Jungle Juice, Jobe's Houseplant Spikes, Peters® Concentrated Liquid Plant Food, Ra-Pid-Gro, Ortho Plant Food

DESCRIPTION: Concentrated liquid applied directly to soil, powdered concentrate mixed with water, or spike, specially formulated for houseplants, containing chelated iron and other micronutrients usually lacking in indoor growing media. Normally should not lead to buildup of salts. Liquid sold in small bottles ranging from 2 ounces upward. Grades tend to be 8-7-6, 10-8-7, 10-5-10, and the like.

USE: Providing nutrients not otherwise available to potted plants.

USE TIPS: Usually formulated to be quickly available to the plant. Often very concentrated so that it can be sold in small containers, it must be diluted according to instructions or else it might harm the plant. Note whether acidic or not.

BUYING TIPS: There is lots of competition for this market, so experiment until you find a product that gives you the best results. Each plant may react differently to the various formulations available. Furthermore, this is an intimate process, and your selection may have as much to do with the way you like to care for your plants as does the actual effect of the fertilizer. Ultimately, houseplant food is not that different from garden fertilizers except in the degree of concentration and the packaging or form.

LAWN FERTILIZER

DESCRIPTION: Sold in all possible forms: pellets, granules, liquids, powdered concentrates to be mixed with water, or powders to be applied dry. Whether synthetic or organic, they come in two general types: *slow-acting* and *fast-acting*.

Many specialized products are made for starting new lawns or greening up old ones in the spring. Starter fertilizers have a higher percentage of phosphorus to promote root development. "Green-up" fertilizers feature extremely high nitrogen content for the leaves.

TYPES: *Starter Lawn Food (10-18-12):* Particularly good for building roots during fall and winter. Added iron prevents leaf yellowing.

Lawn and Tree Food (10-6-4): Good both spring and fall, for both new and established lawns, and for any other leaf crops.

Lawn and Garden Food (10-10-10): Good general use fertilizer.

USE: Keeping lawns healthy and green. This is not just for aesthetics or impressing the neighbors: A healthy lawn is better able to compete with weeds and is more resistant to pests and diseases.

USE TIPS: Follow label directions carefully. Too much fertilizer or too high a concentration of liquid fertilizer will burn and brown off a lawn. Excessive application of nitrogen can cause thatch buildup and poor drought tolerance, and make your lawn vulnerable to diseases. Almost all lawn fertilizers need to be watered in well; failure to do so evenly will result in dead areas where the fertilizers were not watered in and thus did not enter the soil. Lawn fertilizers may be broadcast by hand, applied with a hose attachment (see page 237), or applied with a spreader (see pages 252–53).

Slow-acting lawn fertilizers are best applied only once or twice a year. Organic forms are less likely to burn the lawn. Fast-acting lawn fertilizers produce greener lawns within hours of application, but generally do not continue to fertilize a lawn for more than four to eight weeks, making it necessary to reapply them as often as every month or so during the growing season. This is a case of a choice between instant and delayed gratification, but if you go for the instant kind, you have to have the time and the money to repeat the application often.

Lawns should be fertilized in the spring and in the fall. Most experts recommend early fall fertilizing of lawns to ensure good growth and root development, especially in areas of the country where winters are below freezing. As a general rule, fall is the best time for many other lawn care practices too, such as seeding and sodding.

Remember that rain is going to leach out the chemicals you

put on your lawn, and therefore the repeated, excess application of certain chemicals may pollute your water supply or harm your soil. Caution and moderation are the way to go here.

BUYING TIPS: Which form of fertilizer to buy is pretty much a question of your own preference. Some people prefer to use a dry fertilizer that they then water in well. Others enjoy the practice of liquid feeding. Avoid a fertilizer in which *all* of the nitrogen is supplied by ammonium nitrate or ammonium sulfate—the fast- or quick-release, synthetic, water-soluble forms of nitrogen which act so fast that they break down very soon after application.

MAGNESIUM SULFATE

ALSO KNOWN AS: Epsom salts

DESCRIPTION: White powder containing 9.6 percent magnesium and 14.5 percent sulfur.

USE: Source of magnesium when need is indicated by a soil test or foliage. Most concentrations are spread at a rate of ½ pound per 100 square feet.

USE TIPS: Usually applied as a foliar (leaf) spray to fruit trees in foliage; mix with a spreader-sticker (see page 117). Dolomitic limestone (see pages 14–15), a good source of magnesium, is more often applied to the soil when you have time—this is a quicker treatment.

MURIATE OF POTASH

DESCRIPTION: Granular fertilizer that consists of soluble potash in concentrations of 0-0-60 or 0-0-55. Made from potassium chloride, a potash salt, which actually ranges from 48 to 62 percent soluble potash. Another similar source is sulfate of potash, or potassium sulfate, which has no less than 48 percent soluble potash.

USE: Potassium supplement for accelerating root and tuber growth; typical component of fast-acting, acidic, synthetic complete fertilizers.

USE TIPS: Add only when your soil test tells you that your soil is quite deficient in potash. Also good for melting ice and snow on driveways and sidewalks.

NITRATE OF SODA

ALSO KNOWN AS: Sodium nitrate, Chile or Chilean saltpeter

DESCRIPTION: White, granular substance sold in bags. A salt traditionally mined from natural deposits in Chile or, more recently, produced synthetically by reacting nitric acid with sodium carbonate. Pure nitrate of soda ($NaNO_3$) contains 16 percent nitrogen (16-0-0) and 27 percent sodium (Na). One brand from Chile—Bulldog—is considered natural organic.

USE: Concentrated, highly water soluble source of quickly available nitrogen. Encourages rapid leaf and stem growth.

USE TIP: Use carefully, or you may burn your plants.

BUYING TIP: Old source of nitrogen that was more common before the development of modern synthetic ammonia fertilizer plants.

ROSE FOOD

POPULAR BRAND NAMES: Ra-Pid-Gro®, Peters®, Miracle-Gro® for Roses, Bandini Rose Food®, Osmocote® Plant Food, Verdi-Sol®, Sequestrene® 330 Fe, Rose-Tone®, Ortho Rose Food, Gro-Well Rose Food

DESCRIPTION: Premixed liquids, liquid concentrates, powder concentrates to be mixed with water, pellets, and all of the other forms that fertilizers can come in. Sold as complete fertilizers, rose foods usually have equal or higher percentages of phosphorus, such as 20-20-20, 6-12-6, 8-12-4, or 18-24-16, although there are some exceptions, such as Ra-Pid-Gro® at 23-19-17 and Osmocote® at 18-6-12.

USE: Promoting foliage growth, especially bloom set of roses. Specialized formulations encourage brilliant color.

USE TIPS: Read labels carefully, because many are concentrates that if not diluted properly could easily damage the plants. Others may contain unneeded micronutrients that could change the pH of your soil in a damaging way. If you know your soil conditions, you will be wise to avoid fertilizers that contain additives you may not need.

BUYING TIPS: These products are usually reliable, but at a price. Roses grow best in a soil with a pH around 6.5. To help you maintain this pH level, note the potential acidity equivalent on the label. Liquid rose fertilizers (concentrates and premixed) are readily available to the plant roots and leaves, while pellet and granular fertilizers are not as available but may have the advantage of working over a longer period of time, eliminating the need to fertilize more frequently. Make your choice based on the time you have to spend fertilizing. Sometimes the convenience of application (as with preformulated fertilizers) is worth the extra cost. Roses usually need a yearly dose of cow manure, too.

SULFATE OF AMMONIA

ALSO KNOWN AS: Ammonium sulfate

DESCRIPTION: Granular, acidic fertilizer made from ammonia treated with sulfuric acid, with 20.5 percent available nitrogen (20-0-0). Generally sold in 5-pound bags. Sometimes considered a soil conditioner, as an acidifier.

USE: Fertilizing acid-loving plants; often blended into complete fertilizers as noted earlier in the chapter in the entry for acid-loving plant fertilizers on pages 66–67. Longer lasting but not as quickly available as nitrate of soda (see page 72), but still considered fast-acting. Acidifies the soil (lowers the pH) and feeds sulfur to the plants immediately.

SUPERPHOSPHATE

DESCRIPTION: Bagged white or gray granular fertilizer. During the nineteenth century, superphosphate was made from bone black, a product derived from charred bones, but since then has been manufactured almost exclusively from phosphate rock. Superphosphate is created when rock phosphate, a subtropical mineral deposit found in South Carolina in 1867 (mined in huge open pits there and in Florida, Wyoming, and Tennessee), is treated with either sulfuric acid or phosphoric acid or a combination of the two, making this a synthetic product. A very common kind of phosphorus fertilizer. (Pure mined rock phosphate is an organic fertilizer and is discussed on page 62.)

TYPES: *Normal:* Contains up to 22 percent phosphorus. Made from natural phosphatic material that has been exposed to sulfuric acid. Formerly known as *regular, single, stan-*

dard, simple, or *20 percent superphosphate.* Typical grade is 0-20-0.

Enriched: Derived from natural phosphatic material treated with sulfuric and phosphoric acids. Graded from 0-22-0 to 0-40-0.

Concentrated (also known as *double, treble, triple,* or *multiple superphosphate):* Any grade that contains 40 percent or more available phosphorus, which is the highest percentage of available phosphorus sold. Commonly graded 0-46-0.

USE: Rapidly available source of phosphorus.

USE TIP: Particularly useful when planting bulbs and seeding in lawns.

BUYING TIPS: Superphosphate may be a better buy than bone meal (see pages 59–60) and bulb food (see pages 67–68), at similar phosphate levels.

UREA

DESCRIPTION: Inexpensive source of synthetic nitrogen, derived from natural gas products. Granular, with at least 35 percent but commonly with 46 percent available nitrogen (46-0-0). Acid-forming, nonstaining, and noncorrosive. Sold in bags of all sizes, including 5 pounds. Another similar but slow-release product is *nitroform,* at 38 percent nitrogen.

USE: Foliar feeding and side-dressing of all plants. Also melts snow and ice. Is water-soluble and fast-release.

BUYING TIP: Confusingly called "synthetic organic" by some manufacturers.

VEGETABLE FERTILIZER

ALSO KNOWN AS: Garden fertilizer, garden food, tomato food, vegetable food, etc.

POPULAR BRAND NAMES: Miracle-Gro® All-Purpose, Ra-Pid-Gro®, Gro-Well Garden Fertilizer 5-10-5, Gro-Well Tomato Food 5-10-10

DESCRIPTION: Concentrated powders, pellets, liquids, and granules, with an equal or higher percentage of phosphorus than nitrogen or potash. Perhaps the most common type of fertilizer purchased. Typically 5-10-5 or 10-10-10. Often fortified with micronutrients, including chelated iron. Sold in bags or boxes from 4 to 20 pounds.

USE: To promote the early development of fruiting vegetables, and to help with the bloom set (when the blooms fall and fruit appears). Slightly different formulation than those for blooming ornamental (nonfood) plants.

USE TIPS: Too much fertilizer is worse than too little: Excess nitrogen promotes leaf and stem development at the expense of blooms or fruit, for example. Vegetables benefit from fertilizer at the young seedling stage and again just before bloom set. When fertilizing at these times, follow label directions carefully.

BUYING TIPS: A general purpose 5-10-5 or 10-10-10 is a good garden fertilizer and cheaper than special vegetable foods with their added micronutrients. In fact, some micronutrients, like chelated iron, lower the pH of the soil, and that may be unnecessary in your case. Don't buy it if you don't need it.

WEED AND FEED MIXTURE (LAWN FERTILIZER/HERBICIDE MIX)

POPULAR BRAND NAMES: Twinlight Lawn Food Plus Balan®, Lawn Pro Weed and Feed, Turf Builder Plus 2

DESCRIPTION: Bagged fertilizers that contain both fertilizer and herbicides, and in some rare cases, insecticides.

USE: Promoted as a convenient, labor-saving one-time application, allowing the user to promote lawn growth and fight weeds at the same time.

USE TIPS: This is one instance where convenience can come at a high cost and risk. The government has even issued a warning. The USDA says, in part, "CAUTION: Combinations of [such] materials may be ineffective or even harmful. Their misuse can kill desirable plants or make the soil unproductive. Apply combinations of fertilizer and insecticides or herbicides only on the recommendation of your state agricultural experiment station." Spot control is usually more efficient.

BUYING TIPS: Mixes of fertilizers with weed killers or insecticides are almost always more expensive than the individual products sold separately. Furthermore, performance usually doesn't measure up to the products' claims because the proper time to use pesticides may not be the same as the proper time to fertilize, thereby wasting at least one part of the mix. That makes it even more expensive.

Synthetic Plant Care Products

GRAFTING SUPPLIES

DESCRIPTION:

Grafting wax: Wax compound that is heated, either in a double boiler or by kneading in your hands. Sold in ¼- to 10-pound boxes. *Trowbridge's* is the oldest and best-known kind.

Rubber budding strips: Small rubber strips of different sizes, ranging from ³⁄₁₆ to ⅜ inch wide and 4 to 8 inches long, and from .010 to .020 gauge thick. A wider version with a fastener is made, called a *bud tie.*

Grafting thread: Fine waxed line sold in rolls of hundreds of feet.

Grafting tape (also known as *nurseryman's tape):* A type of adhesive tape that decomposes to prevent damage from girdling. Available ½ to 1 inch wide, in 60-yard rolls.

USE: Holding freshly made grafts in place and protecting them. Covers exposed plant tissue until new tissue grows in. Grafting most commonly done on fruit or nut trees and roses.

USE TIP: This is a difficult process—follow directions carefully.

ROOTING HORMONE

ALSO KNOWN AS: Rooting powder

POPULAR BRAND NAMES: Rootone®, Hormo-Root, Dip 'N Grow, Hormex

DESCRIPTION: Powder containing growth regulators and sometimes fungicides.

USE: Rooting cuttings faster and without rotting or loss to disease.

USE TIP: Dip just the first inch or so of a cutting into the powder and shake off the excess.

BUYING TIP: Because you dip only the end of a stem into the container, even small amounts last a long time.

SOIL INOCULANT

DESCRIPTION: Powder containing live bacteria of the *Rhizobium* genus.

USE: Mixed with legume (bean family) seed prior to planting in order to facilitate the conversion of nitrogen into a readily available source. This process is known as *nitrogen fixation,* and is a primary characteristic of legume plants.

USE TIPS: A little bit of vegetable oil mixed in with the seed helps the inoculant adhere better. Make sure you are matching the correct bacteria to your particular type of plant. Do not use on seed that has been treated with fungicide: The bacteria you just bought will be killed along with the bacteria that the fungicide was intended for.

BUYING TIPS: Especially helpful in soil never planted with legumes before; not usually all that helpful in soils that have already been treated.

STUMP REMOVER

DESCRIPTION: Potassium salt of nitric acid (potassium nitrate), usually in powder form.

USE: When poured onto tree stumps accelerates the natural rotting process, making the stump and roots porous throughout. Holes then can be easily drilled into the rotted stump, filled with kerosene, and the stump set afire, if local laws permit this.

USE TIP: Generally not dangerous to other plants. Check label to be sure.

TREE PAINT

ALSO KNOWN AS: Tar, tree wound dressing, pruning seal, sealer, tree wound spray, tree paint

DESCRIPTION: Black petroleum asphalt base liquid sold in either aerosol form or as a liquid to be brushed on. Some brands contain an antiseptic fungicide, such as copper naphthenate, to help prevent disease.

USE: Seals the stump of a pruned limb or branch against weathering, drying out, decay, pests, and infection.

USE TIPS: We now know that it is unnecessary to paint over the stump of a normally, cleanly pruned limb, as the tree isolates the area and seals it itself, providing a scar tissue that does not allow decaying to advance into the tree. Also, the USDA Forest Service has found that wound dressing does not prevent rot. However, tree paint may be of value to help seal damaged bark or wounded trees, preventing insects or diseases from entering the tree through the wound. It also fills an aesthetic function when a tree has sustained a large prominent scars.

BUYING TIPS: Can also be used to waterproof wooden tubs and planters. Though sold for use after pruning roses and shrubs, it is not needed if the branches are properly pruned at an angle—the slanted cut allows water to run off.

Pest and Disease Control Products

ABOUT PESTICIDES

Synthetic chemical pesticides, which are so familiar to us and so prominently featured in garden centers, are only one set of tools you can use to manage pest problems. Other tools include regular weeding, crop rotation, mechanical control (traps, barriers, and hand picking), biological controls (introducing predator insects or diseases that infect only the pests), naturally derived (organic) products, and cultural controls such as companion planting methods, planting resistant varieties of plants, proper fertilization, and regular watering. In fact, there are so many alternatives that there is a name for them, *integrated pest management (IPM)* (see pages 81–83 for a fuller discussion). Gardeners who practice IPM have come to think of pesticides as only one alternative among many other gardening practices.

Pesticides cannot replace the good gardening habits and techniques mentioned above, despite the constant din of advertising to the contrary. Strong chemicals treat symptoms; good gardening corrects the sources of the problem. It's just not as simple as the ads would have it. Synthetic products can help, but they are no cure-all, by a long shot. In fact, while 224 insect species were listed as resistant to pesticides in 1970, by 1984, 448 were. That's *double*. And now even the Department of Agriculture is reporting that we rely too much on agricultural chemicals. They are good for solving specific acute problems, but many other products that are not synthetic and are every bit as effective, if not more, are available.

Pesticides come in a wide array of types and forms, all of which are explained in the pages that follow. The terms can be confusing, so if you are unfamiliar with them, read the following pages first. Otherwise, go right to the items, starting on page 93.

ABOUT DEFINING PESTICIDES

Garden centers sell a variety of chemical products to rid the garden of the insects, fungi, diseases, animals, or weeds that threaten plants. These include chemical products that are either naturally derived (organic) or synthetically produced. These "garden chemicals" are usually collectively referred to as *pesticides.*

Several specific pesticides are designed for particular types of pests, while others deal with problems that are not pest-related per se. The former group includes chemicals to control insects *(insecticides),* chemicals to control spiderlike mites *(miticides* or *acaricides),* chemicals to control mice, rats, and other rodents *(rodenticides),* and even specific chemicals to control microscopic worms called nematodes *(nematicides).* All of these specialized garden chemicals are sold under the collective term *pesticides.*

In addition to this group of pesticides, a second group sold as pesticides includes garden chemicals or similar products specifically designed to deal with fungal problems *(fungicides)* and other chemicals that help control weeds and unwanted vegetation *(herbicides).* This is how the term *pesticides* refers to both a family of chemicals and to specific ones that do specific jobs.

Many chemical products exist that are not commonly available to consumers and therefore are not listed here. In some cases these products are not available because they are too dangerous to be used by noncertified individuals; in other cases they are hard to find simply because they are generally marketed only to professionals for commercial use. Such items include chemicals for antibacterial use *(bactericides)* and many products for the control of slugs and snails *(molluscicides).* Diseases and viruses are usually controlled through garden management or IPM techniques.

Finally, this is one area where there are so many products available that are new, or new formulations, or slightly different mixtures of the same ingredients, that it would make this book unwieldy to include them all. What are listed are the basic building blocks of pest control. Undoubtedly, some useful items may have been omitted. If you don't see what you want, check with your local Cooperative Extension agent (see appendix C), your garden center manager, or call one of the major manufacturers whose number or address is easily found on similar products. Your local garden center manager will surely be able to assist you, if only to contact the local representative.

ABOUT USING PESTICIDES

Over the last few decades, there has been an enormous increase in the amount of chemicals, in the form of both pesticides and fertilizers, that Americans put on their gardens and lawns. There is no doubt that this has been costly to the environment, and this misuse can cause harmful injury and death. There are now civil and criminal penalties for misuse of synthetic pesticides. Using chemicals safely means taking the time to read and understand the labels and rigorously following the instructions for mixing, application, and disposal. Much information exists on alternatives to this garden chemical dependency, and the alternative products can be found in the same garden center where you buy the chemicals. Remember, garden chemicals are like prescription drugs: They are very helpful in curing specific unusual problems, but may cause their own problems if relied upon on a regular reflex basis.

Finally, keep in mind there is no such thing as a "safe" pesticide, because by definition a pesticide is toxic to *something*.

ABOUT INTEGRATED PEST MANAGEMENT (IPM)

Using chemicals alone as a method of controlling pests is a relatively recent approach to this perennial gardening and farming problem, driven to a certain extent by the development of our consumer- and advertising-oriented society. However, since the advent of popularly available chemical products forty or fifty years ago, we are more knowledgeable about the effects of chemicals on our environment, on natural pest predators, and on public and personal safety. In fact, safe, intelligent use of pesticides and other chemicals need not pose a threat to the environment, animals, or people.

What we are learning about the effects of some toxic chemicals has caused many people to take a new look at how we use them, how we combine them with natural methods of pest control, and to seek methods of pest management that take into consideration the overall effect on the environment and people. The result is *IPM: integrated pest management*.

Rapidly emerging as the most sensible approach to pest control, IPM incorporates the use of chemicals or toxic pesticides into a system designed to utilize natural and physical controls along with the chemical controls. IPM is neither proorganic nor prochemical, though some may call it ecological pest management: It is instead an approach that seeks the best method of controlling garden pests *using all available resources,* though it does generally mean choosing chemicals only after all other methods have been tried. Furthermore, emphasis is placed on finding the *least toxic* method at every stage.

The following are some of the basic building blocks of the IPM system:

• *Planting resistant plants:* It is possible to select food crops that have been specially bred to be resistant to viral problems. For example, tomato plants labeled VF or VFN are resistant to the common diseases verticullium and fusarium wilts and, with the designation VFN, nematodes. Planting resistant varieties is often easier than doing battle with the pests.

• *Good gardening practices:* A healthy plant is less affected by diseases and pests. Good gardening practices such as doing regular soil tests, maintaining appropriate pH levels for each type of plant, using the right fertilizers, planting to ensure sufficient sun and moisture, weeding, choosing the right plant for the right place, and paying attention to general habitat conditions, like humidity and air circulation, produce plants that are more likely to survive an occasional pest problem.

• *Physical controls and traps:* Physical measures can be taken that include things like hand picking (or even vacuuming!) pests from plants, installing barriers (ranging in form from plastic collars made from coffee cups to elaborate fences and row covers), or such simple practices as flushing pests off foliage with water, mulching well, and installing traps.

• *Biological controls and beneficial insects:* Insects such as the ladybug, lacewing, and the praying mantis are natural predators of harmful insects, and can be introduced to your garden (you can purchase them from mail-order catalogs) or conserved. Unfortunately, these insects are usually more sensitive than the pests to the broad-spectrum insecticides in common use.

• *Oils and soaps:* Highly refined horticultural oils are low in toxic chemicals (though they can be dangerous) and act by smothering the pest without the use of poisons, while soaps both smother and destroy some insects and weeds.

• *Research and development:* This ranges from scientists taking products designed to deal with one problem and trying them for others to genetic engineering. A recent example is antitranspirants, which were originally developed to prevent the loss of moisture from evergreen leaves during winter and which are now used to help prevent fungal problems.

• *Choosing toxic chemicals carefully:* Selective use of synthetic insecticides, fungicides, and herbicides can be made in integrated pest management programs, but only if these chemicals work together with the other components in the system, such as the introduction of beneficial insects. For example, you would want to avoid using a pesticide that might kill the ladybugs and praying mantis which are being used to control aphids and other pests. The least toxic chemical is sought out first and its reuse considered carefully; no chemical is used routinely.

• *Analysis of the problems and the solutions:* Much time is given to the positive identification of pests, monitoring of the pest population, level of plant injury, and evaluation of the effect your strategy is having.

ABOUT THE MOST COMMON PROBLEMS WITH HOUSEPLANTS AND GARDENS

COMMON INSECT PESTS: There are over two thousand insects that are considered pests; add to that the fact that many pests exist in different forms at different stages of development, causing different types of damage. Immature beetles, for example, are known as larva, and leafhoppers at the stage just prior to adulthood are nymphs. Many books are available that identify these pests; they should be consulted thoroughly in order to figure out what plagues you. Proper identification of the pest is the most important first step. Here are descriptions of the most common insect pests:

• *Aphids* are small sucking insects that are teardrop in shape, winged or wingless (depending on their life stage), and range in color from light green, gray to dark brown, to black. Aphids are often found on the tender growing tips of plants and flower buds. They are of particular concern as they often carry plant viruses.

- *Spider mites* are small, almost microscopic, sucking animals that are black, orange-green, or red in color. The red spider mite is one of the more common ones. It lives on the underside of plants, thriving when the weather is hot and dry. Often the mite is not visible to a casual observer, but in large numbers their fine webs are evidence of their presence.
- *Scale* are also small sucking insects that may be hard or soft, oval or round in shape, and slow moving in juvenile stages (they are immobile in their adult stage). Types include cottony taxus, oleander, brown soft, oyster, and white peach scale. Many resemble small brown turtle shells attached to the stems and veins of plant leaves. The presence of scale is often indicated by a sticky syrupy substance on the plant. This is actually the honeydew that the scale excretes.
- *Mealybugs* are common sucking insects that are oval and soft-bodied. Their presence is indicated by cottony masses in the axis of leaves, stems, and branches. These masses are actually the nests or egg masses of the reproducing pests.
- *Nematodes* are microscopic sucking worms, some types of which produce hard swellings on plants. Symptoms include slow growth of plants and yellowing leaves. If nematodes are present in container-grown plants or houseplants, it is best to discard the soil and replant in sterile soil.
- *White flies* resemble small moths and can be found on the underside of the infested plants. When the leaves or plant is shaken, the white flies fly around the plant in numbers. White flies are sucking insects and are often a perennial problem on many vegetable crops, such as squash, beans, and tomatoes, as well as begonias, citrus trees, fuchsias, and geraniums.
- *Grubs* are little wormlike creatures that actually may be any of a number of insects, especially Japanese beetles, which spend part of their life cycle as wormlike grubs during their larval stage in the soil. They can do extensive damage to roots and turf. Fortunately, this is usually a vulnerable stage for them, during which controls are quite effective.
- *Beetles* are hard-shelled insects that damage leaves, stems, and roots.
- *Caterpillars* are moths and butterflies in a wormlike stage. They often do major damage to plants, especially the leaves, during their short life stage.

FUNGI: Fungi are plants without chlorophyll. Because they cannot make their own food, they often live as parasites on plants and animals. The garden fungi include *rusts, mildews, molds, smuts,* and a variety of *blights* (athlete's foot and yeast infections are common fungal infections that plague humans). Of the common fungi, the following are likely to be encountered by most gardeners:

- *Powdery mildew:* A fungal problem endemic to many roses, euonymus, lilacs, and garden phlox. It appears as a white film on the leaves late in the season or after particularly wet spells. Since this is hard to prevent and cure and will not kill a healthy plant, it is often wise to learn to live with the problem.
- *Black spot:* A very common fungal problem, particularly on roses. It appears on leaves as yellow spots with brown or black centers.

Fungi are spore-borne, with the spores germinating in the presence of water and the absence of light. A good garden practice to reduce the spread of fungal problems is to avoid watering in the evening or at night. There is no absolute cure for fungal problems on plants once infected, and at best fungicides only prevent the spread of the fungus, though recent experiments with antitranspirants (see page 63)—substances that coat the leaves and prevent spores from attaching or growing—promise hope.

ABOUT TYPES OF GARDEN CHEMICALS

Pesticides are sold in many different forms, which determine the way in which the chemical is applied and how it works.

- *Systemics* are pesticides that are taken into the system of a plant and ingested by insects that suck or eat the plant, therefore working from within the plant. Available in dry, liquid, powder, granular, and concentrated forms, they are absorbed by plants and cannot be leached away by rain or watering. The conscientious gardener should be aware that some systemics can remain in the soil and water table for long periods of time before breaking down, possibly becoming a serious threat to you and the environment, and of course they can remain in food plants.
- *Nonsystemic* pesticides are not absorbed by the plants but instead are ingested directly by the pest, or else work on contact with the insect.

• *Contact* pesticides are those that kill the insect on contact.

• *Selective* chemicals are specifically designed to kill or attack certain insects or weeds without harming other creatures or plants.

• *Nonselective* chemicals are not particular in what they destroy—they kill whatever they touch, and thus can destroy desirable plants (in the case of herbicides) or beneficial insects (in the case of insecticides) when applied incorrectly. Recent gardening wisdom encourages the specific identification of the problem and the use of more selective methods of control. The point is to avoid the indiscriminate use of nonselective chemicals.

• *Baits* contain some type of pesticide and usually a pest attractant, which the pest eats, while others are used as lures with traps.

ABOUT THE FORMS OF GARDEN CHEMICALS

Pesticide packages range in size from a few ounces to 100 pounds, depending on the form and manufacturer.

SPRAYS: Some chemicals are sold to be used as a nonaerosol spray, either prepackaged in a pump or spray container or sold for use in a sprayer (see pages 232–34). These chemicals include:

• *Emulsifiable concentrates,* or *emulsions,* solutions sold as liquids that must be diluted with water (follow label directions carefully). They are produced when the toxicant (the toxic substance) and an emulsifier (a substance that keeps the chemicals together) are dissolved in an organic solvent. The amount of the toxicant in relation to the rest of the mixture is noted on the label as a percentage. The strength of the product is sometimes described in terms of pounds of toxicant per gallon of concentrate.

• *Wettable powders,* very fine powders that are applied after being mixed with water. They remain suspended in the water, not dissolved, so you have to keep shaking the solution as you use it to keep it evenly distributed. Wettable powders, abbreviated *WP* on labels, are made up of an active ingredient (the actual pesticide), often a wetting agent (the substance that causes it to become more easily wettable), and some inert or filler (carrier) ingredients. The amount of the pesticide relative to the filler is shown on the label as a percentage, such as "50W" or "50WP" for a 50 percent concentration. Wettable powders are applied with a sprayer just as emulsifiable concentrates are. Be sure to keep nozzles and filters clean, as they tend to clog up quickly with this kind of material. Mix into a paste and then dilute, rather than just dumping the powder into the water.

• *Flowable liquid* (also known as *flowable powders, flowable formulations, flowable wettable powders,* or *water-dispersible suspensions),* creamy fluids whose active ingredients are suspended in a flowable liquid or paste. They need to be diluted with water to be used as a spray. Flowable liquid is a fairly recently developed form of pesticide, similar to wettable powder in its properties, but it forms a more stable suspension when mixed with water. It still eventually settles out in a sprayer, but more slowly than a wettable powder. Available in a dry form, called *dry flowable powders* or *DF.*

• *Horticultural oils* (also known as *sprayable* or *miscible oils*) contain an emulsifier (see emulsifiable concentrates on preceding page) and can therefore be mixed with water before application. These are often sold with an insecticide added, though not always. They are applied to the plant and work by smothering the insects, such as aphids, mites, and scale. These oils have been particularly helpful in the control of scale on ornamental trees and shrubs.

SPRAY CANS AND AEROSOLS: These are ready-mixed formulas that are sold in spray cans. There are two types and are distinguished by the insects they are intended to control. Many contain oil as a solvent. *Space sprays* produce a fine mist or fog and help control flying insects. *Surface sprays* produce a spray of droplets larger than the former and fall from the air quickly. These are used to control crawling insects.

DUSTS: Powders that are usually made up of particles larger than those of wettable powders. They are applied with shakers and dusters and are not wet when applied. They stick to the surface of the leaves and stems.

BAITS: Food substances to which poison has been added.

GRANULES: Like dusts but are made up of even larger particles. They are applied dry. Watering and rain make them available, but the large particle size makes them slower acting.

ABOUT READING A PESTICIDE LABEL

Pesticides must, by law, include a whole range of information on their labels, telling you clearly what it is, how, when, why, and

BRAND NAME AND TRADE MARKS

CHEMICAL OR COMMON NAMES

ACTIVE AND FILLER INGREDIENTS

SIGNAL WORD

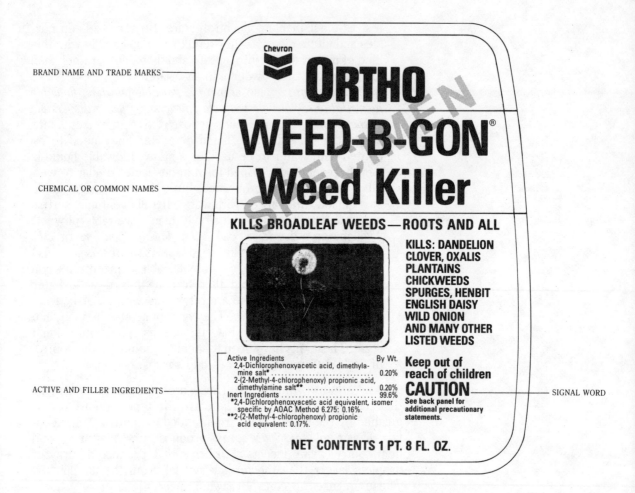

Chevron

ORTHO
WEED-B-GON®
Weed Killer

KILLS BROADLEAF WEEDS—ROOTS AND ALL

KILLS: DANDELION CLOVER, OXALIS PLANTAINS CHICKWEEDS SPURGES, HENBIT ENGLISH DAISY WILD ONION AND MANY OTHER LISTED WEEDS

Active Ingredients   By Wt.
  2,4-Dichlorophenoxyacetic acid, dimethyla-
    mine salt* 0.20%
  2-(2-Methyl-4-chlorophenoxy) propionic acid,
    dimethylamine salt** 0.20%
Inert Ingredients 99.6%
*2,4-Dichlorophenoxyacetic acid equivalent, isomer
    specific by AOAC Method 6.275: 0.16%.
**2-(2-Methyl-4-chlorophenoxy) propionic
    acid equivalent: 0.17%.

Keep out of reach of children
CAUTION
See back panel for additional precautionary statements.

NET CONTENTS 1 PT. 8 FL. OZ.

where to use it, and who made it. The sample label above is typical. This information is officially grouped in the following categories: *product and brand name and identification; active and filler ingredients; precautionary statements* (including the signal word and first aid instructions); *directions for use; directions for storage and disposal; manufacturer's name and address;* and *EPA code numbers.*

PRODUCT AND BRAND NAME AND IDENTIFICATION: The manufacturer's name for this product may suggest its use or it may be the official common name of the chemical. Some formerly trademarked names have become common names, such as diazinon, malathion, and ferbam, all of which are described later on. It is often stated here what type of chemical it is, too, such as "sys-

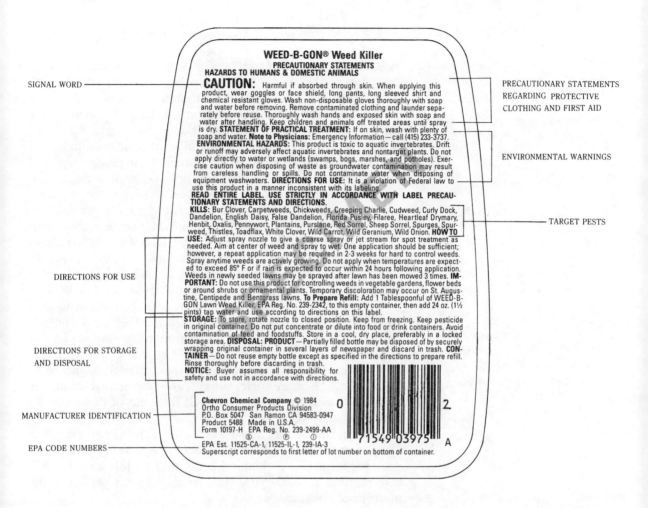

SIGNAL WORD

PRECAUTIONARY STATEMENTS REGARDING PROTECTIVE CLOTHING AND FIRST AID

ENVIRONMENTAL WARNINGS

TARGET PESTS

DIRECTIONS FOR USE

DIRECTIONS FOR STORAGE AND DISPOSAL

MANUFACTURER IDENTIFICATION

EPA CODE NUMBERS

WEED-B-GON® Weed Killer
PRECAUTIONARY STATEMENTS
HAZARDS TO HUMANS & DOMESTIC ANIMALS
CAUTION: Harmful if absorbed through skin. When applying this product, wear goggles or face shield, long pants, long sleeved shirt and chemical resistant gloves. Wash non-disposable gloves thoroughly with soap and water before removing. Remove contaminated clothing and launder separately before reuse. Thoroughly wash hands and exposed skin with soap and water after handling. Keep children and animals off treated areas until spray is dry. **STATEMENT OF PRACTICAL TREATMENT:** If on skin, wash with plenty of soap and water. **Note to Physicians:** Emergency Information—call (415) 233-3737. **ENVIRONMENTAL HAZARDS:** This product is toxic to aquatic invertebrates. Drift or runoff may adversely affect aquatic invertebrates and nontarget plants. Do not apply directly to water or wetlands (swamps, bogs, marshes, and potholes). Exercise caution when disposing of waste as groundwater contamination may result from careless handling or spills. Do not contaminate water when disposing of equipment washwaters. **DIRECTIONS FOR USE:** It is a violation of Federal law to use this product in a manner inconsistent with its labeling.
READ ENTIRE LABEL. USE STRICTLY IN ACCORDANCE WITH LABEL PRECAUTIONARY STATEMENTS AND DIRECTIONS.
KILLS: Bur Clover, Carpetweeds, Chickweeds, Creeping Charlie, Cudweed, Curly Dock, Dandelion, English Daisy, False Dandelion, Florida Pusley, Filaree, Heartleaf Drymary, Henbit, Oxalis, Pennywort, Plantains, Purslane, Red Sorrel, Sheep Sorrel, Spurges, Spurweed, Thistles, Toadflax, White Clover, Wild Carrot, Wild Geranium, Wild Onion. **HOW TO USE:** Adjust spray nozzle to give a coarse spray or jet stream for spot treatment as needed. Aim at center of weed and spray to wet. One application should be sufficient; however, a repeat application may be required in 2-3 weeks for hard to control weeds. Spray anytime weeds are actively growing. Do not apply when temperatures are expected to exceed 85° F or if rain is expected to occur within 24 hours following application. Weeds in newly seeded lawns may be sprayed after lawn has been mowed 3 times. **IMPORTANT:** Do not use this product for controlling weeds in vegetable gardens, flower beds or around shrubs or ornamental plants. Temporary discoloration may occur on St. Augustine, Centipede and Bentgrass lawns. **To Prepare Refill:** Add 1 Tablespoonful of WEED-B-GON Lawn Weed Killer, EPA Reg. No. 239-2342, to this empty container, then add 24 oz. (1½ pints) tap water and use according to directions on this label.
STORAGE: To store, rotate nozzle to closed position. Keep from freezing. Keep pesticide in original container. Do not put concentrate or dilute into food or drink containers. Avoid contamination of feed and foodstuffs. Store in a cool, dry place, preferably in a locked storage area. **DISPOSAL: PRODUCT**—Partially filled bottle may be disposed of by securely wrapping original container in several layers of newspaper and discard in trash. **CONTAINER**—Do not reuse empty bottle except as specified in the directions for package refill. Rinse thoroughly before discarding in trash.
NOTICE: Buyer assumes all responsibility for safety and use not in accordance with directions.

Chevron Chemical Company © 1984
Ortho Consumer Products Division
P.O. Box 5047 San Ramon CA 94583-0947
Product 5488 Made in U.S.A.
Form 10197-H EPA Reg. No. 239-2499-AA
EPA Est. 11525-CA-1, 11525-IL-1, 239-IA-3
Superscript corresponds to first letter of lot number on bottom of container.

0   2

71549 03975   A

temic insect control," and what it is most often used for, such as "kills broadleaf weeds" or other general statements.

ACTIVE AND FILLER INGREDIENTS: Listed, with percentage of volume or weight, by both common and/or chemical names, many also have registered trademarks. These names are found in the entries on the following pages. Many people, even experts, confuse the common or chemical names with trademarked names, such as carbaryl (a chemical name) with Sevin® (a trademarked name). Chemical names are technical terms that describe the composition of a substance. These are the names that you would want to give a doctor in the case of an accidental poisoning. Filler ingredients, usually labeled as inert ingredients, are not necessarily inert in regard to the user or the environment—just trade secrets that are not required to be divulged.

PRECAUTIONARY STATEMENTS: This statement is found on various parts of the label. One of three *signal words*—DANGER, WARNING, or CAUTION—is written in large type on the front of the label and often repeated on the back or sides. Toxic garden chemicals must, by law, include these signal words, or *indicators*, which clearly state the level of toxicity as indicated by the *LD 50 value*, a test that determines the dosage required to kill 50 percent of laboratory test animals, such as mice, rats, or rabbits. Neither chronic toxicity nor whether the chemical might be a carcinogen is indicated. The chemicals available in garden centers are known as *general classification chemicals;* more toxic or difficult to handle chemicals are available only to licensed professionals and are known as *restricted chemicals.* The most toxic restricted chemicals are labeled DANGER—POISON, in red, along with a skull and crossbones.

The most toxic chemicals available over the counter to consumers are marked with the signal word DANGER and are extremely poisonous to humans and animals. May be fatal if swallowed.

Chemicals that are somewhat less toxic carry the signal word WARNING. They are toxic, but kill fewer lab animals at higher dosages than those marked DANGER. Some of these can be fatal if swallowed. Handle carefully.

The rest of the chemicals, which are still less toxic, carry the signal word CAUTION on the label. The warning CAUTION does not mean that a chemical is not toxic; it just means it will take more of it to kill you, your family, or your pets than the more toxic chemicals.

All chemicals, even the less toxic ones, carry the warning "Keep Out of Reach of Children." Handle as if it were very toxic to be on the safe side.

The rest of the precautionary statements include information on hazards to humans and domestic animals, first aid instructions (or "Statement of Practical Treatment"), a "Note to Physicians" with suggestions of more advanced treatment and antidotes (and what *not* to give), "environmental hazards" (actually warnings about where not to use it), and "physical or chemical hazards," such as flammability. If the product is intended for use on food crops, then the amount of time you must wait after application before harvesting fruit or vegetables may be indicated here if it is not noted in the directions for use. The label may also indicate here if any special clothing or safety equipment is required.

DIRECTIONS FOR USE: This is the part you should reread until you are absolutely certain of how to use the product, and above all, how much of it to use. Labels on larger containers of a given product might contain additional useful information, such as an extended list of which pests it kills instead of a general grouping. "Days to Harvest" is the number of days after application you must wait in order to eat fruit or vegetables treated with this product. Whether or not this product can be combined with others would be shown here too.

DIRECTIONS FOR STORAGE AND DISPOSAL: Varies surprisingly from product to product. Most urge you not to reuse the container, among other things.

MANUFACTURER'S IDENTIFICATION: Provided so that you can write or call for more information. Many manufacturers have an 800 number for your convenience and good literature that they willingly send out.

EPA CODE NUMBERS: Both the manufacturer and the EPA give these products identification numbers for additional accuracy when you are inquiring about them. They refer to the chemical and the manufacturing plant and batch, among other things.

GENERAL BUYING AND USE TIPS FOR GARDEN CHEMICALS

Because pesticides are usually poisonous, they must be used sparingly and correctly, both in terms of common sense and with respect to the law. You should make every effort to do so, no matter how small your problem. Should you decide to go with pesticides after trying alternative strategies, you should always proceed cautiously.

• Use the least toxic method of pest management first. It is easier to advance to a more toxic substance if the first does not work than it is to eradicate the effects of a too toxic solution. If there is a safe organic method, you may wish to try that first. If it does not work, go to the next least harmful method. Many books and magazines offer information on this problem. If at all possible, use chemicals no stronger than those that contain CAUTION on the label and avoid those labeled WARNING, DANGER, and POISON (you need a license to apply DANGER—POISON products). Few home gardening problems are so threatening that you need to risk using the more toxic and dangerous chemicals. Each of those words denotes a jump to the next higher level of poison. Stick with CAUTION level poisons whenever possible.

• Identify the pest and determine how destructive it actually is, before deciding what to do. Most Cooperative Extension Services (see appendix C) are more than willing to help with the identification of pests and plenty of literature is available. Many insects, while a nuisance, may not be all that harmful to you or your garden, and in fact the chemicals introduced to deal with them are often more destructive than the discomfort of living with nuisance pests. Try to avoid a knee-jerk reaction to kill all pests.

• Know your chemical. If the specific pest affected or purpose for using a chemical cannot be found in the directions on the label of a product, *do not use that product.* Use only those products that specifically treat the problem you have and nothing else, and only use it on the plants indicated. Read and then reread the instructions. Follow them religiously, including dilution, application, and "Days to Harvest" directions in the case of use on food crops. Pay attention to whatever other chemicals you may be using, including fertilizers, and check with the manufacturer or your Cooperative Extension agent to see if they are compatible. Also check to see if the chemical can be mixed with other pesticides.

• Figure out exactly how much of a material is needed to handle the problem and buy only that amount. It is easier to buy more if it is needed than it is to dispose of unused chemicals. Furthermore, some chemicals lose their effectiveness in storage. Plus, storage can be dangerous too. Overapplication rarely kills more pests (it may even increase some types) and can harm you or your garden. Don't pour excess chemicals down the drain. Never reuse a pesticide container. Most can be wrapped in several layers of newspaper and put in the trash; others have special instructions for disposal on the label.

• Apply toxic chemicals wisely and safely. Do not apply sprays on a windy day. Do not eat, chew gum, or smoke while using pesticides, as this can lead you to ingest the chemical. Wear rubber gloves and clothing that covers your whole body, but avoid natural fiber clothing and shoes (cotton, wool, linen, or leather) because they act as natural wicks and carry the chemical to your skin. Respirators are recommended in some cases. Some gardeners use only one set of clothes for applying toxic chemicals and wash them separately from other clothes. Never use or store pesticides near food, utensils, toys, or children. Never use food utensils for measuring toxic chemicals. Instead, designate one particular measuring cup for this purpose. Remember that small children or pets may eat baits.

• Do not mix two or more chemicals, whether pesticides alone or pesticides with fertilizers, unless you are absolutely sure that no harm will result. In most cases this should not be done. You should really mix only when it is specifically suggested on the label.

IMPORTANT NOTE

The popular brand names listed here are by no means the only names under which these items are sold. Many excellent brands have been omitted. There are over six hundred active ingredients and fifty thousand formulations to choose from. Many new ones are announced daily and old ones removed. A listing here—or omission—is in no way an endorsement of or comment on these products. Dilution rates are indicated as a guide and are by no means to be considered definitive. Only the directions on a pesticide's label should be followed. This book is intended only as a guide and not as the authority on how a chemical should be used or the risks of using it. Neither the authors nor the publishers are responsible for any consequences of using any of the products noted here.

Organic Pesticides

ABOUT ORGANIC PESTICIDES

Pesticides derived from natural sources, while often toxic, are particularly useful in IPM programs. Most of them break down with little residual toxicity, meaning that the toxic chemical does not linger in the soil, water, or atmosphere. Some are based on soap and others on plants, which may be the oldest pesticides around. Remember, just because it is a natural pesticide does not mean it is entirely safe: Some are quite toxic.

Organic Insecticides

DIATOMACEOUS EARTH

ALSO KNOWN AS: Diatom flour, D.E., fossil shell flower

SIGNAL WORD: None—not officially registered as a pesticide.

DESCRIPTION: A white powder composed of finely ground, sharp-edged fossilized shells of diatoms—small-shelled, water-dwelling creatures of the algae family. Can be used as a spray when mixed with water, or used as a dust. Nontoxic.

USE: The microscopic prism-shaped particles' razor-sharp edges easily penetrate many insects on contact, causing them to dry up (desiccate). Sprinkle a band of it around plants that slugs attack. Also used in swimming pool filters and as the abrasive material in scouring cleansers as well.

USE TIP: Use a mask when applying and avoid breathing the dust or getting it in your eyes. Can be fatal to pets if ingested.

BUYING TIP: This is not an expensive product when you consider what it can do relatively safely. Sold in 10-pound bags. Try your local swimming pool dealer if your garden center does not carry it.

INSECTICIDAL SOAPS

POPULAR BRAND NAMES: Safer® Insecticidal Soap, Orthomite Insecticidal Soap

SIGNAL WORD: CAUTION

DESCRIPTION: Products that contain (or are) salts of fatty acids mixed with water and alcohol. They are a direct alternative to synthetic chemical pesticides. Most are sold in liquid concentrates to be mixed and sprayed on the plant, though some are sold in premixed solutions in sprayer bottles. Different formulations of various fatty acids are available for different plants and their pests, such as one for roses, flowers, and houseplants, and another for fruits and vegetables. Gentle to beneficial insects and animals (the birds and the bees); compatible with many biological controls (beneficial predators and the like) and a good number of chemical and organic pesticides; it is incompatible with certain ones that are listed by the manufacturer.

USE: Killing aphids, spider mites, mealybugs, rose slugs, psyllids, earwigs, scales, and whitefly on both garden plants and houseplants, depending on the formulation, which is clearly indicated on the label.

USE TIP: Insecticidal soaps are a contact spray—they kill the insect when they come in contact with it. However, they kill insects only in a certain stage in the life cycle (such as during some juvenile stages before the insects have formed a hard shell). Because of this, it is often necessary to repeat the application at intervals of seven to ten days. Safe to use on food crops right up to harvest.

BUYING TIP: Insecticidal soaps are safe and easy to use, especially those that are premixed and come in easy-to-use pump sprayer bottles. Ivory soap, when mixed with water, often works as well, but you should experiment as it might damage your plants.

NICOTINE SULFATE

ALSO KNOWN AS: Nicotine sulphate

POPULAR BRAND NAME: Black Leaf 40

SIGNAL WORD: DANGER

DESCRIPTION: Alkaloid extract of tobacco, mixed with sulfuric acid when sold as an aqueous solution concentrate, or with lime as a dust, containing 40 percent nicotine. Often combined with an alkaline water or soap solution. Also sold as a smoke for fumigation when combined with a combustible material, and as a wettable powder.

USE: Nonselective contact spray, sometimes a fumigant, for a wide range of insects—none are immune! Its efficiency as a fumigant is increased by a high temperature.

USE TIPS: Leaves little residue, but by the same token has a short shelf life. Can be washed off plants. May harm flower petals. Increase effectiveness by adding a few teaspoonfuls of dormant oil spray (see pages 119–20) per gallon. Nicotine is extremely toxic to humans and nicotine products are usually labeled POISON. A few drops can kill a horse!

BUYING TIP: Selective insecticides are preferable to nonselective ones, as their toxic effects are more predictable.

PYRETHRUM

ALSO KNOWN AS: Pyrethrins, pyrethrin

SIGNAL WORD: CAUTION

DESCRIPTION: Considered a broad spectrum natural botanical

insecticide that works as a contact or stomach poison, it is organically derived in oil form from the ground dried flowers of the African daisy, or oriental chrysanthemum, *Chrysanthemum cinerariaefolium,* grown in Kenya, Rwanda, Tanzania, and Ecuador (and now, as a test, in New Jersey). Sold in pressurized cans or as an oil concentrate for sprays, though can be found in dust form, too. Sometimes mixed with liquid rotenone (see next entry). In use since the mid-nineteenth century. *Pyrethrins* refers to the active ingredients of the plant. *(Permethrin* is a synthetic version.)

USE: In spray form for controlling flies, mosquitoes, springtails, aphids, and whiteflies. Follow label directions carefully so as not to harm plants. Often sold as a household spray for use on insects directly.

USE TIPS: Pyrethrum has a low toxicity to most nonallergic people and animals and leaves no harmful residues on food crops or vegetables ("low residual toxicity"), but skin contact or contamination of water should still be avoided. Some formulations contain petroleum distillates that can be carcinogenic or cause allergic reactions. Use as a last resort after other natural controls have failed. Dispose of empty container according to instructions on the label.

BUYING TIP: Look for the pure dust form if petroleum distillates present a problem for you.

ROTENONE

POPULAR BRAND NAMES: Chem Fish, Derris, Nicouline, Rotacide, Tubatoxin, DX, Prentox®, Noxfire®

SIGNAL WORD: CAUTION (in some formulations); DANGER (in some formulations)

DESCRIPTION: Organic, biodegradable insecticide made from the roots of several types of pea plants in the legume family. Generally sold as a dust or a wettable powder, though sometimes as a spray, to be used as a selective contact insecticide. Moderately toxic to animals (very toxic to swine and fish) but leaves no harmful residues on food or vegetable crops. Sometimes mixed in liquid form with pyrethrum (see preceding entry).

USE: For control of beetles, caterpillars, and other chewing insects. Some mixes may be used as a flea and tick spray for pets, and would be marked as such.

USE TIPS: Tends to break down after a week, which is helpful around harvest time. Avoid contact with skin and keep away from bodies of water, such as fish ponds, and bees. Do not store spray mixture—buy or mix only what you can use right away.

RYANIA

POPULAR BRAND NAMES: Ryanicide®, Triple-Plus (mixture), R-50

SIGNAL WORD: CAUTION

DESCRIPTION: Ground stems of *Ryania speciosa,* a South American shrub. Available as a dust or a wettable powder, often as a mixture with rotenone (above) and pyrethrum (see pages 95–96).

USE: Very effective against European corn borer.

SABADILLA

POPULAR BRAND NAME: Red Devil®

SIGNAL WORD: CAUTION

DESCRIPTION: Dust made from the seeds of a South American lily, sold as a wettable powder or a dust. In use at least since the sixteenth century.

USE: Controlling a wide range of tough pests, especially squash bugs, stink bugs, harlequin bugs, and blister beetles—all hard to control in their adult stage with other pesticides. Commonly used on turnips, collards, and cabbage.

USE TIPS: Can also be used as a spray. OK to use up to the day of harvest. Irritating to mucous membranes, so wear a mask when applying.

BUYING TIP: May no longer be registered with the EPA.

TOBACCO DUST

SIGNAL WORD: CAUTION

DESCRIPTION: Fine granular dust sold in small and large bags. Consists of approximately 5 percent nicotine and 95 percent inert matter in most formulations for consumer use. An old standby, a less refined version of nicotine sulfate (see page 95).

USE: Control of leafhoppers, thrips, plant lice, and other soft-bodied insects.

USE TIPS: Rinse leaves with water after application to avoid burning. Very potent: Use prior to release of beneficial insects in your garden. May turn roses black! May also affect growth and flowering in some plants, so experiment first.

Organic Herbicides

MOSS AND ALGAE KILLER

POPULAR BRAND NAME: Safer® Moss and Algae Killer (previously Cryptocidal Soap)

SIGNAL WORD: WARNING

DESCRIPTION: Liquid concentrate mixed with water and used as a spray. Nonstaining, noncorrosive, with a natural fatty acid base. Similar to insecticidal soap (see pages 94–95). Available in formulations for lawns or for decks, patios, and walls.

USE: For the control of algae, lichens, mosses, etc.

USE TIPS: Can be safely used on roofing, siding, walkways, fencing, trees, and greenhouses. Even works on bathroom fixtures and tiles. Do not spray on plant foliage to control insects.

BUYING TIP: At around $9 a quart, this product may be more expensive than a more toxic substance, but it may be worth the cost if you want an entirely nontoxic product.

WEED AND GRASS KILLER

POPULAR BRAND NAME: Safer® SharpShooter™

SIGNAL WORD: CAUTION

DESCRIPTION: Biodegradable spray made from naturally occurring saturated fatty acids. Works on contact.

USE: Killing weeds and unwanted grass.

USE TIPS: Leaves no residue after forty-eight hours, which means you can plant whatever you actually want in that soil then. Must be applied under the exact conditions specified on the label in order to work.

Organic Fungicides

ABOUT ORGANIC FUNGICIDES

A number of different products are considered organic fungicides that are not necessarily labeled as such, nor listed here. One prime example is antitranspirants, or antidesiccants—used for maintaining the moisture in evergreens and shining houseplant leaves—which also happen to be effective at smothering various types of fungal infestations. See page 63 for a more lengthy discussion.

LIME-SULFUR SOLUTION

SIGNAL WORD: DANGER

DESCRIPTION: Liquid compound of calcium polysulfide sold by the quart, gallon, or 5-gallon container.

USE: Controlling powdery mildew, cane blight, brown rot, and the like on fruit and nut trees, ornamentals, and flowers. Can also be used as an insecticide against scale and as a miticide.

USE TIPS: Apply as a dormant spray as well as in the growing season. Best if used as buds are just starting to swell, but before they break open. More caustic than sulfur—wear a mask and avoid contact with skin when applying.

SULFUR

ALSO KNOWN AS: Wettable sulfur, wettable dusting sulphur, garden sulfur

POPULAR BRAND NAMES: Safer® Garden Fungicide, Flotox® Garden Sulfur, Cosan, Sul-Cide, Magic Dusting Sulfur, Elosal, Kumulus S., Thiolux

SIGNAL WORD: CAUTION (in some formulations)

DESCRIPTION: Fine powder consisting mostly of ground-up sulfur rock. Available in either a wettable micronized powder (extremely small particles) form for use as a dust or in liquid, both as a ready-to-use mixture in a spray bottle or as a concentrate. Sulfur is one of the oldest known garden pesticides (it has been used for thousands of years), and a relatively benign one, though it does smell bad during application.

USE: Controlling powdery mildew, black spot, scab, brown canker, leaf spot, rust, and other diseases on fruits, vegetables, flowering trees, roses, and ornamentals. Like most sulfur products, this works as an organic miticide, too, and kills thrips. Sometimes combined with acephate (see page 117) to control other insects (see labels for details). Also used as a soil acidifier (see page 5). Do not use within one month of using an oil spray.

USE TIPS: No residue. Safe for use on food crops. Extra-fine size of granules makes for better adhesion. Can cause skin irritation, may acidify soil, and may harm beneficial microorganisms and beneficial insects.

BUYING TIPS: *Micronized sulfur* has the smallest possible particle sizes, which makes it cover better. Also, check the label to be sure you are getting pure sulfur.

Organic Miticides

MITE KILLER

POPULAR BRAND NAMES: Safer® Mite Killer, Orthomite Insecticidal Soap

SIGNAL WORD: CAUTION

DESCRIPTION: Liquid spray sold in concentrated as well as ready-to-use strengths, in 8- and 24-ounce plastic bottles. Made from salts of fatty acids, as are the insecticidal soaps. Rapidly biodegradable.

USE: Kills mites once an infestation has begun, especially red spider mites, two-spotted mites, and most sucking insects. Intended for use on houseplants.

USE TIP: Use a flashlight and a magnifying glass to make sure you have covered every area, especially where webbing is found. Most problems are on the undersides of leaves.

BUYING TIP: Other controls include wiping or rinsing off leaves.

Organic Rodenticides

CASTOR BEAN

DESCRIPTION: Seed of the castor bean plant, about the size of a lima or pinto bean. Speckled brown and white, it is often used in necklaces. Though in a tropical climate the plant can grow to become a 40-foot-tall tree with leaves 3 feet across, in the United States it usually grows to a height of only 8 to 12 feet.

Like its seeds, the plant is poisonous to humans and domestic animals. Oil made from the castor plant seed is toxic, too.

USE: The seed, placed in a mole tunnel, is a toxic bait for moles and voles. A repellent spray can be made from a tablespoon of castor oil mixed with 2 tablespoons of liquid detergent and sprinkled over mole-infested areas.

USE TIPS: Do not use if a child might pick up and eat the bean (though it is not toxic to handle). Remove after a month if not eaten by a mole so that a castor plant does not grow. Repellent sprays work best if applied just after a rain shower, for increased penetration.

BUYING TIP: Generally not sold as a rodenticide but sold in seed catalogs for the castor bean plant.

RED SQUILL

POPULAR BRAND NAMES: Scillirocide, Death Diet, Red Quill, Rodine

SIGNAL WORD: CAUTION

DESCRIPTION: A powder or liquid extract made from the bulb of red squill, *Urginea maritima,* which grows in the Mediterranean. It is often used as an additive in rodent baits because it is toxic to rats but not to other animals when used in recommended dosages.

USE: For the control of Norway rats.

USE TIP: Not as harmful to the environment or humans as many similar products.

BUYING TIP: This is not commonly available, but it could become more popular if consumers keep requesting it. An imported item.

STRYCHNINE

SIGNAL WORD: DANGER—POISON

DESCRIPTION: White crystalline powder, somewhat soluble in water and alcohol, extracted from the seeds or berries of the tropical tree and vine family *Strychnos nus vomica.*

USE: Common ingredient in poison baits for moles and gophers in concentrations of less than .5 percent.

USE TIP: Keep baits out of reach of children, pets, and wildlife.

VITAMIN D-3

POPULAR BRAND NAMES: Quintox™, Rampage™, Ortho Rat & Mouse-B-Gon™

CHEMICAL NAME: Cholecalciferol

SIGNAL WORD: CAUTION

DESCRIPTION: Granular bait, pellets, meal, or parafinized blocks, often sold wrapped in disposable paper or cardboard traps. Usually in a mixture containing only .075 percent active ingredients.

USE: Natural rat and mouse control with low toxicity. Causes death in about two to four days.

USE TIPS: Dead rodents are not poisonous to other animals, so this is a fairly safe item to use around pets and domestic animals that might eat them. Good for rodents that have developed resistance to warfarin (see page 133).

Biological Controls

ABOUT BIOLOGICAL CONTROLS

Insects succumb to diseases just like plants and people, and these products increase the naturally occurring disease organisms. Many *microbial control agents, biorational pesticides,* or *microbial insecticides*—which are inherently organic—are on the market and are very easy to use.

BACILLUS POPILLIAE

ALSO KNOWN AS: Milky disease spores, milky spore powder, milky spore disease, milky spores, BP

POPULAR BRAND NAMES: Doom, Japidemic, Grub Attack™, Safer® Grub Killer

DESCRIPTION: A powder of spores applied directly to the soil, usually on lawns, and watered in well.

USE: For the control of Japanese beetles in the larvae stage (grubs), although some brands claim to control oriental beetles, rose chafers, and some May and June beetles as well. Allow one to three years for it to spread completely through your soil.

USE TIPS: Not known to be toxic to humans, nor does it produce any health threats. Harmless to animals, birds, fish, plants, and beneficial insects. Remains active in the lawn only as long as there are sufficient grubs in the lawn for it to feed on. Will not work as a preventive—it only works if grubs are present.

BUYING TIPS: Container should be kept in a cool, dark place. Don't buy it if you think it has been stored improperly—the spores may have become inactive.

BACILLUS THURINGIENSIS

ALSO KNOWN AS: Bt, B.t., BT

POPULAR BRAND NAMES: Dipel, Thuricide, Bactur, Mosquito Attack™, Safer® Caterpillar Killer, Caterpillar Attack™, Bacthane, Biotroe, SOK-Bt, Biotrol, Vectobac (some of these products are meant to control certain insects only—read the labels)

SIGNAL WORD: CAUTION

DESCRIPTION: Microbial insecticide usually sold as a wettable powder and sometimes as a liquid. It contains the spores and toxins produced by the bacteria *Bacillus thuringiensis Berliner,* variety *kurstaki*. Also sold as a dust and bait.

USE: For control of some leaf-eating caterpillars, pupating larvae, cabbage loopers, armyworms, imported cabbage worm, and gypsy moths. Bt is considered one of the most significant biological controls because it is harmless to humans, animals, food crops, and useful insects, and it stops caterpillars instantly. Used on crops such as tobacco, cotton, alfalfa, soybeans, vegetables, shade trees, forested areas, fruit trees, and ornamentals. The bacillus interrupts the digestive cycle of certain larvae, making it a *larvacide* as well as an insecticide. A new variety, 'San Diego,' is being tested to combat the Colorado potato beetle, and another type, var. *israeliensis,* or *Bti,* attacks mosquito and black fly larvae (not adults) on water.

USE TIPS: Compatible with most insecticides, fungicides, and nutritional sprays. Plants must be thoroughly covered, especially the undersides of leaves. Can be mixed with a soap-based solution so it sticks to both sides of leaves. Can be used up to the day of harvest. Apply only when you see insects present—it has no residual effect.

BUYING TIP: Target insects are noted on the label.

BAT HOUSE

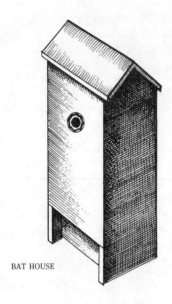

BAT HOUSE

ALSO KNOWN AS: Bat box

DESCRIPTION: Wooden box 17 to 27½ inches high, 8 to 11 inches wide, and 3½ to 7 inches deep, with a slanted roof and an open bottom through which bats enter and leave. The bat house is made of natural finished western red cedar. A single house usually holds twenty to thirty bats, though some models, *macrobat dwellings,* can hold up to one hundred.

USE: Provides a shelter for bats, thus attracting them to your garden. Bats prey on insects, consuming thousands each evening (actually, any birdhouse can be considered an insect control product).

USE TIP: Place the box high up, in a sheltered location near a pond or stream. If there are no bats in your area to begin with, it is unlikely the bat house will attract any, but if you have seen bats flying around at dusk or in the evening, you may want to coax them closer to your garden with a bat box. Especially helpful in areas where bats have lost their natural tree shelters.

BUYING TIP: Bat houses have become extremely popular in the last few years.

BENEFICIAL NEMATODES

POPULAR BRAND NAMES: Scanmask, BioSafe™, Bio-Logic, Grub-Eater

DESCRIPTION: Biologically active insecticide made of microscopic worms called nematodes (principally the beneficial Nc type, *Neoaplectana carpocapsae),* which feed on damaging insects in the soil. May be shipped in a semidormant state, mixed into a gel on a screen that you dissolve with an activator powder mix, or in topsoil or peat mosslike media. Eventually the worms are mixed into a water-based solution that is sprayed or watered onto lawns and gardens.

USE: Controlling insects in lawns, gardens, and houseplants; different nematodes are effective against different pests—check the label.

USE TIPS: Apply directly to the soil in the root zone, not on the leaves of the plants. Follow storage and mixing directions very carefully, as you are dealing with living organisms that are easily affected by sunlight and moisture and soil structure. Keep refrigerated before use, and be sure to use whatever you mix right away. Moist soil is necessary for success.

NEMATICIDE

POPULAR BRAND NAME: Safer® ClandoSan

SIGNAL WORD: CAUTION

DESCRIPTION: Ground and treated crab shells and shellfish waste full of naturally occurring chitin proteins that stimulate the growth of beneficial soil microorganisms, fungi, and bacteria.

USE: Controlling unwanted nematodes by producing enzymes that destroy them as well as their eggs.

NOSEMA LOCUSTAE

ALSO KNOWN AS: Grasshopper spore

POPULAR BRAND NAMES: Nolo, Grasshopper Attack™

DESCRIPTION: Organic insecticide powder made of protozoa spore.

USE: Controlling grasshoppers of the Malanoplus family. Even the eggs laid by the infected grasshoppers infect young nymphs.

USE TIP: Apply by hand or with a seeder. Takes about a year to have maximum effect.

Physical and Mechanical Controls

Traps

ELECTRONIC INSECT KILLER

ALSO KNOWN AS: Bug zapper

DESCRIPTION: Fluorescent or incandescent light inside an electrified metal grid. Some brands are shaped like a lantern. Typical wattage of current in grid is 4,500 to 6,000. Lights are either yellow or black light, a type of ultraviolet light that appears to us as a dull blue. Fluorescent bulbs may be normal ones covered with a *black light blue filter (BLB)*. Higher-wattage models are self-cleaning, meaning that they actually burn off the bugs that hit the grid. Another version uses the same light to attract insects, but has a fan instead of an electrified grid. The fan blows the insects into a container of water with detergent on top of it, and the insects drown. All models come with a variety of brackets and hangers for use indoors and out.

USE: Controlling flying insects in an area about 25 to 70 feet square, although larger models are available. Can be operated twenty-four hours a day, but most effective at night.

USE TIP: Keep grid clean.

BUYING TIPS: There is no doubt that the higher-wattage units are more effective, as are the black light fluorescent bulbs—not the ones with the filters. Nonselective, this device tends to kill many insects that are not pests.

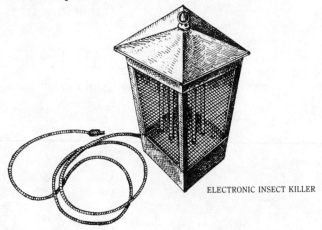

ELECTRONIC INSECT KILLER

MOLE TRAP

POPULAR BRAND NAMES: Victor®, Out-of-Site®

TYPES: Skewer type, scissor type

DESCRIPTION: Metal device about a foot high with spring-loaded blades that is set above a mole burrow and anchored by two

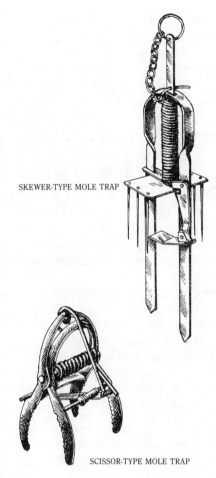

SKEWER-TYPE MOLE TRAP

SCISSOR-TYPE MOLE TRAP

spikes stuck in the ground on both sides of a mole tunnel. When the mole comes along, it sets off the sensitive device and is skewered to death by three sharp spikes, in the case of the Victor trap, or squeezed to death by four scissorlike blades with the Out-of-Site trap.

USE: Control of tunneling moles in the garden or lawn.

USE TIP: With the scissor-type design it is easy to tell if a trap has been triggered. When a trap has done its deed, just remove the trap and pat the soil back down with your foot. It is better not to look at what you have done to the mole, as this is not a scene for the fainthearted. On the other hand, it is entirely nontoxic.

BUYING TIPS: The choice between the two types pretty much depends upon your personal taste: Do you prefer your moles skewered or squeezed? This kind of trap has been around for a while, and is time-tested to be a nontoxic way of killing one mole at a time, but if you have a real infestation you might want to look into putting out castor bean seed (see pages 101–102). Check your local game trap laws—they may dictate what you can do about small animals.

MOUSETRAPS AND RAT TRAPS

DESCRIPTION: Mousetraps and rat traps are the same, except that rat traps are bigger.

TYPES: *Spring-loaded trap* (also known as *spring* or *snap trap):* These are the classic mouse and rat traps that have been around forever. A spring device is set when a U-shaped wire is pulled against the tension of the spring and a short wire is placed over it and onto a flat tin trigger. Cheese or some other bait (including dental floss or a small piece of cloth that a mouse might like for nesting material) is placed on the trigger, and when the mouse or rat goes for it the animal is caught under the U-shaped wire and held there (and if the spring is strong enough, killed there) by the pressure of the spring.

Box trap (also known as *live trap.* Popular brand name: Victor Smiling Cat Repeating Mouse Trap): This is the better mousetrap we've been waiting for! Consists of a metal box with small apertures on either end. When the mouse enters the trap it cannot find its way out again. Available as single models or larger ones that are

REPEATING BOX TYPE MOUSETRAP

reputed to capture as many as a dozen mice at one time without resetting, and without killing them (though they may kill each other or die of loss of body heat).

Glue trap (popular brand name: Tanglefoot): Nontoxic, 3-inch-square up to 7-by-12-inch plastic trays that contain a sticky bait substance. They are placed where rats and mice travel, and the animal is trapped when it walks on the glue, where it dies slowly.

USE: For the control of mice and rats. These are nontoxic and time-tested ways of catching mice and rats. The box type is for areas with an extreme problem.

USE TIPS: Be careful that you don't set off a spring-type trap when you try to set it. Many a finger has been hurt this way. It is also a good idea to put the bait material on the trap before trying to set it, because once the trap is set, you might catch your finger if you press the bait trigger. The only problem with the box-type trap is the problem of what to do with a box full of live mice, although this is a challenge that might appeal to some of the more mischievous gardeners among us. Glue-type traps must be placed where mice travel, usually around the edge of rooms. Both the spring and glue types can be dangerous to inquisitive pets and small children. Disposal of the pest is simple with these two types, as it is just a matter of throwing the trap in the garbage along with the animal stuck to it.

BUYING TIP: All these traps are safe, nontoxic ways of trapping mice. The spring- and glue-type traps are especially inexpensive and efficient; killing a mouse instantly may be more humane than trapping for later dispatch.

PHEROMONE TRAP

ALSO KNOWN AS: Sex traps, Japanese beetle trap, pheromone lures

POPULAR BRAND NAMES: Bag-A-Bug, Japanese Beetle Attack™

DESCRIPTION: Plastic bag or metal or cardboard container underneath a bug-attracting strip containing female Japanese beetle sex pheromone and sometimes floral scents. Trapped bugs fall into container. Strips are yellow and about 15 inches high.

USE: To attract and capture Japanese beetles and other flying insects.

USE TIP: Because the pheromone attracts more insects to the garden than it can kill at once, be sure to place it away from plants that can be eaten by the pest, such as roses and zinnias. This problem makes pheromone traps particularly ill-suited to small urban gardens. In fact, some folks say that the best location for a Japanese beetle trap is in your neighbor's garden—that way the bugs will leave you alone and head over there. Lasts one season.

BUYING TIP: The yellow color of the trap itself is an attractant, but models with both pheromones and floral lures *(double lures)* are better—you just increase your chances.

SLUG TRAP

SLUG TRAP

DESCRIPTION: Plastic cup with lip and a plastic, mushroomlike roof. A *slug barrier* can be made from a strip of copper, which somehow reacts with slug slime to produce an electric shock.

USE: When trap is filled with beer or some other liquid slug-attracting bait, slugs climb into the cup and drown. A safe alternative to placing highly toxic slug bait in your garden or lawn, where it can be eaten by birds.

USE TIP: Stale beer is cheaper and works as well in the traps as the more expensive slug baits. We recommend discount domestic brands over the finer, imported beers. We are sorry to report that no recent studies indicate which brand, in particular, slugs prefer.

BUYING TIP: Cat food and tunafish cans can also be used as slug traps, but at under $2, the slug trap is not that expensive and is slightly more effectively designed, as the cover keeps rain from washing away the beer.

STICKY INSECT TRAP

ALSO KNOWN AS: Flying insect trap, sticky whitefly trap

DESCRIPTION: Small flat piece of yellow material coated with a sticky material that attracts certain insects, such as whiteflies and aphids. May be sold as cards to be placed in holders or hung from hooks. This trap coating (popular brand name: Tanglefoot Tangle-Trap Paste) is also sold separately for making your own traps in aerosol spray, paintable, or spreadable formulations. The color yellow is an attractant.

USE: Not only does this kind of updated flypaper trap insects, it provides an opportunity to identify and count whatever kind of pest is arriving on the scene, acting as an early warning and identification system. Labels identify which insects are attracted to each particular trap, such as flying aphids, thrips, leaf miners, gnats, fruit flies, and leafhoppers.

BUYING TIP: Check out the type of insect each trap attracts.

WIRE CAGE ANIMAL TRAP

POPULAR BRAND NAME: Havahart

DESCRIPTION: Galvanized wire mesh cage that comes in several sizes, from 10 by 3 by 3 inches for mice and shrews, to 42 by 11 by 11 inchs for raccoons. Standard trap for rabbits and squirrels is 30 by 7 by 7 inches.

USE: To capture small animals without harming them. Often used when populations of some animals, like rabbits and squirrels, are particularly high. The animals are released in areas where their populations are lower.

BUYING TIP: Check your local game trap laws—they may dictate what you can do about small animals.

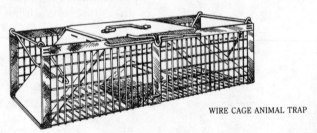

WIRE CAGE ANIMAL TRAP

Barriers

CATERPILLAR TAPE

DESCRIPTION: Plastic silicone tape, 5 inches wide by 40 feet long, with sticky substance on the top part. When attached to a tree, pleats are made every few inches, creating a "skirt" effect. Another type is 3 inches wide by 500 feet long and is completely sticky.

USE: Prevents gypsy moth ("tent") caterpillars from climbing trees—they cannot climb over the smooth surface of the tape. The sticky kind merely traps the caterpillars.

USE TIP: Install carefully.

BUYING TIP: Proven nontoxic control of gypsy moths.

ELECTRIC FENCING

ALSO KNOWN AS: Deer fencing

DESCRIPTION: Thick lengths of wire which conduct pulses of low-voltage electricity; any animal that touches it receives a harmless but unpleasant shock. Wires are attached to fence posts by *insulators;* lightweight custom *fence posts* are available too, as are *insulated gate handles.* Electricity is supplied by house current, a storage or solar battery, and conducted to the fencing by a variety of *fence chargers* or *condensers,* the transformers that change regular electricity into pulsating, low-voltage surges of a fraction of a second—and harmless—duration. Strands are approximately 2 feet apart and usually three strands constitute the fence; they are placed much closer together and closer to the ground when used for protection against smaller animals.

USE: Keeping cattle or horses contained or to prohibit animals such as deer from entering a garden area. Also effective against rabbits, raccoons, and other smaller animals, but this requires more strands of wire.

USE TIP: Deer can make considerable pests of themselves, and electric fences are useful in keeping them at bay. However, deer are also impressive jumpers and may jump over a low electric fence.

GALVANIZED STEEL FENCING

ALSO KNOWN AS: Welded wire fabric

DESCRIPTION: Welded and woven, galvanized 16-gauge steel fencing with various types of mesh. *Rabbit guard, rabbit fencing,* or *garden fencing* has 1-by-4-inch or 1-inch-square mesh on the bottom 12 inches, then 2-by-4-inch mesh on the next 4 inches and 4-inch-square mesh on the top, whether the fencing is 24, 28, 36, 40, or 50 inches high. Sold in 50-foot rolls. Others have just the small mesh on the bottom and 2-inch hexagonal mesh on the top, for economy. Standard *yard fencing,* or *utility fencing,* is usually 14 gauge (thicker than 16 gauge and thinner than 12½ gauge) and has a 2-by-4-inch mesh. *Hexagonal netting,* or *chicken wire,* is sold in 24-, 36-, and 48-inch heights and 75-foot rolls and is made of lightweight 20-gauge wire. Fourteen-gauge steel *fence posts* are sold separately (13 gauge for heavy duty), usually with a green baked-enamel finish, 3 to 8 feet long. Made in either a T shape or a U shape. Packed ten to a bundle.

USE: Barrier for rabbits, pets, and other small animals (and sometimes people).

USE TIP: Where there is a will in the animal world, there is a way. These critters are persistent and will dig under or jump over almost any kind of fence if they possibly can. Try to extend rabbit fences below ground level at least half a foot.

PROTECTIVE NETTING

ALSO KNOWN AS: Anti-bird net, bird control net, bird netting, garden net, tobacco netting

DESCRIPTION: Nets made from synthetic material such as polypropylene in a range of sizes from 20 by 20 feet to 4½ by 75 feet. A ¾-inch mesh is typical.

USE: Placed over fruit trees, fruit shrubs, or plants such as strawberries to protect the crops from birds. Can also be used to cover a lily pond or fish pool to catch falling leaves in autumn. Lasts a few seasons. A heavier version is now available for protecting crops from deer, although it can also be used to keep leaves out of pools, as a snow barrier, and for transporting large quantities of pruning debris. This latter model has a ½-inch mesh, and is also known as a *garden utility net* or a *garden net.* A finer mesh is made for *insect netting,* used primarily on fruit trees.

USE TIPS: Be sure that the net is secured well at the bottom, as birds can get in underneath it. When placing the net over thorny plants like blackberries or raspberries, prop the net up above the plants with a frame to prevent it from becoming stuck on the thorns. Cover tree after fruit set but before ripening starts.

BUYING TIP: Buy a size that is a little larger than you think you need. It is better to have too much than too little.

PROTECTIVE NETTING

TREE TANGLEFOOT®

DESCRIPTION: Viscous goo sold in 6-ounce tubes, 1- to 25-pound cans and pails, caulking cartridges, and aerosol cans. Sticky and nontoxic, made from castor oil, gum resins, and vegetable waxes.

USE: Banding trees and vines to protect against climbing pests such as cankerworms, gypsy moth caterpillars, and ants. The pests get stuck and suffocate.

USE TIPS: Lasts three to four months. Apply a band about 3 to 4 inches wide at 5 to 6 feet above the ground. Put Tanglefoot on banding material for small young trees. Though some people use it, it is not recommended for sealing pruning wounds. If you insist on painting tree wounds, Tanglefoot makes a specially formulated tree paint.

Repellents and Scarecrows

ABOUT REPELLENTS AND SCARECROWS

This is an area of products which contains more folklore than most others. It is very hard to prove the effectiveness of scarecrows and the like, and in fact, some government studies have indicated that the more high-tech devices used to scare animals, such as ultrasonic gopher repellents, are not particularly effective. Some of these items seem to work more on personal faith than scientific principle. And they are nice to have around, out of tradition.

ANIMAL REPELLENT

POPULAR BRAND NAMES: RO-PEL®, Deer Guard®, Hinder®, Hot Sauce Animal Repellent®, Rabbit & Dog Chaser®, Dog and Cat Granular Repellent®, Scent-Off Pellets®, Scent-Off "Twist-On" Buds®, Repel® Dog and Cat Repellent, Repel® Liquid Animal Repellent, Chaperone Squirrel & Bat Repellent®, Scram® Dog & Cat Repellent

DESCRIPTION: Extremely vile-tasting, bitter chemical, either granular or aerosol or powders mixed with a solvent base for spraying. Smells offensive to sensitive animals but not to humans. Also comes in wax buds that are hung from the lower branches of trees and bushes.

USE: Discouraging specific pest animals (ranging from deer to pet cats) from gnawing, nibbling, licking, or biting plants, trees, fences, garbage cans, siding, and furniture. Works without harming the animal—they merely find the odor offensive and move away from it.

USE TIPS: Some brands contain toxic chemicals that must be handled exactly as the label instructs, in terms of both application and storage and disposal. Test on plants or furniture before application. Many need to be reapplied often.

BUYING TIP: Check the label carefully. Some animal repellents carry environmental hazard warnings on the labels. You may find that the environmental condition you create by using the product is worse than the pest you wish to repel. Furthermore, some brands may repel generally beneficial animals, such as bats, along with the pests.

SCARECROWS

ALSO KNOWN AS: Bird repellents, decoys, natural enemy scarecrows, bird scarers, pest scarers

DESCRIPTION: Natural-looking decoys in the form of natural predators of certain garden pests. The inflatable items are made from heavy vinyl, others from molded plastic. All are painted or printed with lifelike detail, with the exception of the scarecat and the monster.

TYPES: *Garden monster:* An unclassifiable model, consists of eight plastic film "tentacles" attached to a stake. Monstrous-looking to pests only.

Inflatable and *plastic owl:* Great horned owl, 18 to 22 inches tall; big orange eyes. Plastic molded type is amazingly lifelike and beautiful.

Inflatable scarecrow: More than 6 feet tall. Resembles a straw man.

Inflatable snake: Six feet long and an inch or two in diameter.

Scarecat (also known as *Le chat* or *cat's head bird scarer*): Either a silhouette of an entire cat or a silhouette of a cat's head. A French product made from flat, black metal, with two clear marbles for eyes. It is hung on a

PLASTIC OWL SCARECROW

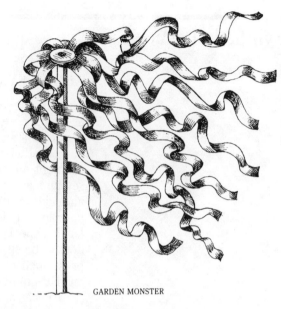

GARDEN MONSTER

SCARECAT

INFLATABLE SNAKE SCARECROW

wire in the garden where it blows in the wind; the movement causes sunlight to glance off the glass eyes. A similar, and perhaps more effective, version is a mobile of highly reflective chrome-plated disks suspended from a hanger or yard-high stake.

USE: The owl and the snake are supposed to scare rodents, such as rats, mice, and rabbits as well as some birds, from the garden and around the house. The snake and the cat are designed to scare birds (especially pigeons), squirrels, and other small animals away from berry patches and vegetable gardens. And the scarecrow is for scaring birds from grain crops.

USE TIPS: Change the position of the snake every few days to aid in its effectiveness against your more cynical pests. Be sure to warn any fainthearted visitors about the snake's presence before they discover it on their own.

BUYING TIPS: It is not entirely clear if these work well or not, but they are generally fun, and certainly traditional, to have in the garden. The solid plastic model owl is more realistic looking to humans and makes for a more decorative object. The cat is probably the least effective and most expensive, considering that a tin can lid performs the same function. However, it is quite nice looking and very popular in France, so maybe that doesn't matter so much.

Synthetic Pesticides

ABOUT SYNTHETIC PESTICIDES

Much has been said in preceding sections of this book about alternatives to the following chemical products. There is no doubt that they provide an excellent service and convenience, but nonetheless, they are very dangerous, not only to the environment but to the consumer, especially if precautions and directions are not followed to the letter. If you should ever have an accident or misuse any of these toxic products, be sure to call your local poison center with the information provided on the label, especially the Note to Physicians. If you go to see a doctor, be sure to take the label or the container with you—the prescribed treatment may be on the label. Also note the code and EPA numbers for positive identification with the authorities.

You can also call the NPTN, the National Pesticide Telecommunications Network, at 1-800-858-7378, twenty-four hours a day, 365 days a year, for information on pesticides and help in responding to pesticide poisoning. Ortho, one of the major manufacturers of these products, requests that you call them collect at 415-233-3737 twenty-four hours a day if you ever have an emergency or accidental spill.

Please note that some garden centers unwittingly sell professional products—that is, *restricted use* chemical products for which the EPA requires that you obtain a pesticide permit or applicator's license number. Be careful. There is a reason for those licenses. These products are very strong, and may be hazardous to you and your environment. This is not to say that the off-the-shelf chemicals are not dangerous: Some were approved for consumer use long ago, when our standards were less demanding and our knowledge less comprehensive. Once-common products disappear from the shelves from time to time as regulations change and research grows in sophistication and the chemicals are discovered to be much more dangerous than originally thought—such as DDT (one of the most popular and widely used pesticides, it is now banned because although harmless to humans, it caused enormous damage to birds). Some of the items listed here will come to the same fate.

For an explanation of the common terms and labels of pesticides, see pages 87–91.

General Use Synthetic Pesticide Products

SPREADER-STICKER

ALSO KNOWN AS: Sticking agent, wetting agent (though not the same as the wetting agent described on page 20)

DESCRIPTION: Highly concentrated liquid petroleum product typically sold in 4- and 8-ounce bottles. A sort of *wetting agent, surfactant,* or *emulsifier.* Also available in an organic formulation. Part of a family of products that are mixed with pesticides to improve or modify their action, called *spray adjuvants.* Another similar product more oriented to the professional market but available to the consumer is a *sticker-extender.*

USE: Increases the efficiency of pesticides (or fertilizers) by reducing surface tension so they can more thoroughly cover plant surfaces (hence, *spreader)* and leaving a film that encapsulates the pesticides, drying to form a shield against rain (hence, *sticker).* An *extender* protects the active ingredients from degradation by the sun, like a sun block, prolonging its effectiveness.

USE TIP: Use at least one hour before rainfall. Note that some additives are quite toxic, even though they are not listed as pesticides.

BUYING TIP: This product is often included in many quality pesticides.

Synthetic Insecticides

ACEPHATE

CHEMICAL NAME: O,S-dimethyl acetylphosphoramidothioate

POPULAR BRAND NAMES: Orthene®, Ortran, Tree and Ornamental Spray

SIGNAL WORD: CAUTION

DESCRIPTION: White, 75 percent soluble powder made for use as a spray, when mixed with water, or an aerosol. Also available as a 9.4 percent emulsifiable concentrate. Works both as a contact and as a systemic insecticide. Absorbed within about twenty-four hours; rain-fast.

USE: Controlling aphids, caterpillars, leaf miners, scale, whiteflies, and many other bugs on potted, flowering, bedding, and ornamental plants and cut flowers. Especially good in combatting fire ants. Sometimes used on roses, trees, and shrubs, too.

USE TIP: Stays in the plant about fourteen to twenty-one days when applied to the leaves as recommended.

CHLORPYRIFOS

CHEMICAL NAME: O,O-diethyl O-(3,5,6 trichloro-2-pyridyl) phosphorothioate

POPULAR BRAND NAMES: Brodan, Dursban®, Eradex, Lorsban®, Pyrinex, d-Con Home Pest Control Killer, Raid Home Insect Killer

SIGNAL WORD: WARNING or CAUTION (granular products)

DESCRIPTION: White granular crystal or fine powder, emulsifiable concentrate, or diluted household spray. Contained in many common household insect sprays.

USE: Insecticide for use against ants, ticks, cutworms, chinch bugs, earwigs, grubs, cockroaches, silverfish, spiders, fleas, dog ticks, and mosquitoes. Also used to control termites, against which it may be effective for up to eighteen years.

USE TIP: One of the most common sources of organophosphate poisoning because it is extremely toxic to fish, aquatic invertebrates, and birds—keep away from water supply.

DIAZINON

CHEMICAL NAME: O,O-diethyl O-(2-isopropyl-6-methyl-4-pyrimidinyl) phosphorothiate

POPULAR BRAND NAMES: Spectracide, Basudin, D-264, Dazzel, Diagran, Dianon, Diaterr-Fos, Diazajet, Diazatol, Diazide, Diazol, Dizinon, Drawizon, Dyzol, D.zn., Fezudin, G-24480, Gardentox, Kayazion, Kayazol, Neocidol, Nipsan, Sarolex (and many ant and roach killers)

SIGNAL WORD: WARNING (spray form) or CAUTION (granular form)—varies with formulation

DESCRIPTION: Comes as an emulsifiable concentrate, wettable powder, granular mixture, or prediluted ready-to-use household spray. A member of the organophosphate family. Extremely toxic to birds feeding on treated lawns. One of the most commonly used insecticide ingredients since the early 1950s, and one of the most toxic available to the consumer. Often mixed with other chemicals, such as fertilizers.

USE: Lawn and garden control of aphids, leafhoppers, leaf miners, sawflies, scale, cutworms, grubs, chinch bugs, and other soil insects. Household uses include cockroaches, ants, fire-brats, silverfish, fleas, sow bugs, springtails, spiders, crickets, earwigs, carpet beetles, and brown dog ticks.

USE TIPS: This is a pretty toxic chemical that has not been tested in every way it is used, because it is in so many consumer products for which it is hard to develop reliable data. However, the EPA recently banned its use on sod farms and golf courses owing to the number of deaths it caused in bird populations. Watering it in thoroughly after application helps some, but then that brings earthworms to the surface which attract birds. It also persists in the insects that birds eat. You should consider this before putting it on your lawn. Try not to use old or improperly stored pressurized containers, as they may explode. Also, certain compounds that are even more toxic are sometimes formed as this product breaks down in storage.

BUYING TIPS: This is such a toxic product that you may want to find alternatives to whatever it is that you think needs it. Check labels of mixtures to see if diazinon is included.

HORTICULTURAL OIL

ALSO KNOWN AS: Dormant oil, dormant spray, summer oil, growing season spray, oils, sprayable oils, miscible oils, white oils, petroleum oils, insect spray, superior oil, oil spray, superior horticultural spray oil, scale oil

POPULAR BRAND NAMES: 90-Par, Volck®, Scalecide

DESCRIPTION: A high-grade, highly refined, light viscosity petroleum product not unlike mineral oil that is sprayed on ornamentals, shrubs, and trees either in early spring (known as *dormant oil)* or late spring–early summer (known as *summer, verdant,* or *growing season oil).* New technical improvements allow it to be used on more plants and for a wider range of seasons. Usually mixed with water—contains an emulsifier for this purpose. May also be made from fish oils or a mixture of borax and kerosene (brand name: Ced-O-Flora). The difference between dormant and summer oils is the viscosity—dormant is thicker, summer is thinner—which may just be the rate at which it is mixed with water by the gardener. Some are sold just as *dormant oils,* the old name. Considered an organic pesticide by many gardeners.

USE: Suffocates certain pests, such as mites, mealybugs, and scale. Dormant oil sprays are applied in March, before new leaves have appeared, for the control of scale, aphids, and spider mites on the stem and trunk. As a summer oil, it is applied in late spring or early summer for the control of aphids, mites, and scale in their crawling stages. Sometimes used as a contact herbicide and, when greatly diluted, as a leaf polish. Can be mixed with compatible pesticides as a spreader-sticker (see page 117), to enhance the pesticide's performance. It works by coating and suffocating the pest.

USE TIPS: Toxic to fish. Flammable—do not store or use near heat or flame—and harmful if swallowed. Wash your hands thoroughly after use. This has been in use for many, many years and no oil-resistant strain of insects has developed. A weak, 2 percent mixture can be used on vegetable crops, but overwintering insects need a strong dose: 3 to 5 percent. Do not try to make your own with mineral or motor oil—they may damage the plants.

Summer oil can be applied when there is little wind or breeze during late spring. Dormant oil must be sprayed on shrubs and trees before new leaves appear, when it is not windy, and when the temperatures are above freezing and are expected to stay there for a few days.

BUYING TIPS: The better-quality oils are light and highly refined, as indicated by a high percentage—87 to 90 percent—of *sulfonation.* The rate at which the oil can pass through a sprayer is noted in its *viscosity,* stated in seconds (sixty to seventy is good). The more refined oils pass through sprayers more easily, and are therefore easier to apply.

MALATHION

CHEMICAL NAME: O,O-dimethyl dithophosphate of diethyl mercaptosuccinate

POPULAR BRAND NAMES: Calmathion, Celthion, Cythion, Detmol MA 96%, Emmatos, Emmatos Extra For-mal, Fyfanon, Kop-Thion, Kypfos, Malaspray, Malamar, Malatol, Home Orchard Spray, Bonide Rose Spray, No-Roach Spray

SIGNAL WORD: CAUTION

DESCRIPTION: Wettable powder or emulsifiable concentrate that makes a clear to amber liquid with a garlic odor. Broad spectrum insecticide, only slightly toxic to mammals.

USE: For the control of aphids, leaf miners, mealybugs, white-flies, scale, and lace bugs.

USE TIP: Harmful if swallowed, comes into contact with your skin, or is inhaled. Wash well after using.

METHOXYCLOR

CHEMICAL NAME: 2,2-bis (p-methoxyphenyl)-1,l,1-trichloro-ethane

POPULAR BRAND NAMES: Marlate, Methoxyclor 25

SIGNAL WORD: CAUTION

DESCRIPTION: Developed as a substitute for DDT; is less harmful to the environment and has very low toxicity to animals and humans. Comes as a wettable powder or emulsifiable concentrate, as well as a dust or aerosol.

USE: For control of chewing insects that attack flowers, shrubs, vegetables, and fruit and shade trees, as well as mosquitoes, ticks, and flies.

USE TIPS: Store in a cool, dry place. Long residual effect.

SEVIN

CHEMICAL NAME: Carbaryl (1-naphthyl N-methylcarbamate)

COMMON BRAND NAME: Sevin®

SIGNAL WORD: CAUTION or WARNING—varies with formulation

DESCRIPTION: Dust or spray, generally containing 5 to 10 percent carbaryl, or a stronger liquid concentrate.

USE: Very broad spectrum insecticide for combating armyworms, cutworms, squash bugs, tomato hornworms, fleas and ticks, certain varieties of beetles, leafhoppers, and numerous other vegetable pests.

USE TIP: Despite the commonness of this product, use it very carefully, following the directions as with all pesticides and taking precautions to keep it out of the home (when using it on animals) and away from bees, to which it is very toxic.

Synthetic Herbicides

ABOUT SYNTHETIC HERBICIDES

Herbicides are products that kill plants or interrupt their growth, and are used to control weeds, brush, or unwanted grass. Most gardeners never need to use herbicides. If you have a weed problem that does not respond to cultivation, hand picking, or other methods of eradication, then you may want to consider using an herbicide that has little or no residual toxicity. There are not too many on the market, as the really effective ones are far too toxic to be used safely: Remember Agent Orange?

TYPES: *Preplanting herbicides:* Used after the soil has been prepared for planting, but before the seed is sown.

Preemergent herbicides: Used after seeding but before germination, to control weeds that might compete with the crop or planting, such as crabgrass.

Postemergent herbicides: Used after a crop or planting is established.

Sterilant (nonselective) herbicides: Kills nonselectively all plants that are treated with it, and is commonly used on walks and patios.

2,4-D

CHEMICAL NAME: 2,4,-dichlorophenoxyacetic acid

POPULAR BRAND NAMES: Agrotect, Aqua-Kleen, BH, "D," D50, Dacamine, Debroussaillant 600, Ded-Weed, Desormone, Dinoxol, Emulsamine, Envert, Envert 171, Super D Weedone, Estone, Fernesta, Fernimine, Fernoxone, Ferxone, Formula 40, Greensweep Weed & Feed, Hedonal, Herbidal, Lawn-Keep, Manccondray, Miracle, Netagrone, Pennamine, Planotox, Plantgard, Salvo, Scotts Lawn Weed Control, Transamine, Tributon, Tuban, U 46, Weedone, Weed-Rhap, Weedtrol, Weed-B-Gon®, Gordon's Dymec Turf Herbicide, Acme Amine 4, Acme Butyl Ester 4, and many others

SIGNAL WORD: CAUTION, WARNING, or DANGER—varies with formulation

DESCRIPTION: In any one of a number of forms, but most often a flowable liquid. A selective herbicide that may be the most common home product of its type in the United States, but also may be reevaluated for cancer risk by the EPA. Often mixed with *MCPP* or *dicamba.*

USE: Postemergent control of most broadleaf lawn weeds, such as dandelions, clover, and plaintain.

USE TIPS: Dilute according to the label, as concentrations may vary. Do not allow this product to contaminate food, feed, or water, and be careful when applying it not to let the spray drift over onto any other plants that may be damaged by it, especially, of course, food crops. May not be compatible with lime-sulfur or oils, and depending on the formulation, should not be used in weather over 80° F.

EPTAM®

CHEMICAL NAME: EPTC (ethyl dipropylthiocarbamate)

SIGNAL WORD: CAUTION

DESCRIPTION: Granular, preemergent herbicide sold in 1- to 20-pound containers and bags.

USE: Control of nutgrass, Bermudagrass, quackgrass, sandburs, and other weeds in lawns and gardens.

USE TIP: Apply within two or three days of cultivation, before weeds germinate.

BUYING TIP: Dacthol (DCPA) is a common alternative product that controls crabgrass as well. Comes as a flowable liquid or wettable powder in addition to the common granular form.

GLYPHOSATE

ALSO KNOWN AS: Grass killer, weed and grass killer

CHEMICAL NAME: Isopropylamine salt of N-(phosphonomethyl) glycine

POPULAR BRAND NAMES: Roundup®, Glifonox, Glycel, Kleenup®, Rodeo, Rondo, Vision

SIGNAL WORD: WARNING or CAUTION—varies with formulation

DESCRIPTION: Sold most often as a concentrated aqueous solution. Nonselective, postemergent, broad spectrum, systemic, foliar spray. Also available in aerosol foam that leaves a residue that indicates where it has been sprayed.

USE: Controlling over fifty types of grasses, brush, vines, and broadleaf weeds after they are grown. Can also be used to control some trees and woody brush. It is one of the safest herbicides on the market because it has little residual toxicity, meaning that it breaks down quickly after application. However, it does kill most plants it touches for up to four weeks.

USE TIPS: Because this product is nonselective, care should be taken so as not to spray desirable plant material around the weeds. Keep people and pets away for any treated area for at least six hours, or overnight. It translocates, meaning that it goes into the roots after killing the leaves. Mix only what you need: The concentrate has a shelf life of many years, but once mixed, it begins to degrade.

TRICLOPYR

POPULAR BRAND NAMES: Brush-B-Gon®, Poison Ivy & Oak Killer

CHEMICAL NAME: Triclopyr (3,5,6-trichloro-2-pyridinyl-oxya-cetic acid) as triethylamine salt

SIGNAL WORD: CAUTION

DESCRIPTION: Postemergent aerosol spray, commonly mixed to a .5 percent acid. Contains foam to help you see where you have sprayed. Largely replaces use of ammate (ammonium sulfamate).

USE: Controlling bushy and woody plants, especially poison ivy and poison oak, in noncrop areas. OK for use on poison ivy in apple and pear orchards. Applied as a spray to the foliage of the offending plant; translocates to the plant roots after killing the foliage. Also kills stumps.

USE TIPS: Takes two to six weeks to show results. Apply to mature foliage. Not hazardous to animals and people when used according to directions. One of the few items on the market that controls poison ivy. Avoid applying directly to lakes, streams, or ponds, or disposing cleanup rags in them.

Synthetic Fungicides

ABOUT FUNGICIDES

Fungi are plants that actually feed on other plants. Contrary to what one might think, fungicides cannot get rid of an established fungus. They are used to prevent fungi from becoming established or to control their spread. Fungi are quite common in all kinds of gardens and especially with fruit trees, which need to be sprayed routinely. Unfortunately, many of these items break down into products that are suspected carcinogens. Some may be removed from the market as studies progress; others will be proven safe.

BENOMYL

CHEMICAL NAME: Methyl 1 -(butylcarbarmoyl)-2-benzimidaz-olecarbamate

POPULAR BRAND NAMES: Benex, Benlate, Tersan 1991

SIGNAL WORD: CAUTION

DESCRIPTION: General purpose systemic fungicide. Usually a white crystalline solid, practically insoluble in water and oil. Sold in concentrated forms in small plastic bottles for the home gardener. Used as a spray.

USE: For the prevention of a variety of fungal problems in the garden, including black spot and powdery mildew on roses, phlox, and lilacs.

USE TIPS: Be careful not to let the spray drift into water or water sources, as it is harmful to fish and other aquatic animals. This is a relatively safe fungicide for the prevention of fungal infection, but it requires intensive application practices. It must be sprayed on the foliage before a fungal problem is apparent and application must be repeated every fourteen days or more frequently if there is rain. Store container in a dry place with the cap securely tightened. Benomyl's effectiveness is lessened if the stored product becomes wet. Keep shaking container so the chemical remains in suspension.

BUYING TIP: Fairly dangerous in case of misuse—may cause nonmalignant tumors.

BORDEAUX MIXTURE

ALSO KNOWN AS: Copper-Fixed, fixed copper, Bordeaux mix, copper dust, liquid copper

POPULAR BRAND NAMES: Kocide, Bordo-Mix, Tri-Basic, CPTS, Copper Bordeaux 22

SIGNAL WORD: WARNING or CAUTION—varies with formulation

DESCRIPTION: Comes in different formulations, but usually sold as a concentrate in wettable powder form. Basically a mixture of copper sulfate and hydrated lime which gets its names (Bordeaux) from years of use in the French vineyards. Low toxic residue—may be considered organic. When copper sulfate is sold in liquid form without lime, it may be called *copper fungicide,* an organic product used in season as a corrective control (applied as disease appears).

USE: Controlling fungal and bacterial diseases such as leaf spots, anthracnose, rusts, molds, and fruit rots found in flowers and small fruit and shade trees. Possibly acceptable for use on organic farms. Considered a general preventive garden fungicide, often used as a dormant spray (meaning not during the growing season).

USE TIP: Dilution rates vary, so follow label directions closely.

BUYING TIP: A relatively safe fungicide that has been around for a long time, but now largely replaced by ferbam (see page 128) and zineb (see page 130).

CAPTAN

CHEMICAL NAME: N-trichloromethylethio-4-cyclohexene-1,2-dicarboximide

POPULAR BRAND NAMES: Orthocide, Captanex, Captaf, Merpan, Vondcaptan, Ortho Home Orchard Spray, Orthocide Captan Garden Fungicide, Bonide Rose Spray, Gro-Well Fruit Tree Spray, Vancide 89

SIGNAL WORD: DANGER or CAUTION—varies with formulation

DESCRIPTION: A protectant-eradicant fungicide, that is, one that prevents fungus from attacking, sold as a wettable powder concentrate that must be diluted. One of the most popular broad-spectrum fungicides in use on crops and seeds of all kinds.

USE: For the prevention of a variety of fungal problems in the garden, including black spot on roses and powdery mildew on phlox and lilacs, and damping off on seedlings. Add a tiny bit to a seed packet of untreated seeds and shake the packet.

USE TIPS: This is a relatively safe fungicide for the prevention of fungal infection, but it requires intensive application practices, similar to benomyl (see page 125). Avoid contact with skin or clothing. Store in a cool, dry place. Wear protective clothing when using. Keep shaking container so the chemical remains in solution.

BUYING TIPS: Not permitted for use on vegetables because it has caused cancer in laboratory animals. It may be used on apples and some other fruit trees. The EPA legislation on this chemical, a probable human carcinogen, has been changed a number of times over the years, so check with the EPA or your local Cooperative Extension agent for the most recent findings.

CHLOROTHALONIL

CHEMICAL NAME: Tetrachloroisophthalonitrile

POPULAR BRAND NAMES: Bravo, Daconil 2787

SIGNAL WORD: WARNING or DANGER—varies with formulation

DESCRIPTION: White crystalline solid usually sold as a wettable powder or liquid concentrate. Also available as a smoke or vapor.

USE: Controlling a wide range of fungal diseases. Considered a broad-spectrum fungicide for use on most vegetables, melons, and much fruit, as well as ornamentals.

USE TIP: Use with care. This is a probable human carcinogen.

DYRENE

ALSO KNOWN AS: Anilazine

CHEMICAL NAME: 2,4-dichloro-6-(O-chloroanilino)=s-triazine

SIGNAL WORD: DANGER or WARNING—varies with formulation

DESCRIPTION: White to tan crystalline solid sold as a wettable or flowable powder. Applied as a spray.

USE: Controlling fungal diseases of turf. Many other uses have been prohibited recently.

USE TIPS: This is a skin irritant—wear protective clothing. Keep away from fish and aquatic invertebrates.

FERBAM

CHEMICAL NAME: Ferric dimethyldithiocarbamate

POPULAR BRAND NAMES: Fermate, Carbamate, Ferbam, Ferberk, Hexaferb, Knockmate, Trifungol

SIGNAL WORD: CAUTION

DESCRIPTION: Wettable powder.

USE: Controlling fungal diseases, such as apple scab, cedar apple rust, peachleaf curl, tobacco blue mold, and others that are common to ornamentals and popular garden flowers. Often applied for general protection against other diseases.

USE TIP: Sometimes recommended as part of a combination spray for apples.

MANCOZEB

CHEMICAL NAME: Zinc ion and manganeze ethylene bisdithiocarbamate

POPULAR BRAND NAMES: Dithane M-45, Manzate 200, Fore, Dithane

SIGNAL WORD: CAUTION

DESCRIPTION: Wettable powder, a mixture of two chemicals (zinc and manganese) that are not normally considered pesticides but which works because it is a *coordination product:* They are effective only when mixed together.

USE: Controlling a wide variety of fungal diseases such as anthracnose, early and late blights, rust, scab, and downy mildew in fruit, vegetable, nut, and field crops, pretty much replacing maneb (see next entry).

USE TIPS: Caution should be taken that it does not get into water, food, or feed. Empty containers should be buried away from water supplies or sources. Store in a dry, dark place with good air circulation.

BUYING TIP: Currently under review by the EPA. Many homeowner products will be affected if it is banned.

MANEB

ALSO KNOWN AS: Akzo Chemie Maneb

CHEMICAL NAME: Manganese ethylene bis-dithiocarbamate

POPULAR BRAND NAMES: Dexol Maneb Garden Fungicide, Security Maneb Spray, Dithane M-22, Manzate

SIGNAL WORD: CAUTION

DESCRIPTION: Wettable, odorless yellow powder that has been replaced in most uses by mancozeb (see preceding entry).

USE: Controlling fungal diseases of vegetables and fruit.

USE TIP: Open dumping is prohibited, so bury empty containers away from all water.

BUYING TIP: Currently being reviewed by the EPA.

TRIADIMEFON

POPULAR BRAND NAMES: Bayleton®, Amiral™

SIGNAL WORD: WARNING (as wettable powder) or CAUTION (depending on formulation)

DESCRIPTION: Dry, flowable (may be abbreviated DF) systemic fungicide in powder form. Also available as granules and liquids of various concentrations.

USE: Fighting majority of diseases of turf and ornamental plants, outdoors and in greenhouses, including flower blight, leaf blight and spots, powdery mildew, and rusts. Particularly good on greenhouse plants such as African violets, carnations, geraniums, and roses.

TRIFORINE

CHEMICAL NAME: Triforine

POPULAR BRAND NAME: Funginex®

SIGNAL WORD: DANGER

DESCRIPTION: Liquid (emulsifiable concentrate) sold in small bottles.

USE: Controlling fungal diseases such as black spot, powdery mildew, and rusts on roses and other flowers.

USE TIP: May be combined with certain insecticides as noted on the label.

ZINEB

CHEMICAL NAME: Zinc ethylene bis-dithiocarbamate

POPULAR BRAND NAMES: Parzate, Dithane

SIGNAL WORD: CAUTION

DESCRIPTION: Wettable powder.

USE: Controlling fungal diseases of vegetables, fruits, and flowers. Applied as a foliar protectant, before disease appears.

USE TIP: Dispose of very carefully away from all water (follow directions on label).

BUYING TIP: Currently being reviewed by the EPA.

Synthetic Miticides

DICOFOL

CHEMICAL NAME: -1,1-bis (chlorophenyl)-2,2,2, trichloreoethanol

POPULAR BRAND NAME: Kelthane

SIGNAL WORD: WARNING or CAUTION—varies with formulation

DESCRIPTION: Wettable powder or amber-colored emulsifiable concentrate.

USE: For the control of mites.

USE TIPS: Avoid contact with skin, and wash thoroughly after using. Should be used with a mask if applied as a mist. Harmful if swallowed. Toxic to fish, and should be kept away from water sources.

BUYING TIP: Currently under review by the EPA and therefore hard to find.

TETRADIFON

CHEMICAL NAME: -4-chlorophenyl 2,4,5-trichlorophenyl sulfone

POPULAR BRAND NAME: Tedion

SIGNAL WORD: CAUTION

DESCRIPTION: Wettable powder or emulsifiable concentrate.

USE: For the control of mites and spiders.

BUYING TIP: Vendex® is a similar product.

Synthetic Molluscicides

SNAIL AND SLUG BAIT

POPULAR BRAND NAMES: Slug-Geta®, Bug-Geta®

SIGNAL WORD: CAUTION or WARNING, depending on the brand

DESCRIPTION: Potent, toxic, granular, pelletized, or thick liquid bait, made of a number of chemicals, such as metaldehyde or Mesurol®.

USE: Poisoning slugs and snails as well as crickets, millipedes, and sow bugs (depending on the brand). Granules are made to be spread across a lawn, but may be placed in special slug traps (see page 109), as may the pellets, which is how they are intended to be dispensed. Liquid form is placed in a chain of drops between berry and vegetable plants—not directly on them—and around flower beds or lawn edges.

USE TIPS: Do not use around food crops or bodies of water. Toxic to fish and wildlife, and, of course, to pets and people. All labels carry the warning to "keep children and pets out of treated areas," which makes it an unlikely choice for a family garden. Certain formulations are actually attractive to dogs, and are marked as such in the label's fine print. Birds that feed on a treated area may be killed. Safer to use in small slug traps than to apply directly.

BUYING TIP: Alternative baits are yeast and water mixtures or stale beer, which are nontoxic, to say the least, although some beer connoisseurs may claim certain inferior brands of beer to be toxic.

Synthetic Rodenticides

CHLOROPHACINONE

ALSO KNOWN AS: Liphadione, LM 91

CHEMICAL NAME: 2-(p-chlorophenyl) phenylacetyl-1,3-indadione

POPULAR BRAND NAMES: Caid, Drat, Microzul, Ramucide, Ratomet, Raviac, Rozol, Topitox

SIGNAL WORD: CAUTION

DESCRIPTION: Chlorophacinone is a pale yellow crystalline material that is sold as a concentrate in oil and dust forms. It is also sold as bait in the form of paraffin blocks and pellets, and as a ground spray (one that is sprayed right onto the soil).

USE: For the control of rodents.

USE TIP: Be sure to check the label for the recommended cautionary practices for application, such as using masks and gloves when handling concentrates of this chemical, and for the most effective form to use for your problem.

CLORECALCIFEROL

POPULAR BRAND NAMES: Mouse-B-Gon™, Rat-B-Gon™

SIGNAL WORD: CAUTION

DESCRIPTION: Bait usually manufactured in paper traps.

USE: Rat and mouse control.

USE TIP: Maintain bait for at least ten days. Do not place any bait where children have access.

COUMAFURYL

CHEMICAL NAME: 3(a-Acetonylfurfuryl)-4-hydroxycourmarin

POPULAR BRAND NAMES: Fumarin, Kill-Ko Rat, Mouse Blues

SIGNAL WORD: CAUTION or DANGER—varies with formulation

DESCRIPTION: A powder that is mixed with cornmeal, rolled oats, or other cereals, is ingested by the rodents, and causes death by internal bleeding.

USE: Used to kill common rodents such as mice and rats.

USE TIP: Should be put out in three to five doses daily for no more than every two days.

PINDONE

CHEMICAL NAME: 2-Pivalyl-1,3-indandione

POPULAR BRAND NAME: Pival

SIGNAL WORD: CAUTION

DESCRIPTION: Sold as a powder concentrate and a premixed bait.

USE: For the long-term control of mice, rats, and other rodents.

USE TIPS: Because it is tasteless and odorless, rodents do not develop bait shyness, making this a popular choice where there is a chronic rodent problem. As with most rodenticides, it is advisable to keep it away from children, pets, and wildlife.

WARFARIN

ALSO KNOWN AS: Wafarin

CHEMICAL NAME: 3(a-Acetonylbenzyl)-4-hydrozycoumarin

SIGNAL WORD: CAUTION or WARNING—varies with formulation

DESCRIPTION: Sold to general public as a ready-to-use bait, but available to exterminators in a concentrated form for mixing with cornmeal. It acts as an anticoagulant (it causes internal bleeding) and has no color or odor.

USE: For the control of mice and rats.

USE TIPS: Keep away from children, pets, and wildlife. Do not store near food or feed. Avoid contact with skin, eyes, or mouth. Use baits only in areas where larger animals cannot reach them. It often takes a couple of weeks before a reduction in the number of rodents is noticed.

Tools, Equipment, and Accessories

Digging Tools and Wheel Goods

ABOUT DIGGING TOOL DURABILITY

These tools are designed to be used for digging as well as turning soil in the garden and include shovels, spades, trowels, and forks. You will find a wide range of digging tools in your garden center, with an even wider range of quality. How durable a digging tool is depends primarily on how the "business end" is attached to the handle, since this is the part of a digging tool that is put under the most stress when the tool is being used. There are three ways in which the tools listed here can be attached to their handles.

TANG-AND-FERRULE: A *tang* is a projecting shank or tongue, in this case, one that comes out the rear end of a shovel or rake head; a *ferrule* is a metal ring or collar that is fitted over the end of a wooden handle after a tang has been inserted into it. Often

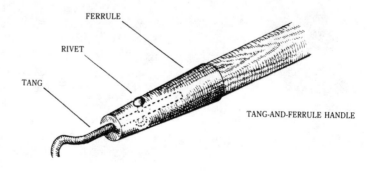

FERRULE

RIVET

TANG

TANG-AND-FERRULE HANDLE

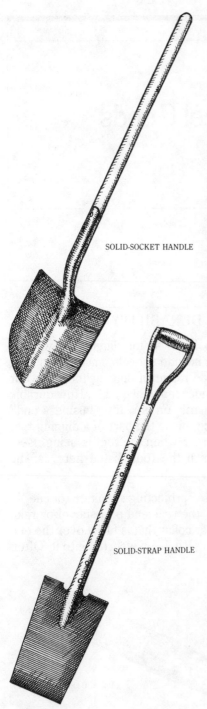

SOLID-SOCKET HANDLE

SOLID-STRAP HANDLE

a rivet or bolt is inserted through the ferrule and the tang to ensure a secure attachment. The tang-and-ferrule method is common in garden tools, but is not as secure a fit as the solid-socket method described next. It is, however, easier and therefore cheaper to manufacture this type of tool. The ferrule should be one long piece; those with a small "extra" collar about 1 inch wide at the end are actually not as good, because the small collar is doing the work that a foot-long piece should do. This kind of tool also may be called a *tanged* or *shank tool.*

SOLID-SOCKET: With this method, a handle is attached to a tool blade via a solid collar that is actually part of the tool blade, having been forged or stamped from the same piece of steel (not welded on). It is wrapped around the first foot or so of the handle or, on the better models, the handle is actually driven into the socket; they may also have a pin or rivets driven through the shaft to hold the handle in. This is sturdier than the tang-and-ferrule method and less likely to bend or break where the handle meets the blade, especially with very long collars. Long, forged solid-sockets are a sign of top quality. However, it is more costly to manufacture because the entire tool must be made from a larger piece of metal than the tang-and-ferrule method just described, and forged versions require hand labor. It is still the best value and recommended for the sturdiest forks, shovels, and spades. May also be called, confusingly, *solid-shank,* or *chucked.*

SOLID-STRAP: In the solid-strap method of attaching the tool blade to the handle, a metal part called a *strap* is extended from the socket up toward the tool handle. The blade, socket, and strap are all forged from one piece of steel, making this kind of tool the sturdiest and most durable. As you might imagine, this is a rare form of manufacture but an excellent find and a highly recommended purchase if you have plenty of heavy work to do, such as digging up shrubs or trees.

All metal tools should be wiped dry after use and coated with a little oil to prevent rust. You can wipe them with a slightly oily rag or spray them with an aerosol lubricant.

Many manufacturers make their most popular models in two sizes, the smaller of which is often called a "ladies'" tool, such as a "ladies' spade," although their "floral" models serve the same purpose. These generally, but not always, are of the same quality and refer only to a lighter weight and smaller head and handle (for working in flower beds), ranging from 15 to 40 percent less. As any tool is an extension of your body, it should fit properly, and these so-called ladies' tools are the way to go to get your fit, if need be. These and children's tools should be of the same quality as the larger tools, but some manufacturers seem to think that smaller tools can be of lesser quality. They are wrong, and these tools should be avoided.

Some manufacturers are now making tools with interchangeable handles, including both hand- and full-sized (one popular brand is Twools™, another is Scotts). This is certainly convenient and may be economical, but be sure to check the balance and the feel of these tools—in some combinations, they may not be as comfortable to use as those that have been specifically designed with a handle of a certain length in mind.

ABOUT GRIPS AND HANDLES

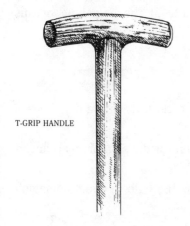

T-GRIP HANDLE

Digging tool handles, or "hilts," come in three types: *straight, T-,* or *D-grip*. Generally speaking, straight handles, just long rods, are useful in longer length (40 to 48 inches) tools where a lot of lifting is done, while D- and T-grips are found in shorter lengths, like 26 to 30 inches, where control or prying is more important, or you're maneuvering in tight quarters. The longer straight handles make it easier to dig deeply and throw farther (the soil, not the shovel!), while T handles are a bit slippery to use as they are awkward to grip, and are not recommended.

D-grips should be made of wood and may be covered with metal for extra protection; heavy-duty models have a reinforcement in the V of the neck while lightweight models are plastic. If the grip is an all-metal piece that is attached to the blunt end of the handle, be sure to check the quality, as this can loosen with time. The best ones are made entirely of wood; the handle is split and formed into a Y, making for a solid and beautiful handle, sometimes reinforced at the narrow part. The *cob* (the crosspiece on the D-grip) should be sturdy, and not turn at all when you grip the tool. Some manufacturers call this a *Y-D grip,* and it is traditional and good.

D-GRIP HANDLE

Ash is the material of choice for wooden handles, though hickory is as good and as common; only the cheaper tools use Douglas fir, which should generally be avoided by the serious gardener. Wooden handles should be free of knots and flaws, and the grain should run lengthwise in even, continuous lines. The closer or tighter the grain of the wood in the handle, the stronger it is. Tubular steel handles are usually too heavy for the average consumer to enjoy, but lighter alloys (usually plastic covered) are found on some fancy models. Replacement handles are available with the end adapted for solid-socket style or ferrule style.

Digging Tools

ABOUT DIGGING TOOLS

There is a wider variety in style and quality among these products than almost any others. Your choice depends largely on the type of gardening you do and the type of soil you have. Acquire slowly and look for quality wherever you can—it will pay off in the long run in terms of comfort and utility for you, and longevity for the tool. As with all metal tools, make an effort to keep these clean, dry, and sharp. See the note at the beginning of this chapter about shovel handle construction.

BULB LIFTER

DESCRIPTION: Wide, two-pronged hand fork with a 6-inch steel blade and a 12-inch wooden handle.

USE: Lifting bulbs out of the garden for division or overwintering, and for transplanting flowers.

USE TIP: Make sure you dig below the bulb to avoid damaging its storage cells.

BULB LIFTER

BULB PLANTER

DESCRIPTION: Tapered metal cylinder from 6 to 10 inches tall, with a D-grip handle right above it or with a long handle (approximately 30 inches long—abbreviated often as an *L.H. bulb planter)* and a foot rest. The hand-held bulb planter is used in a kneeling or stooping position, while the long-handled ones can be used from a standing position. Long-handled bulb planters are often made from a single piece of metal. They all should have

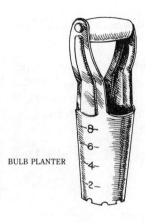

BULB PLANTER

depth markings in inches on their sides. May be confused with the narrow trowel made for this purpose, as they are often called by the same name. A similar model is made for planting zoysia-grass plugs. Another version, called a *sod planter,* is made for planting sod plugs. It has a 2-inch-square cutter and extractor.

USE: Planting bulbs singularly in confined spaces or where there are other plants close by.

USE TIP: The cylinder is pushed into the soil and removed, taking a plug of soil with it, as long as the soil is not completely dry. The bulb is placed in the hole and the plug replaced. Many of these tools have depth markings on the side to help make the correct depth hole for each bulb.

BUYING TIP: Many gardeners prefer a trowel to the hand-held bulb planter, but the long-handled versions are extremely useful for people who cannot kneel or stoop easily.

CROWBAR

ALSO KNOWN AS: Prybar, pinch bar, axle rod, curb-setter, bull prick, bar (*Note:* The term *crowbar* is often used incorrectly for a *gooseneck wrecking bar,* which has a curved end and is 18 to 36 inches long)

DESCRIPTION: Long, straight high-carbon steel bar, about ¾ inch in diameter and about 4 to 5 feet long. Approximately two-thirds of the bar is round, with the working (lower) third square and tipped with either a wedge (triangular) point or pinch point (like that on a chisel). A digger bar, or a fencing crowbar, has a flat end. Crowbars weigh either 12 or 18 pounds.

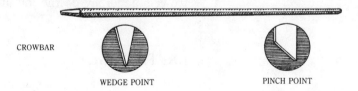

CROWBAR

WEDGE POINT   PINCH POINT

USE: Prying large rocks or root-balled trees out of holes, or maneuvering large stones for fences or curbs (or removing chunks of busted-up sidewalks). It can also be driven into hard soil to start a hole, whether for digging or inserting a tomato stake or bean pole. Some people even use a crowbar to measure the temperature of a compost pile (left in the center of a large "ripe" pile, the tip will heat up to the point where you can't hold onto it).

USE TIPS: When using as a lever to pry out a rock or stump, put a large sturdy piece of scrap wood at the edge of the hole under the crowbar to act as a fulcrum; the bar will otherwise sink right into the soil. Heavier models work best in hard soils and clay, with the weight doing much of the work for you.

BUYING TIP: These things don't age. They make for nice buys at flea markets or auctions.

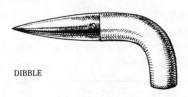

DIBBLE

DIBBLE

ALSO KNOWN AS: Dibber, dibbler, planter

DESCRIPTION: The original dibble was just a cow's horn. Now they are made of solid plastic or cast iron, steel, or metal-covered wood or plastic and are about 8 inches long, pointed and round with a curved, T-, or D- handle just above it, though one with a waist-high handle is also made.

USE: Quick way of making holes for transplants and bulbs.

USE TIP: This is a handy tool if you are setting out numbers of plants or bulbs, but if you are just doing just a few, a trowel will suffice. This is really a tool for large gardens. When planting bulbs, note that the bulb may not rest completely flat in the deep indentation made by the point, thus leaving an air pocket under the bulb. Push the bulb down to nestle it into the soil.

BUYING TIPS: Look for a smooth, comfortable grip. Dibbles are not indispensable tools for most gardeners. A couple of good trowels generally do the job just as well.

EARTH AUGER

ALSO KNOWN AS: Landscape auger, bulb drill

POPULAR BRAND NAMES: Earth Auger, Daffodrill™

DESCRIPTION: Large steel spiral drill bit, 18 to 24 inches long and 1½ to 2½ inches in diameter, designed to fit into a standard power drill (both ¼- and ⅜-inch sizes). Professional models are made for ½-inch drills. Other models are long, open-sided cylinders rather than spirals.

USE: Drilling small holes in the ground for direct access to roots (to install a root feeder, take a soil sample, fertilize, or apply a hose for soaking a newly planted tree or shrub), for installing large stakes, or for planting bulbs and seedlings, in which case the 2½-inch-wide model is used.

USE TIPS: This is the occasion for a cordless drill to shine, owing to the dearth of electrical outlets in your typical garden. Heavy clay or thick sod will require a larger, heavier model. Watch your hole depth when planting bulbs.

BUYING TIP: Definitely a help when planting large quantities of bulbs or small seedlings.

EDGER

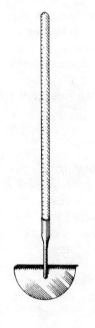

EDGER

ALSO KNOWN AS: Turf edger, half-moon edger, semicircular edger, edging knife, lawn edge trimmer, hand edger

DESCRIPTION: Flat, semicircular blade, about 8 inches across, attached to a handle that may be long and straight or end in a T- or D-grip. The straight top of the edger often has a rolled footrest. Top of the line models have solid-socket construction, and some are made of mirror-polished stainless steel. The rotary edger (see page 203) is for trimming grass borders.

USE: Cutting a sharp edge along garden or lawn walks, borders, driveways, buildings, and sidewalks.

USE TIP: Place the edger about 1 to 2 inches from the walk or area to be edged. Press down by stepping on the footrest. A sharp edge is cut when you pull the handle back toward yourself, creating a slight angle.

BUYING TIPS: Because of the amount of tension that is put on the edger at the shank, it is wise to pay more for a solid-socket type. Highly polished stainless steel slices more easily through the soil than other metals.

FORK

DESCRIPTION: Simply a large steel fork, the size of a shovel, with three to ten tines (or more), depending on the type of fork. Most are tang-and-ferrule construction, but top-of-the-line models are solid-socket type (see "About Digging Tool Durability," pages 137–39, for an extended discussion of methods of

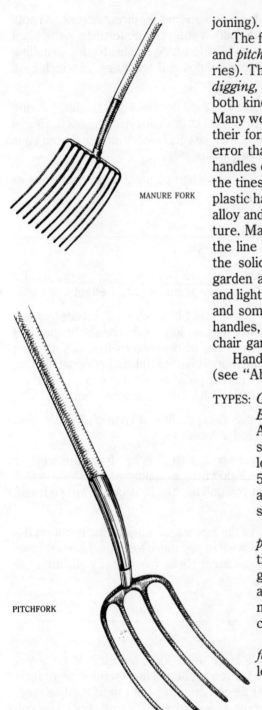

MANURE FORK

PITCHFORK

joining). The shape of the tines also depends on the type of fork.

The four types actually fall into two broad categories, *garden* and *pitch (spading* and *manure* forks are respective subcategories). There is much confusion surrounding the terms *garden, digging,* and *spading. Digging* is a general term that applies to both kinds, but is only accurate as a name for the garden fork. Many well-known and widely distributed manufacturers lump all their forks together under the category of "digging" forks, an error that adds to the confusion. May have lightweight plastic handles or handles that are reinforced with *straps* running from the tines to three-quarters or all of the way up the handle. The plastic handles of high-quality tools are usually filled with a steel alloy and epoxy bonded for extra strength and to exclude moisture. Made of regular or stainless high-carbon steel; the top of the line stainless models are highly polished and the seams of the solid-socket are welded (seam welded), but only in the garden and spading models. A *ladies' fork* is merely a smaller and lighter version (weighing about 1 to 3 pounds) of any model, and some special smaller designs with curved heads and long handles, sometimes called *cultiforks,* are designed for wheelchair gardeners.

Handles are usually D-grip or straight, depending on the type (see "About Grips and Handles," page 139).

TYPES: *Garden fork* (also known as *digging, English garden, English pattern, English digging,* or *English style fork):* A 7- to 8-inch-wide head with four thick rectangular or square tines approximately 12 inches long and a 30-inch-long handle ending in a D-grip, although available with a 5-foot-long straight handle. Most common model. Available in heavy-duty versions that are slightly larger. The square tines may be called *English tines.*

Manure fork (also known as *stable fork* or *apple picker):* Four to ten 12-inch-long, curved, round, fine tines spaced closely together. A similar model with longer tines is a *mulch fork.* The term *stable fork* is usually applied to lighter, almost rakelike models with even more tines, usually sixteen, and may at that point be called a *bedding fork.* Handles are usually 4 feet long.

Pitchfork (also known as *farm, hay,* or *Kansas header fork):* Three to five round, tapered tines about 12 inches long, usually with a 4-foot-long, straight handle attached

SPADING FORK

by either a solid-socket or a tang-and-ferrule. Shorter handles with D-grips are also available. A *Scottish composting fork* is a lighter and smaller version.

Spading fork (also known as *turning, border,* or *digging fork,* though this last is incorrect terminology): Four flat tines, sometimes with diamond or triangular backs. Slightly lighter and smaller than garden fork; sometimes the term *border fork* refers to a lighter, narrower version with wider tines. Usually 42 inches long overall.

USE: The garden and spading forks are used to turn over garden soil, while the other two—pitch and manure—are used to lift and throw light, loose material, such as hay. Forks are often easier to use than shovels for turning and cultivating because it is easier to insert the tines into the ground than it is to shove in an entire shovel blade, particularly if the soil is compacted.

Garden fork: Best suited for turning unbroken soil, breaking up clods, and for heavy cultivation. Use a heavy-duty model for rocky or clayey soils.

Manure fork: Good for lifting manure and other fine material without sifting. More suited to farm use than home garden use.

Pitchfork: Used to lift hay, straw, and leaf mold. Essentially for farm or large garden use.

Spading fork: Turning over already-broken, loose soil for cultivation. Often used for lighter digging, such as lifting out bulbs and perennials, and for harvesting vegetables that grow under the soil surface, such as potatoes and beets.

USE TIP: When cultivating or turning the soil, the fork should be perpendicular to the ground, pushed in with your foot on the footrest, and then pried up.

BUYING TIPS: As with all digging tools, it is important that the length of the handle be comfortable. It should come up just to your waist when fully inserted in the ground. The tool should have good balance and not be too heavy. Unfortunately, American companies no longer manufacture solid-socket or solid-strap garden forks, but many are imported from England. And watch your weight—that is, get a fork that is not too heavy for you to use.

Generally, a spading fork is not as good a buy as a garden fork, if you want only one fork. The flat tines on a spading fork may bend if you hit a rock, and it is difficult, if not impossible, to straighten them. The square tines of the garden fork are less likely to bend, and the fork will do most of the same work of the spading fork. It may not work as well when trying to turn a fine-textured soil, but a spade can then be substituted. Look for high-carbon, tempered steel with a slight "spring" to it. Smaller, hand-sized versions are made, listed under hand forks (see page 164).

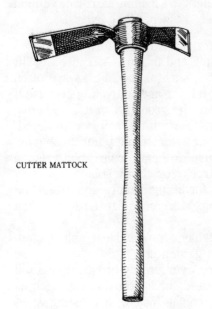

CUTTER MATTOCK

MATTOCK

ALSO KNOWN AS: Grubbing hoe, grub hoe

DESCRIPTION: Sort of a combination serious hoe (see pages 160–63) and ax (see pages 194–95), or pick (see next entry), but with a wider, thicker, duller blade and a heavier wooden handle, larger at the tool end.

TYPES: *Pick mattock* (also known as *trencher* or *trencher pick, garden pick):* Pick on one end, heavy-duty hoe on the other. Weighs about 5 pounds. A smaller, 2-pound model is called a *pick-a-hoe.*

Cutter mattock (also known as *grubbing* or *garden cutter mattock):* Ax on one end, heavy-duty hoe on the other. Weighs about 3½ to 5 pounds.

Garden mattock: Lightweight version of a cutter mattock.

Single-bladed mattock (also known as *adze hoe* or *grubbing mattock):* Rarely available, resembles a wide-bladed adze, with only one flat blade perpendicular to the handle.

USE: Breaking up hard ground and grubbing out roots and rock. Very helpful tool for digging trenches when laying electrical or water lines in a garden, or for removing tree stumps. Mattocks and picks are used for many of the same jobs, but the pick is more useful in initially breaking up very hard soils while mattocks are more useful in lifting rocks and cutting through roots because of its wide blade.

USE TIP: Swing as you would a pick, described below.

BUYING TIP: If you are gardening in a long-neglected garden where the soil is very hard or there is hardpan (a soil that is so hard water cannot drain through), a mattock is indispensable. The lightweight garden mattock should suffice for normal use. Mattocks remain sharp on jobs that would quickly dull an ax or hatchet, such as cutting roots that are surrounded by soil.

PICK

ALSO KNOWN AS: Clay pick, railroad pick

DESCRIPTION: Slightly curved, heavy metal blade from 16 to 20 inches long, with about a 30-inch-long wooden (usually hickory or ash) or fiberglass handle attached in the middle. One end of the pick blade is pointed while the other has a 1- to 2-inch-wide chisel head. When the chisel end is a few inches wide, it may be called a *pick-a-hoe* (pick and hoe), which is sold with a short handle. A *pick axe* (or *pickax)* has a full ax blade on one end and a short pick blade on the other.

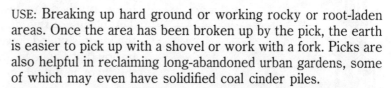

PICK

USE: Breaking up hard ground or working rocky or root-laden areas. Once the area has been broken up by the pick, the earth is easier to pick up with a shovel or work with a fork. Picks are also helpful in reclaiming long-abandoned urban gardens, some of which may even have solidified coal cinder piles.

USE TIP: A pick can be used by swinging the tool in a circular motion at the side of the body, or in an over-the-head motion in which the tool lines up with the center of the body on the down stroke. Allow the weight of the tool to complete the motion as this will require less of your energy and strength, because the weight of the tool does most of the work.

BUYING TIP: Find a pick that is comfortable for you to lift over your head. If the pick is too heavy, just lifting it can be tiring. Picks are not indispensable gardening tools, but for larger gardens and some urban gardens they can be worth the investment.

POSTHOLE DIGGER

DESCRIPTION: Hinged digging blades attached to two long handles.

TYPES: *Clamshell digger:* The most easily found. Consists of two wooden handles, each of which is attached to a curved blade about 12 inches long. A pivot joint is placed between the two blades where they attach to the handles. The blades are plunged into the ground in an open position (that is, when the handles are parallel). The handles are then pulled apart, causing the blades to come to-

CLAMSHELL POSTHOLE DIGGER

gether like a clamshell to scoop up soil that is then lifted from the hole.

Manual auger (also known as *earth auger, posthole auger,* or *posthole borer):* Has two stationary blades that are bent at angles. These are attached to a wooden handle that ends in a crossbar about a yard long. A manual auger works by the blades being screwed into the ground as the crossbar is turned in a clockwise direction. When the blades are full, they are lifted from the hole and emptied. *(Note:* The term *earth auger* also refers to a spiral drill bit that is used with an electric drill for making small holes, described on pages 142–43.)

Lever-action digger (also known as *Canadian, Canadian style, scissor type,* or *universal digger):* One stationary blade attached to a wooden handle with a moving blade attached to a lever about 3 feet up on the handle. The blades of this digger are plunged into the soil and the lever is pulled down, causing the two blades to scoop up soil that can be lifted from the hole and released when the lever is pulled up.

LEVER-ACTION POSTHOLE DIGGER

USE: Digging narrow holes for fence posts and footings for garden structures such as gazebos, arbors, shelters, porches, and the like. Manual augers are effective only in soft soil, not for hard or rocky soil.

USE TIP: Clean digger blades after each use with an oiled cloth. Be sure to oil all moving parts before storing in a dry place.

BUYING TIPS: A must for large estates and farms, but less important in small gardens. If you are installing a fence or garden structures that are supported by posts anchored in the ground you may want to consider purchasing a posthole digger, as these structures usually require some repair maintenance in the future. However, posthole diggers can be rented or borrowed from a neighbor. Lever-action diggers are the most efficient; clamshell models require more energy to use and make a wider hole, but give you more direct control.

The clamshell digger is a durable, reliable tool. With proper care it can last a long time. If you are digging a hole more than 2 feet deep, this is probably the tool for you. Manual augers work well only in loose soil and can make holes only up to 12 inches wide. They work less well, or not at all, in hard or rocky soils. The advantage of a lever-type digger is that it can dig a deep hole that is narrower than one dug by a clamshell digger, the latter always digging a hole as wide as the handle spread required to close the clamshell.

SHOVEL

DESCRIPTION: Probably the gardener's most familiar tools, shovels have a good deal of variety of detail and type. (Spades are a different item and are listed on pages 151–53.) Blade tips may be rounded, pointed, or blunt, depending on the type. Handles vary in length and shape, ending in either a D-grip, a T-grip, or just a slight taper (see "About Grips and Handles" on page 139). The degree of cant, or the angle of the handle from the ground when the blade is flat, varies from model to model.

Steel shovel blades are made one of two basic ways: *stamped* or *forged.* Stamped shovels are stamped out of a large sheet of metal, and contain a crimp, or fold, called a *frog,* near the top of the blade by the handle, to make the blade stronger. These shovels are referred to as *hollow-backed* or *open-back* if the frog opening is left as formed. When a triangular piece of metal is welded over the frog to close and reinforce it, the shovel is referred to as a *closed-back* or *fast-back shovel.*

Forged shovels are rolled out and forged from a single thick piece of steel. They are naturally strong, stronger than stamped shovels, so there is no need for the frog in the blade. Forged shovels, sometimes called *solid-shank* shovels, may be either of solid-socket design or solid-strap design (see "About Digging Tool Durability" on pages 137–38). Top-quality models are made of epoxy-coated, heat-treated, high-carbon steel. Most manufacturers also offer a chrome-plated ceremonial shovel for ground-breaking ceremonies.

TYPES: *Round point shovel* (also known as *pointed, dirt, round-nose, round-point,* or *American pattern shovel):* Pointed, curved blade with an almost 4-foot-long wooden handle;

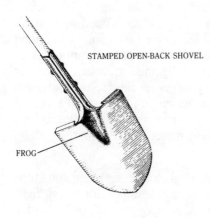

STAMPED OPEN-BACK SHOVEL

FROG

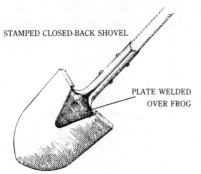

STAMPED CLOSED-BACK SHOVEL

PLATE WELDED OVER FROG

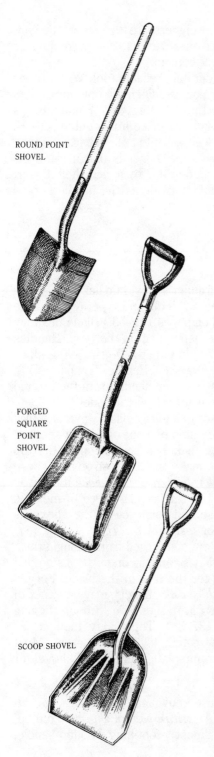

ROUND POINT
SHOVEL

FORGED
SQUARE
POINT
SHOVEL

SCOOP SHOVEL

a less pointed model is called *medium point* and may be broader. The top of the blade, nearest the handle, is often rolled over to form a tread, or footrest. About 8½ inches wide by 11 or 12 inches long. A rare model is the *narrow-blade shovel,* about half the normal size. Some models have serrated front edges to assist in cutting through roots and compacted soil.

Square point shovel (also known as *square-nose* or *square-mouth shovel):* Blunt-ended, flat blade with up-turned sides. May have long plain handles or shorter handles with D-grips. About 9½ by 11 inches.

Scoop shovel (also known as *coal, coal and street,* or *barn and snow shovel):* Much like the square-nose shovel but larger and much lighter. May be made of aluminum or plastic. Almost twice as big as the other types. *Eastern scoops* are smaller than *Western scoops,* which usually have reinforcing ribs in them. Some are more specialized, such as *grain scoops.*

USE: General purpose models are used for digging and moving loose soil or other materials like sand, cement, and gravel from one place to another. The round nose holds more—the wide, slightly curved blade allows you to pick up a good-sized load. Gardeners need at least one of these for tasks such as digging up beds, planting trees and shrubs, and working in compost. The narrow-blade model can be used to dig small trenches or simply as a smaller shovel for smaller gardeners. Square-nose shovels are an excellent construction for when you have to lift material like sand off a sidewalk. Scoop shovels are not for digging but rather for moving loose and light material like snow, sawdust, or trash.

USE TIPS: Clean shovels with an oiled cloth after using and store in a dry place. Shovels are not really designed for lifting light plant material such as straw or uncomposed compost—spades (see pages 151–53) and forks (see pages 143–46) are more appropriate. Though a long-handled shovel has good leverage for lifting, many a handle has been broken when a shovel was used to lift a plant by prying it out.

BUYING TIPS: The lightweight, stamped, hollow-backed shovel is a good purchase for most gardeners, and is the most popular and least expensive. The closed-back models are a bit stronger and generally more expensive. If you want to purchase a higher quality tool that will really last, a forged shovel is worth the investment—the top of the line of any brand is forged. The gardener with a small garden probably does not need a scoop shovel or square-nose shovel, which are used primarily for moving material, but the estate gardener will find these useful—the exception being for snow removal, when either one is a help. In any shovel, look for a good cant, or angle, of the handle to the ground, for ease of use—the larger the angle the less you'll have to bend over. Longer handles also avert bending over. Sockets should be riveted to the handles. Seam-welded sockets are typical of top-quality shovels. Don't buy a large shovel if you have trouble lifting heavy loads—buy the size that's comfortable for you to work with.

SOD LIFTER

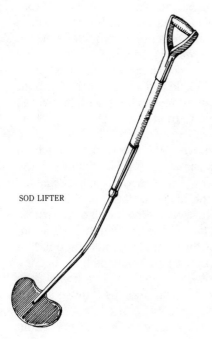

SOD LIFTER

DESCRIPTION: The first cousin of the edger (see page 143). It looks similar, but the sod lifter has a long solid steel shank that is bent at an angle and has no footrest. The handle of the sod lifter often ends in a D-grip.

USE: Lifting sod pieces from a lawn prior to reseeding. Also helpful when cutting a hole in a lawn to plant a tree or to create a bed. When sod is lifted with a sod lifter, less damage is done to it than when a spade or shovel is used, and the sod can be used elsewhere in the lawn.

USE TIP: This tool, which relies on leverage to work, can be a back breaker if used incorrectly. If working on a large area, rhythm and a pattern of motion make using this tool less painful. Use the curve of the handle as a fulcrum to pry up the sod—don't lift with your forward hand.

BUYING TIP: This is not an essential garden tool, but for the gardener who is putting in a border or flower bed or planting trees in a sodded area, it may be worth purchasing. An edger, however, may do a small job just as well.

SPADE

DESCRIPTION: Similar to a shovel (see pages 149–51) but with an almost flat, rectangular blade (or head), usually a shorter handle, and usually a D-grip (see "About Grips and Handles," page 139). The blade is straight or slightly tapered, depending on the type, and may have a small section of the top of the blade bent over to form a footrest, or tread, depending on the model.

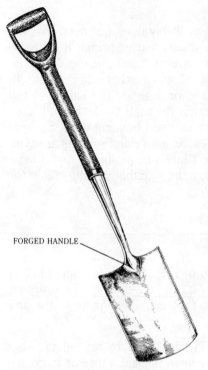

FORGED HANDLE

FORGED STAINLESS STEEL GARDEN SPADE

Professional brands have models that are even further differentiated, by purpose, such as *shrub, drain,* or *balling spades.* For example, drain spades can be as narrow as 5 inches. Spades may have handles that are reinforced with steel straps running from the blade three-fourths or all of the way up the handle, or lightweight plastic-coated hollow steel handles. They are made of regular, high-carbon, or stainless steel; the top of the line stainless models are polished to a mirror finish and the seams of the solid-socket types are welded (referred to as "seam welded"). The plastic handles of high-quality spades are usually epoxy bonded to the socket for extra strength and to keep out moisture.

TYPES: *Border spade:* The smallest, an easy-to-use spade that gets its name from having been used in border gardening, where narrow beds are common. A modified version is sometimes called a *poacher's spade,* with a curved blade and a rounded tip; a *Dutch spade* is a bit shorter and has a slightly curved blade and a T-grip. All are about 5½ inches wide by about 10 inches long, with an overall length of about 36 inches, though the Dutch spade is often longer.

Garden spade (also known as *digging spade):* Medium to large-sized, general purpose spade. The flat or slightly curved blades are usually 8 inches wide and 12 inches long. The top edge of the blade near the handle should be folded over to make two *footrests* (also known as *treads* or *step treads).* Overall lengths range from about 3½ to over 5 feet (on the straight handle models). A smaller, lighter model (about 1 to 3 pounds less) is commonly offered, called a *ladies' spade,* as is a heavy-duty model, with a longer socket and perhaps a more angled blade.

Irish garden spade (also known as *Irish spade):* Longer, more tapered blade than the border spade, with a T-grip handle.

Tree-planting spade (also known as *tree spade, sharpshooter, trenching tool,* or *transplanting spade):* Longest, tapered blade, about 16 inches long, with a very wide footrest at the top of the blade.

USE: Digging, cutting, turning, and lifting soil, especially heavy soil and sod, often when making a lawn edge. Spades are particularly well-suited for cutting through roots and compacted soil when digging planting holes or turning beds. The flat blade is helpful when edging or digging a trench. Border spades are popular with children or older gardeners who appreciate their light weight, as well as for transplanting. Irish garden spades dig deep holes and are the choice of gardeners who like to double-dig their gardens (digging up the soil to a depth of two shovel blades). The extra-wide footrests on a tree-planting spade make it easier to dig deep holes for planting trees and shrubs.

USE TIPS: Keep the cutting edges of spades sharp with an emery wheel, file, or whetstone. Clean spades with an oiled cloth and store in a dry place.

BUYING TIPS: Many gardeners consider the spade to be a more essential gardening tool than the shovel (see pages 149–51), as it can help with so many specific gardening tasks. The length of the handle is important. For the best leverage, the D-grip should be just below waist level when the spade is inserted in the soil. Avoid spades with T-grips, as they are awkward to use, unless you find yourself using two hands for lots of edging, in which case a T-grip has more room to hold on than a D-grip. Look for treads, or footrests on the top edge of the blade. Some of the most amazing spades are made of surgical-quality, mirror-polished stainless steel. They can cost around $100 and are terrific gift items, plus a little easier to use, but a heat-treated carbon steel spade (or even an epoxy-coated one) is just about as good and should last for a few generations—long enough for most of us.

TROWEL

ALSO KNOWN AS: Hand trowel, garden trowel

DESCRIPTION: Small, narrow, hand-held metal scoop, either made from one piece of cast metal or a metal blade with a plastic or wooden handle of one of a variety of colors. Some newer models have specially curved and foam-padded handles or *trigger grip handles* with "triggers" on the bottom side which make them easier to use for people with arthritic joints. Handform manufactures an ergonomic design for arthritis or carpal tunnel syndrome sufferers that features a sideways offset blade and "bent" handle, making it easier to push or scrape without bending or forcing the wrist (it rests against your palm so you don't need to grip it). A curved handle is offered in a one-piece cast aluminum model as a way to avoid blisters, called, unsurprisingly, the *no-blister trowel.* Several makes now come with long handles that

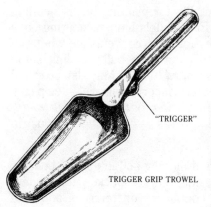

"TRIGGER"

TRIGGER GRIP TROWEL

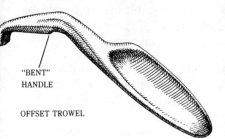

"BENT" HANDLE

OFFSET TROWEL

can be attached as desired in place of the hand-sized handle, and some manufacturers offer *long-handled trowels,* with 2- or 3-feet long, lightweight handles for use by those gardeners who have trouble bending over, or by children. *Houseplant trowels* are made in an almost miniature style, with extremely small blades for use in container gardening.

STANDARD TROWEL
WITH WOODEN HANDLE

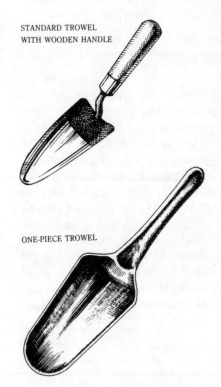

ONE-PIECE TROWEL

TYPES: *Standard trowel:* Two-piece hand tool with a wooden, metal, or plastic handle and metal blade, and a sharp edge.

One-piece trowel: Made from cast lightweight aluminum or other metal alloy or forged heavy-gauge steel. Usually the handle is covered with a colorful plastic grip. The blade on a one-piece steel trowel is often V-shaped rather than curved (adding strength), and the edge is not sharp.

Planting or *bulb trowel:* Constructed like either of the above two, but with a narrower blade, usually 2 inches but no more than 3 inches wide at the top, tapering down to about 1 inch at the tip, and as much as 6 inches long, although some are made even narrower for delicate indoor work with seedlings. The smaller blade allows you to dig a small hole suitable for planting bulbs, bedding plants, or seedlings. Most models have measuring lines stamped into the blades for your convenience when determining how deep to plant each bulb, leading some people to call them *graduated trowels.* May also be called a *bulb planter* (though this is incorrect usage—see pages 140–41), or *planter, transplanter,* or *transplanting trowel.* The narrowest can be known as *rockery trowels,* for use in rock gardens.

USE: Planting, transplanting, and moving soil in garden beds or into containers. They are essential tools, especially for gardening in small spaces such as containers on terraces and roof gardens. Narrow and V-shaped blades are best for digging out weeds and planting bulbs; wider and flatter blades are better for general use with loose soil. Long handles are convenient for gardeners who have trouble bending over or kneeling.

USE TIPS: When transplanting with a trowel it is not always necessary to actually *dig* a hole. Simply insert the trowel into the soil and *open* a hole by moving the trowel from side to side; the curve of the blade forms the hole. Standard metal garden trowels should be cleaned with an oily cloth after use and stored in a dry place to avoid rusting.

BUYING TIPS: Colorful or bright metal trowels are easier to find in the garden. One-piece aluminum or steel trowels are more durable than the standard garden trowels where the blades are attached to a handle by the tang-and-ferrule method (see pages 137–39 for the discussion on handles). Standard trowels with blades made from chrome-plated steel are better buys than those with other metals. Among one-piece trowels, those made from steel are among the strongest and most durable sold. V-shaped blades are strong and less likely to bend. Aluminum trowels are lightweight, a consideration for people with arthritis or some other disability affecting their ability to grip, but the edge of the blade is not as sharp as on other trowels and cannot be sharpened. By all means, get a trowel that won't bend, and of course one that feels comfortable to grip—after all, that's what you do with it. Try all the various grip designs, because they fit individual hands differently from one another. Usually, the larger the grip, the easier the tool is to use. Interchangeable handles are sometimes not well-balanced—try them out before you buy. Finally, you may want to buy several sizes of trowels for use in different jobs.

WIDGER

ALSO KNOWN AS: Nitpicker, nit-picker, everything tool, potted-plant tool, double-ended widger

DESCRIPTION: Plain convex stainless steel strip, ½ inch wide and 7 inches long.

USE: Digging out small seedlings for transplanting and removing small potted plants by pushing the plant down along the side of the pot. Also good for seeding and applying small doses of fertilizer.

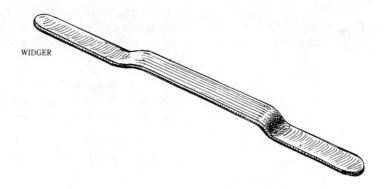

WIDGER

Wheel Goods

ABOUT WHEEL GOODS

The choice between a cart and a wheelbarrow is largely one of personal preference, or feel, though a cart is a bit less maneuverable and needs more room than a wheelbarrow. On the other hand, there are more innovative features to be found in a myriad of makes and models of carts than with wheelbarrows, which remain simple in design. Here is another tool category where it is quite worthwhile to buy the better quality item, or else you will need to replace it sooner than you think.

GARDEN CART

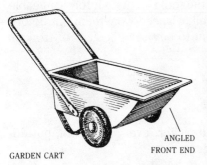

GARDEN CART

ANGLED
FRONT END

ALSO KNOWN AS: Yard cart, utility cart

DESCRIPTION: A cubish, deep-sided container (the "bucket"), about 20 by 40 inches by a foot high, on two wheels, with a metal loop handle, making it larger and deeper than a wheelbarrow (see next entry). Made of sheet metal or wood. Some wooden carts are open on the handle end, and the front end is a board that can be removed for dumping loads (on folding models, all panels are removable). Others can tilt on their axles for easy dumping. Some are designed with an angled front that lies on the ground when tilted down for easy loading. Capacity ranges from 4 to over 13 cubic feet, holding over 300 pounds with ease, but capable of carrying up to 450 pounds. A hybrid version is available that looks like a wheelbarrow with two wheels and a single handle, called a *yard buggy*. Many have spoked bicycle-type wheels for greater weight capacity and maneuverability.

YARD BUGGY

USE: Hauling heavier and larger loads than most wheelbarrows, but because of their double wheels they are not quite as maneuverable. Tilting feature allows for easier unloading and loading than with wheelbarrows.

USE TIPS: Position loads in carts closer to the front of the bucket, balancing them over the wheels to make hauling easier. Keep carts clean and bearings oiled.

BUYING TIPS: Metal carts and the metal parts of wooden carts should be made of heavy-gauge steel that is well protected from rust (zinc-plated is best). Look for large (20-inch) spoked wheels with pneumatic tires, a front panel for unloading, top grade, exterior-stained plywood, and a sturdy, adjustable handle. Choose the size that is right for you—there is quite a range. The yard buggy dumps easily like a wheelbarrow but is able to balance a heavy load like a cart.

WHEELBARROW

DESCRIPTION: A shallow, scooped container (the "tray") about 2 by 2½ feet made of wood, metal (assembled or one piece, seamless aluminum or 18-gauge steel), or heavy plastic (high-density polyethylene), attached to a single 10- to 16-inch wheel. Two long handles made either of metal or 2-inch-square wood are used for pushing the wheelbarrow around the garden. Wheels may be either inflatable or solid rubber, or wooden with a steel surface. A deep model with heavier, wider supports, a sturdier wheel, and higher sides is called a *contractor's* or *concrete wheelbarrow.* Sizes are measured in cubic feet (helpful when you plan to use this for mixing cement): 3 or 4½ cubic feet is a typical small size; the deep models hold as much as 6½ cubic feet. Capacity ranges from 150 to 700 pounds.

WHEELBARROW

USE: Moving heavy loads around the garden, though not as large and heavy as can be moved with a garden cart (see preceding entry). The single wheel makes for easier maneuvering. An essential piece of equipment for any larger garden, and one that should last for years. Deep models are used for mixing concrete as well.

USE TIPS: Keep wheelbarrows clean when not in use. Do not allow water to stand in metal wheelbarrows, as this might cause them to rust. Oil wheels for easier movement. Semirounded front makes for easier dumping. The front brace that connects the two handles immediately in front of the wheel can catch on the ground as you move the barrow along, especially if you hold the handles high and are moving over irregular terrain— and if it does, you and it will come to an immediate and painful stop. Be careful.

Watch out for overloading: If the load shifts, you might injure yourself trying to save it. Better to let it go or just set it down whenever it starts to become unwieldy. Remember, too, that you have to lift half of the weight yourself.

BUYING TIPS: The better wheelbarrows are made of one piece of heavy steel with extra braces on the legs, which are set wide apart for stability. They also have heavy wooden handles that are attached with countersunk bolts. Check the wheelbarrow out for feel and balance. Wide, inflatable tires give the smoothest ride and are a bit easier to use, but can flatten out or puncture under heavy use. Wooden barrows with wooden wheels are great looking but may be a bit rough to use. Plastic models are maintenance-free, of course. In all types, look for good bracing on the legs.

Cultivating, Weeding, and Raking Tools

ABOUT ALL TOOLS

As with shovels (see pages 149–51), cultivating, weeding, and raking tools are generally made either in a tang-and-ferrule or solid-socket style, though smaller tools are also made as one piece. The tang-and-ferrule style is not as strong as the others, but while tools of this design which are intended for light use may work fine, the better-quality tools that are built to endure generally do not use it (see the explanations and illustrations on pages 137–39 under "About Digging Tool Durability").

Metal shaft handles that end with a grip at a slight angle are generally more comfortable to use. The British term for this is *cranked handle*. Hand tools should be designed so that there is clearance for your knuckles when working close to the soil, so check your angles carefully. When investigating tools with interchangeable short and long handles, be sure to check the balance and feel of the tools with *both* handles. Some sacrifice balance for this convenience.

Remember that metal tools should always be wiped dry after use and coated with oil from an oily rag or an aerosol spray, and that their moving parts should be kept lubricated. Cutting edges should be filed sharp from time to time.

Some individual power tools can be duplicated by attachments to multiuse tools; these are not discussed here but are indeed available.

Cultivating Tools

ABOUT CULTIVATING TOOLS

Veteran vegetable gardeners hold cultivating—the loosening of soil around plants—to be one of the most important gardening tasks. Regular cultivating opens up the soil to allow water to reach the roots easily, destroys small weeds, or prevents weeds from getting established in the first place.

There seem to be more types of tools sold in garden centers specifically designed to help with this garden task than any other. It is an ancient job that has provided much grist for the mills of inventors and marketing folks, resulting in a wide array of inventions. Their names may reflect the way they function, the manufacturer, region of origin, or most common use. Some are good, some will disappear after one season, and all are touted as the absolute best. What works for one gardener might not for the next. One thing is sure: There is no one "right" cultivating tool.

GARDENING HOE

ALSO KNOWN AS: Draw hoe

DESCRIPTION: Small, flat metal blade attached at an angle—70 degrees is considered ideal—to a long wooden handle, typically 50 to 70 inches long. The blade of a hoe may be square, rectangular, or triangular in shape, depending upon the type of hoe. The edge may be quite sharp, but not always; corners may be sharp or rounded. The blade is attached to the handle via a long curved shank called a *gooseneck* or *swan neck,* and is held either by the tang-and-ferrule or solid-socket method. Grubbing hoes, or mattocks (see page 146), are sometimes considered types of hoes, too. There are *wheeled hoes* that look like small plows, but they are not commonly found (see pages 167–68).

There are many manufacturers and each may call a slightly different-sized hoe by a different name, and with not much consistency. A typical grouping of specialized hoes that resemble the homeowner type of garden hoe but are a bit larger includes *southern* (also a general category for all of these), *cotton, light cotton, cotton chopper, barn, field, blackland,* and *planter hoes. Note:* Although these hoes can be used for a variety of jobs, including heavy weeding, hoes especially designed for weeding are listed under *weeding hoes* on pages 173–76.

TYPES: *Garden hoe* (also known as *common, general gardening, draw, mounding,* or *digging hoe):* Rectangular blade measuring about 6 inches wide and 4¾ inches high, often with a rounded or scalloped top. Garden hoes are the most common ones sold in garden centers and hardware stores. A slightly larger version, about 7 inches wide and not as high, and with an angular, tapered top, is called a *nurseryman's, nursery,* or *beet hoe.* There is also the *floral hoe,* a narrow, lightweight model suitable for people who don't want the standard weight, or for children. Some models have holes in the blade for the soil to flow through to help pulverize it or for mixing cement *(mason's* or *mortar hoe).* An even larger version, 12 inches wide, is called a *raised bed builder.*

    Eye hoe: The heavy-duty hoe. Has a short, thick handle inserted into an eye in the blade, sort of like a mattock or ax, and is made in a number of similar but slightly different patterns: two normal-looking models, the *American* (7 to 8 inches wide by 6½ to 7 inches deep, available in small, medium, and large models, all with curved shoulders) and the *Scovil* (6½ to 9 inches wide by 5½ to 7½ inches deep, with square shoulders, and either flat or slightly curved—*Scovil* is an old Japanese brand name that may soon be a thing of the past); and more specialized versions such as the larger *grape hoe* (7 inches wide by 10½ inches deep, with almost no shoulders and with an oval eye, developed for working in vineyards), the narrow *grub hoe* (4½ inches wide by 7¾ inches deep, with square shoulders, the heaviest, for compacted or stony soil), and others that vary from

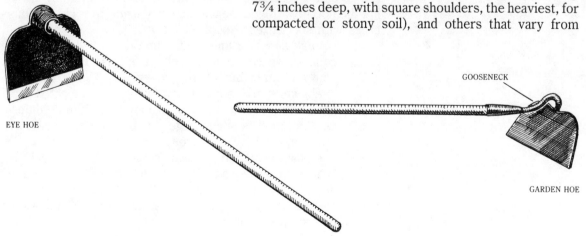

EYE HOE

GOOSENECK

GARDEN HOE

brand to brand, such as the lighter *southern meadow hoe.* All are imported, mostly from Austria and Japan. Handles are 54 inches long, except for the grape hoe, which is 41 inches long.

Onion hoe (also known as *square top onion, nursery, colinear,* or *beet hoe):* Has a wider, higher, narrower blade than the common garden hoe, running about 7 inches wide and 2 inches high. The blade is sharpened on the bottom and the sides, allowing it to be used in two directions. Nursery and beet hoes, according to some, are simply garden hoes with angular sides, like large onion hoes. Available in a hand-sized version, too.

Warren hoe: A pointed blade bent in the center with two smaller points, or ears, near the handle. One model with much larger ears is called a *garden row zipper.*

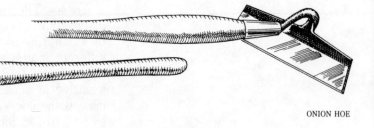

ONION HOE

WARREN HOE

USE: Basically for moving small quantities of soil when planting (hilling and tilling) and cultivating soil, but also for chopping small weeds just below the soil surface, and for very light digging. The broad head is good for moving or tamping down soil. This is the gardener's most basic tool: Break the earth and you can garden. Everything else is extra. Used most often by drawing the hoe toward you, hence the name *draw hoe.* The various types with specialized uses are

Garden hoe: Working around flowers in beds and other confined spaces; general lightweight use for gardeners who find other models too heavy.

Eye hoe: Serious chopping of roots or compacted soil, agricultural and heavy-duty farming work. Subtle differences of models due in large part to tradition—some by crop, others by ethnic group.

Onion hoe: Cultivating in confined spaces, such as between closely planted vegetable crops. Can be used to disturb the soil just under the surface, cutting small weeds, or to just skim the surface of the soil when control is very important.

Warren hoe: Creating rows and furrows. The smaller ears can be used for filling in furrows after the seeds have been laid down. Also good for digging up weeds.

USE TIPS: Only when digging is there a need to use a chopping motion with a hoe; otherwise, just pull it toward you and under the hardened, unworked soil. And keep the inside edge sharp.

BUYING TIPS: If you can find them, hoes with solid-socket handles are better buys for the money than the common tang-and-ferrule type, although the heavy-duty eye hoes are the strongest. Look for forged construction, not welded. The onion hoe is one of the best all-purpose hoes available, and is a wiser choice over the common garden hoe. As with other tools with long handles, the grain of the wood should be tight and run lengthwise. Longer-handled tools are more comfortable to use—they reduce the need to bend—than shorter ones. The head should be the same piece as the tang (forged) or else solidly welded; avoid spot-welded hoes. Replaceable blades are available for some of the more unusual designs. In hand-sized hoes, look for a comfortable shape in the handle, such as an hour-glass design, and good balance. Some of the heavier, more specialized hoes are difficult to find in stores but are carried in the professional catalogs. There seems to be a hoe designed for each hoeing task.

HAND CULTIVATOR

HAND CULTIVATOR

ALSO KNOWN AS: Three-prong cultivator

DESCRIPTION: Commonly three but sometimes more prongs or tines attached to a short wooden or plastic handle. Tines may be flat and pointed, or round, or with angular *harrow-toothed tips,* shaped like arrowheads. Head is attached to handle in either the solid-socket or tang-and-ferrule method (see pages 137–38), although some tools are made that can snap into long or short handles as you want. Prongs may be spring-tooth type, which means they are somewhat flexible.

Grubber is used by some manufacturers to describe a slightly narrower or more lightweight version with no special tips, more like a simple claw; however, this is incorrect: A grubber is used to dig out roots, and is either a knifelike weeder (sometimes called a *soil knife* or *farmer's weeder)* or a type of mattock (see page 146), called a *grubber hoe.*

USE: Hand cultivators are indispensable to gardening, just like hand-held trowels. They are particularly useful when gardening in raised beds, containers, and terrace gardens, especially when working a conditioner or fertilizer into the soil or weeding next to established plants.

USE TIPS: When weeding with a cultivator, be sure to get under the roots of the weed. Clean with an oiled rag for storage.

BUYING TIPS: Hand cultivators should have sharp tines to dig into the soil, a comfortable grip, and a solid-socket construction handle. Using handles that are too small for you may cause blisters. Those that snap into long handles as well may not be well-balanced, so check them out thoroughly before purchasing. Tines should be angled back slightly toward the handle and extend a bit below the line of the handle, enabling you to cultivate the soil by just pulling the tool toward you and be spared having to jam it down, with your fingers hitting the ground each time it enters the soil.

HAND FORK

HAND FORK

ALSO KNOWN AS: Hand-held fork, flower fork, weed fork, digging fork (incorrect)

DESCRIPTION: Head of three or four straight, flat, metal tines attached to either a wooden or plastic handle, or a single piece of cast or stamped metal, such as lightweight aluminum. Hand-sized to a maximum length of 20 inches, though some manufacturers offer *long-handled forks* with 2- or 3-foot-long, lightweight handles for use by those gardeners who have trouble bending over, or by children.

USE: Cultivating in confined spaces, such as small gardens or in containers.

USE TIP: Use as you would a garden fork (see pages 143–46).

BUYING TIPS: Though popular in other countries, hand forks are not considered an indispensable garden tool in this country. This is probably because there is little you can do with a hand fork that cannot be done as well with a good trowel. Though some manufacturers make their hand forks of lesser quality than their full-sized forks, there is no reason for this. Get something sturdy and comfortable.

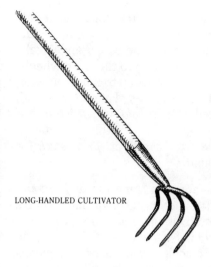

LONG-HANDLED CULTIVATOR

LONG-HANDLED CULTIVATOR

ALSO KNOWN AS: Tined hoe, garden cultivator

DESCRIPTION: Similar to the hand cultivator (see pages 163–64), usually with three, four, or five curved tines and a handle 4 or 5 feet long. Heads are forged or welded, and the tines may have wide, diamond-shaped, harrowtooth-type tips. The handle is attached either by tang-and-ferrule or with a solid-socket (see pages 137–38). A *hook* is a slightly larger and heavier version intended for specialized farming uses, such as harvesting potatoes (called, unsurprisingly, a *potato hook* or *potato hoe),* spreading manure, removing stones and roots, refuse (called a *refuse hook),* and so on. Some models have a U-shaped blade, like an oscillating hoe (see page 174), and are called *cultivator/weeders.* Many brands now are made with handles that snap on and off, and can be interchanged with short handles for hand-held use.

USE: Excellent general cultivation and weeding tool that can be used without stooping.

USE TIPS: Easier to use if you pull the tool toward you. Because the tines of this tool are sharp, you may want to store it with corks on the sharp points. Clean with an oiled cloth before storing.

BUYING TIPS: Among serious gardeners this is an indispensable tool. Look for one with nice weight and balance; forged tools are stronger but welded ones will do in lightly packed soil. Handles attached with a solid-socket are more durable than others. Hooks are often a better buy, because they are heavier and bigger, and some gardeners prefer them for general garden use. Those with snap-on handles may not be well-balanced, so try them out before buying.

POWER TILLER

ALSO KNOWN AS: Rotary tiller, rototiller, tiller/cultivator

DESCRIPTION: A gas or electric motor attached to a tined wheel or a series of tined wheels, with long, straight, or plow-type handles. The smallest tillers have only one or two blade wheels, and the larger tillers have four blades or more; small electric models may be called *power cultivators,* or *tiller/cultivators.* Some models come with special blades that can furrow, aerate, dethatch, or make raised planting rows, or with attachments for

SMALL GAS-POWERED
FRONT-TINED TILLER

snow removal, edging, or trimming. Electric tillers generally have a single shaft or handle, and the tined wheels are below the motor, while gas-powered models tend to be bigger and usually have two regular rubber wheels in addition to the tined wheels. Power tillers come in a wide range of sizes up to 5 horsepower, and dig at adjustable depths up to 8 inches. Tillers come with three basic kinds of tines or tined wheels: *bolo,* which are sort of a universal design for deep tilling; *slasher,* for thick vegetation and roots in soft ground; and *pick and chisel,* or *spring steel,* for general use on hard, rocky ground.

TYPES: *Front-tined tiller* (also known as *front-tine* or *front-end tiller):* Gasoline or electric motor on top of tined wheels (the parts that do the cultivating), sometimes with rubber stabilizing wheels behind, and plow-type handles; the tined wheels propel the machine. Many are 6 to 9 inches wide—smaller and lighter than rear-tine tillers.

    Rear-tined tiller (also known as *rear-tine* or *rear-end tiller):* Largest power tiller, with blade wheels located at the rear of the machine, often propelled by the load-bearing front wheels. Gas-powered motor is above front wheels.

USE: Tilling or cultivating medium or large gardens when the job is too hard to do by hand. Electric and front-tined tillers are more suited to easier-to-work soils, such as in established beds and gardens and soils that have been previously cultivated, and for regular cultivation prior to seeding or for working in soil amendments. Electric, lightweight tillers are for the easiest jobs. Heavier, rear-tined tillers are for areas that may never have been tilled; heavier machines of this type can cultivate even hard-packed, rocky soils that the smaller front-tined models cannot handle.

USE TIPS: Be sure the ground is moist enough to work, but not so moist that it is unable to support the weight of the tiller. Always check the oil before operating—many mechanical problems stem from not doing this. Do not attempt to till soil with tall weeds on it—they will only wrap themselves around the tiller tines; rather, cut weeds before tilling. Remember that this is a powerful machine that can be dangerous if not used carefully. Don't overoil the blades after use. Use it several times a year, spring, summer, and fall, turning in compost and green manures (grasslike plants grown only to be turned into the soil for enrichment), as well as for planting and cultivating. Don't expect a small machine to do heavy-duty work.

BUYING TIPS: Shop around and rent one or two (and try out your neighbors'), because this is one of the more expensive garden tools you can buy. Rear-tined tillers can cost twice as much as front-tined models. Determine if your space is large enough to justify the expense of a tiller. In the past, front-tined tillers were for smaller gardens and rear-tined for larger ones, but many models now overlap a bit. In the larger models, the rear-tined tillers are still easier to control than front-tined. Rear-tined tillers are regular workhorses, doing more than front-tined models, and their wheels do not pass over and compact freshly tilled soil, a problem of front-tined tillers. Light, small tillers of both types are great for churning up the top layer of soil to combat weeds. On any model, see how easy it is to turn. Buy the machine that can take all of the extra attachments you might need. The capability of any tiller is determined largely by the size of the engine and the weight of the machine. The engine should be almost directly over the tines of a front-tined tiller to aid the digging. Look for high-quality, high-carbon steel tines that are adjustable for width, chain drives, easily operated controls, a shielded muffler, and adjustable handles, and try to see how much noise and vibration the motor produces. Rear-tined tillers should have hinged tine covers for safety. If you are using the machine only once a year, consider renting one instead of buying. And if you send away for information, beware: The manufacturers try to outdo each other with volumes upon volumes of brochures. They almost claim to have replaced the hoe and the shovel.

WHEELED CULTIVATOR

DESCRIPTION:

HIGH-WHEEL CULTIVATOR

High-wheel cultivator (also known as *big wheel cultivator):* Sort of a miniature plow designed to be pushed by you rather than pulled by mules. The larger models have wheels as big as 22 inches in diameter and wide, bicycle-like handles, while the smaller ones have a wheel about 8 inches in diameter and a single shaft with one handle. Both have cultivating tines, weeding knives, or plow blades attached just behind the wheel.

Spiked-wheel cultivator (also known as *hand rotary cultivator* (small version), *rotary cultivator, star harrow, star tiller, spin tiller,* or *soil miller):* A popular design among major manufacturers—a set of tined wheels with a long, straight handle. Each brand is slightly different, but two of the more popular brands are the Weasel® and the Crumbler™, which are about 6 inches wide. Others are as wide as a rake (10 inches) with as many as sixteen revolving, spiked disks and resemble reel-type lawn mowers. Some models include an attachment that resembles the U-shaped blade on an oscillating hoe (see page 174) which is dragged through the soil surface, followed by the tines that break up the clods of earth. Others have only two wheels with a foot-long handle, for use in containers. These are all actually miniature tillers (see preceding entry). Large models resemble old rotary lawn mowers with a single crossbar handle. Instead of a leading wheel, there is a barrellike contraption with pointed blades. Cultivating blades can be attached behind this spiked drum.

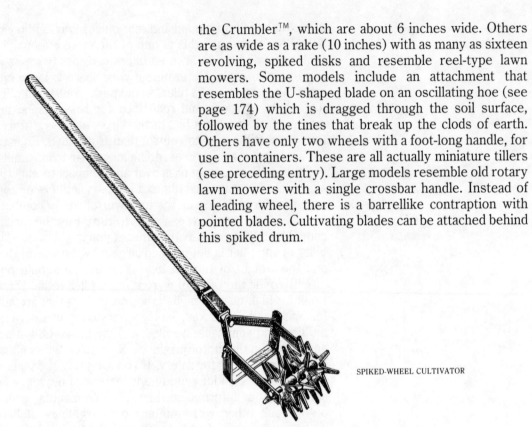

SPIKED-WHEEL CULTIVATOR

USE: Breaking up, aerating, and mixing soil in place when preparing seedbeds, or for mixing in fertilizer or peat. Particularly useful for laying out long garden rows or breaking ground for a new and large garden site. Functions somewhere between a hand cultivator and a motorized tiller. Also offers an alternative for those gardeners who find it physically difficult to handle a regular cultivator, which (like a hoe) you have to lift up and down in a hacking motion. These require only a push-pull motion, or just a push or a pull in the case of the larger models. The spiked-wheel type is for smaller gardens and requires less energy to use than the high-wheel model.

USE TIP: Wheeled cultivators are somewhat less work than hand cultivators. Clean well after using with an oiled cloth.

BUYING TIP: High-wheel cultivators can usually be purchased for under $50. If you garden in long rows or hills, and your soil is fairly loose, it might be worth looking into one. Try to find one that's self-cleaning.

Weeders and Weeding Hoes

ABOUT WEEDERS

Weeds are the plague of most gardens and gardeners. The pervasiveness of weeds leads to an enormous variety of weeders in garden centers throughout the country. These products promise to rid the garden of weeds through prodding, poking, digging, scraping, cutting, slicing, lifting, and more. Probably as much energy and thought has been put into designing a better weeder as that expended for a better mousetrap. What follows are but a few of the weeding tools you will find on the shelves of garden centers, as new ones come out each season.

When using any of these tools, keep in mind that sharp blades make for more effective weeding. Also, once an area has been weeded, allow the disturbed weeds to dry in the sun before removing and composting. Hand-held weeders are designed for small or raised-bed gardens.

ASPARAGUS KNIFE

ALSO KNOWN AS: Fishtail weeder, garden weeder (incorrect), weeder (too general), dandelion digger (incorrect—refers to a larger model, described on page 171)

DESCRIPTION: A metal shaft about 14 inches long with a flat, V-slotted fishtail head and a wooden or plastic handle, like a big screwdriver. The shaft is slightly bent and the head has sharp cutting edges. As the name suggests, this was originally used to cut the tender shoots of asparagus, but it has become a popular weeding tool. A larger version, over 3 feet long, is the dandelion digger. A rarer version has three V slots, instead of one, for pulling, rather than prying weeds out.

ASPARAGUS KNIFE

USE: Designed to reach into the soil and cut off or lift deep-rooted weeds with little disturbance to the area where they are growing, a particular concern with lawn weeds such as dandelion and dock.

USE TIPS: Insert the tool a few inches away from the weed you wish to lift and at a slight angle. Keep the points and cutting edges sharp for better cutting.

BUYING TIPS: Buy a solid, well-constructed asparagus knife. A colorful handle prevents loss when you put it down on the lawn.

CAPE COD WEEDER

DESCRIPTION: Hand tool with a long-necked, L-shaped metal blade attached to a wooden handle. The short part has the cutting edge and is at an angle that varies according to brand. Another similar version, in which the cutting edge is aligned with, not at an angle to, the neck, is known as a *crack weeder* or *joint scraper.* This is sometimes called a *pin point weeder,* or confusingly referred to as a *weeder knife.*

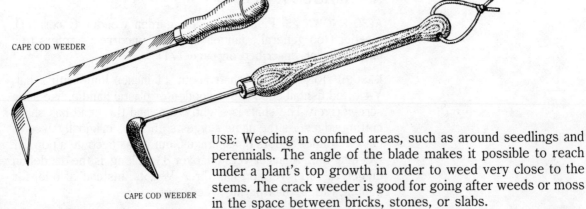

CAPE COD WEEDER

CAPE COD WEEDER

USE: Weeding in confined areas, such as around seedlings and perennials. The angle of the blade makes it possible to reach under a plant's top growth in order to weed very close to the stems. The crack weeder is good for going after weeds or moss in the space between bricks, stones, or slabs.

USE TIPS: Pull the blade toward you just under the surface of the soil. Keep blade sharp for easier weeding.

BUYING TIPS: Because the blade of the Cape Cod weeder curves to the left, this is primarily a tool for right-handed gardeners. It would not appear difficult to manufacture this in a left-handed version, but none seem to be on the market. Crack weeders are not as efficient as you might want, because they can rarely get under the larger weeds.

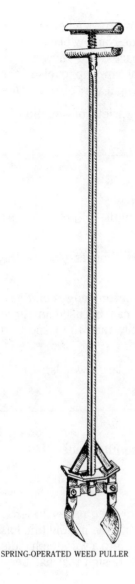

SPRING-OPERATED WEED PULLER

DANDELION DIGGER

ALSO KNOWN AS: Lawn weeder, weed puller, back-saver weeder

DESCRIPTION: Just a larger (it's over 3 feet long) version of the asparagus knife (see pages 169–70) with a fishtail tip. The handle is attached with a tang-and-ferrule design (see pages 137–38). Another version is the *yard arm weeder,* with a yard-long handle and two long, slightly curved, barbed hooks on the tip, sold under a variety of trade names with a play on the words *easy* or *handy,* or under the brand name Weedigger. Other brands use a small fork and fulcrum design. Finally, there are 5-foot-long spring- or lever-operated models that cut, grasp, and pull weeds.

USE: Removing deep-rooted weeds, especially dandelions, and other garden debris without the gardener having to bend over or leave a wheelchair.

USE TIPS: Same as for asparagus knife. Very helpful if you have a bad back or other handicap.

BUYING TIP: The length of the handle provides more leverage than is possible with the asparagus knife, but the tool works the same. If you have trouble with the leverage in the asparagus knife, these are good alternatives.

HEART HOE

ALSO KNOWN AS: Single-tined cultivator, finger hoe, single-finger hoe, one-prong cultivator

DESCRIPTION: Hand tool, generally with a 12- to 18-inch-long wooden handle, with one large (4½-inch diameter) C-shaped, pointed claw with a small heart-shaped blade tip. Not unlike a miniature double-edged plowshare. Also available with a 5-foot-long handle, usually with a C-shaped claw about 9 inches in diameter, and may be called a *biocultivator.*

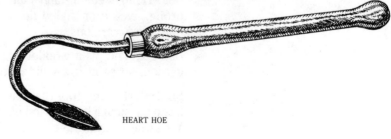

HEART HOE

USE: Cultivating small gardens and window boxes where precise control is needed. Extremely versatile tool. Narrow blade allows for working in tight, difficult-to-reach spaces, and curved neck lets you lift weeds out of the soil. Does not mix up levels of the soil unless you intend for it to do so, making it sort of an *aerator*.

USE TIP: Actually quite useful in a wide variety of situations.

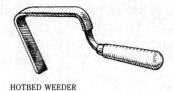

HOTBED WEEDER

HOTBED WEEDER

ALSO KNOWN AS: Ideal weeder

DESCRIPTION: Short-handled, C-shaped, with ¾-inch-wide flat blade, with all three edges sharpened.

USE: Weeding in tight areas, such as greenhouses—hence the name.

USE TIP: Because the hotbed weeder has cutting edges on three sides and straight and curved parts, it can be used in three positions, making it slightly more versatile than the Cape Cod weeder (see page 170).

BUYING TIP: Versatile, but not great with large weeds.

THE ORIGINAL WEEDER

ALSO KNOWN AS: Magic weeder, spring-tooth weeder

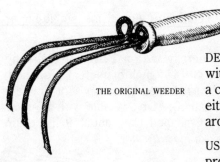

THE ORIGINAL WEEDER

DESCRIPTION: Resembles a hand cultivator (see pages 163–64) with three round curved prongs or tines, but the middle tine has a curl, or spring, in it. The tines fit directly into a wooden handle either 5, 14, or 32 inches long. Venerable design that has been around for years.

USE: Hand weeding and cultivating. The spring in the middle prong gives it an added flexibility and makes it more effective than plain versions.

USE TIP: The plain wooden handle makes it easy to lose in the garden, so paint it a vivid color.

BUYING TIP: Any tool that has remained as popular as this one has over such a long period of time has got to be one of the best. Versatile, easy to use, and effective.

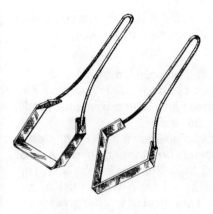

UOO AND VEE WEEDERS

UOO AND VEE WEEDERS

ALSO KNOWN AS: U and V weeders

DESCRIPTION: A short metal blade in the shape of a U or a V attached to a plastic, hand-sized handle. Lightweight (4 ounces!) and less than a foot long. Made of spring steel.

USE: Hand cultivating or surface weeding around crops, and thinning vegetables and plants. They work by cutting roots just below the surface of the soil.

USE TIP: Put sturdy tape on the handle to prevent blisters and give a better grip. Open handle ends provide a convenient design for hanging up when not in use.

BUYING TIPS: Inexpensive weeding tools that are easy to use on young weeds. They are used quite often by commercial growers, which is a good recommendation for the home gardener, but some people find them a little difficult to handle.

WEEDER/ROOTER

WEEDER/ROOTER

ALSO KNOWN AS: Pronghoe

DESCRIPTION: A small hoe with two heads: One resembles a narrow garden hoe, and the other has two, three, or four small prongs. Made as a hand-sized tool, as well as with a long handle.

USE: Particularly well suited for weeding around transplants and seedlings, but also a good general purpose hoe.

USE TIP: The prong side is for getting close to plants, tipping to one side and using just one prong in tight places if need be.

BUYING TIP: One of the most versatile hand tools.

WEEDING HOE

DESCRIPTION: Long-handled tool with metal blade of various designs, with sharp edges on two, three, or four sides, or all around in the case of a curved or round hoe. Designed to be pushed, pulled, and moved from side to side, as opposed to merely pulled, or drawn, through the soil, like the gardening hoes (see pages 160–64). Many different brands make similar items under slightly different names—this is an area of intense competition, artisanal ingenuity, and nuanced designs—which is to say that it is hard to pin down all the various types and names here. And most can cultivate as well as weed, too, just to add to the confusion.

TYPES: *Cavex hoe:* Sharply curved or rounded blade.

Dutch hoe (also known as *Dutch scuffle hoe, push-pull weeder, push hoe,* or *thrust hoe):* Open triangular blade, with a cutting edge on the inside.

Oscillating stirrup hoe (also known as *hula hoe, oscillating hoe, action hoe, pendulum weeder, stirrup hoe,* or *scuffle hoe):* Four-edged blade that looks like a stirrup, hinged so it moves back and forth when pushed and pulled through the soil. This rocking motion gives it the name *hula hoe.* A relatively new design, introduced in 1958.

Rockery hoe: British hand tool with a forged, 4-inch-wide semicircular blade attached to a 7-inch-long handle by a curved metal shank. Designed for use in small, tight areas, such as in rock gardens, which the British insist on calling "rockeries" for some reason.

Scuffle hoe (also known as *glide groom hoe, push-pull hoe, root-cutting hoe,* or *Dutch hoe*—this last term is incorrect): Comes in the widest variety of blade shapes. Blades can be triangular, curved, diamond shaped, or rectangular, with sharp edges on several sides. Some variations have special names, such as *floral* (smaller), *garden* (large rectangular), and *orange grove* (triangular). Other brands are simply called by their shape, such as *crescent hoe* or *colinear hoe. Note:* Almost all multi-edged weeding hoes that use a push-pull motion to cut weeds just below the surface (at their roots) might be called *scuffle hoes.*

CAVEX HOE

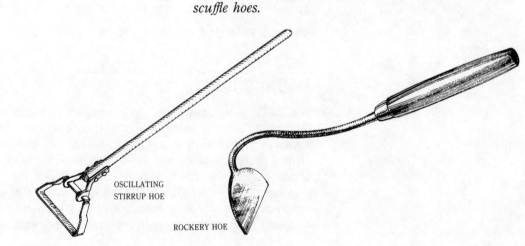

OSCILLATING
STIRRUP HOE

ROCKERY HOE

Swoe (also known as *shuffle, scuffle,* or *cultivation hoe):* Odd rectangular, about 5 by 3 inch, almost triangular blade, sharp on three sides, in either a hand-weeding version with a foot-long handle, or a longer, stand-up version that looks like a golf club. The blade of either model is at an angle to the handle, attached by a long tang. True Temper calls their hand version the *Swoe Jr.* and the stand-up version *Swoe Sr.* Basically a modified scuffle hoe.

Weeding hoe (also known as *rabbit ears, planting hoe,* or *three-prong cultivator):* Double-headed blade. One side resembles the blade of a narrow garden hoe, while the other is made up of two or three long prongs or points,

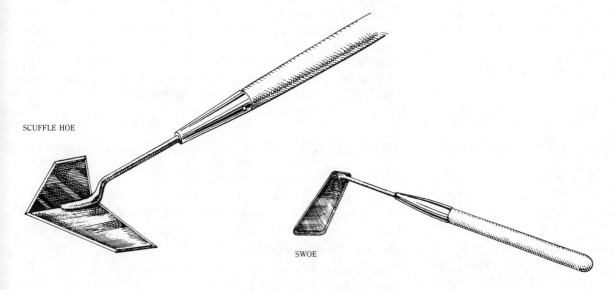

SCUFFLE HOE

SWOE

or a triangular blade. The prongs break up crusty soil and rip up weeds, such as dichondra. Another version is triangularly shaped, with no ears, called a *triangular hoe,* and if it is on the end of a long, curved neck, it is called a *gooseneck hoe.* Still another version is the *Southern Belle,* with a rectangular blade on one side and a triangular blade on the other, sort of like a mattock (see page 146). In fact, it might be called a *mattock hoe.* Hand-sized versions are available, too.

USE: Cutting off and removing small weeds in frequently cultivated beds before they become established, especially those found just below the surface. The multi-edged design allows for cutting in any direction; the large oscillating models work well in heavy soil while the basic scuffle designs work best in light, sandy soils and under mulches—in fact, they don't disturb mulch as they work. Hand-held models are useful in cold frames and greenhouses. Swoes (and some of the other models, depending on the gardener) can easily be used for traditional hoeing chores, such as making furrows and general cultivation.

USE TIPS: Keep all blade edges sharp. Dry off tool after use, and do not leave it lying about—someone might step on the business end and get clunked in the face with the handle.

BUYING TIPS: A good second hoe to have, in addition to a regular gardening hoe. As for which type, this is really a case of personal preference, though of course the smaller blades are handier in confined gardens. The variety of designs reflect the industry-wide effort to develop the ideal weeder. Oscillating hoes work just below the surface and are a little bit less work because less soil is being displaced. The swoe is available in stainless steel, for truly serious weeding. Always look for one-piece forged blades and necks instead of spot-welded ones.

WEED SLICER

ALSO KNOWN AS: Hand weeder, gooseneck hoe

DESCRIPTION: A 6-inch-wide triangular blade attached at an angle to a 5-inch-long wooden handle by a curved metal shank (called a swan neck) about a foot long. Usually a sturdy, forged steel item. Left- and right-handed versions available.

USE: The razor-sharp blade slices through weeds just under the soil surface. Especially good for hard-to-reach places in a small garden, and "intensive" gardening. Design lends itself to a variety of detail work.

USE TIPS: Keep blades sharp for easier weeding. This is another hand tool that is easy to lose in the garden, and because of the sharp blade, it can be dangerous with children around. Be sure to paint the handle a bright color.

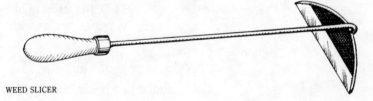

WEED SLICER

Rakes

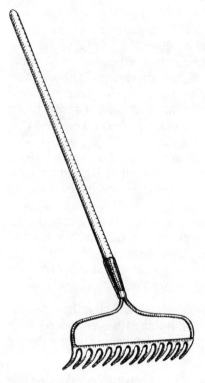

BOWHEAD GARDEN RAKE

GARDEN RAKE

DESCRIPTION: A row, over a foot long, of solid steel tines a few inches long, set perpendicular to a long, usually wooden, handle. Lightweight handles are made of tubular aluminum. Most garden rakes are attached to the handle in the tang-and-ferrule way, but a few can be found attached using the solid-socket method (see page 138). Small versions, as small as 6 inches wide, may be called *floral* (or *flower), children's,* or *ladies' rakes.*

TYPES: *Flathead rake* (also known as *level head rake):* Made of forged, high-carbon steel. A long center tine is bent back to form the tang that is used to attach the rake to the handle, causing the rake head to fit flush with the handle to form a T. Hand-held, "miniature" models are available, too.

Bowhead rake (also known as *bow* or *bow holder rake):* Attached to the handle by way of two steel rods or tangs that run from each end of the rake head, bow out, and are inserted into the handle. Traditional design.

USE: Leveling out soil for lawn or garden seeding. The hard teeth help break up soil and remove debris. Also useful for spreading gravel, sand, or topsoil. An essential garden tool. When pressed into a seedbed, makes small holes about 1 inch apart, for planting seeds.

USE TIPS: When using the rake for leveling a bed, allow the rake handle to slide freely through the forward hand while pulling and pushing it with the hand nearest the far end of the handle, gripping firmly. If you grip it firmly with both hands, the rake head follows only the present contours of the bed and will not level it. The straight back of the rake can be used for final smoothing. Always leave the tines facing down when not in use in your garden.

BUYING TIPS: If you can find a garden rake with solid-socket construction, definitely buy it. Some gardeners feel that the slightly lighter bowhead rake adds a desirable spring to the raking motion. If you want to buy one of the smaller versions, make sure the handle is long enough for you to use comfortably.

LAWN RAKE

LAWN RAKE

ALSO KNOWN AS: Broom rake, leaf rake, fan rake, sweep rake, spring lawn rake

DESCRIPTION: Long wood, flat steel, bamboo, rubber, or plastic tines fanned out from the wood or aluminum handle of the rake so that it resembles a wide broom, about 20 inches or so wide. The tips of the tines are bent slightly downward. The width of some metal models can be adjusted for easier raking around shrubs and in flower beds. Steel rakes may have a spring brace on their backs for additional strength. Bamboo rakes are available in a large range of sizes, including a small one with a 6- or 8-inch fan for raking in beds and around shrubs. The width on some brands is adjustable from 7 to 24 inches. Recently a rake with wheels like a reel-type lawn mower (see pages 248–49) was introduced for people with back problems (it works on both the push and pull strokes). There has long been a model with a bend in the handle, called a *back-saver rake,* which is easy to use without bending your back. Other versions have a rectangular shape, often with rubber tines. *Floral* and *shrub rakes* are simply narrower and of lighter construction.

USE: Raking leaves, twigs, grass clippings, and other light debris. A basic, indispensable garden tool. Rubber tines are used where their flexibility is desirable to prevent damaging shallow-rooted plants.

USE TIPS: Store in a dry place. To make bamboo rakes pliable before use (if they have dried out in storage) they should be soaked briefly in soapy water. This should be done especially at the beginning of a season. Don't use stiff wire-tined rakes on a lawn, or you may rip up your grass.

BUYING TIPS: Although any well-made model is a good buy, this is one of the few cases where the cheaper product—bamboo rakes—is as good a buy as others, because they can be so easily and cheaply replaced, and some gardeners even prefer the feel of the natural material of the bamboo rakes. They are also gentler on the lawn than metal, though rubber tines are the most gentle and flexible in regard to the terrain. Plastic rakes don't rust, but check to see that the handle is securely attached to the head with a screw. Steel rakes must be of top quality only, or they are likely to come apart.

LEVELING RAKE

LEVELING RAKE

ALSO KNOWN AS: Grading rake, lawn rake, hay rake

DESCRIPTION: A 2- to 2½-foot-long board with a series of holes in it, through which sharpened 4-inch dowels (usually of ash) protrude to form the tines. The handle is stuck into a hole in the rake head and secured with metal braces. Resembles the old wooden *hay rakes,* though those intended for raking grass or hay usually have more closely spaced teeth. Also made in aluminum and magnesium, for professionals. Although the term *lawn rake* is used correctly here, this more often refers to the fan-shaped bamboo rake described in the preceding entry.

USE: Particularly useful in creating a level surface on a seedbed or lawns in preparation for seeding, just after spading has left large clumps of soil. Lighter models are used to remove grass clippings and clumps of leaves, fallen fruit, and, of course, cut hay.

USE TIP: Same as for garden rake (see page 177). This rake is not as strong as the garden rake and is intended for kinder, gentler jobs.

BUYING TIP: Be sure that the handle and the wooden tines are secure.

THATCHING RAKE

ALSO KNOWN AS: Cavex rake, multipurpose rake, lawn rake, adjustable rake, dethatching rake

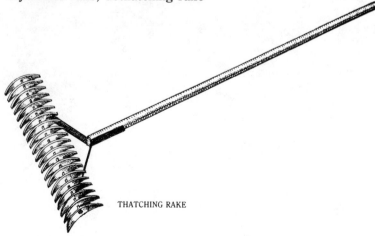

THATCHING RAKE

DESCRIPTION: A specialized design composed of about twenty crescent-shaped blades attached 1 inch apart with the curved side of the crescents pointed out. The angle of the bladelike tines is usually adjustable to fit the height of the grass. Some brands have a tilting head for self-cleaning.

USE: Removing dead and matted grass (thatch) from a lawn, permitting better growth.

USE TIPS: When removing thatch, adjust the head of the rake so that the tines ride above the soil and do not cut into it. You can clean tines easily by pushing with the head down a bit. Be prepared to work hard—when this rake cuts into thatch, it takes some effort to pull it through.

BUYING TIP: Make sure that the rake is well constructed and the rake head is attached securely to the handle. This is a specialty tool, and not every gardener needs it.

CHAPTER 7

Pruning, Cutting, and Trimming Tools

ABOUT PRUNING, CUTTING, AND TRIMMING TOOLS

All cutting tools perform better if they are kept sharp. This is not just a case of being professional or perfectionist; it also makes them safer. Sharpen each one according to its size and design: Use a hand-held whetstone or a file, or take them to a professional sharpener (look them up in the Yellow Pages under "Sharpening Services"). The best blades are "hollow ground" (slightly concave) and are more difficult to sharpen yourself.

Be sure to wipe cutting tools dry after each use, coat them with oil from either an oily rag or an aerosol spray, lubricate the moving parts or hinges, and store them in a dry place.

Pruners and Shears

ABOUT PRUNING AND HEDGE SHEARS

This is the kind of tool where good quality is immediately apparent to the user: Good ones cut better. Ones made of top-quality steel cut and last longer, too. Good gardeners know when to use pruning shears instead of hedge shears—the former is for removing whole branches, and the latter is for superficial cutting. Each type of cut affects the plant differently. Keep both kinds of shears clean and wiped with an oily rag or sprayed with a penetrating lubricant aerosol such as WD-40.

Shears made especially for trimming grass are listed in their own section (see pages 202–204).

FLOWER GATHERER

ALSO KNOWN AS: Cut-and-hold shears, flower shears (also see next entry), flower gathering scissors

DESCRIPTION: Very closely resembles regular kitchen scissors, except that one blade is thick and serrated and the other is a small, sharp, blunt-ended blade that slices into it. Other types have a setback over the cutting blade which holds the cut stem. Some brands are designed with a thorn remover and stem crusher in the handles. Large handles should allow use by both left- and right-handers. Made with a 28- or 31-inch-long pistol grip as well as hand-sized.

USE: Cutting flowers for display. Cuts and holds the bloom in the same move. Long-handled models are excellent for gardeners who have difficulty bending and reaching, such as wheelchair gardeners. Handy also in rock gardens, for hanging plants, climbing plants, or reaching over greenhouse benches.

USE TIP: Blunt ends mean you can drop these into your pocket.

FLOWER SHEARS

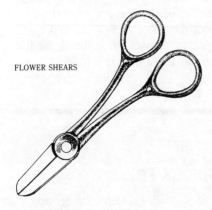

FLOWER SHEARS

ALSO KNOWN AS: Freehand snips, Japanese flower shears, Japanese flower arranging shears

DESCRIPTION: Extra sharp and sturdy scissors, some models of which have giant loops called *butterfly handles,* for the insertion of your entire hand. Other models, called *flat-end scissors,* have one broad, blunt-ended blade and one slightly hooked one. Japanese models with butterfly handles are called *Ikebana shears* and have a black, Parkerized finish; they come in either the short-bladed *Koryu* style or the thin, long-bladed *Ashinaga bonsai hasami* style (see page 306).

USE: Trimming or cutting flowers and small plants. Models with large loops are for use with gloves on, or more importantly, if you have trouble gripping, because of arthritis or other conditions.

USE TIPS: Try not to cut too much woody or extra-thick material, a job more appropriate for pruning shears. If the rivet becomes loose, see if you can tighten it by hammering it down on a metal surface.

BUYING TIPS: Better than kitchen scissors because they make a cleaner cut, helping the flower stem draw water in a vase. Flat-end scissors can go in your pocket or tool kit without danger. Butterfly handles are good for gardeners who have difficulty gripping.

HEDGE SHEARS

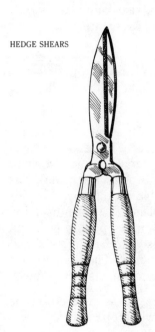

HEDGE SHEARS

ALSO KNOWN AS: Hand hedge shears, hand shears

DESCRIPTION: Large scissorlike device 12 to 28 inches in length overall. The long, straight handles may be wooden or metal with rubber grips, and the blades can be straightedged, curved, serrated, or wavy. Most shears have a notch in one blade close to the pivot that allows you to cut larger branches. (The curves, serrations, or waves hold branches in place as the blades are closed; without this design feature, branches tend to spring out of the blades' grasp.) Forged and occasionally stainless steel blades are available in better models. Rubber bumpers at the pivot point absorb the shock of the two handles coming together. Light models are available, as are long-handled versions.

USE: Trimming hedges and cutting branches up to ½ inch thick. A notch near the pivot point is for slightly larger branches. Hedge shears are not intended for general pruning, where branches and limbs should be cut individually. Hand hedge shears cut through thicker branches than power shears.

USE TIPS: Hedges should be trimmed so that the top is narrower than the bottom, and not squared off. Tapering allows the sun to reach the entire surface of the hedge so it fills in evenly. Longer blades are best for cutting evenly. You can hang shears that have a hole in a blade on a nail.

BUYING TIPS: Hedge shears are not for general pruning, so buy a pair only if you have a hedge. Rubber bumpers, which should be replaceable, make the shears less taxing to use, as does a lighter weight. Shears with serrated or wavy blades hold the branches better and are easier to use. Handle shape and finish vary from brand to brand and model to model, so pick them up and try them out first. Look for those with an adjustable locknut at the hinge, so you can adjust the tension of the cutting motion.

LONG-REACH FRUIT AND FLOWER PICKER

DESCRIPTION: A 5-foot-long aluminum pole with a squeeze grip handle on one end and scissorlike blades on the other (anvil style, where one blade has a cutting edge while the other has a flat surface against which the cutting blade works). Attached to these blades are two metal strips that come together when the blades meet in order to hold the stems of the fruit or flowers so they can be lowered after cutting. Another basic version of a fruit picker is a simple wire or cloth basket with tines on one side, on a 15-foot-long handle. This is also known as a *fruit harvester* or *fresh-fruit picker*. Head sold separately.

LONG-REACH FRUIT AND FLOWER PICKER

USE: A helpful tool for cutting dead stems, spent rose blooms, and general garden cutting in beds and places not easily reached with pruning shears. Because the cut material does not drop into the bed (it is held between the metal strips on the blade), it is very helpful for people who have trouble bending over to pick things up or for cutting from thorny plants. It is also useful in water gardening, allowing you to reach into a pool to pick out, for example. dead lily blooms or debris. The basket-style fruit picker is used just for that: picking ripe fruit. The basket holds the fruit as long as it is larger than the openings in the mesh.

USE TIP: Be sure that whatever is being cut is grabbed by the clamping side of the blade, or else it will drop.

BUYING TIP: At under $50, this is a good investment for most gardeners. Even small gardens have areas that are difficult to reach with hand pruners, and where using a ladder is not a good solution.

LOPPER

ALSO KNOWN AS: Lopping shears, two-handed pruning shears, two-handed shears, clopper

DESCRIPTION: Long-handled pruning tool that looks like pruning shears (see next entry) with arm-length handles (12 to 28 inches long), and comes with either a curved bypass cutting head or an anvil-type cutting head (see description at pruning shears, page

186). Loppers may be made entirely from one piece of steel or have wooden handles and high-quality steel blades. Recently some constructed from other materials, such as fiberglass, have appeared, and still other new models have gears *(geared* or *gear drive loppers)* or *ratchet* devices that look like an offset hinge, for cutting thicker branches than those possible with standard models. These may be referred to as *multilevel* or *compound action loppers,* versus the normal *single-level* type. *Two-handed pruning shears* often refers to loppers that have extraordinary cutting capacity. *Vine pruners* are lightweight models, and specially designed long, telescopic-handled models are available, such as the *pulley lever lopper.* Better models have shock absorbers.

LOPPER

USE: Pruning branches that are thicker or tougher than those that can be cut with pruning shears easily, that is, those between ¾ and 1½ inches thick. Loppers' longer handles give more leverage for heavier cutting than the short handles of pruning shears, and compound action loppers can cut still thicker branches.

USE TIPS: Do not twist loppers when cutting, as this will bend the blades, preventing clean cuts in the future. If you are having trouble cutting through a branch with loppers, don't force them; go for the pruning saw (see pages 192–93). Place the anvil blade on top when cutting with anvil-type loppers.

BUYING TIPS: The choice between wooden or metal-handled loppers depends upon the feel of the tool and your own preference, but the anvil type should be avoided in favor of the bypass type with forged blades. Bypass loppers make cleaner, closer cuts. Try them out and see how they feel. Many gardeners like the balance of the newer all-metal loppers, but if you are cutting branches over your head, you may feel that they are too heavy for you, and many find the fiberglass handles not quite as durable as those made of wood or metal. As with pruning shears, the longer the blade, the thicker the limb they can cut. Most loppers are graded by weight, with the heavier ones capable of doing the heavier-duty jobs and being usually of better quality. Ratchet models give you more force, which is a consideration if you don't have the strength for heavy pruning with regular models. Chrome alloy steel resists rust better than other types. Hinges that are slightly offset keep the branch being cut from slipping out of the blades, as does a hooked end.

PRUNING SHEARS

ALSO KNOWN AS: Pruners, hand pruners, secateurs, pruning snips

DESCRIPTION: Resembling pliers or short, heavy-duty scissors, pruning shears consist of hand-sized handles, a pivot point with a spring, and one or two strong cutting blades. The spring causes the cutting end to remain open when the handles are not squeezed together. The shears usually have a lock for storage in a closed position. Usually sized by the maximum thickness of the branches they can cut, such as ½, ⅝, or ¾ inch. Some smaller ones are made with short handles, sometimes called *pocket pruners,* and are often recommended for women's smaller hands. *(Pocket pruner* also refers to a plain scissors design with blunt ends that can be carried in your pocket.) The more exotic-looking designs have blades at a slight angle to the handle, or offset, for easier access to branches and reduction of wrist fatigue (it is easier to get the right cutting angle). The most refined design has one grip that rotates to fit the angle of your hand as it moves through the squeezing motion, reducing friction and the possibility of blisters as well as fatigue (the manufacturer claims a 30 percent reduction in effort). Better quality shears also have small shock absorbers, sap grooves (slots in lower blades for draining sap), wire-cutting notches, ergonomically shaped handles, and replaceable blades or other parts. Left-handed versions are available, as are *long-reach extensions* that enable wheelchair-bound gardeners to prune with ease thanks to an added lever. *Pneumatic shears,* operated with one hand and powered by compressed air, are also available from professional sources.

TYPES: *Anvil shears:* One cutting blade and one solid, flat-faced "anvil" that the cutting blade touches when squeezed shut. The cutting blade is straight, made of cast or stamped steel, and may be coated for longer life and less sticking. The anvil is usually brass, which is softer than the cutting blade, and may be replaceable. Some have a "swing" anvil that is hinged in such a way as to give the pruner a wider opening and also produces a slicing action to the cut. Many models have a ratchet device for additional force and are called, not surprisingly, *ratchet anvil pruners.*

    Curved bypass shears (also known as *blade-on-blade, double-cutting,* or *hook-and-blade shears):* Two slightly curved blades that cut when their surfaces pass each

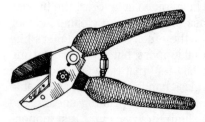

ANVIL PRUNING SHEARS

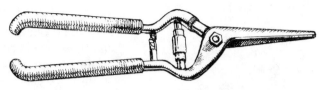

CURVED BYPASS PRUNING SHEARS

other, just like a pair of scissors. Some manufacturers call the lower blade the anvil blade. Made of cast, stamped, or forged steel, including stainless steel. May be coated. May also have a convenient *wire-cutting notch* near the hinge. Left-handed versions available, but not from many manufacturers. Lightweight version may be called *floral pruner.*

Straight bypass shears (also known as *grape shears, thinning shears, minishears* or *houseplant minishears*— if small—*all-purpose snips,* or *utility shears):* Cut like curved bypass shears, but the blade edges are straight, rather than curved, resembling stubby kitchen scissors. Cast, stamped, or forged steel, including stainless steel. A particularly pointed model may be called *needle-nose pruners.* Usually smaller than the other shears.

USE: Cutting small branches up to approximately ¾ inch thick (though generally for diameters less than ½ inch thick) and twigs from woody plants. Smaller pruning shears are designed to be used on less woody plants and small green wood. An essential tool for any gardener. Anvil types are generally used for casual or light pruning and bypass types for serious and closer pruning, though *ratchet anvil pruners* have more force for thick or tough woody plants, and there is less risk of bending, or springing, the blade than with bypass pruners. Straight pruners are good for detail work on flowers.

USE TIPS: Keep blades sharp. Pruning shears work best when the spring and the pivot area are oiled before or after each use. Don't twist them when you have difficulty cutting through something—you'll bend the blades, and they can't be bent back. Never try to cut a branch that is too thick for the shears or you will bend the blade (anvil types can cut a bit thicker branches with less danger of bending). If you can't squeeze through with one hand, the branch is too thick—use your loppers (see preceding entry). Cut at a diagonal to the grain for less resistance. This and the trowel are the most often lost tools: Paint the handles bright orange or yellow or buy them with brightly colored grips so they are easier to spot in the garden, or use a holster (some brands of shears, such as Felco, make their own). Curved blades keep the branch from slipping out as you squeeze. Making good clean cuts is essential to preventing disease.

BUYING TIPS: Anvil-type shears smash the branch when cutting and leave a stub when cutting off branches or sprouts. They are better suited to cutting up branches that have already been pruned from the tree or shrub. However, they are quite common and usually the cheapest; unfortunately, they are also often cheap in quality, though high-quality ones can be had. Look for the kind that have offset pivots which cause the blade to slice along the anvil, and for replaceable anvils. Try to find those with hardened and tempered edges.

Curved bypass shears are the most efficient type, as they give the cleanest and closest cut, right down to the trunk or branch, leaving no stub. Wire-cutting notches are very convenient if you have lots of plant ties, and if you prune for long periods of time, the rotating grip is helpful. Look for a pivot adjustment that allows you to align the blades perfectly. Felco of Switzerland makes ergonomically designed, red-handled shears that are the industry standard; they are often referred to as "Felcos" without any more description (Felco has been making them for over forty years). They have hollow-ground, replaceable blades, as a top-quality shear should have. Models 9 and 10 are left-handed. Straight bypass shears are good for light work where the space may be confined, such as with houseplants and small shrubs.

Many concerns for any type of pruning shear are similar. Ratchet-style shears have more strength in their cut and require less effort from the gardener, an important consideration for arthritic gardeners. Small shock absorbers are also helpful. Pruning shears are sold in a variety of grades determined by weight, design, and the overall quality of the tool, and you can generally bet on getting what you pay for. Left-handed shears are manufactured and very advantageous if you need them. It is unclear if Teflon®-coated blades are an advantage, though they may reduce sap buildup, but then so does a regular wiping or a "sap groove" in the blade.

Shears with thumb-operated locks are easier to use, as they allow you to lock and holster or pocket the tool between cuts.

Make sure the lock is in a place where it doesn't give you blisters, especially at the heel of your hand; it is more convenient if you can operate it with one hand while holding the shears. Shears that come apart for sharpening or blade replacement are a good idea. The longer and wider the blade, the thicker the limb the shears will cut. Look for stainless or forged steel, as opposed to cast or stamped, which are slightly rough. Buying quality pruning shears means more than buying a tool that is durable and will last; quality pruning shears produce a clean cut that is better for the shrubs and trees you are pruning. Get good ones.

Saws

BOW SAW

ALSO KNOWN AS: Buck saw (usually in context of carpentry), tubular saw, log saw

DESCRIPTION: Metal frame in the D shape of a bow, with a thick blade connecting the two ends. Available in a small range of sizes, and in two D shapes: tapered to a point at one end, and a basic, even D shape. The variously sized teeth are slightly offset to accommodate green wood. Some blades are disposable, others are longer lasting and sharpenable hardened steel. Wooden-framed bow or buck saws, now known as *frame saws*, were indispensable tools for cutting firewood in the past.

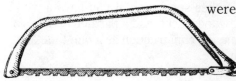

BOW SAW

USE: Cutting firewood or branches 10 to 20 inches in diameter. Each cut can only be as deep as the bow frame.

USE TIPS: Keep blades sharp and well oiled. Because of their thin blades, bow saws cut faster and easier than other handsaws. When cutting heavy branches, make a cut from the bottom of the branch about 2 inches closer to the trunk than where the final cut will be made. This prevents the bark from skinning beyond this point when the branch falls. If you intend to do a lot of light pruning, buy a tapered bow saw rather than a basic D-shaped one. This prevents the end from hitting other branches while cutting; however, a tapered saw is not good for cutting thick firewood.

BUYING TIP: A bow saw is a good investment for those people with large gardens and many trees, and especially for those who cut their own firewood.

CROSSCUT SAW

TYPES: *Two-person* (or *two-man) saw*
One-person (or *one-man) saw*

DESCRIPTION: The two-person crosscut saw has a 6-foot-long blade with a combination of two kinds of incredibly large teeth, both pointed and rectangular (called "rakers") and two 11-inch-long wooden, removable handles attached to the ends of the blade with nuts and bolts. The one-person model is similar, but only about 3 feet long, and has a vertical grip attached to the top of the blade.

USE: For serious and quick tree-felling and log-cutting. A very efficient tool with two people sharing the labor.

USE TIPS: Never push on a two-person crosscut saw, as this will bend the blade and cause it to bind in the log or tree. Wait until your partner has finished his or her pull, then *pull* the saw back toward yourself. When cutting a log on a buck (an X-shaped log stand) it is better to start the movement of the saw before the blade makes contact with the log. This gets the mutual movement of the partners going and gently lines up the cut.

BUYING TIP: Such a saw makes sense only if you have a wood-burning stove, lots of firewood to cut, and a partner to help you saw. If you are doing some log construction as a one-time activity only, then try to rent one.

CROSSCUT SAW

HIGH LIMB CHAIN SAW

ALSO KNOWN AS: Chain blade high-limb cutter

DESCRIPTION: A linked chain (like a bicycle chain) with carbon steel blades on each link, attached to long pieces of rope, one

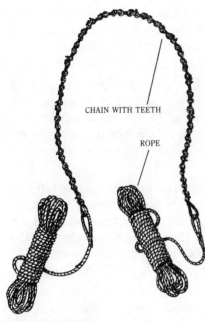

CHAIN WITH TEETH

ROPE

HIGH LIMB CHAIN SAW

of which has a weight on the end. The chain and one rope are thrown over a limb with the chain positioned on the limb itself. When the cords are pulled back and forth, the blades of the chain cut through the limb.

USE: Cutting branches that are hard to get to by ladder or beyond a long-reach pole saw (see next entry).

USE TIPS: Add your own rope for really high limbs (and good luck throwing the saw up there). Do not stand directly under the limb that is being cut. This may seem obvious but is a common mistake.

BUYING TIP: Though not something you would need often, if you have many trees it may be worth purchasing for a rare use that would otherwise mean calling in expensive professionals.

LONG-REACH POLE SAW AND LOPPER

ALSO KNOWN AS: Pole pruner, long-reach pruner, telescoping tree pruner, pole tree-trimmer, tree pruner, pole pruning saw, telephone tree-trimmer, tree trimmer, pole pruner/trimmer, pole pruner/saw

DESCRIPTION: A long sectional or telescoped pole made of wood, metal, or fiberglass, with a 16-inch or so long pruning saw or a pruning shear or lopper (may be called a *clipper),* or a combination of both, depending on the brand, on one end. Can be as much as 20 feet long. The shear is operated by a large lever attached to a long cord that is pulled by the operator at the tail end of the

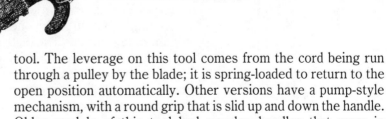

LONG-REACH POLE SAW AND LOPPER

tool. The leverage on this tool comes from the cord being run through a pulley by the blade; it is spring-loaded to return to the open position automatically. Other versions have a pump-style mechanism, with a round grip that is slid up and down the handle. Older models of this tool had wooden handles that were in sections, but today most are light, telescopic poles made of metal or fiberglass which are easily extended by twisting the pole.

(Names are used differently by each manufacturer, and some products with the same name may be quite different, i.e., one may have only a pruning shear while another might have only a saw, while a third has both.)

USE: Pruning limbs and branches that cannot be reached by hand-held tools or are inconvenient to trim by standing on a ladder. The shear cuts branches up to ¾ inch diameter. The pump-style pole pruner is excellent for the wheelchair gardener. A good telescopic handle enables you to prune branches up to 18 feet high.

USE TIPS: Stand to the side of branches you are cutting or sawing, not below them. If you try to prune a branch that is too large for the blade to cut, the blade may become stuck in the branch. Check the label to see the maximum-size branch the shear or lopper can cut. Remember to look down and around from time to time, or you'll get a crick in your neck. And wear goggles.

BUYING TIPS: Fiberglass poles are often preferable to metal ones, especially when pruning near electrical wires (metal poles are illegal in some states). If you have trees or tall shrubs in your landscape, this is an indispensable tool. Teflon-coated saw blades—a very good idea—are now available. Double pulleys are a definite advantage with the shear. Tie a handle to the end of the rope to make it a bit easier to grip.

PRUNING SAW

ALSO KNOWN AS: Tree saw, gardener's saw

DESCRIPTION: The most common pruning saws are curved steel blade saws about 14 inches long with amazingly large, sometimes razor-sharp triangular teeth and straight, pistol-grip, or D-grip handles. Some steel blades are Teflon coated. One model, a *duplex saw,* is straight, with tapered blades 18 inches long that have teeth on both sides: one side is for coarse cutting and the other for fine cutting. The teeth are usually angled so that you cut on the "pull" stroke, enabling them to be designed with more aggressive teeth than if they cut on the "push" stroke. They also cut faster and don't get gummed up with green wood. Four to 8 teeth per inch is standard, with the lower number better for green woods and the higher number better for hard or dry woods. Available in either *fixed,* sometimes called *rigid,* or *folding* models (in which the blade folds back into the handle like a big

FOLDING PRUNING SAW

DUPLEX PRUNING SAW

pocketknife), sometimes called *collapsible saws.* Rigid models are sometimes called *single-* or *double-sided,* depending on their design.

USE: Cutting branches from 1½ to 10 inches in diameter.

USE TIPS: When pruning large branches, it is a good idea to make an initial cut 1 to 2 inches deep into the bottom side of the branch closer to the trunk than where the final cut will be. This prevents the branch from ripping the bark beyond this point, should it fall before the final cut is completed. Use the folding type if you are working on ladders, so you can put the folded saw in your pocket or holster when not in use. Folding saws are a bit safer and more likely to hold their extreme sharpness because the blade is protected when folded up.

BUYING TIPS: Many gardeners have found pruning saws with the double-sided blade a good investment because they need both fine and coarse cuts (more teeth per inch yields a finer cut; fewer teeth, a coarser cut). The curved blade saws, however, are easier to use as the curve allows for a smoother sawing rhythm. A medium tooth gauge of around 8 to 10 teeth per inch does most of the work required in home gardens. Tooth edges should be beveled for sharpness. Check out the saw for balance and the feel of the grip before purchasing. Look for a saw with a small hang-up hole near the tip.

Knives and Other Hand Cutting Tools

ABOUT KNIVES AND OTHER HAND CUTTING TOOLS

Every gardener should have at least a good pocketknife for jobs such as opening plastic bags, sharpening stakes, cutting cords and string, and many similar jobs that pop up while gardening.

However, garden centers usually carry many specialized knives that are in some cases invaluable.

Before using any large cutting tool that you swing, such as an ax or machete, take note of surrounding objects that you might hit by mistake. Bushes or low branches might deflect a tool into you, or there may be some garden furniture in the way. Above all, keep children and pets away; because you are focused on your work, you might not notice them until too late.

AX

AX

ALSO KNOWN AS: Axe

DESCRIPTION: Wedge-shaped cutting tool, approximately 4½-inch-wide, 8-inch-long, made from tempered steel with a handle 20 to 36 inches long, usually of hickory or white ash, though available in fiberglass. The handle is attached to the head through the eye (a hole or socket in the butt end of the ax head). Some newer models, called *splitting axes,* have spring fingers on the sides that help split wood more easily.

TYPES: *Single-bit ax:* Only one cutting edge with a flat butt end. The handle is curved and saddle-horn shaped at the end for leverage and to prevent your hands from slipping off. Most popular model is the *Michigan-style ax,* with a head weighing about 3½ pounds. Other similar popular patterns are *Dayton,* with a slightly flared cutting edge, and *Jersey.*

  Double-bit ax: Two curved cutting edges instead of one and a straight handle.

USE: Cutting down trees, removing their limbs ("limbing"), cutting roots, sharpening stakes and poles, and for chopping and splitting logs. The blunt end of the head can be used for driving wooden stakes.

USE TIPS: Move your hands correctly to ensure that the momentum of the ax head does the work and not your back. Spread your hands at either end of the handle at the top of the swing and slide the forward hand back down the handle during the swing so that both hands are at the base when you hit the wood. *Hammer wedges* (small triangular bits of metal) should be driven into the head end of handles if the head is loose. Do not use the "heel" end of the head for driving metal objects.

BUYING TIPS: Buy only axes with heads made of tempered steel, as these hold an edge better than those that are not tempered. Avoid axes with painted handles, because imperfections in the wood or the grain of the wood may be covered up. The grain of the handle should run lengthwise and be thin and close together. Knots or swirls in the wood mean the handle is weak; you should avoid tools with these imperfections. An ax is an impact tool, so the handle, which takes the impact, is as important as the cutting head. Newer fiberglass handles do not necessarily give the tool the proper balance between head and handle. Finally, a double-bit ax is a loggers' tool and not recommended for the home gardener—it is very dangerous to use.

BUSH HOOK

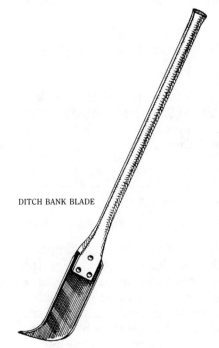

DITCH BANK BLADE

ALSO KNOWN AS: Bush ax, bush knife, bush hog, brush knife, brush hook, brush cutter, bank blade, slashing hook

DESCRIPTION: A heavy-duty tool consisting of a short, wide blade with a hooked end. The blade may be *single edge* (sharpened on only one side) or *double edge* (sharpened on both sides). The blade is attached to the handle with a heavy metal collar forged onto the blade, though one version, a *ditch bank blade,* is usually bolted to the handle (it has the same blade but with a cutting edge on its entire circumference). Handles are heavy and from 35 to 40 inches long. Sort of a large, heavy alternative to the machete (see page 198). A smaller version, called a *bill hook,* is used to harvest sugarcane or for the rough pruning of bushes; other versions are used to harvest corn (they may be called *corn knives)* and still more versions are called by whatever a manufacturer might invent, which allows for a fair amount of imagination.

A smaller version is a *weed* or *brier hook,* which is simply a hook with a sharp inside cutting edge and a long handle. It cuts when the hook is pulled toward you; handy for wheelchair-bound gardeners. Another variation is a sort of hybrid of an ax and a bush hook, called a *clearing ax.* It has a steel bow with a short, replaceable blade instead of the solid blades noted here.

USE: Clearing heavy weed bushes and shrubs, as well as trees up to 1½ inches thick. They are particularly useful in clearing overgrown lots or wooded areas in preparation for a future garden.

USE TIP: Keep the blades sharp because, like machetes, a dull bush hook is more dangerous than a sharp one as it can bounce off the brush it's cutting and possibly inflict you with a nasty gash.

BUYING TIP: This is an item to rent if you have an unusual clearing job ahead of you.

FOLDING PRUNING KNIFE

DESCRIPTION: Usually a slightly curved, wooden or plastic handle about 4 or 5 inches long into which folds a curved blade with a hawkbill hook in its tip.

USE: A well-cared-for folding pruning knife is a valuable tool for cutting twigs, small woody shoots, and any other cutting job that requires a small knife. The curved tip of this knife holds the limb and makes it easy to cut when the knife is pulled toward you.

USE TIP: Keep the blade sharp and clean.

BUYING TIP: A folding pruning knife is not just a cheap pocket-knife—a good one costs from $40 to $50. Quality here goes up pretty much with cost. Wooden handles are preferable to plastic. Check the tool out for feel and balance.

FOLDING PRUNING KNIFE

GRAFTING KNIFE

ALSO KNOWN AS: Horticultural knife, gardener's knife

DESCRIPTION: Folding or stationary (nonfolding) pocketknife with an extremely sharp blade less than 3 inches long. The plastic or wooden handles are approximately 4 inches in length, and the blades generally have a straight cutting edge with a curved top side, although curved blades are available. Some models have a stubby brass blade called an *opener,* which is used to hold bark open for the insertion of a graft. A wide range of similar types of horticultural knives are made for professionals, such as *nursery knives.* A smaller bladed knife with a blunt or stubby point is a *budding knife.*

USE: Taking cuttings from plants, called *scions,* which are then grafted onto other plants or root stock, or for budding.

USE TIP: Good clean cuts produce the most successful grafts, so keep grafting knives particularly sharp.

BUYING TIPS: Grafting is not done casually, and a sharp grafting

GRAFTING KNIFE

knife is definitely required. The criteria for buying a grafting knife are the same as for buying any knife—good feel and balance, a comfortable grip. A wooden handle is preferable to a plastic one. Also, the highest quality steel is more easily kept razor sharp. Look for a combination model with two different blades and a small brass opening blade, for spreading bark apart at cuts. This is probably not something needed by the beginning gardener.

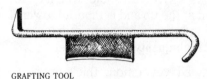

GRAFTING TOOL

GRAFTING TOOL

DESCRIPTION: Heavy steel rod, from about ½ to 1 foot long, in either of two versions: with a 2¼-inch-wide convex blade on one end (which may be called a *grafting chisel),* or with a 4-inch-long concave blade in the middle (of the longer version); both have hooked ends (two, in the case of the larger model).

USE: Splitting and holding open trees for grafting.

USE TIP: Make sure you know what you are doing before attempting to graft trees, or you may easily damage them.

BUYING TIPS: The smaller version may be included in a *grafting kit,* which might also include a *grafting knife, grafting wax, grafting tape, rubber budding strips* (for holding the graft together), and instructions for making grafts (see page 76 for information on grafting equipment).

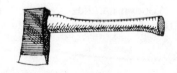

HATCHET

HATCHET

ALSO KNOWN AS: Camp ax or axe, kindling ax or axe, hand ax

DESCRIPTION: Hammer-sized single-bit ax (see page 194), usually with a wooden handle, or one solid piece of metal. Heads are about 6 inches long and 3 to 3½ inches high.

USE: Many garden uses, such as cutting poles, trimming stakes for flowers and vegetables, driving stakes into the ground for row covers and cloches. The name *camp ax* comes from its earlier common use for setting up camp, chopping wood for the campfire, and chopping and driving the tent stakes.

USE TIP: Leather holsters make the use of hatchets easier and have saved many a hatchet from being lost in the weeds where it could be stepped on.

BUYING TIPS: Similar to the regular ax. Look at the grain of a wooden handle and, whether you buy a hatchet with a wooden handle or one that is solid steel, check for weight and balance. The head should be of tempered steel.

MACHETE

DESCRIPTION: Huge knife, around 18 to 27 inches long and 3 inches wide, with wooden or plastic riveted handle; weighs 2 to 2½ pounds. The blade is curved at the tip and is tapered toward the handle, making it tip-heavy and therefore giving momentum to the swing. Blade should be high-quality carbon steel.

USE: Excellent for cutting tangled vegetation, thick grasses, vines, bamboo, saplings, and thin, woody weeds, as well as for harvesting sugarcane, one of its most common uses. It is perfect for clearing an overgrown lot or garden, tropical or not. In a jungle or other tropical setting, it is more common and more useful than shoes. Short, thick blades can be used for chopping almost anything.

USE TIP: A machete with a dull blade is more dangerous to use than a sharp one—it might bounce or glance off woody material and inflict a serious cut on the user. Extra-sharp machetes also don't seem as heavy.

BUYING TIPS: Heavy steel machetes found at army surplus stores may be a better buy than those that have been manufactured to be sold as garden tools. Wooden handles wear better and are often more comfortable than plastic ones.

MACHETE

MAUL

ALSO KNOWN AS: Splitting maul

DESCRIPTION: Looks like a heavy-headed ax (see page 194), and it is—almost twice as heavy. Made of high-quality steel. The cutting edge is much more flared and curved than an ax's, and the "heel" side is quite thick—just like a sledgehammer. Thirty-six-inch-long handle (wood or fiberglass) is typical; *Oregon maul* is a common style, named after an old brand. Weighs about 6 to

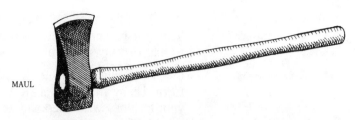

MAUL

8 pounds. Some makes have a straight triangle for a head, instead of the modified ax style. An enormous cast-iron model with a hammerlike head 6 inches wide and 6 inches long is called a *fence post maul.*

USE: Splitting firewood and pounding stakes. Its extreme wideness makes it excellent for splitting wood along the grain, and the weight makes it easier to take advantage of its momentum than that of an ax. The wider the head, the faster it splits logs (but the heavier it is to heft). A fence post maul is used only for pounding wooden posts.

USE TIPS: Be careful when using a maul to pound something, as you can cut yourself with the cutting edge on your backswing— this is a very heavy tool. Eliminates the need to use a wedge— you can use the maul's extra width to cut all the way through a log lengthwise.

SCYTHE

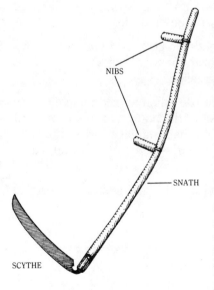

NIBS

SNATH

SCYTHE

DESCRIPTION: You may recognize this tool as the one carried by Father Time. It has a long, slightly curved wooden or aluminum handle, known as a *snath (snaith,* in England, as well as *snade, snead, sneathe,* or *batt),* to which are attached two short, straight wooden hand grips called *nibs.* The steel blade is 24 to 34 inches long and just barely curved, with the sharp cutting edge on the inside; a short metal rod called a *grass nail* crosses the inside corner of the blade and handle junction to prevent grass from catching there. Replacement handles, or those designed for specific jobs, such as lighter or heavier cutting, are available separately. Straight-handle models are made, too, and are a matter of personal preference. Blades are available in three weights: *grass, weed,* and *bush* (grass blades are the longest and heaviest). Many fine blades come from Germany and Austria. A lighter model with a straight snath and only one nib is called a *scythe hook.* A similar lightweight English version is called a *scythette,* and its handle has no grips; it may also be called a *grass hook,* which is actually a long-handled sickle (see next entry).

USE: These days, used to cut areas with tall grasses, weeds, or light brush. The scythe is an old farm tool, used for centuries to harvest hay and grain crops.

USE TIP: Swing the blade by rocking your entire body back and forth. Using the arms alone to move a scythe will quickly tire you; farmers who used the scythe for harvesting grain developed a rhythm that made using this heavy tool easier.

BUYING TIPS: Look for fine, high-carbon steel and heat-treated blades. This beautifully shaped and balanced tool can also be rented, which is a good thing to do because these days most gardeners do not have much use for one. However, you may enjoy owning a cutting tool that looks as if it came from an old farm or a museum. A lighter, cheaper alternative is the swing blade or grass whip (see below).

SICKLE

SICKLE

ALSO KNOWN AS: Hand scythe, grass hook, reaping hook, bagging hook

DESCRIPTION: A sharply curved blade, sharpened on the inside (also may be finely serrated), with a short, usually wooden handle. It may be familiar to you, shown with a hammer, as the symbol of the USSR. Models with long, straight handles are available, but rare, and have straighter blades.

USE: Excellent for cutting weeds or grass too high for a lawn mower or in areas that a mower cannot reach. A *rice sickle* is made for particularly heavy grasses.

USE TIPS: The sickle is easy to use when moved in an elliptical pattern with the pulling motion at the bottom of the movement doing the cutting. Keep in mind that you have to bend over to use this; if you have a lot of ground-level cutting to do, use a scythe (see preceding entry).

BUYING TIP: Look for a heavy steel blade and a comfortable wooden handle.

SWING BLADE AND GRASS WHIP

ALSO KNOWN AS: *Swing blade*—weed cutter; *grass whip*—grass cutter, stand-up grass cutter, weed whip, grass hook, grass trimmer, weed cutter, weed hook

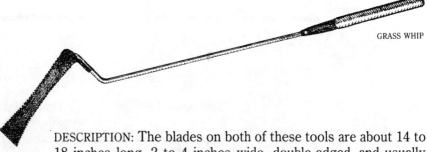

GRASS WHIP

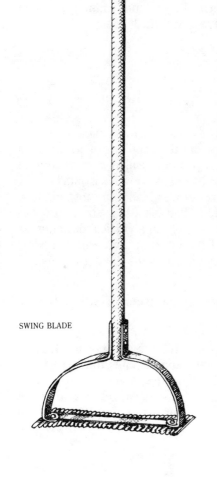

SWING BLADE

DESCRIPTION: The blades on both of these tools are about 14 to 18 inches long, 2 to 4 inches wide, double-edged, and usually slightly serrated. The blade of the *grass whip* is attached at only one end to a metal handle with a plastic or rubber grip, making it look like a giant golf club. A heavier-duty version is called a *brush cutter* (as are a few other different tools). The wooden handle of the *swing blade* is attached with two metal strips, or brackets, to both ends of the blade, forming a D. Some manufacturers consider a modified model with a short hooked blade and a 45-inch handle in lieu of the 36-inch handle a *bean* or *soybean hook;* it is quite similar to the *weed* or *brier hook* (see at bush hook, page 195), or even the same thing.

USE: Both of these tools are used for cutting weeds and grasses, but the swing blade is heavier and made for heavier plants. The grass whip is for woody or hard-to-reach weeds, or thorny bushes, and is helpful for those who cannot bend and reach easily.

USE TIPS: The grass whip is held in one hand and moved in a 75-degree arc with the power of the downstroke doing the cutting. The swing blade is used similarly with either one hand or two, though many experienced gardeners prefer to use it with only one hand. Keep blades clean. A good, cheap alternative to lawn mowers for small lawns. Watch out for surrounding bushes, furniture, trees, lights, and of course, children: Your swing is very, very wide, and you're bound to cut things you don't mean to, even if you are experienced. Take a good look at the distance of your swing when you start, and by all means keep inquisitive children away; they have a way of sneaking up on you when you are concentrating on your work.

BUYING TIPS: Grass whips can be found with smooth-edged blades, but the serrated edges cut better as they give a greater cutting surface. The swing blade is a standard farm tool, but may not be as indispensable to most gardeners. This is a tool that can be rented if needed only once. Consider it a lighter-duty, less expensive version of the scythe (see pages 199–200), easier to handle and keep sharp. Look for high-carbon steel blades.

Grass and Weed Trimmers

ABOUT GRASS AND WEED TRIMMERS

Trimming has always been one of the more arduous garden chores (second only to weeding), and grass and weed trimmers have proven essential in this task. They allow you to cut where lawn mowers can't go, such as up close to buildings, trees, or paths. The manual trimmers are relatively easy to use in small gardens, but for a garden with many areas to trim, the new power trimmers are a blessing.

GRASS SHEARS

ALSO KNOWN AS: Hand shears, grass trimmers, hand trimmers, floating blade grass shears, vertical grip hand trimmers, garden shears (this last term is incorrect and misleading)

VERTICAL SQUEEZE GRASS SHEARS

DESCRIPTION: Scissor-type blades that cut by passing over one another like household scissors, but the handles are arranged so they are squeezed in a vertical position, called *vertical squeeze* or *pump action* style, with the blades cutting horizontally. The top blade "floats" over the fixed lower blade on most models. Most handles are plastic coated. The blades of some new designs can be swiveled so that they cut in a vertical direction as well as horizontally, and are Teflon coated. Some new models designed for people with gripping problems have a hand-sized trigger grip.

USE: Trimming grass or weeds around trees or structures.

USE TIP: Wear gloves to prevent blisters.

BUYING TIPS: A comfortable grip is the most important feature to look for, and the better models have handles that are plastic or rubber coated. The new designs that swivel or use large triggers may be easier for an arthritic gardener. Floating top blade is the sign of a better shear, but the choice is largely one of personal "feel."

LONG-HANDLED GRASS SHEARS

LONG-HANDLED GRASS SHEARS

ALSO KNOWN AS: Long-handled hand trimmers, border shears, lawn shears, lawn trimmers, light edgers, edging shears

DESCRIPTION: Quite similar to grass shears (see preceding entry) but with a metal handle about a yard long. On some models, two wheels at the rear of the blades allow these trimmers to be rolled along the ground and operated from a standing position. Seven- to 9-inch blades. True *edging shears* have blades that cut in line with the handles (vertically) for edging; those with blades that cut horizontally are true *lawn shears*.

USE: Trimming grass and weeds from a standing position.

USE TIPS: Keep blades sharp and wear gloves to prevent blisters. Clean blades after use. Remember not to trim the grass too closely.

BUYING TIPS: Check for comfort of grip, above all. Plastic-covered grips are easier to use. These shears are particularly helpful if you have trouble bending and stooping, or even kneeling, and can even be used from a wheelchair. Quality shears are edge-hardened and hollow-ground.

ROTARY EDGER

ALSO KNOWN AS: Rotary turf edger, lawn edger, single-wheel edger, two-wheel edger

DESCRIPTION: One or a pair of hard rubber or plastic wheels attached to a metal wheel with sharp, pointed cutting teeth. Made with a 4- to 5-foot-long handle. When the wheels are rolled along the ground, the movement forces the teeth to cut. This edger works by cutting, unlike the semicircular plain edger (see page 143). Also available in a power version that works like either a string trimmer (see pages 208–209) or a small gas-powered lawn mower with a vertical blade.

USE: Trimming grass and weeds along paths and plant beds and the like. May be adjustable to cut a trench ⅝ to 1½ inches deep.

USE TIP: Keep wheels cleaned and oiled.

BUYING TIP: Models on which the blade depth can be adjusted for deep-rooted weeds are more expensive and not always necessary.

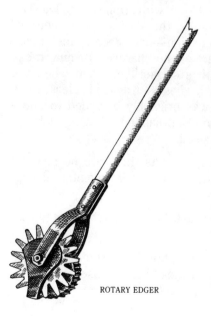

ROTARY EDGER

SCISSOR-TYPE GRASS SHEARS

DESCRIPTION: Resemble a pair of heavy-duty household scissors, with the blade and handles being made from one piece of metal. The handles are usually plastic-coated and spring-loaded to force the shears open after each cut. Blades cut by crossing over each other.

USE: Trimming small amounts of grass and weeds around trees or structures.

USE TIP: Wear gloves, as these shears are prone to cause blisters.

BUYING TIP: The horizontal squeeze action required to operate these shears is more difficult than the vertical squeeze movement required by regular grass shears (see page 202), but they are less expensive and good for use as standbys in small areas.

SHEEP SHEAR TRIMMER

SHEEP SHEAR TRIMMER

ALSO KNOWN AS: Grass shears, sheep shear pattern trimmer, singing grass shears, English clipping shears, English garden shears, short-handled grass shears

DESCRIPTION: Commonly made from a single piece of fine carbon steel, sheep shears consist of two 5½-inch-wide triangular blades at the end of a bent metal loop, with straight handles. The bent loop acts as a spring, holding the shears open when not cutting. The simplicity of the design—one piece of metal, and self-sharpening at that—is part of the charm of owning these shears. These blades cut with a scissorlike action when the handles are squeezed. This design has been around at least since the nineteenth century, and was originally designed to shear wool from sheep. Available in a left-handed version. Makes a pleasant ringing sound when used.

USE: Trimming small areas of grass. As there are no pivoting parts—only bending ones—these are easy to maintain if kept free from rust.

USE TIP: Extended use may cause blisters if you don't wear gloves when trimming.

BUYING TIP: This is a simple, straightforward tool, but people with difficulty gripping may find these hard to use.

Power Trimming and Cutting Tools

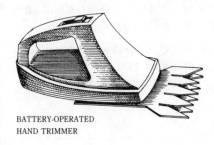

BATTERY-OPERATED
HAND TRIMMER

BATTERY-OPERATED HAND TRIMMER

ALSO KNOWN AS: Cordless hand trimmer, electric grass shears, electric shears

DESCRIPTION: Plastic-housed motor with two metal blades having sharp triangular teeth extending horizontally from it, about the size and shape of an eggbeater. The teeth on the top blade move over the bottom blade, which is stationary. Uses rechargeable batteries and is cordless. Cuts a swath about 3 to 4 inches wide.

USE: Designed only for light trimming jobs, such as the grass around trees, not for heavy weeds or woody plants. Useful for someone who has difficulty gripping. Charge lasts 30 to 55 minutes.

USE TIP: Do not try to force these trimmers to do heavier work than they are designed to do. The blades should be replaced when they become dull.

BUYING TIP: Cordless electric trimmers are relatively inexpensive, at under $50. These trimmers are helpful for light trimming or as an aid to someone with difficulty gripping.

BLADE-TYPE POWER TRIMMER

ALSO KNOWN AS: Combination edger and trimmer, power edger, brush cutter

DESCRIPTION: A variety of blade types have appeared over the years for this popular item, including a straight piece of metal similar to a miniature rotary mower (see page 249), a double blade with triangular teeth similar to the battery-operated hand trimmer (see preceding entry), or a circular, serrated blade like a circular saw. The gas or electric motor may be mounted above the blade or at the end of the handle. These trimmers have long metal handles for operation from a standing position. They were among the first power tools introduced.

USE: Heavy lawn trimming work along walls, such as brush or thick and woody weeds.

USE TIPS: The model with the spinning metal blade is capable of flinging stones and other objects, so it is necessary to wear protective clothing and goggles when using it. For the same reason, it is a good idea not to use these machines near other people, especially small ones, or pets. Most of these should be used with a lunging, chopping motion for larger branches.

BUYING TIP: Metal blades can cut woody material that the string trimmers (see pages 208–209) cannot. If you are cutting only green weeds and grass, the string trimmers are better suited to the job and safer to use.

CHAIN SAW

DESCRIPTION: Gas- or electric-powered saw with a wide, 10- to 20-inch-long blade called a *guide bar* surrounded by a continuous cutting chain that revolves around its edge. Gasoline-powered saws tend to be heavier duty and are available in a wide range of sizes and capabilities, from those for home use to production models used in professional logging operations. Gas engines are rated by displacement (measured in cubic inches, running from about 1.6 to an enormous 8.3), with the higher numbers indicating more power. Chain saws have four types of teeth: *chipper* (most common), *chisel* (typical on professional models), *semi-chisel* (a good combination of chipper and chisel), and *automatic sharpening* (for specially equipped saws). Replacement guide bars are available, as are chains.

Electric chain saws are powered by electric motors. They are quiet, do not use volatile fuels, are easy to start, and emit no exhaust fumes. *Gasoline chain saws* are powered by gasoline engines. The range in size is from small and lightweight to the large heavy logger machines. Pull-cord or electronic push-button ignition.

CHAIN SAW

USE: Heavy pruning, felling unwanted or overgrown trees, and cutting up firewood. The latter is the most common use of chain saws among homeowners.

USE TIPS: This is one of the most dangerous tools you might own, so be absolutely sure to use it correctly and carefully. Double-check the manufacturer's instructions. The contact point of the blade and the tree or log should be right up near the motor—otherwise the moving chain might pull you and the saw into the tree, causing you serious injury. Be especially careful when felling a tree over 4 inches thick: Make sure the saw does not bind in the cut, and be prepared to get back quickly when the cut goes through and the tree begins to fall. Be sure to keep the chain tension properly adjusted. Keep your blade sharp; *saw sharpener kits* are available. Keep well-lubricated with special oils.

BUYING TIPS: Be sure to consider your needs carefully before buying a chain saw. A small bargain saw that cannot stand up to the work you need it for is no bargain in the end, especially the bottom-of-the-line electric ones. A good electric chain saw that can do the job well should cost as much as a comparable gasoline one. A chain brake that stops the saw automatically should it become bound (or if your hand hits it) is a feature definitely worth paying for, but it is unfortunately not usually found on the smaller models. Look for a toothed cutting guide where the blade meets the motor on the larger chain saws and better small ones. This is used to anchor and stabilize the saw at the cut. Also look for solid-state ignition, a tip guard, antivibration devices, an automatic oiler, a nose sprocket (to reduce friction at the tip), and a compression release button, which makes for easier starting of gas models. The grip and oil button should be comfortable to you; the location of the oil button is of particular concern to left-handed people, as it is often designed to be pressed with the operator's right thumb. Electric chain saws are fine if you are no further from an electrical source than 150 feet; the advantage of gasoline saws lies in their portability and power, but they are noisy and fuel is volatile. They are the way to go, however, if you have lots of firewood to cut.

POWER HEDGE SHEARS

ALSO KNOWN AS: Power shears, garden trimmers

DESCRIPTION: Two back-to-back sets of blades about 2 to 3 feet long, with many large, moving, pointed teeth, with a gas or electric motor and handle. Resembles the beak of a swordfish. Normally cuts from both sides.

USE: Trimming hedges with branches up to ¼ inch thick, though some professional models will cut up to ½ inch thick.

USE TIPS: Trim the top of a hedge so it is narrower than the bottom, allowing sunlight to reach the bottom branches. When

POWER HEDGE SHEARS

working with an electric trimmer, be careful not to cut the power cord.

BUYING TIPS: Electric trimmers are lighter and quieter to use than gasoline-powered ones but are limited by the length of the cord. Look for double-insulated, UL-approved makes. Look also for an adjustable handle, for better balance when cutting in different positions. Blades may be made from stainless steel or forged steel, but while stainless steel is slightly better than forged steel, the advantage is so slight that the cost difference makes forged steel a better buy.

STRING TRIMMER

ALSO KNOWN AS: Rotary trimmer, nylon cord trimmer, nylon string trimmer, grass trimmer, weed trimmer, flexible line grass trimmer, line trimmer

POPULAR BRAND NAMES: Weed Eater®, Weed Wacker, Weed Wizard®

DESCRIPTION: A long-handled tool, either straight or slightly curved, with one, two, or three heavy nylon monofilament strings on a spool that are spun at high speed by an electric (regular or battery-operated) or two-cycle gas engine. They weigh upwards of 3 pounds. The strings act as a blade. The heavier-duty models are usually gas powered and have straight shafts. The cord is reeled out as it becomes frayed or broken, either by a button on the handle *(push button feed)* or by bumping the head on the ground *(bump feed),* although some *automatic feed* models are available. String trimmers are a revolutionary form of power trimming created in 1974 by George Ballas. Some gas-powered models can also take a metal sawtooth blade for heavy brush cutting. Trimmer line is available by itself in various thicknesses from .040 to .130 inch and in lengths from 40 to over 1,000 feet (that's just a 1-pound box of the thinnest line). Curved shafts are found on most light-duty models.

A recent variation is a nylon trimmer that mows as well as trims. This is a traditional-looking gasoline-powered mower

STRING TRIMMER

with the motor mounted behind the nylon reel and between two large wheels. This "nylon mower" may in time replace the classic rotary mower.

USE: Cutting weeds and long grass but not woody material. Particularly good for trimming near buildings, trees, and other solid structures in the garden. Some models double as edgers when turned on their sides; others are designed specifically as edgers. Cuts a path from 7 to 20 inches wide, depending on the model.

USE TIPS: While generally safer to use than metal blade trimmers, nylon cord trimmers are not without hazard. The nylon cord can sling stones and debris, so appropriate clothing, heavy boots, and goggles should be worn, and no pets or people should be in the area. Some manufacturers even offer shin guards. Though string trimmers do less damage to trees than ones with metal blades, they are still capable of knocking off tree bark or damaging flowers and shrubs through carelessness. A plastic or metal tree guard (see page 288) is recommended for young trees. Don't try to work a multiple-line trimmer with only one line.

BUYING TIPS: There is a large choice of makes and models on the market today. The tool should feel comfortable to use: Check the handle length, controls, and overall feel, and above all, the balance. Note if it is easy to replace the string. Models with the engine mounted on the upper end of the handle are slightly better balanced, and this position keeps the engine clean; straight shafts are more easily handled and a bit more powerful and durable. Models with more than one "whip" have a larger cutting capacity. Larger models carry more string. A built-in clutch that prevents the cord from turning when the motor idles is an important safety feature. Look for models with "bump feed," which means that the head of the tool is simply bumped on the ground to release more cord while the motor remains on. Other models require that you shut them off in order to hand-feed new cord. Automatic release models often release more than you might need, wasting cord. Electric trimmers are generally preferable to gasoline ones if your area is not so large, as they are so much more quiet (gas models are actually banned in some areas) and vibrate less. A 20 to 25 cubic centimeter gas engine is usually sufficient for most lawns and gardens; electric models have a narrow range of $\frac{1}{8}$ to about $\frac{3}{4}$ horsepower. Look for the most amperage. This is fast becoming considered a basic homeowner tool.

Maintenance Tools and Equipment

ABOUT GENERAL MAINTENANCE TOOLS AND EQUIPMENT

This is one area of the garden center where there is plenty of overlap, so here is a broadly inclusive category for lawn and garden items. Although it could be argued that shovels (chapter 5) can just as easily be used for maintenance as for planting, this is how these items are usually arranged.

Watering Equipment

ABOUT WATERING EQUIPMENT

Every garden, large or small, needs to be watered. While this is a simple and usually relatively passive task, figuring out your needs can be daunting. Garden centers sell a confusing variety of watering equipment and accessories (collectively known as *watering goods),* but basically all you need is a good hose, a watering can, a good nozzle, and if your space demands it, a sprinkler. The many other watering accessories can be purchased as you discover a special need for them.

Watering should be done on a regular and careful basis. Most gardens (especially a vegetable garden) require at least 1 inch of water a week. However, too little water is often worse than none at all, because shallow watering causes plants to be shallow-rooted, leaving you with plants that will not survive periods of drought. *When* you water can be as important as *how much* you water, since fungal infections are spread by spores that develop in the presence of moisture and in the absence of light—so it is best not to water at dusk or at night. Plants that are particularly susceptible to fungal problems (such as roses, lilacs, zinnias, and phlox) should be carefully watered at soil level, taking care not to wet the foliage. It is wise to choose watering accessories that can help you garden with this type of concern in mind.

Plumbing fittings, including garden hose accessories, are described in terms of *male* and *female,* which refers to the screw threads. Female threads are on the inside, while male threads are on the outside. Female threaded parts seem bigger because they actually house the threads, while male threads seem smaller because all that is present is the threads. Another way to remember which is which is to remind yourself that male threads *go into* other fittings, while female threads *receive* other fittings.

BUBBLER

BUBBLER

ALSO KNOWN AS: Soaker, irrigator, bubble soaker

DESCRIPTION: Rounded, fist-sized nozzle that mixes air with water which is dispersed in a gentle flow.

USE: Watering trees and large plants one spot at a time, when you want to give a well-targeted, good soaking. The bubbler is left on the ground wherever the water is needed.

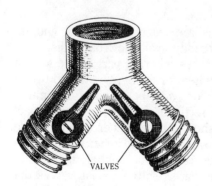

VALVES

DOUBLE HOSE SHUTOFF

DOUBLE HOSE SHUTOFF

ALSO KNOWN AS: Y-connector, 2-way hose shut-off, dual shutoff coupling, Siamese shutoff, two- or 2-hose adapter, twin shut-off, Siamese coupling with shutoffs

DESCRIPTION: Brass, zinc, or plastic accessory that screws onto a male-threaded faucet and into two female hose couplings; contains two shutoff valves in each leg of the Y, similar to the shutoff valve (see page 223).

USE: Separate control of two hoses from one faucet.

BUYING TIP: Get the best heavy-duty quality make you can find.

DRIP IRRIGATION SYSTEM

ALSO KNOWN AS: Spaghetti-type irrigation system, landscape or garden watering system, drip watering system, microtube system, emitter system

DESCRIPTION: Network of small hoses—¼ to ½ inch in diameter—with numerous small *dripper heads,* or *emitters,* tiny spray heads, and associated accessories designed to be custom assembled for each individual garden layout. They are usually made of black plastic, to prevent sun penetration and algae formation. Each brand is sold with its own accessories of *dripper heads, hose adapters, T-couplings* and *connectors* (for tapping into the supply line), *elbow connectors, hole punches, hole plugs, clamps* or *mounting clips, spikes* or *support stakes,* and *distributors,* complete with several built-in valves, and of course, *tubing,* or *line.* You may also need (or the kit may include) a *vacuum breaker, filter, pressure regulator* with hose bib connector, and *wall clips.* Usually you can find these bundled into a one-package starter kit. Smaller diameter (¼ inch) kits are for containers, and larger (⅜ and ½ inch) for gardens. Should come with appropriate connectors for a spigot or indoor faucet, and an antisiphon device. A sort of miniature version is a *drip ring,* which fits around the trunks of potted trees or plants; models are made for 6- to 16-inch diameter containers.

USE: Slow, even, efficient watering system that delivers water only to planted areas, and then only to the root zone, a drop at a time (though some accessories include misters and small sprinklers). Minimizes evaporation and delivers water at the prescribed rate and amount for your plants. Also used for application of fertilizers. Cuts wasted water dramatically. Used on potted plants, hanging baskets, planters, trees, shrubs, and vegetable gardens of all types.

USE TIPS: The latest systems are easily assembled, and the component parts should be readily available from a display at your local garden center. In cases where a part of the system is higher than the faucet, or when fertilizing, be sure to use an antisiphon *backflow preventer* or *vacuum breaker* (a common plumbing device) to prevent fertilizer from being drawn back into the home water system should there be a drop in pressure. You may also require a *pressure regulator* to lower the pressure to an ideal level. Both of these should be sold along with the other parts of the system; they are relatively small valves that screw into the hose line near the faucet. If your water source is a pond or other body of water where algae are present, use a *filter,* which should also be a readily available component, to trap the algae. Drip irrigation is particularly useful with vegetable gardens, but less so with flower gardens.

BUYING TIPS: Start with a small system and experiment, because you can always add to your system as you become more familiar with it. Look for systems that promise to deliver uniform flow and clog-free operation through the use of devices such as a pressure- (or flow-) regulation valve (PRV), or large, specially designed dripper openings. They should be unaffected by temperature.

DRIP IRRIGATION SYSTEM

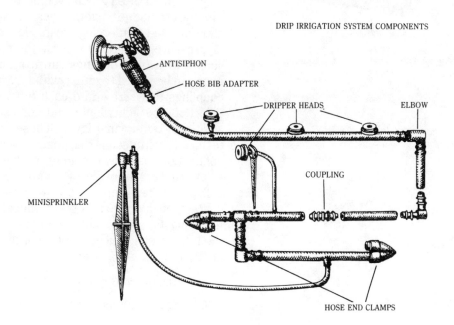

DRIP IRRIGATION SYSTEM COMPONENTS

ANTISIPHON

HOSE BIB ADAPTER

DRIPPER HEADS

ELBOW

COUPLING

MINISPRINKLER

HOSE END CLAMPS

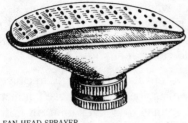

FAN HEAD SPRAYER

FAN HEAD SPRAYER

ALSO KNOWN AS: Fan sprayer, fan spray, flaring rose

DESCRIPTION: Metal or plastic nozzle, wide and triangular in shape. It has a very wide spray head with many small holes with a narrow, threaded end that attaches to a hose. Some models have a spike attached which allows them to be left on in a particular area for deeper soaking, like a stationary sprinkler.

USE: Delivering a large quantity of water in a gentle spray. Ideal devices for watering in seeds and seedlings, as well as roses and other delicate flowers.

USE TIP: Be sure that the area is well soaked when watering in seedlings; shallow watering encourages transplants to be shallow rooted.

BUYING TIP: These are inexpensive devices, but the slightly more expensive ones with built-in valves that shut the water on and off are easier to use.

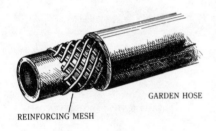

GARDEN HOSE

REINFORCING MESH

GARDEN HOSE

DESCRIPTION: Plastic, rubber, nylon, or vinyl flexible tubing $\frac{1}{2}$, $\frac{5}{8}$, or $\frac{3}{4}$ inch in diameter, usually available in 25-, 50-, or 75-foot lengths. Most often green in color, but also found in red or black. Most are made of several plies of materials and many include an integrated reinforcing mesh. Hoses are rated by the amount of pressure required to burst them, indicated in pounds per square inch (psi). Ratings run from 50 to 600 psi. Lengths of hose can be joined together with threaded brass, steel, or plastic couplings that screw into each other. Two-ply vinyl hoses are sold that are lightweight and consist of a vinyl core with an additional outer vinyl layer. Those with plastic couplings may feature a grip design that makes tightening and loosening the connection easier by providing a flange to push with your thumb.

A *flat hose* is made of a vinyl or other plastic weave that collapses when empty and can be reeled up in a more compact space than a regular hose. A miniature version for use with houseplants, called a *house hose,* is designed to be hooked up to the kitchen sink faucet (in place of the aerator) and has a trigger at the foot-long wand end.

USE: Carrying water throughout the garden.

USE TIPS: It is a good practice to roll up hoses when not in use, because leaving them out exposes them to the deteriorating rays of the sun. Be careful not to damage plants when dragging the hose through the garden; stakes or hose guides (see page 216) help prevent this from happening. And don't bang the couplings against stone, or you'll have some leaks.

BUYING TIPS: Price determines quality when purchasing garden hoses, and you should buy the best quality possible; 500-pound (psi) burst strength is a main criterion for the best. Hoses with larger diameters deliver more water faster to the garden, making ⅝-inch-diameter hoses a good buy. As most leaks occur at the couplings, look for good crush-resistant couplings of heavy-duty cast brass. Only the best-quality vinyl is both flexible, kink-resistant, and durable. The best rubber or vinyl hoses are reinforced with a synthetic mesh layer, or ply. The higher the number of plies to the hose, the better the quality; 4 is tops, though 3 is good if the mesh is thick.

Note that nylon and vinyl are more sensitive to the sun, and deteriorate after much exposure. They generally have lower pressure capacity ratings than rubber hoses; some are rated as low as 50 psi, which indicates a hose of very low quality. Two-ply vinyl hoses are lightweight and are some of the cheapest on the market, but they kink easily and are not very pliable, making them very annoying to use; they are not worth the money saved. In all hoses, look for ones sold with a 4-inch plastic *hose collar* to keep the hose from kinking at the faucet, or buy one as an accessory. At least one manufacturer offers a lifetime guarantee, which is hard to beat. Rubber hoses are more expensive and heavier, but they are more durable, resisting sun, cold weather, and kinks, and are generally considered the best—quite worth the extra expense.

GOOSENECK COUPLING

ALSO KNOWN AS: Gooseneck hose swivel connector, gooseneck connector, gooseneck swivel connector

DESCRIPTION: Brass coupling with female threads on one end and male on the other, which is at a 45-degree angle and, in most brands, swivels. Simply an extension of a spigot, but one that puts the threads on an angle and allows it to move with the hose.

GOOSENECK COUPLING

USE: Allows for easier connection of a hose and may save on hose wear at the spigot.

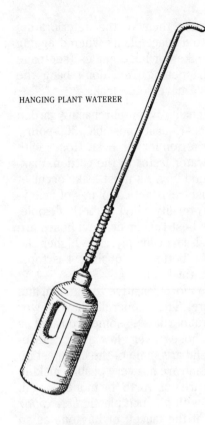

HANGING PLANT WATERER

HANGING PLANT WATERER

DESCRIPTION: Quart or half-gallon plastic bottle with a small, J-shaped, yard-long tube. Either one of two types: one that you squeeze, or one that has a sliding pump grip, like a trombone.

USE: Watering and fertilizing hanging plants up to 9 feet above the floor. Excellent for wheelchair gardeners.

USE TIP: Practice over a sink to see how much water comes out with a squeeze, or else you may find yourself taking an impromptu shower.

BUYING TIP: Inexpensive, handy item.

HOSE GRABBER

DESCRIPTION: Simple loop of heavy-gauge steel wire that is stuck into the ground; loop is a double ring that springs apart to hold a hose by tension.

USE: Holds nozzle end of a hose in a position for spraying one spot you wish to soak, such as a newly planted shrub. Easily set up and removed.

BUYING TIP: An inexpensive alternative to a sprinkler.

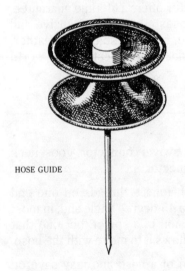

HOSE GUIDE

HOSE GUIDE

DESCRIPTION: Metal or wooden rods, which may be plain or encircled by a large roller or made of three small rollers, designed to be inserted into the ground. Some models have a hook or curved top that prevents the hose from riding up and over the guide. Others are quite ornamental, with sculpted leaf tops and the like.

USE: When placed in the ground near plant beds and plants, prevents the hose from being pulled over the bed and damaging plants as it is dragged through the garden. The hose just rubs against the guides.

BUYING TIP: Though excellent hose guides are sold in garden centers, they can also be made easily by the gardener. Strong bamboo stakes or metal rods driven in the ground can suffice.

HOSE HANGER

HOSE HANGER

DESCRIPTION: Basically a large hook or double hook with a wide, partially curved support designed to be attached to a wall, though there is a wide variety of models available. Made from galvanized, epoxy-coated, or painted metal as well as plastic. Capacity ranges from 50 to 150 feet.

USE: Garden hose storage. The hose is coiled over the hook. The curved support holds the hose in a coil form instead of pinching it, as a simple hook would do.

USE TIP: Ideal for winter storage of hose in a garage or shed.

BUYING TIP: Make sure you get a model sturdy enough to support the weight of your hose.

HOSE REEL CART

HOSE REEL

DESCRIPTION: Large spool, or reel, that is either attached to a wall or is part of a cart with two wheels. The *hose reel cart,* or *trolley,* allows you to move the hose from place to place in the yard. Capacity is about 150 feet of ⅝-inch hose, more of smaller hoses. *Estate* models hold up to 400 feet and have four wheels, like a wagon; other, fancy models have an accessory storage tray for nozzles and couplings. Reel carts usually have a 4- to 6-foot leader hose that attaches to the water supply. Made of galvanized or enameled steel, or heavy plastic, or a combination of materials. There are few alternative designs, though attractive ceramic pots with an interior cone (known as *hose pots)* can be found; the hose is coiled within.

USE: Storage of hoses in a coiled position off the ground and out of the sun (presuming they are installed under shelter), avoiding sun damage as well as garden tripping hazards. In the case of the cart type, also provides convenient transport of a heavy hose to distant gardens and out-of-sight storage.

USE TIPS: When reeling in the hose, be sure that it does not kink. Install it out of the sun's reach. Cart type may offer some relief to gardeners who do not have the strength or ability to carry a heavy coil around the garden.

BUYING TIPS: Buy a reel that is large enough for the length of hose you wish to store. Cart-type hose reels are complicated and are available in a range of styles and qualities; buy the sturdiest you can afford. Poorly constructed hose reel carts do not last long and often bend after normal use.

MALE HOSE COUPLING

HOSE MENDER

HOSE REPAIR ACCESSORIES

DESCRIPTION: A variety of items are available to replace or repair most parts of garden hoses.

TYPES: *Couplings:* Sets of male or female threads that are secured to a hose end with two screws, or an expanded collar (known as a *clincher coupling)* that is pinched down with pliers for one of three reasons: to attach two lengths of hose to one another after a damaged section is cut away (male and female threads); to a nozzle (male threads); or to a faucet (female threads). Usually made of nylon or other plastic, top-quality models are made of brass and a metal ring with a clamp for tightening that is then screwed down upon them. A specialized version of a coupling, called *mender,* has clamps on both ends and is used for patching two pieces of hose together where a leaky section has been cut out, and can be the clinch or the clamp type (sometimes called the *clam shell* type), or a new quick-connect style (see page 221).

Tape: Plastic tape with strong adhesive for temporary repairs of small leaks.

Patch kit: Small package containing rubber patch material and cement for patching pinholes.

Washer: Small package of flat donut-shaped rubber pieces that fit inside the hose fitting and help seal the connection made when the parts are screwed together.

USE: Replacing or repairing damaged hose parts.

USE TIPS: Clincher-type couplings need to be pinched down very carefully, sometimes with the aid of a hose clamp. The clamp types are easier to use. Replace washers often, as they tend to wear out. It is a good idea to keep a few on a small wire attached to a spigot.

BUYING TIPS: A good-quality hose can be repaired easily and for less money than is required to replace it. None of the replacement coupling parts are very expensive, and sturdy, top-quality plastic (not rubber) may work as well as solid brass parts. Experiment to find out which replacement parts are easiest for you to use.

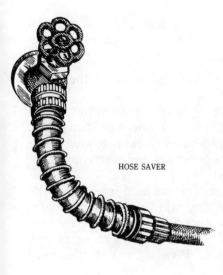

HOSE SAVER

HOSE SAVER

DESCRIPTION: Short length of hose wrapped in heavy steel spring, with couplings on either end. Attaches to faucet and hose end.

USE: Prevents kinking of hose at faucet by maintaining a gentle bend.

BUYING TIP: Excellent accessory that is often part of newer hoses, sometimes in an all-plastic version.

NOZZLE

DESCRIPTION: Hand-sized plastic or metal devices that attach to the male end (the smaller end, with external threads) of a hose. Various settings control the shape and force of the spray or stop the water altogether; many ingenious devices are available.

TWIST-TYPE NOZZLE

TYPES: *Twist-type nozzle* (also known as *spray* or *straight nozzle):* Straight shaft made of metal or plastic. Spray is controlled by twisting the shaft. Most common kind.

Pistol-grip nozzle (also known as *spray gun nozzle):* Water is turned on or off by squeezing or releasing a trigger. In most models, the spray is adjusted by screwing a knob at the top of the trigger to control how far the trigger can be compressed when it is squeezed. Others have a rotating or twist-type spray head that is adjusted by twisting the shaft of the head. A modified version, called a *trigger nozzle,* looks like a gun and is very comfortable to use.

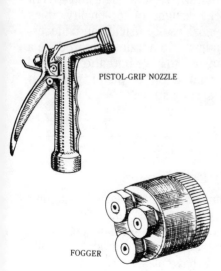

PISTOL-GRIP NOZZLE

Cleaning nozzle (also known as *sweeping, sweeper,* or *power nozzle):* Not adjustable. A small aperture causes water to spurt out with extreme force.

Water Breaker™ *nozzle:* Large, round aluminum or plastic nozzle with many small holes, like a kitchen sink aerator. Reduces a full volume of water to a soft, rainlike spray without increasing pressure. Smaller ones are made for low-pressure sources. A trademark (held by the Dramm Company) that aptly describes what it does to water: breaks it up into a fine, gently spray.

Fogger nozzle (also known as *misting head, fog nozzle,* or Fogg-It—a brand name): Finely machined brass nozzle with three small holes that create a fine mist. Four degrees of spray fineness available.

FOGGER

Seedling nozzle: Finely machined, cadmium-plated brass nozzle with one small hole that produces an extra-fine mist.

USE: Controlling the shape, volume, and force of the water coming out of a hose.

Twist-type nozzle: Can be set at a particular spray pattern and left on, such as when watering beds or transplants.

Pistol-grip nozzle: Excellent for quick spray jobs where spray consistency is not important and where quick on-and-off action is needed.

Cleaning nozzle: High-pressure tool intended to be used for cleaning patios, driveways, or sidewalks, and is not at all suitable for watering plants or gardens.

Water Breaker nozzle: Normal watering of plants, particularly in greenhouses. Popular with professional growers.

Fogger nozzle: Watering delicate flowers such as orchids, or wilting plants.

Seedling nozzle: Watering delicate seedlings.

USE TIPS: Nozzles are helpful hose attachments for washing off foliage or when light watering is required for seedlings and transplants. Hand-watering a lawn with a hose and nozzle is wrong, though; a sprinkler is the best way to achieve the 1 inch of water necessary to avoid shallow watering.

BUYING TIPS: The best nozzles are made of solid brass, which can last a lifetime. Less expensive nozzles are made of plastic or brass-plated zinc, which can rust where scratched, and are not as sturdy, although some recent designs of top-quality, thick plastic are very good. Cleaning nozzles are usually an unnecessary investment, as the other, adjustable nozzles can produce a spray almost as hard. It is not unwise to have both the twist and the pistol types of nozzles on hand. Look for pistol types that can be set to hold a particular spray pattern.

PAIL

ALSO KNOWN AS: Bucket, utility pail

DESCRIPTION: Hot-dipped galvanized metal or plastic container, open on one end, with a slightly curved, hooplike wire handle. Plastic versions may have one or even two specially channeled lips, or spouts, for easy pouring. Some fancier models actually have two lips. Extra-fancy models have plastic grips in the middle of the wire handles for carrying comfort, and a molded grip on the bottom of the pail to aid in pouring. Plastic models also come in a variety of colors, such as red, black, white, beige, brown, and green.

USE: Carrying water of all kinds and styles, including frozen water if need be, as well as fertilizers, pesticides, fruit, vegetables, compost, sand, and gravel. Secondary uses include carrying tools and even toys.

USE TIPS: Bend your knees when lifting. Carrying a full pail of water while in a hurry is generally conducive to a condition known as "wetfoot." Even if you do manage to transport the water without a spill, the abrupt stop when it is set down often sends a small wave over the edge. Practice, and carrying smaller quantities, rather than caution, is the best solution to this ancient problem. Drain metal pails completely when not in use.

BUYING TIPS: Plastic pails with reinforced shoulders can carry a heavier load that those without. In metal pails, look for a wire-reinforced top, hot-dipped galvanized finish, double-locked welded seams, and riveted ears.

QUICK-CONNECT HOSE SYSTEM

ALSO KNOWN AS: Snap-together watering system, Gardena® system, snap adapters

DESCRIPTION: Plastic devices based on a small connector that snaps onto garden hoses or accessories (like sprinklers) quite easily. Some models have a built-in valve that automatically shuts off water flow when accessories are removed. Invented in Germany a number of years ago by Gardena, a West German company, there are now quite a few manufacturers with their own similar products. Systems include adapters for attachment to conventional accessories, taps or faucets, more hose, two other hoses (Y-coupler), 4-tap distributor, and other accessories of the same manufacturer, such as sprinklers and nozzles—the entire range of hose accessories. It can also serve as the basis for an entire drip irrigation system (see pages 212–13).

USE: Quick connection of hose accessories without force or having to turn off the water at the faucet.

BUYING TIP: This is an inexpensive item and makes for a very easy-to-use system. Look for shock-resistant plastic that won't break if you step on it accidentally.

RAIN DRAIN

ALSO KNOWN AS: Rain spout lawn protector, downspout drain, downspout control

DESCRIPTION: Heavy-duty vinyl tube with many small holes that is installed, coiled up, at the foot of downspouts (or drains or leaders); the vertical pipe that leads down from gutters. Recoils automatically when rain has stopped. Similar item is a permanent stone or plastic (solid or water-filled) flat triangle called a *splashblock* about 28 inches long.

USE: Rainwater forces the device to unroll and is sprinkled over the lawn instead of gushing out and eroding it. The splashblock merely diverts water a few feet away from the bottom of the downspout.

RAIN GAUGE

DESCRIPTION: Plastic or metal cylinder with measurement markings along the side. Some types have a colored ball that floats inside. Made to be attached to a fence post or a stake away from buildings. A smaller version with a stake is made for measuring sprinkler output—it is easy to move from location to location.

USE: Measuring the amount of rainfall or sprinkling water a garden receives, particularly over a period of time, like a week. Bright floats allow you to read them from afar.

USE TIPS: Make sure you position the gauge for the most accurate reading. Remove during cold weather when water might freeze and damage the gauge. Keep it clean of insects and debris. Determine the goal of water per week that you need, such as 1 inch, and add what the rain doesn't supply.

BUYING TIP: The most accurate gauges have tiny calibrations and small capacities, at least at the bottom, and may be tapered for this purpose.

ROOT WATERER

ALSO KNOWN AS: Root irrigator, root feeder, tree feeder, tree feeding needle, deep root waterer

DESCRIPTION: Steel tube, just under a yard long, with holes in

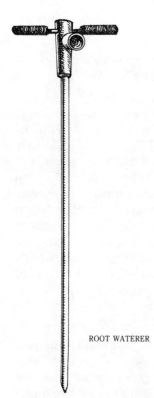

ROOT WATERER

the end, which is inserted into the soil; the other end is attached to a hose. Some root waterers come with fertilizer chambers at the top for cartridges that allow you to fertilize as you water trees and shrubs. The cartridges are supplied by the waterer manufacturer.

USE: Delivering water and fertilizer directly to the root areas of trees and shrubs where it is needed most. Ideal when compacted soil is a problem.

USE TIP: Insert the probe at the edge of the circle around the tree where the branches end, known as the *drip line.* Move the waterer about 6 feet every hour or so until you've gone around the entire tree, using moderate water pressure. Particularly useful during drought periods.

BUYING TIP: Root waterers are excellent devices that deliver the water where it is needed most, eliminating the problem of shallow-watering trees and shrubs as well as mud puddles. Models with handles are easier to insert into the soil. If you want to use the waterer for applying fertilizer, look for one that has a chamber at the top for this purpose.

SHUTOFF VALVE

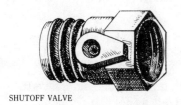

SHUTOFF VALVE

ALSO KNOWN AS: Shutoff coupling, hose accessory

DESCRIPTION: Brass, zinc, or plastic accessory that screws into female hose couplings and contains a small twist piece. One particular make is a short rubber nozzle that shuts off whenever it is dropped onto the ground, called a *water miser.*

USE: Allows you to stop the water flow without having to go back to the spigot when you want to change nozzles or other accessories. Y connectors allow you to run two separate hoses from a single water source, controlling the water flow in one or both of the attached hoses independently of one another.

USE TIP: Shutoff valves save time and labor when they are attached between hoses that are connected together. When connected to the spigot, though, shutoff valves are no easier to use than turning the faucet knob.

BUYING TIP: Brass is usually the best quality and most durable. If you have extremely good water pressure, plastic may not be sturdy enough.

SOAKER HOSE

ALSO KNOWN AS: Soil soaker, leaky pipe system, porous pipe, weeping watering system, drip hose, oozer

DESCRIPTION: A hose that contains thousands of small holes or is made of porous material so that water seeps out of it along its length rather than just at the end, as with a conventional garden hose. Sort of a hose that "leaks" over its entire length. The first types of soaker hoses were made from canvas, and can still be found in some garden centers. Others are made from plastic with small holes along one side, while some of the newer models are made from porous foam, vinyl, or rubber (often recycled rubber). Designed to be buried as deep as 14 inches or laid in a garden bed, and can be left there indefinitely—freezing should not bother it. Sold in 25- to 500-foot lengths. Accessories include *feeder sets* and *flow regulators.* Should be rated in number of gallons per hour per foot. A similar product is a two- or three-tubed flat garden hose with small holes throughout one side, sometimes called a *sprinkler hose* or a *sprinkler soaker hose.*

USE: Even, gentle watering of plants that ensures that the root area receives the most water. Watering with a soaker hose is healthier for most plants than using a conventional hose and nozzle or sprinkler as it avoids the problem of spreading fungal diseases caused by wet foliage. It also makes better use of water, as there is less runoff—it just seeps into the ground alongside the hose.

USE TIPS: Adjust the water pressure to avoid bursting the hose. If you are using a buried soaker hose, wrap the open end with a plastic bag. This prevents dirt from clogging up the hose. If you are using a flat soaker hose with holes on one side, face the holes toward the ground to avoid wetting foliage.

BUYING TIPS: A good-quality soaker hose may cost more, but lasts longer. The newer rubber or vinyl hoses are more expensive, but they are more durable in general and do not rot or decay when buried, making them good buys. In either a soaker hose or a sprinkler hose, look for one with removable end caps so that you can flush them out occasionally.

SOAKER HOSE

SOIL CORE SAMPLER

DESCRIPTION: Hollow aluminum rod about 1 inch or less in diameter and about 3 feet long, with a T-handle. Eight inches from the open end is a short step sticking straight out.

USE: Taking 8-inch core of soil from your lawn to check the moisture content (to see if you are watering properly) as well as the texture. Other things you can check for are turf quality, the presence of pests, root depth, and thatch buildup, and of course you can use the soil for testing (see soil test kit, pages 237–39).

USE TIP: Can also be used to plant tiny crocus bulbs.

SPRINKLER

DESCRIPTION: Metal or plastic device that attaches to the end of a water hose and disperses a gentle spray of water over the garden or lawn. There is a wide array of types and models, rated by the square foot or dimensions of the area they can water, such as 2,600 square feet, or a diameter of 30 to 80 feet.

TYPES: *Impulse sprinkler* (also known as *impact, pulsating, pulsator,* or *pulse sprinkler):* A small nozzle shoots water straight out, which is then deflected by a spring-loaded arm. The arm bounces back and forth, breaking up the stream of water into droplets and moving the sprinkler head slightly each time. The radius can be adjusted to cover full or partial circles up to 100 feet in diameter— well over 5,000 square feet. Usually designed to be staked into the ground, whether at ground level or on a stand as much as 6 feet high. Mechanism made of brass, bronze, plastic, or stainless steel; the base is made of the same materials and is a stake, a ring, or a platform. Rainbird is the most common brand used by professionals, who sometimes use this brand name as if it were a generic term.

Oscillating sprinkler (also known as *oscillator sprinkler):* Curved sprayhead tube, 8 to 20 inches long, which oscillates slowly from side to side as it is driven by water power. May have a built-in timer for automatic shutoff and a stationary setting. Typically waters from 2,600 to 3,600 square feet in an area 55 by 66 feet. Usually on a "sled" base.

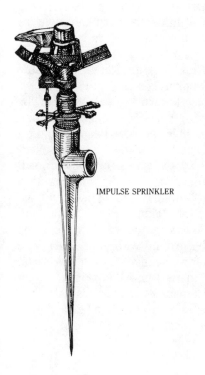

IMPULSE SPRINKLER

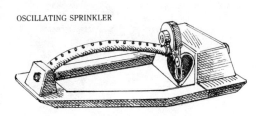

OSCILLATING SPRINKLER

Pop-up sprinkler: Small impulse or stationary sprinkler head inside a plastic or metal cone which is designed to be permanently buried in the lawn surface as part of a permanent built-in lawn watering system. Water pressure pops the head up over the surface a few inches.

Revolving sprinkler (also known as *whirling, whirling head,* or *rotating sprinkler):* Two or four arms, parallel to the ground, that revolve and disperse water through nozzles at the tips of the arms. Most have simple sled bases and must be moved from area to area of the garden; some have spikes of various heights up to 4 feet. Most models can water a circle (some can do a square) up to about 50 feet in diameter (and down to a few feet, if you keep the water pressure low). *Traveling sprinklers,* revolving sprinkers on a wheeled base, have water-powered motors that move the sprinkler along as it waters, either following the hose pattern laid out and coiling up the hose as they go *(wind-up type)* or dragging the hose behind them *(tractor type).* These can water areas as large as 20,000 square feet.

Stationary sprinkler (also known as *fixed, hose-end,* or *static sprinkler):* No moving parts; the simplest model. There are some that resemble the rose heads found on the spouts of watering cans (see pages 228–29) called, if they protrude a bit, *turret sprinklers,* or showerhead-like *ring sprinklers;* others are simple devices that merely deflect the water coming out of a hose and have a 6-inch-long metal spike for staking in the ground, and may be called *spike sprinklers* (some spikes have steps for pushing them into the ground with your foot). The simplest models are either a 3½-inch-diameter cast-iron piece with a small hole in its top, called a *centrifugal sprinkler,* or a spray head made of two circles with eyelets for spiking the sprinkler in place, called a *double eyelet, twin dome,* or *twin spot sprinkler.* These all can

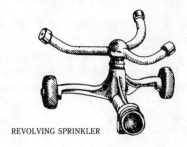

REVOLVING SPRINKLER

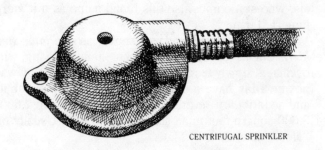

CENTRIFUGAL SPRINKLER

DOUBLE EYELET SPRINKLER

water an area from a few feet to 30 feet in diameter and in square or rectangular patterns, depending both on their design and on the water pressure.

USE: Watering lawns. Much better than hand-held nozzles, but not as efficient as soaker hoses or underground systems. With the wide variety of sprinklers on the market, it is easy to find one that sends out water in the same shape as the area to be watered. Stationary sprinklers are for the smallest areas.

USE TIPS: Sprinklers should be drained of water (or as much as can be drained) and stored in areas that do not freeze at the end of the season. Holes should be cleaned regularly to prevent clogging and assure an even spray. Adjust the volume of water that your sprinkler puts out to that which the soil can absorb easily. If it is delivered in too high a volume, much is not absorbed and the excess just runs off. On the other hand, too little water coming from the sprinkler just means that it takes longer to water the garden. Buy a rain gauge specifically designed for this or place a large open can, like a coffee can, in the range of the sprinkler as a measuring guide, and try to give your garden or lawn 1 inch of water per week. Be careful not to water foliage of plants susceptible to fungal problems.

BUYING TIPS: The better sprinklers are made of brass and stainless steel, while the cheaper plastic sprinklers are not as durable. Traveling sprinklers (the revolving type) are good for people who are unable to move the sprinkler around the lawn as needed or are not going to be present to do their own watering. However, these are among the more expensive models on the market. Some traveling sprinklers even shut off when the job is done. With oscillating sprinklers, look for those that have brass nozzles that screw into the holes along the oscillating tube. They can be easily cleaned, and replaced if they break; the end plug should be removable for cleaning, too. And they should have a filter to prevent clogging. Cheaper oscillating sprinklers hesitate at the extremes of each watering cycle, putting excess water down and causing puddles to form; make sure you get a model that is engineered to avoid this. The impulse type is the one most often used by professional gardeners. Look for models with many points of adjustment, such as a baffle plate to limit height, and part circle operation. Know the measurements of the areas you wish to water before buying—some can cover many thousands of square feet. If need be, look for one with an adjustable pattern. Try to find sprinklers that use as little water as possible, called *low gallonage sprinklers.*

WATER CONTROLLER

ALSO KNOWN AS: Water timer, water computer, water meter

DESCRIPTION: Small plastic box containing a meter that measures the volume of water flowing through, or the amount of time a faucet is open. Designed to be attached to a faucet with a female coupling end and to a hose with a male coupling end. Depending on the model, contains electronic or mechanical dials and indicators of settings.

USE: Automatic watering. Settings control turning on and shutting off water at predetermined times and/or volumes. Particularly useful for people who travel often. Electronic models can be set for multiple tasks over a long period of time; mechanical models are more like glorified oven timers and can be set only at the time of each watering to shut off automatically, usually within a range of two hours.

USE TIPS: The accuracy of a water controller is easily affected, so check the device by using buckets or a rain gauge (see page 222). The type of sprinkler you use may also affect the accuracy of the water meter settings. It is a good idea to get a *moisture sensor* as well, to prevent watering on rainy days.

BUYING TIPS: Better water meters have a bypass or override setting that allows you to set them for a continuous flow for manual watering, or to stop them on rainy days. Top models should have an *antihammer device* that prevents hammering (the knocking or rattling of pipes that occurs when water is suddenly shut off), which can damage your pipes.

WATERING CAN

ALSO KNOWN AS: Sprinkling can

DESCRIPTION: Plastic or metal cans of a wide range of sizes (from 2 pints to 2 gallons) with a spout on one end and a handle on the other. The spout end is usually capped with a round or oval sprinkling head with many small holes, known as a *rose,* which can point either up or down; it either screws or slides on. *Long-reach watering cans* have spouts as long as 36 inches. A variation on this style, called a *watering box,* is a large boxlike container with a short, flexible hose. Handles and roses are sometimes made of brass.

USE: Light watering, such as that needed when setting out trans-

ROSE

WATERING CAN

ROSE

LONG-REACH WATERING CAN

plants or watering in seeds. Also useful for applying liquid fertilizers. An oval rose that points up provides a gentle sprinkle for delicate seedlings and plants; it points down for other watering. A round rose that faces forward is an all-purpose head for watering established plants. A variation made for hanging plants is called a *hanging plant waterer* (see page 216). Watering boxes are for watering difficult-to-reach plants. Long-reach cans are useful in greenhouses, wide beds, or wherever plants are a bit hard to reach, or where you want to avoid watering the foliage and just get to the roots with fine spray.

USE TIPS: Metal cans, particularly those made of galvanized metal, should be dry when stored, as most eventually corrode if stored with water in them. Watering cans should not be used for applying any kind of pesticide—they should be used for water and fertilizer only. Plastic cans in particular might absorb any toxic chemical put in them. If you must apply pesticide this way, designate one watering can just for that purpose. The capacity of English-imported cans is noted in imperial gallons, which are about 1 pint larger than ours. Smaller cans are easier to use for hard-to-reach plants, especially those that are high up. Watering boxes are easily stored owing to their efficient shape.

BUYING TIPS: Plastic watering cans are usually cheaper than metal ones, and do the job well. Watering cans made from heavy-gauge galvanized steel (the best are treated with zinc chromate), which last very well when cared for, have been manufactured for more than fifty years and are still the most popular. Check to see if the seams are reinforced. Rose heads, especially brass ones that screw on, can be replaced with different types, and are therefore more desirable. Cans with long spouts tend to be better balanced; a crosspiece helps when carrying a full load. Brass and copper watering cans are attractive and very durable when they are kept clean and dry during storage, but are much more expensive. Always look for a well-balanced can that has a solid spout, the end of which should be at a higher point than the water level in order to prevent spilling. A collar around the top opening is further insurance against spilling. Unless you have only one or two plants to water, get something that holds at least a couple of quarts. Remember that large cans are quite heavy when filled and that they may not fit under your faucet for filling, so measure first.

WATER SIGNAL

DESCRIPTION: Small paperlike marker, about an inch high, with a point.

USE: Stuck in container soil to indicate if moisture is present or if the soil is dry, i.e., needs watering. Changes color accordingly from green to yellow.

WATER WAND

ALSO KNOWN AS: Spray wand, rain wand, garden soft spray, soft spray wand, soft sprayer, hose extender, hose extension, extension wand, showerhead nozzle, shower arm, water breaker, trigger-release lance, lance

DESCRIPTION: Watering and fertilizing device made of a lightweight metal pipe, from 1½ to about 3 feet long, that attaches to the end of a hose. On one end is a type of nozzle or spray head (or *rose),* and on the other is a grip with some type of water shutoff valve, often a pistol grip. Those designed for fertilizing as well as watering contain a clear plastic chamber on the grip end which delivers fertilizer diluted with the water that flows through the wand. Fertilizer is usually supplied by a solid *fertilizer tablet,* sold for a particular type of plant. Many water wands, such as the Gardena Watering System, have a variety of attachments that control the type of spray. The shortest models—16 inches—may be called *patio plant wands.*

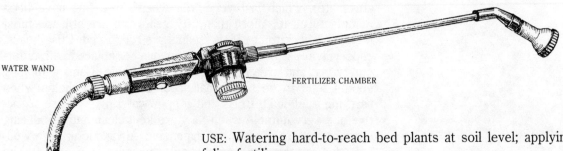

WATER WAND

FERTILIZER CHAMBER

USE: Watering hard-to-reach bed plants at soil level; applying foliar fertilizers.

USE TIPS: Keep the holes in the spray heads clean and unclogged. Drain water from the wand when storing. Change rubber washers in the connectors frequently to prevent leaks.

BUYING TIP: This is one gardening device where plastic does not signal poor quality.

WATER WICK

DESCRIPTION: Small, porous clay cone with length of wick material attached. Other versions incorporate a wick in a reservoir-type pot, or include cones as part of an irrigation network, like a drip irrigation system (see pages 212–13). On the other extreme are plain wicks (soft woven line not much different from a shoelace) that have one end hardened with a little plastic (again, like a shoelace).

USE: Continuous and unsupervised watering of houseplants. Wick end is placed in a bowl of water and the cone in the soil of a small plant container. Water is wicked into the soil as needed.

USE TIP: Start with moist soil. The amount of water that a wick can deliver is sufficient for maintenance, but not for soaking a whole pot of soil.

Fertilizing and Pest Control Equipment

ABOUT FERTILIZING AND PEST CONTROL EQUIPMENT

Keep in mind that the toxic chemicals in pesticides of all kinds should not be mixed with fertilizers or, in some cases, with each other. Equipment should be kept thoroughly cleaned and, in many cases, dedicated exclusively to the use of a particular pesticide (mark the containers well). Measuring cups used for pesticides should be treated with the same respect (some are made especially for this purpose). Nozzles, either *hollow cone* (circular spray pattern) or *flat fan* (flat oval spray pattern), should be removable for cleaning. Remember that dusts are applied with dusters, while wettable powders are dissolved in water to be applied as a liquid spray.

Most sprayed products, whether liquid or dust, should be applied only when there is very little wind. Always wear appropriate protective clothing and determine if a respirator or face mask is necessary.

BACKPACK PUMP SPRAYER

BACKPACK PUMP SPRAYER

ALSO KNOWN AS: Knapsack sprayer

DESCRIPTION: A metal or plastic rectangular tank worn on the back just like a backpack. Capacity ranges from 3½ to 5 gallons. Similar to the compression sprayer (see pages 233–34), but designed to be carried on your back instead of lifted by hand, permitting a larger capacity. A hose and wand with a nozzle on the end come out of the top, and a pressure lever comes out the bottom on one side or the other. The user holds the wand with one hand while pumping the pressure lever with the other hand.

USE: For heavy chemical application over large areas. Often used by professional foresters who need to spray large areas of forest and do not wish to be constantly refilling a smaller sprayer.

USE TIPS: Clean nozzles and tank well before storing. Because backpack sprayers hold more solution than others, do not put in more chemical than you really need for a given job. To do so is obviously wasteful and may even be dangerous, as the disposal of such a concentrated chemical is very difficult to do safely (the liquid is concentrated because it was intended to be sprayed, or dispersed lightly over a large area). If poured in one place, it may enter the water supply.

BUYING TIPS: Heavy duty—not often needed by home gardeners. You might consider this item if you have large wooded areas that require regular spraying, because it is more convenient than a compression type that you have to put down and pick up every time you change locations. Look for a large pumping handle, which is easier to use. Don't get too large a size: A gallon of water weighs about 8 pounds. Look for a model that can be easily converted to be used by either left-handed or right-handed people.

BARK SPUD

BARK SPUD

DESCRIPTION: Hand tool with a 2-by-4-inch flat metal blade, sharpened on its three sides, and a short wooden handle; overall length is about a foot. Usually solid-socket construction.

USE: Removing bark from dead or old trees or fence posts to eliminate insect attraction. Heavier models can be used like a big knife to hack off small branches and the like.

CAN SPRAYER

CAN SPRAYER

ALSO KNOWN AS: Bottle sprayer, hand sprayer, plunger duster, piston duster

DESCRIPTION: Hand-held sprayer consisting of a metal tube about 10 to 12 inches in length, into which a plunger is inserted, much like a bicycle pump. At the other end of the sprayer is a can or bottle that holds the chemical to be sprayed. Works with a pumping action, much like an atomizer. Some are *intermittent sprayers* (spray only on the forward motion) and others are *continuous sprayers* (spray steadily because of pressure built up from pumping).

USE: Spraying liquids, be they pesticides, fertilizers, detergents, water, or any other household or garden liquids.

USE TIPS: If the sprayer is used for toxic chemicals it should not be used for other things, especially not fertilizer or any foliar spray. Only oil-based sprays should be used in intermittent sprayers.

BUYING TIP: Look for models with adjustable nozzles that are easily cleaned and corrosion-resistant.

COMPRESSION SPRAYER

COMPRESSION SPRAYER

ALSO KNOWN AS: Pump sprayer, pump-type sprayer, compressed-air sprayer, pressure sprayer, sprayer/mister, hydraulic hand sprayer

DESCRIPTION: Metal or plastic tank, usually about 2 feet tall and about 8 inches in diameter, equipped with some kind of pump. Capacity ranges from 1 to 4 gallons of liquid, but 1½ gallons is typical. A short hose is attached to a wand with a spray head with an adjustable nozzle and a squeeze handle. Chemicals are mixed to the correct dilution rates before being poured into the tank. The sprayer is then closed and the pressure in the tank is pumped up by hand. Perhaps the most common type of sprayer. A smaller version, a *pressurized hand sprayer,* is a sturdy quart-sized plastic bottle in which compression is provided by a vertical hand pump knob on top, and a cordless electric model is now available as well.

USE: Applying chemicals to the garden or lawn, or in the case of the smaller ones, misting plants. Because of their light weight and portability, compression sprayers are used in areas of a garden beyond reach of a hose.

USE TIPS: Toxic substances should not be used in sprayers that are also used for fertilizers. Fine mist spraying should be done only on a windless day. Mix only the amount of chemical that you need and use it up completely before washing out the sprayer. Many plastic compression sprayers use a leather plunger cup (the disk that builds up the pressure when the sprayer is pumped) that needs to be kept oiled to ensure a tight fit and good pressure. If possible, take the sprayer apart to clean it. Don't ever leave a compression sprayer in the sun or near a heat source—it might explode, or in any case release its contents with much more pressure than you intend. Always let the pressure out when you are done using it.

BUYING TIPS: Plastic tanks can absorb chemicals; metal tanks do not. Plus, metal wears better. If you have a need for a compression sprayer only infrequently, or for very small amounts, the cheaper plastic types will probably be satisfactory, though there are a few excellent plastic makes on the market with permanently fused couplings and removable filters. Look for a nozzle with a setting that produces an extremely fine mist—you'll use less chemical. High pressures (up to 150 pounds) are helpful in creating fine mists.

HAND-CRANKED DUSTER

DUSTER

DESCRIPTION: Small plastic or metal housing with a container for pesticide and a pump or crank handle.

TYPES: *Pump duster* (also known as *hand pump* or *plunger duster):* Looks like a bicycle air pump, with a rigid tube instead of a hose. Capacity ranges from a few ounces to a few pounds.

Hand-cranked duster (also known as *crank, hand crank,* or *rotary duster):* Plastic or metal hopper with a crank on one side and a long, wide barrel. Squirrel-cage type fan. Capacity ranges from less than 1 to over 9 pounds. Tubes have flat ends for dispersal of dust, and may be supplied in various shapes and models.

USE: Dispersing dusts over foliage at close range (around 2 feet) in small gardens and greenhouses. Pumps are used for the most accurate applicators.

USE TIPS: Simple to operate, as most pesticide dusts can be used without mixing, especially as opposed to a sprayer, where they must be mixed with water for each use. However, dusters are not as accurate or efficient as liquid sprayers. Make sure you use them only when a wind is not blowing. Pump-type dusters can spray the undersides of leaves

BUYING TIP: Generally inexpensive. All parts should be noncorrosive.

FERTILIZER SIPHON

ALSO KNOWN AS: Hose-on

DESCRIPTION: Small metal or plastic device with female threads on both ends. Designed to be screwed onto a faucet and connected to a garden hose, with a small hose that comes out its side that is placed in a container of liquid fertilizer. The force of the water running from the faucet through the garden hose draws the fertilizer mixture into the flow through natural siphon action.

USE: A simple way to fertilize while watering. Especially useful when applying concentrated fertilizers, as it eliminates premixing.

USE TIPS: Should be clean of all products and dried for storage. Sometimes siphon devices can be used for applying pesticides, but those used for this purpose should never be used for fertilizing. The water to fertilizer ratio can range from 16 parts water to 1 part fertilizer, to 1 tablespoon of fertilizer per gallon of water that is being applied to the garden—so read the directions.

BUYING TIP: Siphons made of brass are usually better than those of plastic.

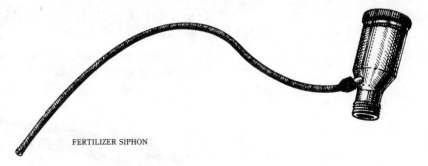

FERTILIZER SIPHON

HAND SPRAYER

HAND SPRAYER

ALSO KNOWN AS: Utility sprayer, pressure mister, sprayer/ mister, plant mister, plant sprayer, trigger sprayer, sprayer dispenser, all-purpose sprayer

DESCRIPTION: From pint- to quart-sized plastic or metal bottle with trigger spray head, adjustable from a wide, fine mist to a coarse spray to a steady stream of liquid. An adjustable model that makes mist only is called a *mister.* The pumping action of the trigger sucks up the liquid from the bottom through a small tube. Triggers and longer tubes are sold separately for dispensing from your own gallon containers.

USE: Spraying water or anything mixed with it, such as fertilizers or pesticides, in small quantities and at targeted areas. Good for misting tropical plants. Not bad for wetting clothes when ironing, either (just make sure that there are no unwanted chemicals inside when you start on your fine garments).

USE TIPS: Don't mix fertilizers and pesticides. If you ever use these for strong chemicals, note this on a label and try to use the container for this only.

BUYING TIPS: Prices vary widely—this should be an inexpensive item. However, better ones can be taken apart for cleaning.

HERBICIDE APPLICATOR

POPULAR BRAND NAME: Killer Kane

DESCRIPTION: Yard-long plastic tube with small plunger on one end. Herbicide tablet is inserted into tube that is then filled with water; when plunger is pushed in by pushing the tube down onto it, herbicide is released. The amount that is released with each "hit" is adjustable.

USE: Accurate application of herbicide to dandelions and crabgrass in a lawn.

BUYING TIP: One of the safer and more economical ways to apply herbicide, as nothing is likely to go astray of the intended target.

HERBICIDE APPLICATOR

HOSE-END SPRAYER

HOSE-END SPRAYER

ALSO KNOWN AS: Hose sprayer, lawn and garden sprayer (incorrect—too general)

DESCRIPTION: Glass or plastic container with spray nozzle (usually made of plastic) built into a top designed to be attached to the male end of a hose. Like a big atomizer, the container holds the product to be sprayed. There is some type of valve to control the outflow, and while most nozzles on these sprayers are set to disperse the mixture only at a certain ratio, some nozzles can be adjusted to change the ratio of the product to water. The nozzle usually controls the type of spray as well. Should contain an antisiphon backflow-preventer device so chemicals don't get sucked back into the home water supply should there be a drop in water pressure. The container may hold only a pint or two, but the solution is made from a concentrate that can be diluted to make up to about 100 gallons of chemical spray. Many chemical products are now available in plastic containers with caps that act as disposable hose-end sprayers. Those designed for use with fertilizers are larger than those intended for pesticides.

USE: Spraying concentrated fertilizers or pesticides, depending on the design.

USE TIPS: Sprayers that are used for pesticides should not be used for fertilizers. Containers and nozzles should be washed thoroughly and dried after each use. Follow the dilution ratio carefully for the sprayer and chemical product you are using.

BUYING TIPS: Inexpensive and efficient product. Determining the correct dilution rate is often the most difficult part of using these sprayers, so purchase a sprayer with clear instructions and measurement marks on the container that are easy to read. Sprayers that have nozzles which can change the dilution ratio cost more, but may be worth the price. Glass containers may be breakable, but they do not absorb the chemicals that are put into them. Inexpensive and very helpful. Products in disposable hose-end sprayers are very convenient but, because they are prediluted, are likely to cost more per use.

SOIL TEST KIT

DESCRIPTION: A wide variety of kits are on the market, with an equally wide range of prices and types. Some are electronic probes *(pH meters),* some are paper products (usually *litmus tests),* some are elaborate portable laboratories with test tubes, filters, funnels, and testing chemicals for over five hundred tests, and some are low-priced kits that test only for one nutrient at a time. A professional accessory is a *soil probe* or *soil core sampler,* a long tube with a large T-handle for taking core samples of soil.

USE: Testing soil for pH (degree of acidity or alkalinity) and, in the cases of the more advanced kits, nutrients. The end result guides you in your choice of fertilizers and soil conditioners in your effort to build the right soil for your garden. Directions are supplied with each kit, but typically you dig out a small sample of soil and mix it with water and the various chemicals supplied, then watch for it to turn a particular color. Litmus paper tests are made by simply putting the paper in contact with the soil and waiting for it to turn a color that indicates a particular pH level.

USE TIPS: Follow directions carefully, and take soil samples properly. Most tests require that you dry out your soil first, which may take a few days. The most inexpensive probe-type meters may be inaccurate—back up your readings with a full test.

BUYING TIPS: For the average gardener, it is easier and more accurate to send a soil sample to your local Cooperative Extension office (see appendix C), though some of the tests, like the meter or litmus paper roll, are very simple to use.

TROMBONE SPRAYER

ALSO KNOWN AS: Slide-type sprayer, slide sprayer, slide pump sprayer, lance, spray lance

DESCRIPTION: A type of pump consisting of two tubes, one inserted in the other, which are pushed and pulled apart. (The British term for the spraying tube is *lance.*) One end of the

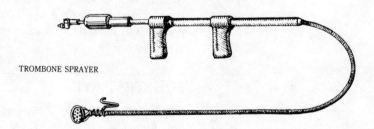

TROMBONE SPRAYER

sprayer is attached to a hose that is placed in the container of the chemical being sprayed. The pushing and pulling of the cylinders builds up pressure that then propels a long stream out of the sprayer. The pump works with both the push and pull stroke, making for an even spray. The nozzle can be adjusted to emit anything from a fine mist to a long jet.

USE: Spraying trees or tall shrubbery. These have the longest reach of all the sprayers.

USE TIP: Keep nozzles cleaned and moving parts well oiled. Empty and clean completely before storing.

BUYING TIPS: The best of the trombone sprayers is made of brass, with the nozzles also of brass. Some models have a grip-type handle attached to both of the sliding tubes that makes it easier to pump.

Composting and Mulching Equipment

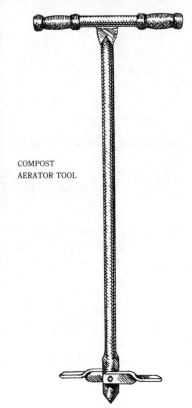

COMPOST
AERATOR TOOL

ABOUT COMPOSTING AND MULCHING EQUIPMENT

The following products are sold at many garden centers to help the gardener recycle organic material that all too often is simply thrown away or to process material into an easily decomposable state.

COMPOST AERATOR TOOL

ALSO KNOWN AS: Compost tool, aerator

POPULAR BRAND NAME: Compostool

DESCRIPTION: A 30-inch metal shaft with a T-handlebar about 12 inches long, usually with vinyl grips. The tip has small hinged paddles that fold up flat when the tool is inserted into a compost bin or pile. The paddles open up to turn the compost as the tool is pulled and twisted out of the bin.

USE: To open, aerate, and turn a compost pile. The tool is considerably easier to use than a fork.

USE TIP: Keep clean and dry when not in use. Use every few days.

BUYING TIP: Check around, as the same tool may be sold at different places at prices ranging from $13 to $20.

COMPOST BIN

COMPOST BIN

ALSO KNOWN AS: Composter

DESCRIPTION: Wood, solid metal, wire, or plastic container where organic material, such as leaves, grass clippings, and kitchen garbage, is kept during the process of decomposition. Many ingenious designs have been developed around the world for the purpose of making compost. Some plastic bins resemble barrels or large garbage cans with vented sides. A drum version, called a *compost tumbler,* is mounted on a metal frame, allowing the drum to revolve and turn the compost, which speeds up the decomposition action without your having to use a fork or other tool. The simplest model is just a large, vented, heavy-duty garbage bag. Composters usually are covered to keep out rain, and have holes that ensure air circulation and ventilation, a necessity for proper decomposition. Sides afford an element of insulation, increasing the heat within, and have some sort of opening for easy removal of compost.

USE: Contains both compost and the heat compost generates (from the bacteria breaking down the organic matter); certain designs (the drum models) facilitate the composting process with movement and any design with a cover helps keep the compost dry. Most can make compost in around twenty-one days.

USE TIPS: Place on a level surface, and make sure it is located in a place convenient for the continuous addition of raw material. Core temperatures may be over 160° F, so be careful to keep it away from any materials, organic or inorganic, that should not be exposed to such levels of heat.

BUYING TIPS: Because of all the competition and innovation in this field, be sure to shop extensively for the best deal. Drum-type models should revolve easily; some of the better models hold as much as 18 bushels. Popular commercial models go for around $100, but many garden books have designs for bins you can build yourself. Perhaps the easiest are either made from a cylinder of wire mesh or by cutting holes in a 30-gallon garbage can. Still, the more refined models do speed up the process and require less room and effort than the cruder homemade versions. Look for something that is easy to remove the compost from, and easy to stir up.

COMPOST STARTER

ALSO KNOWN AS: Compost maker

DESCRIPTION: Bacteria and other microscopic soil organisms in a powder form, sold in containers (2 pounds is typical) as well as tablets. Some brands are for composting specific materials only, such as for leaves or grass clippings.

USE: Added to the compost pile or bin to speed up the process of decomposition and to assure a balanced blend of essential nutrients.

USE TIP: Use the appropriate amount for the size of your compost bin and wet in well.

BUYING TIP: Compost starters are available under a variety of trade names, so shop around. Prices vary a great deal, and smaller packages may or may not be a bad deal, depending on how much compost can be created per pound of the product used—some 2-pound boxes make half a ton of compost, others make 2½ tons; one brand's 6-ounce package is good for "tons" of compost, and so on.

GARDEN SIEVE

GARDEN SIEVE

ALSO KNOWN AS: Soil sieve, riddle (British term)

DESCRIPTION: A steel mesh screen strung over a rectangular or round frame, with legs in the case of larger models, or merely a plastic tub with an open grid for a bottom. The frame may be made of plastic, metal, or wood. Before they were commercially manufactured, gardeners made their own sieves from ¼ inch galvanized mesh (such as hardware cloth) nailed to a wooden box frame. One type, called a *Roto-Sieve,* has a crank on its top, sort of like an oversized flour sifter/turntable.

USE: Sifting out large particles from compost before using it in flower beds or soil mixes.

USE TIP: If compost is too wet, it is sticky and does not sift well. Compost should be moderately dry and crumbly for sifting.

BUYING TIPS: Look for a sturdy, well-made sieve constructed from material that will not rust. You may wish to have a couple of sieves with different mesh sizes. On the other hand, it is not difficult to make your own, and a flour sieve is good for small quantities of very fine soils, needed for indoor seed starting.

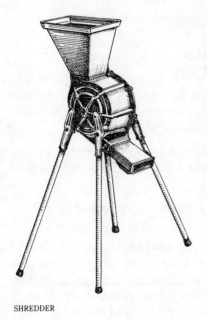

SHREDDER

SHREDDER AND CHIPPER

ALSO KNOWN AS: Mulcher, grinder

DESCRIPTION: Gasoline or electric motor with a cutting mechanism contained inside a chute, into which you feed leaves or branches.

A *shredder* has a spinning interior drum with small *hammers* (known as the *hammer mills system)* or nylon lines called *flails* that break up organic material when it comes in contact with them. Shredders work well on leaves, small twigs, and other light plant material. They tend to be small, consisting of a plastic or metal tube, about a foot and a half in diameter, on legs that make them waist high, with a ¼ or ½ horsepower electric motor. Some popular models weigh about 15 pounds and can be placed directly over a plastic bag, garbage can, or compost pile. They can reduce eight large trash bags of leaves to one.

Chippers are armed with a blade or many blades that transform heavier woody material, including large branches, into a load of chips. These tend to be large and some models can be enormous, almost industrial machines.

Shredder/chippers are machines that shred leaves and other plant material as well as chip woody material. Machines that are sold as shredder/chippers usually work with some type of blade mechanism, but some machines have two separate chutes, one for shredding and one for chipping, with both hammers and blade(s).

USE: Shredding and chipping garden debris, both to rid the garden of large piles and to create raw material for compost (the smaller pieces) or mulch (the larger pieces). Shredded compost material decomposes much more rapidly than if left whole.

USE TIPS: Shredders and chippers can be hazardous machines, and safety precautions should be followed strictly, such as using goggles and gloves and keeping hands away from the blades and hammers. Wear tight-fitting clothes to prevent anything from getting caught in the mechanism. Don't force a machine to chip larger branches than it is intended to accommodate.

BUYING TIPS: Most gardeners can get by with one of the smaller electric shredder/chippers unless they have a large estate. Shredder/chippers at bargain prices are probably not a good buy—expect to pay $100 to over $200 for a well-built, versatile, reliable machine. Twelve- to 16-gauge steel is a sign of quality, as opposed to sheet metal. Look for safety features such as lids and baffles or feeding chutes that make it impossible to insert your hand near the cutting devices (these features include small diameter chutes, or chutes longer than your arm, and the like). Check out the size of the shredding hopper, the height of the shredder section, and the maximum diameter wood it can take—in short, the ease of feeding. Narrow feeder chutes are safer but slower to use. This is a major purchase, so ask for a demonstration of the machine you are considering. Wheeled units are more convenient to use. Look also for cleaning access.

WORMS

ALSO KNOWN AS: Red wigglers, *Lumbricus rubellus,* bed run worms

DESCRIPTION: Red earthworms, usually around 6 to 8 inches in length.

USE: Help break down kitchen scraps and other compost material rapidly. Result is known euphemistically as *worm castings* (see page 12) and is an excellent soil conditioner.

USE TIP: Prepare a tub with plenty of vegetable scraps and composting material before purchasing these worms. Check a book on organic gardening for information on raising them.

BUYING TIP: Though available through mail-order firms, the survival rate of the worms is higher if you can purchase them from a garden center. Fish bait shops are an alternative source.

Lawn and Yard Care Equipment

AERATOR

ALSO KNOWN AS: Soil digger

DESCRIPTION: A long-handled metal tool with two or four hardened steel spikes on the working end and a crossbar grip. The spike end is forced into the soil by stepping on the tool, much as one would a shovel.

TYPES: *Sod coring aerator:* Spikes are hollow tubes that remove plugs of earth when forced into the lawn.
    Spiked (or *spike*) *disk* (or *disc*) *aerator:* Consists of a disk with numerous spikes protruding from it that is

LAWN AERATOR SANDALS

rolled over a lawn by pulling or pushing, by hand or with a small tractor.

Lawn aerator sandals: Spiked platforms that are strapped onto your shoes like roller skates and worn while you walk around the lawn (such as while mowing).

USE: Opening up sections of lawn where the soil has become compacted by traffic or nature, or for cultivating heavy soils without disturbing the soil structure. Also may kill some grubs.

USE TIPS: Hollow tube spikes should be kept open; remove any plug of soil that becomes trapped in them. Remember to remove aerator sandals from your feet before entering your house— they're not great for floors.

BUYING TIP: If the entire lawn is in need of aeration, it is time to consider tilling and reseeding or sodding. The spiked disk aerators cost more than most gardeners can justify.

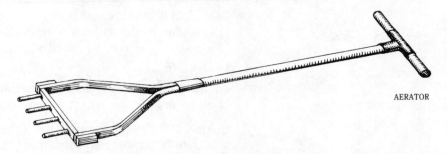

AERATOR

BAGS AND ACCESSORIES

ALSO KNOWN AS: Lawn and leaf bags, garbage bags

DESCRIPTION: Large black, gray, white, brown, or green plastic bags, varying in thickness from 1 to 4 mil and with an average capacity of about 6 bushels or 30 gallons, the size of a standard large garbage can. Available up to 55-gallon capacity. Some brands are enormous, up to 45 by 96 inches, sometimes called *banana bags.* Now available in biodegradable plastic. Accessories include a plastic hoop, about 2 feet in diameter, which clamps onto the edge of the opening of the bag to hold it open for loading, and a stand or small two-wheel cart, or caddie, similar to a baggage cart, which holds the hoop and bag. Enormous plastic bins that look like giant garbage cans are used by professional landscapers, but can be found in some garden centers, especially those that have their own landscaping business. They are usually green.

USE: Bagging leaves, grass, or garden clippings for disposal. Hoops and carts make the process more efficient, especially for people who have trouble lifting large objects. Biodegradable bags are required in some communities where they are trying to cut down on landfill debris.

USE TIPS: If you are planning to use plastic bags for hedge trimmings, be sure to cut the branches into very small pieces or they will pierce the bags and prevent you from filling them with any appreciable quantity. When disposing of concrete or plaster rubble, or gravel fill, just put a little in each bag so you can handle them easily.

BUYING TIP: Professional bins are not all that expensive. 1.5 mil bags are light and tear easily; 3 or 4 mil is heavy duty. Look for bags with no seams. A reusable alternative to bags is a 7- or 10-foot-square piece of reinforced plastic or burlap, with handles, which lays flat on the ground while you sweep or rake leaves and garden refuse onto it; the corners are easily gathered together for transportation. These are often sold in packages as *totes,* or *burlap squares* (see page 284).

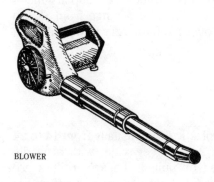

BLOWER

BLOWER

ALSO KNOWN AS: Leaf blower, blower/vac

DESCRIPTION: Electric- or gasoline-powered 5 to 10 horsepower motor with a large tube or accordion hose attached, much like a powerful canister vacuum cleaner with the hose attached to the outflow vent. Some of the smaller blowers are designed to be hand held and are more often powered by electricity (some also may have shoulder straps). Cordless models are available, and may be called *electric brooms.* Larger (usually gas-powered) blowers designed to fit on the back with straps are known as *backpack blowers.* The largest are wheeled contraptions resembling lawn mowers. A number of attachments that resemble large vacuum cleaner heads fit onto the hose; some work as misters or sprayers. A variation of the blower is the *power wand,* a multipurpose tool with the motor at the ground end that has a blower attachment, though certain models have *gutter cleanout* attachments. Some are convertible to vacuums, complete with a cart for the leaf bag.

USE: Blowing away leaves, debris, water on patios and tennis courts, and even light snow, as a substitute for a vigorous sweeping, shoveling, or raking. Vacuums can pick up light debris like leaves and some models shred them for mulch. Replaces both rake and broom for the handicapped or gardeners with bad backs.

USE TIPS: Wear goggles and ear protectors when operating a blower. The latter are especially important if you are operating a powerful gasoline-driven blower, which is quite noisy (and is banned in some areas). Never point the nozzle of a blower toward people.

BUYING TIPS: If you want to blow debris and leaves from beds but leave the mulch, look for one of the less powerful blowers, probably an electric one. If you have heavy leaf work to do, consider the more powerful gasoline-powered blowers. Look for a 16-gauge cord on electric blowers, and adjustable speed. The throttle should fit your hand; some models are adapted for left-handed users. Air speed is one feature by which to measure blowers, if you need to compare. Those who garden in small spaces can find little justification for the expense of this power tool in any case. Test them to get the feel, first. Certain models have the power unit at ground level, which may be harder to use because of clogging with leaves. Electric models are much quieter and vibrate less than gas-powered models. Shop around—there is much competition here. Prices can range from $25 to $75 for average models up to over $150 for very powerful ones.

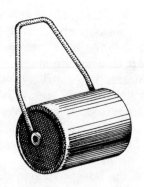

LAWN ROLLER

LAWN ROLLER

ALSO KNOWN AS: Roller

DESCRIPTION: Large metal or plastic drum, usually from 14 to 24 inches in diameter and from 2 to 3 feet wide, with a handle attached so it can be pushed or pulled. Today's rollers are hollow and are designed to be filled with water when they are used, making them lighter to transport and store. Old-fashioned ones were filled with cement, and were often homemade.

USE: Preparing a lawn for seeding or sodding or for rolling out sod after it is planted to ensure good root contact with the soil.

USE TIPS: Roll a seedbed both horizontally and vertically to ensure a smooth, level surface. Adjust the amount of water to a weight that compacts the soil properly—when walking on the lawn after rolling, you should leave slight footprints.

BUYING TIP: Rent a roller instead of buying one, unless you are likely to reseed a lawn or seedbed regularly.

LAWN SWEEPER

LAWN SWEEPER

ALSO KNOWN AS: Push-type lawn sweeper, lawn sweep

DESCRIPTION: A long drum about 8 inches in diameter and 20 to 30 inches long, fitted around an axle, with rows of bristles and two wheels on either end. A canvas hopper trails behind to catch leaves or grass clippings that are thrown back by the bristles when the sweeper is pushed over the lawn. The handle holds or is part of the hopper and may be attached directly to the wheels. Hoppers hold 6 to 9 bushels of debris. Some larger models are designed to be towed behind a riding mower or lawn tractor.

USE: Cleaning up grass clippings and leaves.

USE TIPS: Keep all metal parts cleaned and oiled. Sweepers work best on level and dry lawns.

BUYING TIPS: A good lawn sweeper is a definite labor advantage over raking and much quieter than a blower. Sweepers with handles attached directly to the wheels are sturdier. The hopper floors of better sweepers are made of steel or fiberglass to reduce wear and friction. Narrower models do a better job on uneven terrain.

PUSH BROOM

DESCRIPTION: Push-type brooms with large bristled heads mounted to long wooden or fiberglass handles.

TYPES: *Heavy-duty broom* (also known as *street, street sweeper type, barn,* or *outdoor broom):* Fourteen- to 18-inch-wide head, usually with two sets of five rows of tough fiber bristles, sometimes over 6 inches long. This is what you see used by professional street sweepers. Bristles made of African basswood, palmyra stalks, or plastic, and are suitable for wet or dry use.

Sidewalk-and-garage broom: At 18 to 24 inches, wider than the heavy-duty model, with shorter palmyra fiber bristles about 4 inches long. A steel version with plastic bristles is available for caked-up dirt or debris, in models up to 36 inches wide. Made for wet or dry use.

Floor broom: More finished wooden head than the above types, with Tampico fiber or plastic bristles usually around 3 inches long. Eighteen to 24 inches wide.

Porch-and-patio broom (also known as *lawn broom):* One-foot-wide steel head with stiff 3-inch-long plastic bristles.

USE: Sweeping patios, terraces, garages, walks, and driveways. Also for sweeping clippings and leaves from thick, well-mowed lawns.

USE TIPS: Store brooms with the bristles up to prevent them from getting bent. Move the handle to the opposite side if the bristles are worn on one side.

BUYING TIPS: A good push broom is reinforced where the handle is attached to the head, usually with a metal shank screwed to the handle. Handles that are just stuck into a hole in the head are likely to work loose. Braces can be purchased separately.

REEL MOWER

ALSO KNOWN AS: Push mower; push-reel, hand-reel, hand-push-reel, or power-reel mower; beater bar type mower; cylinder mower

DESCRIPTION: Five to eight curved blades, 14 to 18 inches long, mounted on a reel approximately the same size as the large wheels found on either of its ends. The blades rotate as the mower is moved, cutting grass as they are drawn over a stationary blade (the "bed knife"), like a pair of giant scissors. This was the conventional design for all home lawn mowers before rotary power mowers were introduced after World War II. The reel mowers available today are lighter than ever and the handles are made from metal instead of wood. The power reel mower has the same basic design, but is driven by a gasoline engine above the reel. Most models are easily adjusted to different cutting heights.

USE: Cutting grass that is not too long. Manual reel mowers are ideal for cutting small lawns, such as those in urban areas. And they are quiet. Models with fewer blades are fine for mowing bluegrass and creeping fescues; more blades are suggested for Southern types, such as Bermudagrasses.

REEL MOWER

USE TIPS: The reel mower works quite well if the blades are kept sharp, producing a superior, more efficient cut than that provided by a power rotary mower, which cuts only with the tips of its blades. The bed knife should be adjusted so that the entire length of the cutting blade makes contact with it when the mower is pushed. To check the bed knife, insert a piece of paper between the blade and the bed knife. It is well adjusted if the paper is cut the full length of the blades when the reel is turned. Reel mowers are better suited to lawns that are mowed regularly, as they do not cut tall grass well.

BUYING TIPS: Look for a reel mower that is lightweight but still well made. Power reel mowers are preferred by many gardeners and turf specialists because they cut grass cleaner than rotary mowers (see next entry) owing to their scissorlike cutting action. Make sure that the mowing height can be adjusted. Manual reel mowers are more easily stored than power mowers, and use no fuels—other than refreshments for the person doing the pushing. Look for all-steel construction.

ROTARY MOWER

DESCRIPTION: Either an electric or gasoline motor mounted on a metal casing below which rotates a propellerlike blade with a diameter of 18 to 24 inches. Mostly gasoline powered, rotary mowers are the most common design of power mowers today. Electric mowers may be either battery-driven or plugged into an outlet by a long cord. Battery-powered mowers run for about forty-five minutes on a charge. Gasoline mowers are driven by either a two-cycle or four-cycle engine with an average strength of 3 to 4 horsepower.

ROTARY MOWER

TYPES: *Walk-behind* (also known as *walking mower):* The most common type. The higher-priced gasoline rotary mowers are usually self-propelled (that is, the motor not only turns the blade but drives the wheels as well), while the less expensive ones must be pushed. Smaller models have flip-over handles, which save you from having to turn the mower around at the end of each pass. Mowing height on most models can be adjusted. Some models either can be converted to or are *mower-mulchers* that cut the grass clippings very finely so they can settle down on the soil where they act as a mulch that decomposes and returns nitrogen to the soil. If you don't cut your grass often, however, you may want to rake them up or bag them because long clippings tend to mat. Two basic bagging designs are made: *rear bagging,* in which the grass clippings are spewed into a bag that hangs from the handles of the mower, or *side-discharge,* which spews them onto the lawn or a side-mounted bag.

Riding mowers (also known as *lawn tractors):* Self-propelled mowers that you sit on and drive. Often rotary types and usually feature the blade housing, or *mower deck,* under the seat, but some, called *front-cut mowers,* have the blade housing in front, making for a more maneuverable mower that can also cut underneath fences, bushes, and trees. The width of cut usually ranges from 26 to 42 inches. In all cases, a *grass catcher,* usually a canvas and metal or plastic container that trails along behind the mower, is a recommended accessory for catching the clippings. There is as much competition among manufacturers of riding mowers as there is for automobiles, it seems—with as many features to choose from: width, clutch, automatic transmission (hydrostatic drive), control panel, steering (wheel or levers), diesel engine, engine access for maintenance, four-wheel steering, warranties, and the number of optional attachments, like snow blowers. These are a matter of personal choice.

Nylon string mower (also known as *trimmer/mower):* The newest type of mower is quite different from standard rotary models. This is a large string trimmer (see pages 208–209) on wheels, and may be either gas- or electric-powered. It does not have a metal blade but rather a rapidly spinning nylon cord. This design may prove to be a safer lawn mower to use. Another new string type is a *floating mower,* which actually floats on a cushion of air and has no wheels. After a long, hot day mowing a large lawn with a heavy, conventional mower, many gardeners wish to float, too, for which a large swimming pool is recommended; at that point, they themselves might be considered yet another type of "floating mower."

USE: Cutting lawns, especially larger lawns with long grass (stemming from extended time between mowings). Riding mowers are helpful when you have more than ¾ acre to mow.

USE TIPS: Keep the blades of rotary mowers sharp, or else the grass will be beaten and bruised instead of cut. The oil in gasoline-powered mowers that have reservoirs is essential to their operation, and should be checked regularly and changed completely once during the mowing season. The rotating blade is extremely dangerous and capable of slinging stones, so safety precautions should be followed when using these mowers such as wearing shoes, long pants, and keeping children away. Rear bagging–type mowers allow you to maneuver a bit more easily, but leave the grass catcher off if you mow often: Grass clippings are a good source of nutrients. Always determine the best length for your grass, and keep in mind that much damage comes from cutting it too short.

BUYING TIPS: The electric or battery-powered rotary mowers are best suited to small lawns that are mowed regularly. Gasoline-powered rotary mowers capable of cutting tall or tough grasses are generally heavier duty than electric mowers. Self-propelled mowers are helpful for large hilly areas or for people who have trouble pushing. Some gasoline-powered mowers come with push-button electronic ignition instead of pull-cord starters, but you pay dearly for this convenience. Check to see how comfortable the controls are. When buying any model, but especially the larger ones, be sure that you understand which attachments are standard and which must be purchased as extras. *Leaf shredders* are one of the most useful attachments for those gardeners who have lots of trees. Look for blades that are attached to the drive shaft with a *half-moon key,* or *Woodruff key*—it will shear off if you hit a big object, instead of severely damaging the entire drive shaft and engine. Although two-cycle engines are better for hilly terrains owing to their lighter weight, the choice is largely one of size: of lawn and of mower, as well as of the person doing the work. Two-cycle engines are smaller and lighter, but four-cycle engines are more efficient.

Look for the following safety features: a rear deflector, which is a hinged flap on the rear of the mower that stops flying rocks and sticks from hitting you; a similar deflection guard at the grass-clipping discharge opening; and a well-placed exhaust system and muffler—namely, away from the grass catcher bag. All-steel construction is best.

Wide selections of riding mowers may be found at specialized outdoor equipment dealers; many garden centers do not sell riding mowers because this requires another expertise and maintenance capability, as well as a lot of space. Be sure to buy equipment from a reputable dealer with a well-known service department. Avoid buying from dealers who are only into power equipment a little bit: They may not be able to service you promptly or well. Front-cutting riding mowers are more expensive. With all riding mowers, check to see what other attachments, such as snow blowers, are available, and how easy it is to attach or remove them. The turning radius is an important point of comparison (less is better). Above all, test-drive the mower to see how it feels.

SOD TAMPER

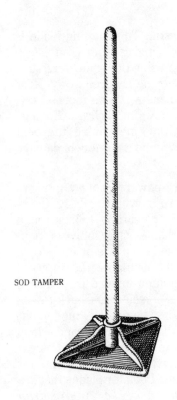

SOD TAMPER

ALSO KNOWN AS: Lawn tamper, tamper

DESCRIPTION: Heavy, flat metal square of about 8 to 10 inches, with a 4-foot-long perpendicular handle in the middle. Models vary in weight from around 11 to 25 pounds.

USE: Leveling and tamping down sod after it is planted, seedbeds before seeding, or sand and gravel before pouring concrete or laying brick. Does many of the same jobs a roller does (see page 246).

USE TIP: Work in an overlapping pattern to ensure a smooth and level surface.

BUYING TIP: Unless you are a professional sod layer, or doing it for a lot of neighbors, this tool may be better to rent than to buy.

SPREADER

ALSO KNOWN AS: Seed sower, seeder (these two names are used only when the spreader is used to broadcast seed), lawn spreader

DESCRIPTION: Hand-operated device carried like a front pack, or a cartlike device pushed over the lawn like a lawn mower, both of which have hoppers made of steel, structural foam plastic, regular plastic, or canvas.

TYPES: *Broadcast spreader* (also known as *rotary* or *rotary broadcast spreader):* Canvas or metal hopper that holds material to be broadcast, below which is a ridged, revolving, circular disk. There are two basic types—hand-driven and wheeled. The hand-driven broadcast spreader, also known as a *shoulder* or *hand spreader,* is suspended from the shoulder by straps and the broadcast platform is turned by a hand crank on the side as you walk along. The wheeled model, called a *push* or *rotary broadcast spreader,* is similar (and much more common), except that the hopper is on a metal cart and the broadcast platform is turned by the movement of the wheels as it is pushed. Hoppers on wheeled spreaders can be tall

BROADCAST SPREADER

DROP SPREADER

cylinders, holding as much as 5 gallons or 60 pounds. Spreads material as wide as 30 feet.

Drop spreader (also known as *wheel drop spreader):* Two-wheel cartlike device that drops the material through an opening in the bottom as the spreader is pushed over the lawn. A control lever that opens (to a particular size) and closes the drop mechanism is located on the handle of the spreader. Spreads material only to the width of the hopper, about 20 inches. Capacity of the hopper ranges up to 75 pounds.

Organic spreader (also known as *manure spreader):* Perforated steel drum, about 2½ cubic feet capacity, that holds manure or other organic material. Holes are cut so there is either 48 or 63 percent open space through which the material falls as you roll it over your lawn or garden.

USE: Spreading fertilizer, seed, lime, pesticide, or other powdered or pelleted materials over a garden, field, or lawn.

USE TIPS: Broadcast spreaders tend to concentrate the material near the spreader. Because of this, it is important to overlap when broadcasting to get an even coverage. Drop spreaders disperse material more regularly and evenly than the broadcast spreaders, so it is important *not* to overlap. On the other hand, drop spreaders cover less ground with each pass than broadcast spreaders; they are more accurate but more work. Spreaders should be cleaned and oiled after each use.

ORGANIC SPREADER

BUYING TIPS: Broadcast spreaders are more efficient for large areas because they scatter seed and other material over a wider space. However, drop spreaders are more reliable in the amount and the evenness of material dispersed, making them a marginally better buy. Be sure to check that the spreader you purchase can handle the types of material you are using. Plastic spreaders are more rust-resistant. Many larger professional models are available for gardeners with extremely large areas to cover. Look for models with easily operated gates. Steel bargain models are likely to corrode very quickly and should be avoided.

Starting Products and Gardening Aids

Seed Starting Products

ABOUT SEED STARTING PRODUCTS

In late winter and early spring, about the same time that the seed displays begin to make their annual appearance, garden center shelves contain bags of starter soils, seed flats, seed flat heaters, light units, peat pots, soil blockers, and myriad other products to help you start your own plants from seed. Most gardeners find growing plants from seed a fun, not to mention therapeutic, activity in late winter. Perhaps because it is often done in the house, or because it is more of a hobby than a utilitarian job, there is enormous competition in this area, resulting in a bewildering variety of types and models and packaged sets. Chances are there is a specialized product for any problem you might encounter in this delicate work.

AUTOMATIC TIMER

DESCRIPTION: Clock mechanism that is plugged into an electrical outlet. Many different types are available. The simplest are mechanical—just a twenty-four-hour clock dial and box with a plug—and the most sophisticated are electronic, capable of controlling a number of devices at once.

USE: Remote, automatic control of electrical devices, such as growing lights. Turns the light unit on automatically in the morning and shuts it off in the evening.

USE TIP: If you are using light units for growing seedlings, set the timer to simulate the day length at the time of the year that the seeds would germinate and grow outdoors. For example, if you are growing seed indoors in February that would normally be sown outside in April or May, set your timer for the April and May day length and not the shorter February time.

BUYING TIP: Check around before purchasing a timer. Good timers may not cost as much as bad ones, so be sure to ask for advice before making your choice.

CAPILLARY WATERER

DESCRIPTION: Variety of designs that consist of a large reservoir of water that is delivered as needed to pots by capillary action via a spongelike mat *(capillary matting)* or wicks. Most waterers have a tray covered with channels for the water; the mat sits on top of the channels and the pots are set on top of the mat. The reservoir may look like a coffee urn.

USE: Long-term, consistent watering of seedlings.

USE TIPS: Make sure the tray is on a level surface. Experiment to determine the rate and volume of water your plants require.

BUYING TIP: Often used with houseplants by people who travel for long periods.

HEATING CABLE

ALSO KNOWN AS: Heating wire, soil cable

DESCRIPTION: Electrical wire, covered with lead and hooked into a thermostat, that is pluged directly into a grounded electrical outlet.

USE: Placed under soil in seed flats (see page 262) to control the temperature when starting delicate seedlings.

USE TIPS: Though the wire is covered with lead to protect it and you from electrical shock, you should be careful when digging near a heating cable with metal tools. It is important that the heating cable be attached to an electrical plug with a third prong for grounding, and that this be plugged into a properly grounded outlet. Note that if a grounding adapter is used, the short green wire must be screwed into the wall outlet. Be sure to bury the thermostat in the ground.

BUYING TIP: The less expensive heating cables have thermostats that are part of the cable, while the more expensive ones have thermostats that are separate from the cable. The latter is the safer design.

HEATING MAT

ALSO KNOWN AS: Heat mat, propagation heat mat

DESCRIPTION: Two rubber mats with electric heating wires sandwiched between them. The heating wires are attached to a thermostat that is in turn plugged into an electrical outlet. Supplied with transformer for low-voltage current. Usually rectangular, but available in long and narrow shapes for windowsills.

USE: Providing consistent, gentle bottom heat, essential to good seed germination.

USE TIP: Thermostats may not be accurate. It is a good idea to insert a thermometer into the seed flat itself to check the temperature of the flat and adjust the thermostat accordingly. Check your gardening books for ideal temperatures.

BUYING TIP: Do not buy a heating mat that does not come with a thermostat. Many gardeners have grown plants from seed for years without a heating mat with thermostat, but many experienced gardeners swear by them. If the conditions under which you are growing plants from seed do not provide a uniform temperature, or temperatures vary greatly, a heating mat is worth investing in.

LIGHT AND MOISTURE METERS

DESCRIPTION: Small, hand-held meters. Sometimes both functions are combined in a single unit, but more commonly they are sold separately. Moisture meters have a probe, either on the end of a cable or as part of the meter body.

USE: Estimating light and moisture content in soils and growing areas; particularly useful under artificial conditions, such as with light units or greenhouses. May also help discover problem conditions that affect especially sensitive plants. The primary use of a light meter is to check the difference in intensity of light from the center to the edge of an area lit by fluorescent tubes. One way to compensate is to rotate the position of the plants. Some moisture meters, usually sold as part of a system, are connected to water computers that turn the water supply on and off as needed, their prime purpose being to prevent automatic sprinkler systems from going on when it's raining.

USE TIP: Always wipe off the tips of the probes after use.

BUYING TIP: Once you have learned the proper level of moisture for your plants, you may find that your finger can replace the probe.

LIGHT UNIT

ALSO KNOWN AS: Growing light, growing lamp unit, plant light, propagation light

DESCRIPTION: Basically a standard fluorescent light fixture that has been adapted to the special needs of indoor plant growing. Typically a two-lamp fixture, mounted in a reflective metal hood. Some models come as part of a unit that includes one or two shelves for plants, and a frame that holds the light at the right distance above them. Twenty-four to 48-inch-long 20 or 40 watt *wide spectrum* (or *full spectrum* or *continuous spectrum)* fluorescent tubes, sometimes called *grow lights,* are used, though one "cool white" and one "warm white" is recommended by some experts. Some brands claim to last 24,000 hours.

USE: Providing the light required for plants to make their own food, or photosynthesize, indoors and away from sunny windows. Light units are also ideal for starting plants indoors, as they provide consistent light that can be controlled at this delicate stage in a plant's life.

USE TIPS: The amount of light produced from fluorescent lamps diminishes toward their ends, and as the plants must be close to the fixture, you must place the plants with this in mind. You must also change the height of the fixture as the plants grow to keep them at the same distance. Plants also need a period of darkness, so plant light units should not be on all the time. An automatic timer (see pages 254–55) is useful to control the amount of light the plants receive. It is important that the period of light the plants and seedlings receive be fairly consistent and mock natural day length conditions. Units can be covered with plastic to help retain humidity, the lack of which is often a problem during the winter heating season. Specialized grow lights work best with flowering houseplants; vegetables are less fussy. Do not use *white* or *daylight* tubes.

BUYING TIPS: Light units are more efficient if there are two 4-foot fluorescent tubes. Units sold specifically for plants are more expensive than the same unit sold for general lighting use, but you usually still need to get the "wide spectrum" lamp at a garden center. Because they are a bit costly it is a good idea to use them in tandem with a regular "cool white" lamp. If you buy a regular fixture, you need to make the frame and shelves yourself—not a difficult task for some people, but for those with little time or inclination to build or assemble, the ready-made unit is a big advantage.

EXPANDED
PEAT PELLET

PEAT PELLET

PEAT PELLET

POPULAR BRAND NAME: Jiffy-7®

ALSO KNOWN AS: One step disk, growing cube

DESCRIPTION: Small brown disk, about 1½ inches wide and ¹⁄₁₆ inch thick, made from compressed peat and wood fibers, that is sterile and pH balanced. Expands on contact with water to become a combination small pot of peat and growing medium. Peat pellets are encased in a light plastic netting that keeps the peat intact. Jiffy-7s expand to 1⅔ inches square, but a deeper Jiffy-7 (extra-depth pellets, no. 727) expands to 2⅜ inches square. Another version is a block of cubes stamped out of a whole sheet of this material; some brands include fertilizer and use a gel instead of a net to hold it all together.

USE: Self-contained pots and planting medium all in one, for starting slow-growing annuals and vegetables from seed. Once the seedlings have grown and have been thinned to only one plant per "pot," the pot itself is set directly in the garden, avoiding transplant shock.

USE TIPS: Tepid water causes disks to expand more quickly. To allow the gel to work best, allow the disks to sit for a few hours after expanding. Once seeds begin to germinate, the medium should be kept evenly moist, and any pot material above the soil line should be trimmed off so it does not wick water away. Sow several seeds per pot to compensate for poor germination; thin to one seedling.

BUYING TIPS: A real convenience if you are just starting to grow plants from seed, as there is no soil to mix nor pots to fill. The plastic nets on Jiffy-7s do not decompose, and because they remain in the soil some gardeners prefer other types that decompose over time.

PEAT POT

PEAT POT

POPULAR BRAND NAMES: Jiffy-Pots®, Fertil Pots

DESCRIPTION: Small pot made from compressed peat and wood fiber and sometimes fertilizer. Standard sizes include 2 inches square, 2¼ inches round or square, and 3 inches round or square. One hundred percent biodegradable. *Dwarf pots* are a bit wider and less tapered than normal; *Long Tom* pots are taller.

USE: Starting seeds, particularly with sterile soilless mixes. The pot is planted directly into the garden when the seedling is ready, avoiding transplant shock as well as the work of repotting. Especially suitable for bedding plants and vegetables that normally may be hard to transplant.

USE TIPS: Remove any small part of the pot that sticks above the soil level when setting the plants into the garden—otherwise it acts as a wick, drawing water away from the plant and into the air. Sow several seeds per pot and thin to one after germination.

BUYING TIP: Peat pots are about the same price as the peat pellets (see previous entry) but you need to fill peat pots with a growing medium, making them ultimately just a little more expensive.

PLANTING LINE

DESCRIPTION: Length of cord with a stake at either end and a winding mechanism, usually a reel. Many different lengths offered in the range of 50 or 100 feet. Stakes made of metal, wood, or plastic. Line may be natural hemp or plastic coated, and is often sold on a convenient reel, like kite-flying string.

USE: Laying out a garden: This allows planting row crops in a straight line. Pull line taut above the soil surface.

USE TIP: Keep your line relatively clean by trying to use only on dry soil; moist soil sticks to planting lines.

BUYING TIP: This is the kind of item that is manufactured as a convenience only. It is very easy to make yourself.

PLANT MARKER

ALSO KNOWN AS: Flower markers, plant labels

DESCRIPTION: Plastic, metal, or wooden stake just under a foot long with a flat area, about 1 by 3 inches, which can be written on. Metal markers have one or two long wire prongs that are stuck in the ground, with an angled top that has an etched zinc band for writing on with a special black carbon pencil. Others, often called *pot labels,* are thin, flat plastic or wood pieces from 4 to 12 inches long and ⅝ inch wide, angled to a point for insertion in the soil; sometimes the longer ones are called *garden stakes.*

USE: Labeling plants, either as a marker of a freshly seeded row of vegetables or to identify prize flowers. Also handy as a reminder of when something was fertilized or treated with a pesticide. Small wooden pot labels are good for seedling pots.

BUYING TIPS: Top-quality metal markers are made of zinc, aluminum, or galvanized steel. Plastic may look good, but it is breakable. Wooden ones tend to rot in a season, and are more suitable for temporary jobs, such as indicating where seeds have been planted.

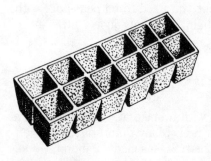

SECTIONED FIBER SEED TRAY

SECTIONED FIBER SEED TRAY

POPULAR BRAND NAME: Jiffy Strip®

DESCRIPTION: Compressed 2¼-inch-square fiber pots attached at their tops to form a tray, or strip, of twelve units, like a large ice cube tray. Commonly sold with plastic trays that they fit into perfectly and that contain drainage holes for excess water. Some are designed especially to fit onto windowsills, called *windowsill sets.*

USE: Growing seedlings, when filled with a growing medium.

USE TIPS: Growing medium should be premoistened before sowing seed. Sections can be cut apart and completely buried in the garden (where they will disintegrate naturally) instead of transplanting. Trim off any part of pot above soil line. Sow several seeds in each section to compensate for poor germination; seedlings should then be thinned to one seedling per section.

BUYING TIP: Fiber planting trays are as inexpensive as individual peat pots (see page 259), and more convenient to use.

SECTIONED STARTING TRAY

SECTIONED STARTING TRAY

ALSO KNOWN AS: Compartmentalized tray, seedling flat, seedling tray, growing tray, plug tray, planter flat, plug seedling tray, cell pack, cell tray

DESCRIPTION: Lightweight plastic or biodegradable paper tray divided into separate cubes, like a muffin tin, for growing individual seedlings. Cells are 2 to 3 inches deep and up to 3 inches square or round; round ones are also available as small as 1 inch deep and 1 inch in diameter. Trays vary in size from small six packs (approximately 4 by 8 inches) to approximately 12 by 20 inches. Some have a flat tray underneath to catch excess water.

Some more elaborate *self-watering* models, with drainage holes and capillary matting (see capillary waterer, page 255), are sold with outer trays without drainage holes that they fit into like a sleeve. The seedlings are watered indirectly—water put in the bottom tray is pulled up into the starting tray. A high, clear plastic cover is provided for extra climate control at the germinating stage in the case of *propagating trays.* The plainest version is a *seed pan,* which looks like a casserole dish.

USE: Growing seedlings for transplanting.

USE TIPS: Sow a couple of seeds in each compartment to compensate for poor germination. If more than one seed germinates, they should be thinned out, leaving only one seedling in each section. Remove the clear plastic cover as soon as the seeds germinate. All the plants in each tray should have the same watering requirements and planting times for ease of maintenance.

BUYING TIPS: Sectioned trays are more expensive than the single flats often used by many professional growers. Sectioned trays, however, are worth the extra money because they prevent root competition among seedlings, as roots can develop only within the confines of each section—thus reducing transplant shock. Plastic trays are a good investment, as they can be reused year after year. The self-watering trays are easy to use and worth the extra cost. Look for stiff, solid fabrication that will not easily break. Using your old coffee cups or yogurt containers is good for recycling, but not as easy. And they are hard to carry out to the garden for transplanting.

SEED FLAT

ALSO KNOWN AS: Seed tray, nursery flat

DESCRIPTION: Shallow, rectangular plastic or fiberglass tray approximately 12 by 20 inches and about 2 to 3 inches deep, with ribs and usually drainage holes. When sold with a clear plastic top, may be considered a *propagator,* which is then usually packaged with other seed starting products, such as the pots and other items listed here.

USE: A place to put peat pots or other small containers. Can also be filled directly with soil and seeds, though this is not recommended. Some are sectioned to hold small pots.

USE TIPS: Avoid overwatering, especially if your flat has no drainage holes. When peat pots of seedlings are placed in a seed flat, apply no more water than the pots can absorb in less than one half hour. Professional growers with little greenhouse space to waste plant seeds directly into seed flats, but seedlings' roots can then intertwine, and there is considerable transplant shock when they are cut apart and moved into larger containers.

BUYING TIPS: Look for seed flats that are sturdy and do no bend if the weight of the pots is unevenly distributed in the flat. Foam plastic has greater structural rigidity, making it easier to carry a loaded flat. Plastic resists rot, mildew, fungi, and other damage.

SEED GROWING KIT

ALSO KNOWN AS: Seed starter kit, seed starting kit

DESCRIPTION: Prepackaged group of products containing all of the necessary items for starting plants from seed. They often contain pots, flats, planting medium, a thermometer, labels, and fertilizer. The number of seedlings you can produce with one of these kits depends upon the size of the kit.

USE: Simple and sure germination setup.

USE TIP: Follow the general directions for growing plants from seed. If your kit does not have directions, use a gardening book.

BUYING TIP: It is usually cheaper to buy these prepackaged kits than it is to purchase each item separately. If you prefer peat or fiber pots to plastic, or peat disks, look for seed growing kits that have just what you want.

SEED SCOOP

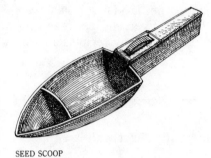

SEED SCOOP

ALSO KNOWN AS: Seed planter, seed sower

DESCRIPTION: Small hand-held scoop that resembles an ice cream scoop with a divider across the middle that has a small open space at the bottom for seeds to pass through. The space behind the divider serves as a hopper for the seeds, which pass underneath the divider one at a time. Smaller versions look like big test tubes, palm-sized powder compacts, giant hyperdermic needles, or long and narrow shoehorns. This last item is an English import known as a widger (see page 155)—some people call it the *everything tool* because it is not limited to seed planting, but is more often used for digging.

USE: Planting small quantities of seeds evenly.

USE TIP: Can also be used for applying small amounts of granular fertilizer.

BUYING TIP: The least expensive version is the clear plastic tube, though it could be argued that this is only one small step up from using seed packets or pieces of cardboard folded into a V shape, which are, of course, still less expensive.

SEED STARTING MIX

ALSO KNOWN AS: Soilless mix (see pages 7–8)

DESCRIPTION: Lightweight soil substitute, usually light brown in color with white specks. The white specks are either vermiculite or perlite (see pages 19 and 18), and the brown is peat (see pages 16–19) and other organic material. Contains no soil, and is sterile, having been exposed to high temperatures to kill off the bacteria. Retains moisture extremely well.

USE: Starting seeds. Constant moisture is essential to the germination and growth of seeds. The sterile soil prevents the problem of damping-off, a fungal disease that kills seedlings.

USE TIP: Wet thoroughly before using. It is more difficult to moisten after seed has been sown than before sowing. Tepid or warm water is absorbed more quickly than cool or cold water.

BUYING TIPS: Mixes that contain perlite are preferred to those that contain vermiculite, because vermiculite, which is lighter than perlite, tends to rise to the surface when water is applied. Most sterile starter mixes on the market are fairly reliable, so just look for those within your budget. Even cheaper is mixing your own from milled peat and perlite, or any recipe found in a good general gardening book.

SEED-SPACING TEMPLATE

DESCRIPTION: Large, lightweight plastic sheet with large holes in a regular pattern, such as every 6 inches.

USE: Placed over the ground, provides an accurate guide for planting seeds in an exact pattern.

USE TIP: Mark where the edge of your template falls so that you can maintain your pattern when you move the template over to cover the adjacent area.

BUYING TIP: It is just as easy to mark off measurements on a line, or to make a similar item from a large sheet of cardboard or a notched piece of wood.

SEEDER

ALSO KNOWN AS: Row seeder, garden seeder

DESCRIPTION: Single wheel with a long handle and a large hub; the hub contains a hopper and a release device for seeds. A larger, two-wheeled model simultaneously furrows, covers, and marks the next row.

USE: Sowing row crops. As you walk along your garden, the seeder releases seeds at a preset rate, so you don't have to bend over or kneel.

USE TIPS: Be sure to set the rate and walk at the pace necessary for the proper dispersion of each kind of seed.

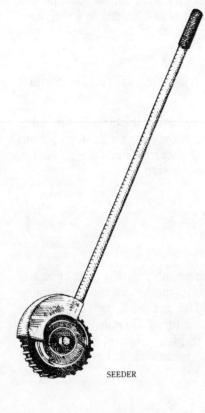

SEEDER

BUYING TIPS: Reduces the need for thinning, and of course is much faster than hand planting.

SOIL BLOCKER

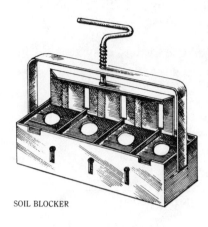

SOIL BLOCKER

ALSO KNOWN AS: Soil block, soil block maker

DESCRIPTION: Small metal device that compresses soil or planting medium to form four tight 2-inch soil blocks. Another version, a *soil cuber,* makes twenty ¾-inch cubes at once. Four plastic blocks, called *cube attachments,* make ¾-inch holes in the large blocks in which the small cubes can be dropped. A spring-held lever forces the soil or medium out of the blocker neatly.

USE: Makes cubes that are both the planting medium and the transplant container, an efficient way to grow plants from seed without transplant shock. Once the seed has sprouted in small cubes it can be dropped into the larger cube made by the soil blocker.

USE TIPS: The moister the growing medium, the tighter the cubes, and the more likely they will hold together while the seed germinates and grows. Seed germinates better in the smaller cubes than in the soil blocks. Special blends of peat, humus, and vermiculite are available that make ideal blocks.

BUYING TIP: Not many different makes are available, but prices do vary.

THERMOMETER

DESCRIPTION: Dial or small mercury-filled tube with calibrations in centigrade or Fahrenheit degrees suitable for indoor or outdoor use. Some are mounted alongside a barometer or *hygrometer* or *humidistat* or *humidity meter* (for measuring humidity). A *soil* or *garden thermometer,* a large specialized version with a long spike like a meat thermometer, is made for measuring the temperature of compost piles (one brand is called a *hot bed soil thermometer,* and it is over a foot long). A *minimum-maximum* (or *min/max) thermometer* has markers that show the low and high temperature points each day. A special accessory is a *temperature alarm* that you can set for minimum or maximum temperatures.

USE: Measuring air temperature or, in the case of soil thermometers, soil temperature. Both help you avoid planting your vegetable garden too early in the season or leaving certain plants in too late in the fall. Humidistats help you maintain the proper level of humidity in your home or greenhouse.

BUYING TIP: Make sure you get one that is easy to read in relation to where you intend to place it—on a greenhouse wall, outside a window, or whatever. A must for greenhouses.

Planting Containers and Accessories

ABOUT PLANTING CONTAINERS

Most garden centers devote a large area to planters, pots, and containers made of clay, wood, plastic (many of recycled plastic), metal, cement, and ceramics. Which material is best for pots and planters depends primarily on personal taste. The most notable point of comparison is this, though: The more porous the material a pot or planter is made of, the more quickly the soil or planting medium dries out. That is, if two pots are the same size, one made of clay and the other of plastic, the soil in the clay pot needs to be watered more often than the soil in the plastic pot, although now some terra-cotta planters have a self-watering feature, like many plastic ones. This is particularly important when gardening in dry and hot places, like roof gardens. And clay pots are harder to clean than plastic pots. Still, the old debate over whether clay pots are better than plastic ones remains unsettled for many gardeners.

Beyond their inherent qualities is the question of weight. Outdoor pots and pots for larger plants must be heavy enough to resist wind. Hanging plant pots need to be light. You may want to put a heavy planter on a *plant dolly* (or *plant caddy, planter base,* or *coaster),* a small platform with four sturdy casters, so that it can be moved.

Remember that all planting pots must have drain holes so excess water does not rot the plant's roots. You may want to use a saucer to catch any water that flows out. Pot dimensions are given as the diameter at the top, and sometimes the height as well, though some dimensions are not given if the design is extreme, such as with the flat planter used for forcing bulbs or starting seedlings, called a *bulb pan.*

BASKET PLANTER

BASKET PLANTER

DESCRIPTION: Half- or quarter-sphere frames constructed from concentric circles of wire connected by perpendicular wires, or of solid plastic. Quarter-sphere models may be called *wall baskets* or *English hayrack flower baskets*. Other items that do the same job with much charm are unglazed pottery faces and other decorative shapes with one flat side that goes against a wall.

USE: Lined with peat moss or other fibrous material and filled with soil for hanging plants. Quarter-sphere models hang from a wall, like a picture, while half spheres hang free. Those made of solid materials, like plastic and pottery, do not need a moss lining.

USE TIPS: Fill the basket with a growing medium that holds moisture well (one with a lot of humus). Plants can also be placed through the wires from the outside, inserted into the peat moss on the sides of the basket to produce a fuller planter, usually a very striking effect. If possible, water by submersing the basket completely, which gives it a really thorough soaking.

BUYING TIP: Wire frames provide a suitable base for hanging baskets, but only if you can supply ample water. Look for sturdy construction, and if it is made of painted metal, an even, solid paint job.

CERAMIC PLANTER

DESCRIPTION: Cast terra-cotta in a wide range of sizes and designs, both freestanding and wall hanging. Some have a vitreous glaze, adding an even wider range of colors. Some are fired in such a way as to be frost-proof, meaning they can be left out over the winter, with no danger of cracking.

USE: Typically used as an accent piece on a terrace, patio, or in the home.

USE TIP: May add just the right focus to a deck or terrace, so one or two are better than a whole collection.

BUYING TIP: Good-quality ceramic planters, especially those with beautiful decorative detail and a nice glaze, are more expensive than other types, so choose carefully. Those with drainage holes are more desirable than those without, as holes cannot be added, though a layer of gravel can be placed in the bottom if need be.

FIBERGLASS PLANTER

ALSO KNOWN AS: Tub

DESCRIPTION: Lightweight containers in all kinds of shapes and sizes, from small urns to large tree containers. Many are painted to look like wood, stone, or ceramic material. Some are designed to match furniture or architectural detail.

USE: Substitute for heavier containers, especially where weight is a consideration, such as on a roof or balcony. Will not weather, chip, or peel. The great variety of design possibilities makes these fit into specific decors, unlike other kinds of containers.

USE TIP: Drainage holes can be drilled in fiberglass planters if they do not have them.

BUYING TIP: What fiberglass container you should buy depends largely upon your taste, need, and ability to pay. Those that most closely resemble wood or stone are usually more expensive. Try to buy one with drainage holes.

HALF WHISKEY BARREL

HALF WHISKEY BARREL

DESCRIPTION: A wooden barrel, cut in half, that actually was used to make whiskey (or wine), though some are made just for planter use. All are made of hardwood staves or strips held together with metal bands, about 2½ feet in diameter at the top, and slightly narrow at the bottom; about 2 feet deep. The inside of the barrel often has been charred as part of the whiskey aging process. Sizes vary, but a typical big one holds about 3 cubic feet of soil.

USE: As large planters. Can also be used to create a miniature water garden if the residual whiskey or wine is thoroughly washed out first to avoid intoxicating the fish.

USE TIPS: Whiskey barrels used for aging whiskey and wine must be cleaned well with warm water and a stiff brush before they can be used as planters or for miniature water gardens, but it is not necessary to remove the charred section from the inside of the barrel. The charred sides actually "sweeten" the soil or water in the barrel—they absorb many unwelcome chemicals that tend to build up in soil. The staves in the barrel swell when wet, allowing the barrel to hold water for water gardening (lily pads and goldfish—why not?), though it may take several days for this to happen. If you are planning to use a whiskey barrel as a planter, drill several ½-inch holes in the bottom for drainage first. Because the metal bands that hold the staves in place are not treated to prevent rust, it may be a good idea to paint them.

BUYING TIP: Look for half whiskey barrels that have not been allowed to dry out and whose bottoms are not warped. When a whiskey barrel is overdry the staves are not tight and the metal bands become loose. Compare prices at different places, as the markup can vary greatly. You should have to pay no more than $25 for a half whiskey barrel—remember, they are discards from whiskey manufacturers.

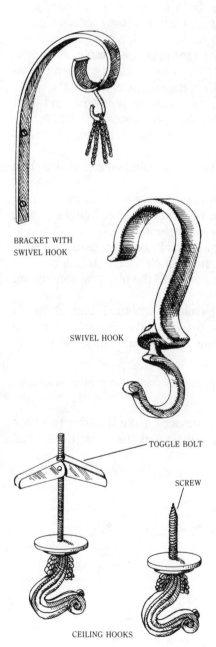

BRACKET WITH
SWIVEL HOOK

SWIVEL HOOK

TOGGLE BOLT

SCREW

CEILING HOOKS

HOOKS, HANGERS, AND BRACKETS

DESCRIPTION: Many ingenious designs are available, and most fall into the categories that follow. However, there are too many odd ones to list, such as those that stick on windows or hold hanging plants. Be sure to browse through several displays and ask for suggestions from the garden center if you aren't satisfied with what you see.

TYPES: *Brackets:* Decorative L-shaped or scroll hook of various sizes that is mounted on a wall and may be hinged, from which a hanging basket is suspended. Some models have a small scroll at the outward end in which you insert an S-hook, while others have a swiveling hook built in. Some of the best looking are made from wrought iron, though brackets made from all kinds of metal or wood can be found in a wide range of prices. They are adjustable to fit. Place pulleys at the base and tip, and with a cord and a cleat you can raise and lower a hanging basket to your level, especially handy if you're in a wheelchair, or to a high ceiling.

Ceiling hooks: Simple hook with a flanged base, like a big cup hook, usually made of cast aluminum in a decorative style (this may also be known as a *swag hook).* Sold with either a screw (for solid ceilings) or a toggle bolt (a winged device for hollow ceilings). Both kinds are generally used with a lightweight decorative chain and often sold in plastic bubble packs. A special design of ceiling hook is made for use on suspended ceilings. It slips over the thin metal runners that hold the ceiling panels. All are used with hanging baskets.

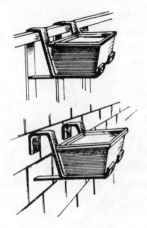

PLANTER BOX BRACKETS

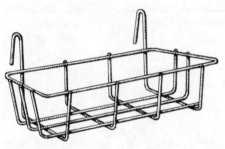

HANGOVER

POT CLIP

Macramé: Multiple strands of decorative woven rope or yarn, ranging from 2 to 6 feet in length; the strands come together at one or several points to hold potted plants. A metal eye at the top provides for hanging from a nail or hook.

Planter box brackets (also known as *hangovers, window box brackets,* or *flower box brackets):* Sturdy metal arms that hook over a deck, stair, fence railing, or windowsill, or attach to a wall to support a planter or window box. Most are adjustable, with a sliding assembly to accommodate the width of the railing as well as the width of the planter. Smaller versions for holding round pots are also available, called *hang-a-rounds.* Models for direct attachment to a wall are available, too, called *pot clips,* or *flowerpot holders.*

Pulleys: Grooved wheel assembly that can be attached to a ceiling.

S-hooks: Wrought iron, plastic, or steel strand, usually about ¼ inch thick, in the form of an S. Ranges in size from about an inch to half a foot.

Shelving: Lightweight metal shelving, usually 3 or 4 shelves to a unit, about 36 inches long and high.

Swivel hooks: These rotate so the plant can get sun on all sides.

Track: Long metal channel, about 1 inch deep, in which special hooks or eyes can slide; S-hooks or chains are hooked into each one, and the plant suspended by the chains.

USE: Hanging or supporting plants in containers near windows or on exterior walls.

USE TIPS: Hangers with swivel devices make it easier to rotate plants so that different sides are toward the light. Hooks and

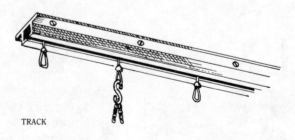

TRACK

hangers with pulley devices make it easier to lower heavy pots and planters for watering and care. Measure your rails and planters before purchasing support brackets.

BUYING TIP: Hardware stores and gift shops also carry ingenious plant hanging items. Shop around.

JARDINIERE

DESCRIPTION: Decorative ceramic or stoneware jar that comes in a wide variety of shapes, sizes, and colors.

USE: Dresses up houseplant containers. Not often used for outdoor plants.

USE TIPS: Few jardinieres have drainage holes, so plants should not be planted directly in them but rather in containers, such as plain pots, that fit easily inside the jardiniere. A layer of gravel should be placed in the bottom to act as a reservoir for excess water underneath the plain pot. The container holding the plant should never sit in water unless the plant is a bog marginal (bog marginals are referred to as "plants that love wet feet").

BUYING TIP: A purchase determined by budget or aesthetic considerations only.

PLANT TRAY

DESCRIPTION: Shallow, clear or colored plastic tray with ribs and no drainage holes. *Window* or *windowsill trays* are designed to fit on windowsills, and are therefore long and narrow. Typically 20 or 22 inches long by 3½ to 10 inches wide. Usually sold with small aluminum brackets to hold them in place.

USE: Supporting flowerpots or other containers in a moist environment when filled with gravel, sand, perlite, or vermiculite. The gravel or other material holds a supply of water away from the roots to prevent rot and to maintain high humidity.

USE TIPS: Even in a greenhouse these are helpful, especially a window greenhouse. Collect sand or rocks from a favorite vacation spot and you'll have even more to enjoy.

BUYING TIP: Clear plastic for some reason is often more expensive. Search out the thicker, stronger trays.

PLASTIC PLANTER

DESCRIPTION: Commonly made of polyurethane and available in almost any size and shape. Color range is wide, but a popular color resembles terra-cotta. Many models, called *self-watering* or *reservoir planters* or *pots,* are available with a built-in reservoir for water in the bottom. This may be internal and airtight, or else a saucerlike attachment, with a capillary or wick system that draws up the water as needed. The better models have aeration ducts that maintain the proper humidity level in the soil, and sensors that shut the water on and off. *Hanging pots* are deep containers with attached saucers and three wires and a hook for hanging.

USE: Any type of planting. Those that look like terra-cotta are ideal for designs that call for this appearance but where weight is an issue, such as on roofs and balconies. Self-watering planters are good for people who find it hard to water regularly, with some models capable of going a month between waterings.

USE TIPS: Plastic is not porous and soils and media in these containers do not dry out as quickly as soil in a more porous clay pot, an important consideration in hot, dry places. But watch out for overwatering, the primary cause of houseplant failure, if you don't have a self-watering model. Soil should always be separated from water reservoirs by stones or else the roots will rot. Add a layer of charcoal to the bottom to absorb toxic chemicals and salts.

BUYING TIPS: Plastic pots are often less expensive than fiberglass ones. The choice of plastic pots is pretty much up to your needs and taste, though color is an important consideration. A good thick layer of gravel in the bottom may give a similar but less efficient effect as a more expensive built-in reservoir.

RED CLAY FLOWERPOT

DESCRIPTION: The quintessential flowerpot, available in the standard tapered shape, with a ridge that extends about one-fifth of the way down from the top, since time immemorial. The ridge indicates the level to which it should be filled with soil. Size ranges from tiny 2-inch-deep pots to those more than 3 feet deep. Standard-model clay pots are unglazed and unpainted, though glazed and painted clay pots are available.

RED CLAY FLOWERPOT

USE: Containers for houseplants or terrace or roof garden plants. Often houseplants in clay pots are summered outside in the garden or on the patio.

USE TIPS: Because clay pots are porous, the soil they contain dries out more quickly than soil in less porous pots. Clay pots are the only ones that "breathe." Experienced gardeners know when to water plants that are growing in clay pots by being observant of the color of the pot. As the soil dries out, the pots become lighter in color. The salts found in fertilizers and some water sources may build up on clay pots, appearing as a white chalky residue on the surface of the pot. If the pot is to be reused, this salt should be scraped off and the pot washed in a solution of warm water and chlorine bleach to remove other bacteria and fungi that may be on or in the clay. Pots that are kept wet develop algae, which appear as a green film. Algae are usually not harmful and can easily be washed off if the pot is reused for another plant. Note that pots do absorb heat quickly in hot weather, which may bake plant roots.

BUYING TIPS: Clay pots may not necessarily be any better than ones made from plastic or other materials, but they do seem to be the choice of serious gardeners, primarily because they absorb excess water and thus help resist damage from overwatering. They are less expensive than ceramic or stoneware pots and are generally considered more earthy and attractive.

STRAWBERRY JAR

ALSO KNOWN AS: Strawberry pot

DESCRIPTION: Urn or jar with an open top and holes in the sides. Most commonly made from unglazed fired red clay, but also made from glazed stoneware or other materials such as plastic or fiberglass. Size ranges from only 8 inches in height to as tall as 3 feet. Another version is a redwood *patio tower* with slats instead of holes, in either a slight pyramid or bookcase style.

USE: Traditionally used for growing strawberries, but also used to grow a miniature herb garden or a collection of succulents or other small houseplants, including African violets and miniature English ivy.

USE TIPS: Strawberry jars should be planted in layers. Soil should first be placed in the pot up to the first holes, plants then put in the holes, and soil added until the next level of holes is

STRAWBERRY JAR

reached. A cardboard collar or tube made from paper towel rollers taped together should be placed in the center of the pot from top to bottom and filled with the small gravel such as is sold in pet stores for lining bird cages or aquariums, before the pot is filled with soil. The tube is removed when the pot is completely filled and planted, leaving a gravel core through which the pot can be uniformly watered. You may want to use soilless mixes because they are lighter, and put this planter on rollers so you can rotate it to give all sides some sun.

BUYING TIPS: The material you choose is strictly a matter of personal preference. Glazed stoneware pots are usually more expensive. Hand-thrown, unglazed, Italian clay strawberry pots are common and often not expensive.

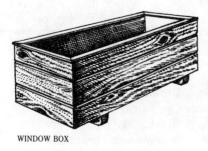

WINDOW BOX

WINDOW BOX

ALSO KNOWN AS: Estate planter box

DESCRIPTION: Rectangular planter made of metal, plastic, wood, fiberglass, cast cement, terra-cotta, or ceramic. A standard window box fits on or hangs from a windowsill, and is as long as 3 feet and as wide and deep as 8 to 10 inches. Plastic and metal window boxes come in an assortment of colors, though green is the most common. Though not all boxes do, they should have two or more 1-inch drainage holes in the bottom, and feet to create a gap under the holes. Redwood and cedar are the most common woods used.

USE: Growing decorative plants outside windows and along balcony or porch railings.

USE TIPS: Many wooden or plastic window boxes are sold without drainage holes, but they should be drilled in the bottom before being used. Also, put the box on something to create a gap under it if it has no feet. Soil in window boxes dries out quickly, so frequent watering is essential for most plants. Be sure to place them where they are convenient for watering. A soil mix high in humus (see page 6) holds moisture longer. Metal boxes on sunny sills tend to heat up to dangerous levels, harming plant roots. Treat any wood other than cedar or redwood with a preservative that does not contain pentachlorophenol (also known as "penta"), such as Cuprinol. Special brackets (see page 269) are available for attaching window boxes to railings or fences as well as windows.

BUYING TIPS: Buy the deepest window boxes you can find (a minimum depth of 10 inches is preferred) and that your space can hold. The deeper the box, the longer it takes for the soil to dry out. Even though you can drill holes in window boxes that do not have them, it is better to buy boxes that already do. Color is an important consideration—many shades of green clash with the natural green of plant foliage. Window boxes in earth tones, if they go with the color of your house or apartment, are often good choices. Also, the more lightweight the box, the easier it is to mount outside your window—no small consideration. The only woods that hold up well to weathering are redwood and cedar.

WOODEN TUB OR CONTAINER

WOODEN TUB

ALSO KNOWN AS: Redwood planter, cedar planter

DESCRIPTION: Rectangular or octagonal container, usually held together by metal bands and sometimes lined with plastic or galvanized tin. Available in a variety of sizes from flowerpot size to large tubs that can hold a tree or shrub. Made of rot-resistant redwood, cedar, teak, or treated pine or other softwoods.

USE: Attractive, natural-looking containers for plants and shrubs. A carefully chosen collection of wooden containers on a terrace can give continuity to the overall design.

USE TIPS: If a wooden planter is not lined, a heavy plastic garbage bag can be placed on the inside in order to slow down the decay of the wood (be sure to put drainage holes in the plastic liner). If the planter does not have drainage holes, drill some before planting. Even a rot-resistant redwood planter can have its useful life doubled by using a plastic liner. The soil in unlined wooden planters tends to dry out more quickly than in lined or solid containers. Do not use treated wood planters for growing any edible plants—the treatment is usually toxic.

BUYING TIPS: Wooden containers have an insulating value that keeps soil from drying out as fast as it does in other types of containers. Look for lined planters with drainage holes. Avoid those treated with toxic preservatives, such as those used on decks (CCA is the most common), but if you must, get one that is treated for contact with the ground. Never even bother with creosoted wood—it is toxic to plants. The best planters are made of disease- and rot-resistant redwood or cedar. While teak is an excellent material for the construction of wooden planters, much of it comes from the commercial harvest of naturally grown teak that has been destroying tropical rain forests. Gardeners in particular should be concerned about this and avoid purchasing teak products that are produced from wild teak; look for teak labeled as "grown in managed forests."

Stakes, Supports, and Fencing

ABOUT STAKES, SUPPORTS, AND FENCING

Stakes and supports are used with all kinds of plants and to solve many different problems, so there is a wide array of types available.

There is no such thing as just plain "fencing"—each type has its specific function. Some are used to keep pest animals at bay, and are noted in chapter 4. Others are used for defining areas or for creating shade, and are noted here.

ANCHOR

DESCRIPTION: Short stakes made of wood, metal, or plastic, designed to be driven into the ground with a mallet or hammer.

USE: Holding down plastic sheeting, whether it be landscape fabric used as mulch (see pages 27–28), row covers (see pages 286–87), or protective netting (see page 112).

USE TIPS: Drive in deeply for extra holding strength and shield exposed end with rocks or potted plants to limit the chance of someone tripping over the stake.

BORDER FENCING

ALSO KNOWN AS: Trim fence, bed guard, folding fence, flower border

DESCRIPTION: Small decorative fence of welded, plastic-coated or enameled wire, or of wooden pickets. Vinyl coated in green or white. Commonly sold in 8-, 10-, and 12-foot lengths, folded into sections, or in 20- and 25-foot rolls, 8 to 32 inches high, and

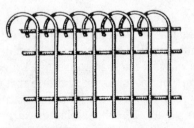

BORDER FENCING

in a variety of styles, such as round tops, angular tops, or Gothic tops. Picket patterns usually have model names like Colonial or Cape Cod. Wooden lattice panels also available. Also available is a 36- or 48-inch high version, called a *lawn guard*.

USE: Marking off flower beds and protecting them from people, pets, and lawn mowers.

USE TIP: If low fencing is to be placed near a popular shortcut, try to notice if people are tripping on the fence rather than going around it. If so, replace with a higher fence.

BUYING TIP: Avoid untreated pine fencing, as it will rot after just one year in the soil.

PLASTIC EDGING

EDGING

ALSO KNOWN AS: Plastic border, landscape border, grass stop, grass edging, lawn edging, border edging, bed divider, lawn border

POPULAR BRAND NAMES: Easy-Edge®, Sureedge

DESCRIPTION: Several different types available. Semirigid polyethylene, galvanized steel, or aluminum sheet, 4 to 6 inches high, meant to be driven into the ground vertically. The plastic version has a tubular edge that, when pushed into the ground, should just touch the surface (a small L on the bottom edge keeps the plastic from coming back up). Plastic models available in black, white, green, or redwood color, sold in rolls of 20 and 100 feet. Steel and aluminum come in the same lengths, silver or green in color, and usually in 40-foot lengths. Also available in 6-inch and 12-inch-high scalloped cedar slabs in 10- and 20-foot sections or in 3-inch diameter *pegs* or *logs* 4½ to 10 inches high, joined by a wire or rubber sheet in 3-foot sections. Still other types are made of pressure-treated pine (in a green-gray color) with decorative picket tops, or fake plastic "pegs." Better brands have a T or flared bottom to keep it from coming out.

USE: Making borders for flower beds and lawns. A particularly good way to keep creeping grass out of perennial beds and off walks.

USE TIP: Push metal or plastic in slowly so it does not buckle. The edging should be pushed into the soil deep enough to block any invasive roots and for a lawn mower to pass over it.

BUYING TIPS: Black plastic edging with the tubular top has largely replaced green metal and other forms of plastic edging and is considerably more durable. Some brands are guaranteed for twenty years. Avoid promotionally priced lightweight metal edging, as it is likely to bend when it is being installed.

PLANT STAKE

DESCRIPTION: Long thin piece of bamboo, hardwood, or steel tubing covered with PVC, ranging in size from small pencil diameters to 1 inch thick and from 2 to 8 feet long. Wooden and bamboo stakes may be either painted or unpainted. Usually sold in packages or bundles of 10 to 25, sometimes including an assortment of mixed sizes. *Tree stakes* are either of two kinds: 6-foot-long and 2- to 3-inch-thick pieces of rot-resistant cedar, or else sturdy 1-foot stakes that look much like tent stakes. Both are used with *guy wires* (lengths of galvanized steel wire) that are wrapped around the trunk with a rubber sleeve for protection and attached to the stakes. Rough-textured natural *fernwood poles,* made from the roots of large ferns, are also available. These are a few inches in diameter and 18 to 36 inches long.

USE: Holding up tall or heavy plants, like hollyhocks or tomatoes, and shrubs. Tree stakes keep newly planted trees from blowing over in high winds before their roots are established. Fernwood poles are used for houseplants.

USE TIPS: When tying plants to a stake, secure the tie or twist or string to the stake before tying it to the plant. This prevents the tie from slipping down the stake. Especially with vegetable crops like tomatoes, it is important that the tie be loose around the plant's stem. If it is too tight, the plant will strangle as it grows or the tie will cut into the stem. Use natural fiber string or twine to tie the plants. String or twine made from synthetic material will not decompose if left in the garden, and is harder to work with. Look for natural fiber materials such as jute or cotton; paper-covered wire is better than plastic ties.

BUYING TIPS: Determine how you are going to use the stakes and whether you will be using them for many years or not. If you need the stakes for a temporary job, buy the cheaper bamboo stakes. If you are planning to use the stakes for several years, the more expensive PVC-covered steel tubing is worth the extra money.

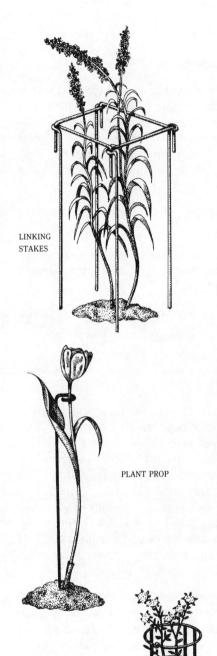

LINKING
STAKES

PLANT PROP

PEONY SUPPORT

PLANT SUPPORT

ALSO KNOWN AS: Cage, hoop, perennial support, flower support, flower support ring, border support

DESCRIPTION: Rust-resistant or plastic-coated stakes or wire hoops, loops, or grids with vertical wire legs, of various designs. *Peony supports* are single or double wire hoops attached to heavy vertical wires 24 or 35 inches long, making a cylinder. *Grow-through flower supports* have a large round grid, or frame, over the top of which plants grow. Another version has just a single stake with a small loop at the top, called a *blossom* or *bulb support, plant prop,* or *loop-stake.* And some, *link* or *linking stakes,* are just straight wire pieces available in three lengths, from about 1 to 3 feet, that are linked together as the gardener wishes, custom-designed for each plant or garden. *Tuteurs* (French for "tutors") are 6-foot-high supports for vines and climbing plants. All are usually dark green and available in a small range of sizes. Some designs fold flat for winter storage.

USE: Holding up top-heavy plants that have a tendency to flop over, whether due to their own weight or heavy winds and rain. Blossom or bulb supports are for single top-heavy flowers. The grow-through flower support, or grid, is more suitable for taller perennials. Linking stakes are most helpful in borders and beds.

USE TIPS: Place the supports over the plants just as they start to grow. Push the vertical wire in the ground around the plant so that the plant is centered in the hoop or hoops. Note that it is darn hard to push a full-grown plant with large blooms through a small opening, so put supports out when the plant is beginning to grow, not afterward, though linking stakes can be installed after plants have grown.

BUYING TIPS: Peony supports are not very expensive at under $2 for a single hoop and under $3 for a double hoop, although a homemade version using chicken wire is a good alternative, and it doesn't show that much. The chicken wire (about 1 foot square) is placed over the plant just as it starts to grow and is raised up by the lower leaves as it grows. The blooms appear above the wire. Linking stakes are the most versatile. Look for strong wire and smooth coatings. Though more expensive than tying plants to stakes, supports are easier.

PLANT TIE

POPULAR BRAND NAME: Twist-em®

DESCRIPTION: Thin wire sandwiched inside a ¼-inch-wide paper, usually green. Sold in reels ranging from a few feet to 250 feet long as well as in packages of precut pieces about 6 or 8 inches long. Alternatives include soft, natural *jute twine* (green or natural beige color), *vinyl ribbon, nylon loops,* and *foam-coated, cushioned wire,* some of which stretch as the plant grows. Most can be found in the color green.

USE: Temporary and gentle holding of plants against supports and stakes.

USE TIPS: Avoid sturdy plastic ties because they are more likely to restrict the growth of woody plants. Wire ties are easiest to use and can be tied with one hand.

BUYING TIP: Natural jute or sisal twine is generally cheapest and also biodegradable.

RIGID PLANT TRELLIS

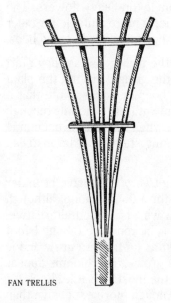

FAN TRELLIS

DESCRIPTION: Sold in a variety of shapes, including the old-fashioned *fan trellis,* a wider-bottomed *flair trellis,* a rectangular *ladder* design, and the *diamond grid trellis,* also called *lattice.* Made of aluminum, plastic, fiberglass, or wood. An *arbor* (or *trellised arch)* is sort of a three-dimensional trellis that spans a walk like a freestanding doorway or arch, and a *tunnel* is a longer version. A *bean and pea tower* is merely 6-foot-long stakes bunched together at the top like a skinless tepee. An *A-frame trellis* consists of two 5-by-8-foot metal frames covered with a large mesh nylon net, and a similar rigid trellis is made of large panels that unfold like a Japanese screen.

USE: Supporting climbing or vining plants that cannot adhere to a wall. In some cases, you may not want vines on the wall (to avoid damage by invasive roots) or, in other cases, the trellis may create a natural wall of its own. Trellises also allow you to harvest vining vegetables without bending over.

USE TIP: Be sure that the trellis is well secured, particularly when growing woody or heavy vines. Excellent for those who have trouble reaching ground level, such as wheelchair-bound or elderly gardeners.

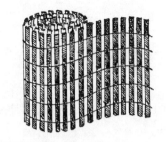

SHADE FENCING

SHADE FENCING

ALSO KNOWN AS: Snow fencing, shading fence

DESCRIPTION: Small, ⅜-inch-thick wooden boards, called *laths,* 3 to 6 feet long by about 1 inch wide, bound together with several rows of wire, twisted on both sides of each lath. Often stained or painted red or maroon. Sold in rolls of 50 feet. A similar type of protective fencing is woven from thin, chemically treated freshwater reeds, called *reed fencing.* It comes in 6-foot-high rolls 15 and 25 feet long.

USE: Breaks wind enough to control the drifting of snow and sand. Also functions as a simple windbreak for small shrubs and trees—an application particularly useful in areas where the winter winds can be damaging. Can also be used to shade newly planted seedlings or hardwood cuttings.

SPIRAL ALUMINUM TOMATO STAKE

SPIRAL ALUMINUM TOMATO STAKE

DESCRIPTION: Thick wire spiral with straight pointed end, 5½ feet tall and ½ inch in diameter, which can be stuck in the ground near a tomato plant.

USE: Holding tomato plants upright without tying: They grow through the tunnel that is created by the spiral.

USE TIP: Make sure the main stem is placed inside the spiral before branching occurs. Keeping sucker growth (buds and stems that appear between the main stem and a branch) pruned is more important with this kind of stake. Sucker growth not only saps the strength of the plant, but can create a bushier plant than this type of stake is designed to accommodate.

BUYING TIP: These are more expensive than other types of stakes. Try one out before deciding whether you want to use it for all your tomato plants.

TOMATO CAGE

ALSO KNOWN AS: Tomato stake cage

DESCRIPTION: Rust-resistant metal or plastic frame, 48 or 54 inches high, shaped like a cone, with the larger end of the cone on the top, or like a straight cylinder or rectangle. Several concentric wire rings are held together by vertical metal wires.

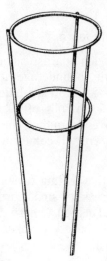

TOMATO CAGE

Some are made from pieces of large wire mesh formed into 18-inch cylinders.

USE: Supports tomatoes and other fruiting plants, eliminating the task of staking and tying.

USE TIP: Cages should be placed over the plants shortly after they have been transplanted into the garden, before they become too big to be easily caged.

BUYING TIP: Unless you grow hundreds of tomatoes, cages are not an expensive purchase. They can be used for many years and are much easier to use than stakes and ties.

TRELLIS NET

DESCRIPTION: Plastic netting designed to be strung between poles or posts.

USE: Temporary trellis for climbing vegetable crops, such as cucumbers, beans, and peas. Reduces the amount of space needed in the garden. They also make harvesting from vines easier.

USE TIP: Place poles and posts that are used to support nets close enough together to support the weight of the crops. Test and experiment to determine the best distance, and install so that they hold well.

BUYING TIP: Gardeners in the past made their own net vegetable trellises by stringing twine between upright poles. Plastic net trellises simplify this task, and they can be used for many more years than twine. Make sure the net you are buying can support the weight of the crop that you wish to grow on it.

WALL ANCHOR

ALSO KNOWN AS: Vine hanger, vine support, vine nail, wall nail, garden wall tie

DESCRIPTION: Extra-sturdy 1¼-inch nail (a masonry nail) with a soft lead arm, or clip, about an inch or two long. Another version is a small fiber disk with a 2-inch-long wire tongue, sold with a tube of weatherproof adhesive. The simplest version is a long steel wedge with a hole in the wide end, called a *vine eye.* Another type is the *pole pin,* a sturdy, long U-shaped pin that is pushed into soft wood.

USE: Holding up vines or other climbing plants on masonry or wooden walls.

USE TIPS: Bend the holding arm before attaching to a wall. Make sure you follow adhesive directions, leaving a thick pad of it between the wall and the anchor.

WIRE FENCING

DESCRIPTION: Welded wire fences are available with large mesh and fence posts in 36- and 48-inch-high models, sold in 50-foot rolls. *Hex netting,* also known as *poultry netting* or *chicken wire,* is available in 50- and 150-foot rolls, 24, 36, and 48 inches wide, of lightweight galvanized, woven wire. *Diamond mesh* is available galvanized or vinyl coated, usually with a 2½-inch woven mesh made of medium-weight wire, in 50-foot rolls, 36 or 48 inches high—it looks like the much stronger and heavier *chain link fences.* Welded mesh has square openings in various sizes, including ½ by 1 inch, 1 inch square, 2 by 1 inch, and 4 by 2 inches, and is available in 36- and 48-inch heights, sold in rolls 50 and 100 feet long. Some fencing labels refer to the "gauge" of the wire used, meaning the weight or thickness. A higher number is lighter weight: Below approximately 14 to 16 is heavy, and above 20 is lightweight.

USE: Containing animals and people on your property, or excluding them.

BUYING TIP: Welded fencing is stronger than woven fencing, and wire fence material that is galvanized after welding is better protected against the elements.

Protective Materials and Season Extenders

BURLAP

ALSO KNOWN AS: Wind shield, windbreak, plant protector

DESCRIPTION: Loosely woven, light brown cloth traditionally made from natural jute fiber, available in 7-ounce and lightweight 5-ounce versions. Sold in sheets from 20 inches square to 120 inches square or in rolls up to 125 yards long and in widths of 36, 40, 48, or 60 inches, called *bulk,* or *continuous, burlap.* May be treated (to prevent rot) or untreated. Very loosely woven (½-inch) untreated burlap is sold in 3-foot by 10-, 25-, 50-, and 100-foot rolls for use over newly seeded lawns. It decomposes after the grass grows through it. Longer rolls, 45 inches by 250 yards, are sold as *lawn netting* and may be made of twisted paper cord. Plastic version is also available. *Erosion cloth* is a term sometimes used to refer to the 5-ounce, lightweight, wide (or "open") mesh version. Available also in 8- to 12-foot squares, with grommets in each corner and reinforced edges for use as a leaf carrier; may be called *totes*.

USE: Seven-ounce rolled burlap is used to construct wind shields to protect sensitive plants from cold, damaging winter winds and snow. Sheets are used to wrap root and soil balls when transplanting or moving woody shrubs and trees. Smaller sheets, about 8 feet square, can be used for carrying large loads of raked leaves or other garden debris. Five-ounce erosion cloth and lawn netting are staked or pinned down on newly seeded or bare lawns, especially on gentle slopes and embankments.

USE TIPS: When wrapping root balls, wet the soil around the plant well to keep the soil in a compact ball. Be sure to use natural twine to bind a natural burlapped root ball, so that it decomposes after planting. Most burlap products, especially the lightweight version, are biodegradable and disintegrate naturally after one season—considered an advantage by most users. Remove lawn netting after grass sprouts if you don't want to wait. Do not use as a duster: The dust will go all over, not as directed, and is likely to pose a hazard to you.

BUYING TIP: Natural burlap is easier to use as it is more pliable than plastic, which does not allow plant roots to breathe and does not decompose in the ground.

CLOCHE

ALSO KNOWN AS: Season extender, plant protector, tepee, plant cover

DESCRIPTION: Plastic, glass, or fabric cone that is placed over a single plant, several plants, or an entire row of plants in a garden. Similar in theory to a cold frame (see next entry), but portable. Light passes through the material so that the green leaves can still photosynthesize. Many ingenious designs are available, from galvanized wire mesh covered with plastic to paper on wire hoops, as well as the familiar molded or formed

CLOCHE

plastic. A newer kind is a set of interconnected clear plastic tubes that are filled with about 3 gallons of water, forming a ribbed cone (sold under the brand name Wall-O-Water). The water retains heat from the day and releases it at night, acting as a temperature moderator and insulator.

USE: Protects young, tender crops during the early (and late) season from late (or early) frosts and cold winds. It is also used to extend the season into the cooler weather in the fall and to protect seedlings from birds, insects, and hard rains. Crops such as tomatoes, peppers, and other transplants can get a head start when a cloche is placed over them.

USE TIP: Be sure to remove the cloche when the day temperatures are particularly warm (75° F or over), as the plants may heat up too much. Replace the cloche when the temperatures begin to drop.

BUYING TIP: If you plan on using cloches for several years, buy the higher-priced fabric or solid plastic ones that will last, and store carefully between seasons. It will be worth the investment.

COLD FRAME

DESCRIPTION: Essentially a miniature greenhouse, consisting of an open pit dug in the ground up to 2 feet deep by about 3 or 4 feet long and wide, with a wooden (rot-resistant redwood most often), plastic (polycarbonate), or aluminum frame around the sides and a hinged glass or clear plastic top. Some models come with thermostatically controled tops that automatically open when the temperature reaches a certain point, or other automatic venting systems, or it can be a simple homemade job.

USE: Allows you to winter over tender plants as well as to start and protect seedlings in the spring. Can double during the summer as a small compost bin when it is not being used for plants.

USE TIPS: Cold frames should be opened when the day temperatures begin to climb, otherwise you risk a premature cooking of the plants within. Watch out that you don't drop the top and break the glass; plastic glazing is advantageous in this respect.

BUYING TIPS: Cold frames are so easy to make that most people (even those who are not handy) can put one together in an afternoon, using scrap lumber and old windows. However, the polycarbonate ones sold commercially are excellent—they even insulate a bit—and won't break if you drop the tops or accidentally step on them when chasing an errant shuttlecock or baseball. Look for ones with wind-protected vents.

ROSEBUSH PROTECTOR

ALSO KNOWN AS: Winterizer, plant protector, season extender, rose collar, rose cone

DESCRIPTION: Two basic types: one solid and one open. The solid one is a Styrofoam plastic cone about 1½ or 2 feet high that resembles a large wastebasket with a flange. Stakes, which are supplied, are driven through holes in the flange to hold the cone down. The open one is fiberglass screening or corrugated plastic in the form of a cylinder a foot high and from 1 to 1½ feet in diameter. It is filled with a light, insulating mulch, such as peat moss, peanut shells, or the like.

USE: Protecting rosebushes from winter weather extremes.

USE TIPS: Carefully prune your roses first. Clean and store properly to get long life out of your protectors.

ROW COVER

ALSO KNOWN AS: Fabric row cover, floating row cover

POPULAR BRAND NAME: Reemay®

DESCRIPTION: Essentially a sort of cold frame (see pages 285–86) brought to the plants instead of the other way around. Made of lightweight, translucent, spun-bonded polyester material in rolls between 5 and 6 feet wide and 250 to 2,550 feet long. Sunlight (75 percent) and water (almost 100 percent) penetrate easily. Some are slitted to prevent overheating during periods of temperature fluctuation.

USE: Protects seedlings from animals, flying pests, and seasonal temperature extremes (early spring and late fall) to a certain extent, while still allowing light and water to enter. Also helps retain moisture and heat in a seedbed.

USE TIPS: Support with some kind of light framework or stakes. Though the manufacturer claims that the material is so light it can be placed loosely over new plants or seedbeds, letting the plants push it up as they grow, tender seedlings might not be

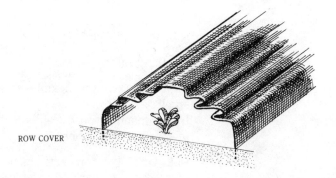

ROW COVER

strong enough to do this and could get damaged. Remove the fabric once the seedlings are established to avoid heating up the bed too much.

SHADE FABRIC

DESCRIPTION: Loosely woven black polypropylene fibers sold in 6-foot rolls in lengths up to 300 feet. It is graded according to the density of shade it provides, ranging from 30 to 92 percent (commonly 53, 63, and 73 percent). Price varies accordingly, with the densest costing roughly twice as much per square foot as the most open. The fabric is rot-proof, mildew-proof, UV ray resistant, and chemical resistant. *Shading compound* is a concentrated paint that is used on glass greenhouses to temper the sunlight. A different kind of compound is used on plastic. *Greenhouse film* is UV resistant plastic sheeting, 14 to 40 feet wide, sold in 100-foot rolls, used for the same purpose; it is secured with staples and *greenhouse tape,* an adhesive tape specially formulated for this purpose.

USE: Primarily for shading tender new seedlings and transplants but also for covering a planting bed where cuttings are rooting.

USE TIP: It is easier to install above a planting bed if it is attached to a wooden frame.

BUYING TIPS: As with many products sold by the roll, larger ones are cheaper to buy by the foot. Look for shade fabric that is UV tested, as this indicates it does not break down under sunlight.

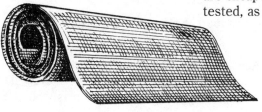

SHADE FABRIC

STEEL MESH TREE PROTECTOR

POPULAR BRAND NAME: Tree Tender®

DESCRIPTION: Soft, flexible, stainless steel mesh that is sold in small pieces 2⅜ inches by 7½ feet. Secured with clips supplied by the manufacturer. Can be cut to fit. Another version is made of sturdy foam rubber.

USE: One layer protects against rodent damage; multilayered wrap protects bark from string trimmer and mower damage. The open weave permits natural ventilation but discourages insect larvae development.

TREE SUPPORT KIT

DESCRIPTION: Collection of three 18-inch hardwood stakes, three 12-inch rubber sleeves (probably sections of old hose), and 30 feet of heavy galvanized wire. Others may include 6-foot cedar stakes instead, usually in urban areas.

USE: Holding a newly planted tree upright without damaging it.

USE TIPS: Wrap the wire around the stakes securely so that it really holds the tree if tension is placed on it. Position the hose around the tree's trunk, then wrap securely with the other ends of the wire. The hose will prevent the wire from cutting into the tree's bark. Place colorful ribbons on the stakes to prevent people from tripping over them. Remove after one year.

BUYING TIP: This is another item that is easily made at home, but is packaged merely as a convenience.

TREE TUBE

ALSO KNOWN AS: Tree guard

POPULAR BRAND NAMES: Ross Tree Gard®, Clark's Weed Whacker Guards

DESCRIPTION: A plastic tube slit along the side, sold in 36-inch lengths.

USE: Snaps onto trunks of young trees to protect them from insect and animal damage, as well as from excessive sun, like tree wrap (see next entry), but, because it is stiff plastic, it also protects street trees from minor bike or dog abuse, and provides particularly good winter protection. A new specialty model only 6 inches high has been developed for protecting against nylon string trimmers.

USE TIP: Remember to remove the tubing as the tree grows too big for it, although one advantage to slit tube or spirals is that they expand easily with the growth of the tree.

TREE WRAP

ALSO KNOWN AS: Tree paper, tree collar

DESCRIPTION: Waterproof paper, plastic fiber, vinyl, foam rubber, or burlap in widths from 3 to 6 inches. The woven wraps are sold in rolls of 100 or 150 feet, while the plastic wraps may be in 2- and 3-foot-long spirals. The paper type is dark brown kraft paper sandwiching a layer of weatherproof asphalt and given a "crepe" finish.

USE: Wound in a spiral around the bottom 6 feet or so of the trunks of small trees. Protects trees, especially young, newly planted ones, from damage by insects, pets, deer, rabbits, and weather (sunscald, windburn, or early frost), as well as from loss of moisture.

USE TIPS: Paper and natural fiber burlap are easier to work with and better for the tree than synthetic material, which when used as a tight fabric wrap does not expand as the tree grows, and if not removed, will constrict the tree. Tie with jute twine, which will rot off over time and not harm the tree as it grows. Solid plastic spirals should be avoided as they neither breathe nor decompose. Trees with lenticles (breathing pores) should not be covered with plastic tree wrap.

Personal and Miscellaneous Gear and Equipment

Protective Clothing and Gear

ABOUT PROTECTIVE GEAR AND SAFETY ITEMS

As tame a pastime as it may appear to be, gardening is not without its dangers—power tools, tools with sharp edges or blades, and toxic chemicals are some of the things that can be hazardous to the gardener who does not consider safety when using them. Many of the items listed here as personal gear are in fact safety items, designed to protect the gardener from harm. On the other hand, some are designed to make the gardener's job easier, or to help infirm or elderly gardeners get around an uncomfortable job. Both kinds are important.

When shopping for safety items, do not sacrifice quality for price. Be sure the items you are buying meet your own rigid standards for fit and function, and look for labels of government approval as well, such as OSHA (Occupational Safety and Health Administration) or ANSI (American National Standards Institute).

EAR PROTECTORS

ALSO KNOWN AS: Earmuffs, hearing protectors

DESCRIPTION: Similar to large audio headphones: two semi-

EAR PROTECTORS

spherical cups that are sound-insulated and foam-lined for easy fit. They fit over the ears and are held in place by a plastic or metal band that is worn over the top of the head.

USE: Prevent damage to the ears from the noise of power tools.

USE TIPS: Gasoline-powered tools such as lawn mowers, gas-powered string trimmers, chipper/shredders, generators for hedge trimmers, rotary tillers, and chain saws are particularly noisy and can cause damage to the ears. Ear protectors should be worn when using these tools and machines. Keep your eyes open for possible warnings from other people, because you won't be able to hear them when operating these types of equipment.

BUYING TIP: Try on ear protectors to test for comfortable fit and to test the level of noise they absorb.

HARD HAT

ALSO KNOWN AS: Safety hard cap

DESCRIPTION: Metal or reinforced plastic cap with a short bib visor in the front and a web lining. Available with transparent face shields (made of either plastic sheet or metal mesh) or ear protectors, in which case may be called a *safety helmet.*

USE: Protecting your head during overhead tree pruning or major clearing projects.

USE TIP: Adjust headband for snug fit.

BUYING TIP: Though not a standard item for all gardeners, it is recommended if you do a lot of heavy pruning. If you find that your are wearing a hard hat with your goggles and ear protectors, you may wish to look for hats that have these features built in. Consider the temperature when buying a hat with a face visor—a wire mesh face shield is cooler than a solid plastic one. Many different makes are available. Look for one that meets ANSI standards, the government test.

PROTECTIVE GOGGLES

ALSO KNOWN AS: Safety goggles, eye protectors

DESCRIPTION: Oversized plastic glasses with covered sides,

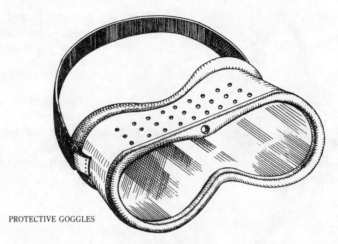

PROTECTIVE GOGGLES

large enough to fit over regular glasses, with rubber or elastic headbands that hold them in place. The side pieces also have vent holes to prevent the goggles from fogging up, though some goggles are now made of nonfogging plastic.

USE: Protect eyes from dust or flying particles of wood, grit, stone, or any other object that could damage the eyes. They are to be worn when using most power tools, such as chipper/shredders and string- or blade-type weed cutters, as well as large cutting tools such as axes and hatchets.

USE TIP: Goggles should be kept clean for better visibility. Certain power tools kick up so much debris that the goggles can become dangerously clogged, actually blinding you and possibly leading to an accident.

BUYING TIPS: Safety goggles are an essential gardening item if you use axes or power tools. Try them on before purchase to ensure a comfortable fit. Wear them for a few minutes to see if they fog up, and don't buy them if they do. Goggles should protect from dust and dirt as well as impact, and are marked as such. If you wear glasses, get a pair of goggles that are large enough to fit over them. There is no question that protection of your eyes is worth spending money on. Don't worry about finding great bargains here.

RESPIRATOR AND DUST MASK

ALSO KNOWN AS: *Respirator*—Breathing mask, gas mask; *Dust mask*—Pinch mask, face mask, painter's mask (this term is incorrect and misleading)

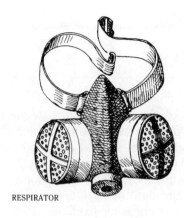

RESPIRATOR

DUST MASK

DESCRIPTION: Respirators are heavy-duty rubberized plastic devices that are strapped to the head and fit over the mouth and nose. A round filter cartridge is on each side. Some models, called "full-face" models, have a face shield that covers the entire face. Government specifications for whatever it can filter out are clearly indicated on the filter package.

Dust masks are only a few inches wide, fit loosely over the mouth and nose, and are held by a thin rubber band around the head. They are made of compressed paper fibers, are usually white, and a thin metal strip above the nose section of the mask is pinched tight for a more secure fit around the nose. The term *painter's mask* is incorrect as it generally does not protect against inhaling spray paint. Also available are slightly heavier plastic or rubber masks, roughly triangular in form, into which you insert small replacement filters; they provide a slightly snugger fit around the mouth and nose. Only a few designs are government approved.

USE: Respirators are used to filter out fine dust, mists, or toxic vapors, depending on the filter type. This kind of respirator is essential if you are using toxic chemicals; be certain to check the specifications of the filter cartridges. Dust masks are used to block out larger dusts and powders, but they do not filter out toxic vapors or mists.

USE TIPS: All masks must fit properly in order to do any good. Every gardener should keep good-quality paper dust masks on hand to wear when mixing soils, working with milled peat, and particularly for mixing soilless mixes that throw off a lot of dust, which can cause respiratory problems. *Paper dust masks are disposable and must be discarded after each use.* Clean a respirator and change its filter per directions.

BUYING TIPS: Depending upon the type of gardening you do and your exposure to toxic fumes, a respirator may not be necessary, but it is easily available these days and not too expensive. It seems a worthwhile investment in your health, even if used rarely. Dust masks, however, are inexpensive essentials. You must match the type of respirator to the job at hand. Filter cartridges are marked by their capacity for masking out dusts, mists, vapors, or fumes. Look for government approval, from either NIOSH (National Institute of Safety and Health) or MSHA (Mine Safety and Health Administration) or both. If your local garden center or hardware store cannot provide these items, check the Yellow Pages under "Safety Equipment" or "Industrial Supplies."

Comfort and Convenience Items

STAKES

BOOT SCRAPER

BOOT SCRAPER

DESCRIPTION: Many varieties, most of which fall into two categories: mat and brush type or H bar type. The former is like a metal doormat, with several rows of metal teeth instead of fiber or rubber, and the latter is a simple, flat, 6-inch-long piece of metal suspended between two uprights not more than a foot long. Stakes are driven into the ground through the uprights to hold it securely. Sometimes the mat kind has brushes fixed on either side, and instead of metal teeth, a wire brush that is replaceable. Certain models have waist-high handles, helping those of us who have trouble balancing on one leg, whether from lack of strength or mere exuberance.

USE: Forcibly removing mud from the bottoms and sides of boots.

GARDEN BOOTS

DESCRIPTION: High-top rubber boots with sturdy soles reinforced in the instep for digging (pushing a shovel by stepping on it) and a patch over the anklebone. Easily removable and waterproof.

USE: Allow unworrisome accumulation of mud on the feet, while keeping them dry.

BUYING TIPS: Typically black; most of the best models are English. Be sure to look for reinforcement where you push the shovel with your instep, and a sole pattern that does not hang onto mud.

GARDEN CLOGS

DESCRIPTION: Colorful clogs that look like wooden Dutch shoes, but are made of a rubberlike plastic. They have cushioned insoles that can be removed so that the clog can be cleaned with a hose.

USE: Gardening shoes that hold up to moisture and repeated cleanings.

USE TIP: The clog will outlast the insole, which is replaceable.

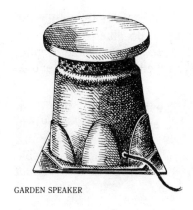

GARDEN SPEAKER

GARDEN SPEAKER

DESCRIPTION: Electronic hi-fi speaker in a decorative, weather-proof housing, often cylindrical and intended to be partially buried.

USE: Providing music in your garden from a remote source, usually your interior radio, tape deck, or record player.

USE TIPS: It is unclear which kind of music plants prefer. Watch your volume. Be careful not to disturb the neighbors.

GARDENING APRON AND TOTE

ALSO KNOWN AS: Gardener's apron

DESCRIPTION: Heavy canvas or cloth with pockets for small hand tools, plant labels, seed packets, notepad, pencils, and the like, designed to be worn like a kitchen apron or, in the case of the tote, like a holster on a belt.

USE: Keeping small and often-used gardening tools and accessories handy when not in use. Particularly useful during spring planting days.

USE TIPS: Aprons can be used for storage of these small necessities whether being worn or not. Hang the apron in an "open" position; this has the advantage of keeping the apron loaded and ready whenever you actually put it on. You may want to dedicate a belt to the gardening tote, so you can put it on over your gardening outfit, rather than having to take your own belt off each time you want to use the tote.

BUYING TIPS: Heavy-duty canvas aprons with many pockets and double seams are the best. Shorter aprons allow free movement, especially if you need to kneel, so the length should not go beyond the knees.

GARDENING GLOVES

ALSO KNOWN AS: Work gloves, protective gloves, garden gloves

DESCRIPTION: Constructed from cloth, canvas, leather, rubber, or some form of pliable plastic, lined or unlined. Gloves designed for pruning thorny brush or roses or picking fruit have long gauntlet-type cuffs to protect the arms and are coated with a plasticlike material that thorns cannot penetrate. They may be called *fruit picker gloves.* Lightweight, disposable plastic gloves are also available. So-called *ladies' gloves* are available in gingham, floral, and polka-dot patterns as well as plain, and tend to run in smaller sizes.

USE: Protect hands from blisters, dryness, cuts, and other damage that might occur during gardening, and provide a better grip in cold weather. Heavy plastic gloves made of *neoprene* are required for handling toxic materials, and lightweight, disposable ones for merely irritating chemicals. *Real* gardeners do *not* wear gloves to keep their hands clean!

USE TIPS: Wear the appropriate glove for the job you are doing. If you are transplanting delicate seedlings, don't wear heavy gloves that dampen your sense of touch. Unlined cloth gloves are good for light work and leather gloves that provide a good grip are for heavier or dangerous work. Check the directions for cleaning, because only some leather gloves can be washed. Most leather gloves that are soiled and damp become stiff and difficult to use when they dry, and should be treated with saddle soap or Murphy's Oil. Some pigskin resists this stiffness. Cotton gloves can be rinsed out in a rain barrel or sink. Gloves with holes in them will no longer prevent blisters and should be replaced. Models with lots of little rubber dots are excellent for gripping muddy tools and may wear longer.

BUYING TIPS: Gardeners should have several pairs of gloves. Check the gloves for a comfortable fit that is neither too tight nor too loose. Design varies greatly from brand to brand, and some makes offer a range of sizes, including those designed for women and men. The better designs take the natural curve of your grip into account. Look for material that resists cuts, snags, and punctures; goatskin is used in top-of-the-line products. Sheepskin, with its natural lanolin, is a real comfort if you can find it, and such gloves tend not to impede your dexterity (other skins, like goatskin, may offer the same quality, depending on the make). Look also for reinforced palms and seams. Work gloves are not an expensive investment, but generally the better gloves cost a little more (around $10 for good leather work gloves) and are worth it. When you find a pair that fits just right, you may want to buy several pairs right then.

GARDENING HAT

GARDENING HAT AND SUN VISOR

DESCRIPTION: Wide-brimmed, lightweight hat made of cloth, palm, plastic, straw, leather, or even paper and cardboard, in a wide variety of styles. A Panama hat is woven out of light straw.

USE: Personal, extremely portable sunshade. Wide brims keep gnats away.

USE TIPS: A hat or visor is essential protection against the harmful ultraviolet rays of the sun. Wear one as much as possible. And never underestimate the role of fashion in your choice of hats: A snappy-looking gardener is a better gardener, they say. Also, you might scare away some pest birds with some of the more adventurous or unsuccessful designs.

BUYING TIPS: Should be flexible, and a good-quality hat should "breathe" to keep you cool during hot days. There are no substitutes for genuine palm in terms of strength.

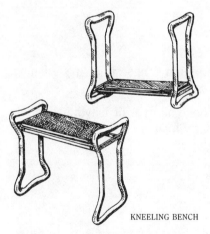

KNEELING BENCH

KNEE PROTECTORS

DESCRIPTION: Several products are sold that protect the knees from damage while gardening.

TYPES: *Kneepads:* Shallow rubber cups that fit directly over the knee and are held in place by straps that go around the leg. Sold in different weights and densities.

Kneeling pads: Rectangular foam rubber pads about 9 by 18 inches. Most have an elliptical hole that serves as a handle for carrying.

Kneeling bench (also known as *kneeler stool, bench/ kneeler,* or *garden stool):* A combination bench and kneeling pad design, this has become quite popular in recent years. Consists of a tubular metal frame about 20 inches high that supports a padded seat about 20 inches wide. When the bench is positioned with the cushion up, it is a comfortable, portable seat. When it is turned upside down, it becomes a kneeling pad with high handles for assisting the gardener in getting up and down. A bench or seat design is available with wheels, for scooting along as you garden, called a *garden scoot.*

USE: Reducing the pain of kneeling. The kneeling bench is particularly helpful to elderly gardeners and all those who have difficulty kneeling and bending.

USE TIP: It is probably a good idea to protect your knees even if you have no knee problem. Whether using a pad or not, stand up and stretch often while gardening.

BUYING TIPS: Rubber kneepads are convenient because they are attached to you and don't have to be carried around, but many gardeners complain about the slight discomfort caused by the strap that holds them on. The more expensive designs, with their heavier, denser material, tend to be worth it. Cheaper ones that don't work well make you pay with real discomfort. (One alternative is a homemade solution: Make large pockets for sponges on the knees of your gardening pants. Ready-made pants like this are available via mail-order.) Foam kneeling pads are light, inexpensive, and easy to use, but they have to be moved each time you move. The kneeling bench is more expensive but its combination design makes it versatile. It is particularly attractive to elderly or arthritic gardeners who find kneeling and bending difficult.

LAWN TWEEZERS

ALSO KNOWN AS: Cleanup caddy

LAWN TWEEZERS

DESCRIPTION: Lightweight aluminum tongs about a yard long with a hinge near the end. Plastic hand grips.

USE: Picking up litter without bending over or leaving a wheelchair, or reaching through thorny bushes

POISON OAK AND IVY CLEANSER

DESCRIPTION: Bottled salve.

USE: Applied within two to eight hours after exposure to these menaces, it removes the poison oil from your skin, actually preventing the dreaded rash. Relieves itching, slows spreading, and helps heal if applied to a rash directly.

TOOL HANGER

ALSO KNOWN AS: Tool hook

DESCRIPTION: Small steel tubing and brackets of various de-

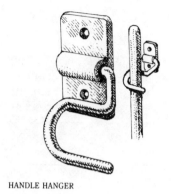

HANDLE HANGER

signs. Longer brackets may have small balls welded on to keep tools apart. Some are designed to fit into the holes of Pegboard® while others are cliplike devices that slide over the top of a board which is in turn anchored to a wall. Another type, best for smaller tools, is a metal grid with specially made hooks. A popular design is a loop of tubular steel with both ends pointing out and up; it is attached to the wall at the center (a smaller version is merely a piece of stamped metal with two hooks). For larger tools there are *handle hangers* that look like large hooks placed sideways with hinges at the top—a long, straight tool handle is inserted in the hook by lifting it away from the wall and is held in place by friction.

USE: Holding tools on a wall.

USE TIPS: Draw an outline for each tool, or put a label above each hanger, so you can always fit the tools back where they came from. Make sure any supporting boards are securely anchored—a half dozen garden tools can be very heavy and quite dangerous should they fall. Hang pronged tools with their sharp tips facing the wall.

BUYING TIPS: Hangers are useful because they help avoid a dangerous clutter of tools on the floor, and keep the tools away from moisture as well. However, in many cases, large nails driven partway into a thick board, such as a two-by-four, that is in turn anchored securely to a wall, can do just as well. Look for systems that do not require two hands to use.

TOOL HOLSTER

TYPES: *Sheath, Scabbard, Utility belt*

ALSO KNOWN AS: *Utility belt*—Tool belt

DESCRIPTION: Leather or canvas pouch that attaches to a belt, or in the case of a utility belt, a wide leather belt with hooks and compartments that goes over a regular belt.

USE: Keeping frequently used tools close at hand, especially knives, hatchets, pruning shears, and tree saws. Particularly useful for tools that are used throughout the garden, such as pruning shears, or those used when you are on a ladder.

USE TIP: Small items like pruning shears and pruning knives are less likely to be lost if they are placed in a sheath worn on the

TOOL HOLSTER

belt. Can be considered a safety item if you are working from a ladder.

BUYING TIP: Though most gardeners have no need for a heavy utility belt, any gardener with pruning shears and pruning knives will find the purchase of a quality holster a good investment. Look for well-sewn seams that are also riveted, and expect to pay between $5 and $10 for a good one.

TRUG

TRUG

ALSO KNOWN AS: Sussex trug, garden basket

DESCRIPTION: Shallow basket made of wide wooden strips, with short wooden feet and a large handle. Typically about 1 foot to just under 2 feet in length; size may be measured in capacity (e.g., 2 pints, 1.5 gallons, and 3 gallons). Made also of polyethylene.

USE: Handy way to bring small garden tools or your vegetable and flower harvest along with you as you work in the garden.

BUYING TIPS: Top-quality models are often English, made from chestnut and willow. Other common good materials are northern ash weavings and oak handles.

Birdhouses, Feeders, and Food

ABOUT BIRD EQUIPMENT

Almost all garden centers have a section devoted to birds, with birdhouses, bird feeders, birdseed, and other items designed to attract birds to the garden. Most gardeners get a particular thrill when birds find the garden pleasing enough to inhabit it. Furthermore, the presence of birds (and their singing) in a garden reminds gardeners that they are participating in a natural world that is larger than the dimensions of the garden itself. Though some birds become pests, and products are sold to rid the garden of them (see chapter 4), most birds are quite beneficial to gardens, consuming mosquitoes and other insect pests. In even the smallest garden (on apartment balconies, too) there is room for a bird feeder or a small birdhouse.

BIRDBATH

DESCRIPTION: Shallow basin that holds water, of almost infinite variety in design and detail. Some are classic and simple bowllike designs, others whimsical animal motifs (including one that recently appeared, ironically, in the form of a cat). Most birdbaths are set on a pedestal to keep them out of the reach of cats. Birdbaths can be made of stone, glazed clay, terra-cotta, cement, plastic, cast aluminum, brass, and still other materials.

USE: Attracting birds to your garden. Water is essential to attract birds, and a birdbath provides this water and is at the same time an attractive garden accessory.

USE TIPS: Place birdbaths in somewhat open areas so that birds can see any approaching cats while they are bathing. This is particularly important for basins that do not sit on pedestals or stands. Keep filled with fresh water and wash the bath out if algae begin to grow. In areas of the country where winters are harsh, basins should be heated with an *electric birdbath heater* or emptied of water. If not stored inside, they should be wrapped in plastic. Freezing water will expand and crack even a stone birdbath.

BUYING TIP: Cheap plastic birdbaths are not a good buy. Besides looking cheap (this should be considered a permanent decorative item), they are light, and the water-filled basin makes them top-heavy. There are almost unlimited alternatives. Shop for one that will complement your garden and be a focal point.

BIRD FEEDER

DESCRIPTION: A tremendous array of designs exist, from the whimsical and rustic to the extremely high tech, but all bird feeders consist of some type of chamber that holds birdseed and some place for birds to perch while feeding. Bird feeders can be round cylinders, rectangular boxes, or covered top shelters in which the seed is placed in a feeding tray. They are made of plastic, wood, glass, metal, and combinations of all these materials. Some are even designed to be mounted on a window. Most have some device for preventing squirrels from feeding, a *squirrel baffle,* a large plastic disk that fits on the support pole or hangs above a wire-held feeder. A *seed catcher,* a large saucer that attaches to the pole under the feeder, catches any stray

BIRD FEEDER

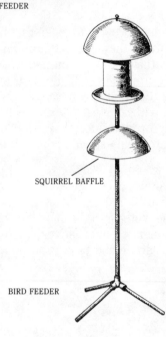

SQUIRREL BAFFLE

BIRD FEEDER

seeds that might fall. Baffles also are used for excluding heavier "nuisance" birds, such as blackbirds or pigeons.

USE: Bird feeders are most often used to attract birds to the garden during off-seasons, such as winter, when other food is scarce. Some feeders, however, are designed to attract a particular type of bird during seasons when they migrate through your area. Other feeders are used to attract particular types of birds in the spring in the hope that they will nest in or near your garden. Always keep your feeder full during its season(s) of use.

USE TIPS: Squirrels are the enemies of bird feeders, as they will enter and devour all the seed if at all possible. Place bird feeders in locations that make it difficult for squirrels (and cats, of course) to get to them, such as on metal poles and away from branches and climbable parts of buildings. Or add a squirrel baffle. Be mindful that sunflower seeds act as an herbicide and will kill your grass.

BUYING TIPS: Other than buying a sturdy, well-made feeder, particular consideration should be paid to whether the feeder is squirrel- or cat-proof. Squirrel baffles are sold separately, too. Look for models hung from wires or poles with circular squirrel guards. Bird feeders that have wide platform areas give squirrels a place to perch while raiding a feeder, and should be avoided. Window-mounted models may work better with one-way mirrors so you don't scare the birds away. The feeder should be able to adequately dispense the size of birdseed you wish to put in it. For example, finches, wrens, and many small birds feed on thistle seed and small grains. If the dispensing part of a feeder is too large, these smaller seeds will not be held well. Sunflower seed cannot be dispensed if the openings are too small. Buy feeders that will attract the specific birds you want. This information should be included in the packaging but can also be found in reference books.

BIRDHOUSE

DESCRIPTION: Made of wood, clay, plastic, or metal, birdhouses are constructed in certain sizes, shapes, and even colors to attract the specific type of bird they were built to accommodate. For example, the very social purple martins prefer to live and nest in groups and are attracted to white, well-ventilated, multicompartment houses that will house six to twenty-four nesting couples, usually perched on top of a tall pole (which has to be

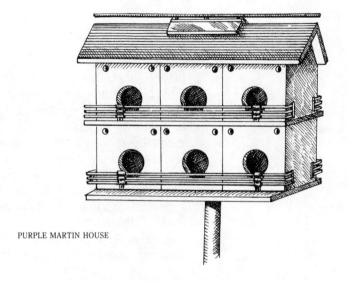

PURPLE MARTIN HOUSE

taken down, or the house lowered, each winter for cleaning). The wren, on the other hand, prefers to nest in a solitary small house that is protected by lush plant growth. The size(s) of the hole(s) in birdhouses determine(s) what birds will live in them, too. For example, house wrens and pygmy and brown-headed titmice use a house with a 1-inch hole; chickadees, Carolina wrens, tufted and plain titmice, and small woodpeckers need a small hole 1¼ inches in diameter; while bluebirds and swallows want a hole that is 1½ inches in diameter. As for materials, a popular type is a sawdust/clay/concrete mixture that looks and feels like wood or dried mud, the normal stuff birds make nests of. Also popular are those with genuine thatched roofs. Of all the woods, cedar lasts longest. Many have openings for cleaning out the houses.

USE: Attracting birds by providing a place for them to nest in your garden. Since many birds nest in the same place year after year, once you have housed nesting birds they should be with you for many years. Attracting nesting birds that are known to eat bugs is a great natural way of controlling many garden pests.

USE TIPS: Birdhouses should be placed in areas where cats cannot reach them. If this is not possible, then you must find ways to cat-proof the house, such as wrapping a wooden pole in a sheet of galvanized tin about 3 feet high to prevent cats from climbing up. How high a birdhouse is placed and what direction it faces are important considerations for getting the tenant you want to occupy it. This information can be easily found in your library, in most popular field guides and books and articles on attracting wildlife. You might also try checking your local Cooperative Extension bulletins.

BUYING TIPS: Look for sturdy birdhouses. Know specifically what birds you want to nest in your house, and buy one that is stated to have been made for that particular bird. Shop around, as prices do vary considerably. Martin houses, being bigger, are generally more expensive than others. Check your reference books to find out what size hole you need for the birds you want to attract, and measure the holes before buying—often they are not marked. As for "manufactured" wood versus natural, it seems to be a matter of personal preference. The birds are not choosy. What's important is that the house endures, and the clay/concrete mixture seems to be the sturdiest; furthermore, squirrels and predator birds are unable to enlarge the hole.

BIRDSEED

DESCRIPTION: Grains and seeds, usually mixed, including sunflower, safflower, peanut hearts, millet, sunflower chips, thistle, and cracked corn. Mixtures of different types of grain and seed are blended to match the diets of certain types of birds. Some garden centers sell the seed unmixed so that you can buy and mix your own, depending on the type of birds you have or want to attract.

USE: Placed in bird feeders primarily to supplement birds' diets during times when other food is scarce, such as in winter.

USE TIPS: Select the type of seed to attract the birds you want most. Avoid unshelled sunflower seeds if you have a squirrel problem, as this is their favorite. Mixes that contain unshelled sunflower seed are for larger birds. The shells of sunflower seeds contain a natural herbicide and kill vegetation if they collect on the ground under a feeder.

BUYING TIP: Birdseed is not expensive, so experiment to find those mixes that attract the birds you want. With a little research, you can easily learn what types of seed certain birds prefer.

HUMMINGBIRD FEEDER

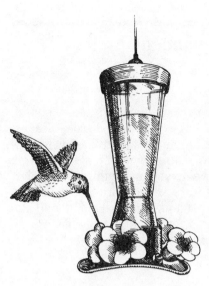

HUMMINGBIRD FEEDER

DESCRIPTION: There are several types of hummingbird feeders on the market but all have several things in common. Each has a reservoir for holding a liquid sugar mixture (often sold as *hummingbird nectar*). All or part of the feeders are red, as this color attracts hummingbirds. Feeding tubes that resemble the trumpet-shape flower that hummingbirds naturally take nectar from are attached to the sides. Feeders may have a single or several feeding tubes or fountains (small holes that the hummingbird sticks its beak into).

USE: Attracting this fascinating bird to the garden.

USE TIPS: If the liquid reservoir on your feeder is clear, a little red food coloring can be added to the nectar to help attract hummingbirds. Learning something about the hummingbirds in your area will help you attract them to your garden. For example, hummingbirds migrate through the northeastern United States in late summer, so this is the best time for putting out feeders there. Remember that hummingbirds feed from flowers, so the feeder should not be placed higher than where the birds will naturally look for it.

BUYING TIP: Hummingbird feeders are not expensive. Most will attract hummingbirds if they are in the area at all, but ones designed to be bee-proof are better.

SUET BALLS AND CONES

DESCRIPTION: Suet balls are made of animal fats or lard compressed into a small ball and embedded with birdseed. The ball has a string or a wire attached so that it can be hung from a tree. Suet cones are large pinecones that have been dipped in animal fats and sprinkled with birdseed.

USE: Supplement to birds' winter diet, when food is scarce. The suet itself is supposed to be helpful to the birds during cold weather.

USE TIPS: Note that suet balls and cones are primarily for winter feeding—they become a dripping mess in warm weather. A metal collar is necessary to act as a squirrel guard.

BUYING TIP: Suet balls are an inexpensive and easy way to feed birds in winter. As inexpensive as they are, some people find them a nice home project to make themselves.

Bonsai and Flower Arranging Tools and Equipment

ABOUT BONSAI

The enduring Japanese art of growing miniature trees, bonsai, is very popular in all parts of this country. The tree's leaves, branches, and roots are clipped regularly and trained with copper wire, forcing the plant to mature without getting large. Specialized tools have been developed to make this work easier.

Bonsai plants need gentle care. If you are not a serious bonsai hobbiest and receive a plant as a gift, take a course at a nearby botanic garden or search for some good books on the subject, of which there are many.

BONSAI PLANTER

DESCRIPTION: Shallow round, oval, or rectangular dish, usually of glazed ceramic material but also of plastic, with drainage holes. Commonly sold with matching saucer.

USE: Growing bonsai plants.

BUYING TIP: Although any container with drainage will do, these are more likely to fit the art form.

BONSAI SNIPS

DESCRIPTION: Specially adapted snips for more control and precision in the detail work required by bonsai gardening. More specialized tools may be found—these are the basics.

TYPES: *Scissors* (also known as *beginner's shears* or *bud shears*—these have small finger loops): Black wrought iron or carbon-steel scissors with short blades (about 1 inch—known as *Koryu* style) and long handles, either with small finger holes on the end or with large butterfly loops for the entire hand. Overall length about 6 inches.

Shears (also known as *trimming, Ikebana,* or *flower arranging shears):* Like scissors, but with slightly longer blades (about 2 inches) and butterfly handles—called *Ashinaga,* or more correctly, *naga ashi bonsai hasami*—*hasami* means "shears" in Japanese.

Branch nippers (also known as *concave cutter*): Black

KORYU STYLE BONSAI SCISSORS

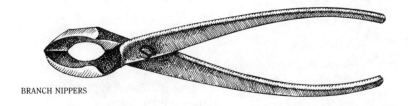

BRANCH NIPPERS

wrought iron pincers, with wide, beveled, curved jaws, about 1 inch long and ¾ inch wide. Resemble wide pliers. Long handles; tool is about 8 inches long overall. Variations include a *spherical cutter,* a *knuckle cutter,* and a *root cutter.*

Wire cutters: Resembles above-mentioned scissors, but 1-inch blades are thicker. Handles have finger loops at end.

USE: Maintaining bonsai plants with precision. The *scissors* are for leaf trimming; *shears* for cutting small branches and leaves; *branch nippers* for making concave cuts when removing branches; and *wire cutters* cut wire close to the branch. Choice of model is largely one of individual discretion.

BONSAI TROWELS

DESCRIPTION: Miniature versions of trowels (see pages 153–55) and scoops, usually made of one piece of metal.

USE: Careful moving of soil in bonsai planters (see page 306).

CEMETERY CONE

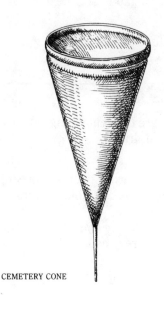

CEMETERY CONE

ALSO KNOWN AS: Funeral cone, cemetery vase

DESCRIPTION: Small plastic, galvanized steel, tin, or cast-iron cone, about the size of a jumbo soft-drink cup or ice-cream cone, often filled with a small bouquet of plastic flowers. Usually dark green. May have a spike on the bottom or a bracket on the side.

USE: Displays flowers on or near a gravestone. Attaches permanently to gravestones or is stuck into the ground nearby. Holds plastic or real flowers.

USE TIP: One of the best ways to leave flowers at a gravesite.

BUYING TIP: Usually carried only by those garden centers located near a cemetery.

CUT FLOWER PRESERVATIVE

ALSO KNOWN AS: Cut flower food

DESCRIPTION: A type of fertilizer and conditioner for cut flowers in granular form.

USE: When mixed with water in a vase, can preserve cut flowers an extra week or so by cutting down on bacterial growth, which also keeps the water clear.

FLORAL FOAM

ALSO KNOWN AS: Foam brick, floral base, floral foam brick

POPULAR BRAND NAME: Oasis

DESCRIPTION: Stiff green Styrofoam block, sold in 6-inch cubes, that can be cut to size. Is treated with a floral preservative and may come with adhesive on one side for anchoring in a vase. *Dry floral foam* is similar, but is intended for use with dried and silk flowers (and plastic flowers, too, if you must). A similar product that is less common is *floral clay,* which works in much the same way as foam.

USE: Holding the stems of cut flowers in the bottom of a floral arrangement. Stems are merely stuck into the foam at any angle. The foam is first floated on water until it is saturated, then held down with waterproof adhesive floral tape (see next entry) made for this purpose.

USE TIP: Helps retain water and extend flower life.

FLOWER ARRANGING ACCESSORIES

DESCRIPTION: A variety of items that are convenient ingredients in floral arrangements, both fresh and dried.

TYPES AND THEIR USES:
  Floral wire (also known as *florist's wire)* comes in green, straight, and coiled forms and is used to hold flowers in place in arrangements and corsages.
  Floral tape (also known as *stemming tape* or *stemming wire)* is used to conceal the wires, especially on corsages.

Floral picks hold flower stems in the foam.

Floral adhesive, usually sold in 1-inch-wide tape form, holds the foam securely to the bottom of the vase.

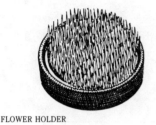

FLOWER HOLDER

FLOWER HOLDER

ALSO KNOWN AS: Flower pin, needlepoint flower holder, *kenzan* (Japanese), floral holder, frog, flower frog

DESCRIPTION: Small, heavy, flat or domed disk or rectangle with many 1-inch spikes, usually green enamel or brass. Round ones are as small as 1 inch in diameter, with 4 inches a common size. May have a lead-weighted base surrounded by rubber. Some models on adjustable pedestals are made for putting short-stemmed flowers in with longer ones. An older version with notched copper hooks that look like hairpins instead of spikes is called a *hairpin frog.* Circular, interlocking models are called *sun-and-moon* flower holders.

USE: Holding the stems of cut flowers in the bottom of vases for floral arrangements such as *Ikebana.* Domed models are for splays of flowers.

BUYING TIP: Permanent and reusable, as opposed to floral foam (see page 308). Brass spikes are the most desirable, though galvanized steel does fine.

CHAPTER 11

Garden Ornaments

ABOUT GARDEN ORNAMENTS

Garden centers that years ago limited their selections of garden art to designer urns, fancy teak chairs, benches, or a few pieces of sculpture are now selling all manner of lawn and garden ornaments, including gnomes, flamingos, and whirligigs.

The use of lawn and garden decorations has long been more popular in the South. Ironically, however, many of the major manufacturers are in the North, including Quebec, which is quite seriously north. The ornaments themselves have been sold in New England since the late 1700s.

These garden variety "objets d'art" give gardeners an opportunity to display their taste in public, leading one to ask, At what point does kitsch become art? This is a difficult question to answer, especially for a buying guide such as this. Excess and flamboyance may actually help develop our collective sense of taste. However, instead of the usual garden experts, it is more likely that archeologists, art critics, art historians, social commentators, and psychologists could provide answers—perhaps not definitive ones, but certainly more profound ones. Even some of the religious objects may be chosen for the same unspoken reason many of the animal or fantasy symbols are: some sort of basic, intimate desire for protection and a wish for continued fertility of the garden. It could be the sort of thing that taps into our collective unconscious and identification with archetypal symbols: We've moved on from totems, rocks, and petroglyphs, but not far—this is simply the modern version. As for the whimsey involved, this seems to be a way to keep the child within us alive, tying in with the theme of endless rejuvenation that is so appropriate to a garden. Anyway, it's probably something like that, but maybe not.

A final note: Once caught up in a collecting frenzy, some gardeners have difficulty curbing the impulse. In answer to the often-asked question, How much is too much? it appears that the answer is, according to one distinguished Southern gardener, "When it looks like you're selling the stuff!"

BARNYARD ANIMALS

HEN WITH CHICKS

DESCRIPTION: Cast either in plastic or cement in the shapes of familiar farm animals such as roosters, hens, chicks, ducks, ducklings, lambs, and sheep. Also available as wooden cutouts, painted, or covered with polyester imitation wool (in the case of sheep), or a sort of furry material that expands when wet to resemble the three-dimensional real thing. Sheep come in two styles: with heads down at grass level (grazing position) or up (looking position), and in small (1 foot), medium, and large (2½ feet) sizes. Some large sheep may also have a bell at their necks.

USE: To create a bucolic or "cute" effect.

USE TIP: Move your animals around the garden or lawn every day to create the illusion that they are alive. Excellent gift item, especially the fur-covered ones of the cuddly type.

BUYING TIPS: If you are buying a family of chickens, be sure to get the hen with the chicks, and not the rooster, even though he may be more colorful, in order to be biologically correct. Those animals that are curled up and looking out at the viewer are much more cuddly appearing than those that are in the standing position. Sheep with their heads in the "up" position generally cost $2 more, for no apparent reason. Large polyester-on-plywood pigs and sheep can cost as much as $70. Some sheep come in a set with Little Bo-Peep.

CARTOON CHARACTERS

DESCRIPTION: Disney characters and other familiar cartoon friends. Recent introductions to lawn and garden decor, they are almost always made of colorful plastic. Snow White and the Seven Dwarfs are sold as a unit of approximately eight pieces.

USE: Personal expression in public. These objects reflect your interest and personality more than most of the other ornaments.

USE TIP: Bambi may not go with more serious garden or landscape concepts.

BUYING TIP: Cartoon characters are among the most affordable of the lawn objects on the market. If you are on a limited budget but wish to collect, this would be a good place to start.

CLASSIC SCULPTURE AND FOUNTAINS

DESCRIPTION: Figures and shapes of a variety so diverse as to be impossible to list here. Though derived primarily from Western European stock classic art styles, it ranges in style from the Greek to the Colonial to the representational to the abstract. The most popular include small svelte figures of nymphs and cherubs as well as a series of sea horses or scallop shells plumbed internally for cascading water. Pumps may or may not be included; some models are wired for lighting. Often edged in turquoise.

USE: Adds a touch of class to a garden.

USE TIPS: The higher the waterfall, the louder the noise. Do not place near popular nap locations.

BUYING TIPS: Some regional preferences may be reflected in the stock your garden center carries, such as a fountain in the shape of an oil well for the oil-producing areas of our country.

CLASSIC FOUNTAIN

FAT FANNY

ALSO KNOWN AS: Gardening girl

DESCRIPTION: Wooden cutout of a rear view of a woman in a polka-dot dress bent over so that all you see is the polka dot–clad rump and two short legs, although now there is a thinner, bikini-clad version. Male version also available, sometimes called *Fat Freddy*. Sizes range from 16 to 24 inches high.

USE: To show the general public that you have a sense of humor.

USE TIP: Most effective when seen from a distance at high speed—excellent for those people who live near a major highway.

FAT FANNY

BUYING TIP: Look for well-painted wood that will stand up to the weather.

FLAMINGO

FLAMINGOS

DESCRIPTION: Invariably pink, large plastic or cement birds that usually stand a yard tall and are usually sold in pairs. The body is often cast or molded while the legs are extremely thin metal, plastic, or wood stakes made to be stuck into the ground. Some models are made with only one leg to imitate the flamingo's natural resting position, while others have two, to imitate a natural feeding position. *Herons* are a similar-looking but all white bird available in some garden centers.

USE: Adds a touch of drama to a yard. The farther away from the natural range of the subtropical flamingos you live, the more drama they add to your garden. Tropical colors give a sense of Miami Beach.

USE TIP: Flamingos should be taken in during the winter, as they appear particularly out of place in the snow. Furthermore, flamingos allowed to weather outside during the winter may lose their pink color, leaving the bird looking drab, which then quite defeats their purpose, as drab is not dramatic. Herons should be placed near a body of water to appear more natural-looking, as they do not add as much drama as flamingos.

BUYING TIP: It is a matter of personal taste as to whether the one-leg or two-leg model is preferable, but some gardeners find that the one-leg models make them nervous.

GAZING GLOBE

GAZING GLOBE

ALSO KNOWN AS: Reflective ball, witch's ball, lawn ball, buzzard ball, mirror ball

DESCRIPTION: Mirrorlike glass ball, 8 to 14 inches in diameter, usually placed upon a pedestal. Available in several colors, usually including sky blue, red, green, silver, and gold. Pedestals, which are also sold for birdbaths, may need an *extension* to hold the globe, and come in white or various shades of brown. They are made of concrete or clay.

USE: To attract attention. Rumored to kill weeds by reflection, but this is unproven at this time.

USE TIPS: Do not place near an active play area, as globes are made of glass. Bring inside during hailstorms.

BUYING TIPS: Look for the slightly irregular, hand-blown globes. Molded globes have seams and are of lesser quality.

GNOMES

ALSO KNOWN AS: Dwarfs, dwarves, elfs, elves, trolls, leprechauns

GNOME

DESCRIPTION: Elfish statues of "little people" in odd clothes and with old faces, ranging in size from less than a foot to around 20 inches high, though one model is 39 inches high; made of cast cement, bonded marble, plastic, or painted plaster. They may be the natural color of the material from which they are made or they can be painted to look more or less lifelike, depending on your taste. Some are wired with lights. Gnomes come with a variety of props, such as garden tools, pails, lanterns, golf clubs, watering cans, a large snail, a book, flutes, and an accordion. Props and poses can either reflect the owner's interests, personality, or some imagined and longed-for identity. Folklore has long linked these "little people" with the earth, trees, and water. Gnomes are European in origin and one of the better quality lines, Heissner Gnomes, has been manufactured in Germany since 1872. This may be the "Old World" that people so often link with "charm."

USE: Adding charm to your garden, and for good luck. A British scholar considers these phallic symbols.

USE TIPS: Gnomes tend to do well when partially hidden behind foliage or low branches, appearing to peek from behind plants. Remember that dwarfs and gnomes are social creatures and a single one does not look natural—place them in natural groupings of three or more.

BUYING TIPS: Though nothing lasts longer than concrete, the colors may fade. Only the very expensive makes are painted very accurately. Materials are largely a matter of personal taste. Gnomes should be bought to scale: Small gardens should have smaller gnomes than large gardens. If you want a lot of dwarfs, your best deal is to get a set of the Disney characters, such as Snow White and the Seven Dwarfs (see pages 311–12).

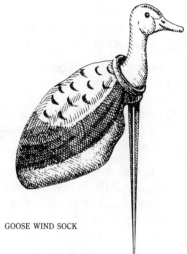

GOOSE WIND SOCK

JOCKEY HITCHING POST

GOOSE AND DUCK WIND SOCKS

DESCRIPTION: Large fabric socks printed to look like ducks or geese, attached to stakes that are stuck into the lawn. When the wind fills the fabric body of the birds they undulate and appear to be moving like the real thing; they hang limply when there is no wind. These work on the same principle as the fabric carps that are used in Japan to celebrate the birth of a boy child. Popularity began on the East Coast seashore.

USE: Adds movement to ornamentation in order to draw attention to your yard. Also tells you if the wind is blowing or not, and from which direction.

USE TIP: Use in groups of half a dozen or more, just as geese tend to land and feed in flocks.

JOCKEY AND SERVANT HITCHING POSTS

DESCRIPTION: Cast-iron, plaster, plastic, or cement statue of a 3- to 4-foot-tall jockey or servant in formal (red topcoat and tophat) or riding attire. His right arm is raised and often contains a small lamp or a ring for tethering a horse or mule. Until recently the jockey was black, but generally they are now white, reflecting a positive, though very minor, step in evolution of our society's race consciousness. Other hitching post lawn ornaments include the head of a horse with a ring through its nose, or a simple pole with a ring attached to the top.

USE: Originally to provide, perhaps, the mystique of the Old South, now nothing more than pure ornamentation, used primarily at the end of a walk or driveway.

USE TIP: Existing black jockeys may easily be painted white.

BUYING TIP: Not considered trendy.

JUST PLAIN BIZARRE ANIMALS AND FIGURES

DESCRIPTION: Large marine creatures (such as fish, clams, or sea horses) in chomping action, little dogs with their back legs raised (to be posed in an appropriate place, such as near the wheel of a car when it is parked in the driveway), other dogs (usually basset hounds) with "Welcome" or "Beware of Dog" painted on their ears, guttersnipes (urchins) in a variety of

BIZARRE MARINE FIGURE WITH NYMPH

poses, little sports players in action, seamen, drunkards, and servants. A new appearance has been made by dinosaurs, appropriately labeled "Tyrannosaurus," "Stegosaurus," and the like.

USE: To have something unusual on your lawn that your neighbor doesn't have yet, or to get otherwise taciturn visitors to ask you questions about your garden. Considered by some gardeners as necessary for providing a finishing touch to their landscaping. There is no logical explanation for the popularity of the little sports players as garden ornaments.

USE TIP: Manufacturers are coming up with new items all the time, and though the first time you see one of these it will seem extremely strange, as more and more people buy this new strange item it will become a familiar sight in our suburban landscape.

BUYING TIP: Expect a short life for your new and strange item because its uniqueness is bound to wear thin or completely off after a while. Frequent visits to garden centers will ensure that you will be one of the first people on your block to have the newest and the weirdest.

MUSHROOMS AND TOADSTOOLS

DESCRIPTION: Cast cement sculpture in a variety of sizes from 6 inches to as much as a yard high, available in single, double, and triple versions. May be painted in a variety of bright or even garish colors, including polka dots, or may be left unpainted, such as is often the case with cast cement. *Toadstool* refers to relatively flat-topped mushrooms.

USE: Making a complementary setting for gnomes, deer, and other decorative lawn and garden creatures.

USE TIP: If the top and the stem of the toadstool are two separate pieces, be sure that they fit together well. This could be a safety concern in the matter of larger, heavier models, not only for the nearby gnomes, but also for children or other visitors to your garden who might bump it.

BUYING TIP: If your other statuary is unpainted, choose toadstools that are also unpainted. Otherwise, the effect is an inconsistency similar to that of being lost between Kansas and the Land of Oz.

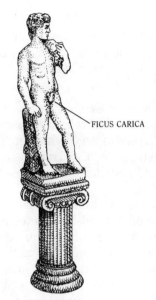

FICUS CARICA

DAVID ON PEDESTAL

JAPANESE LANTERN

NUDES

DESCRIPTION: Statues in plastic, cement, and stone without clothing, fig leaves, or loincloths. Many items also sold in covered versions—even Michelangelo's *David* is available with or without a fig leaf. Many consumers today are turning over a new leaf on what is acceptable in garden statuary, and are boldly displaying copies of classic nude sculptures, wood nymphs, Pans, and gods and goddesses. Only the Virgin Mother and Snow White seem to have escaped this revealing trend. May be sold as fountains. Available on both Ionic and Doric pedestals.

USE: To demonstrate your taste and standards of expression on a level wholly different from the other lawn ornaments noted here.

USE TIP: If you are shy about venturing into the exciting world of nude statues, you may wish to start out by positioning one modestly behind a small bush.

BUYING TIP: Expect to pay more for nudes: Art comes at a price.

ORIENTAL OBJECTS

DESCRIPTION: Japanese lanterns, fat Buddhas, meditating Buddhas, dragons, Japanese scholars, miniature pagodas, temple guard dogs, samurai warriers, Tiki gods, Tiki torches, and arched footbridges. Made of cast cement or bonded marble, natural cement color or artificially bronzed. Derived from traditional Japanese garden decor.

USE: To add a touch of the exotic to your landscape.

USE TIP: Do not mix samurai warriors with Buddhas.

BUYING TIP: Although "Tiki" generally implies a South Pacific style, some of the designs resemble Easter Island god-sculptures.

RELIGIOUS FIGURES

ALSO KNOWN AS: Saints and shrines

RELIGIOUS FIGURES AVAILABLE: Jesus, Mary, St. Joseph, St. Anthony, St. Fiacre, St. Francis, St. Jude, St. Patrick, St. Theresa (or St. Theresa of Avila)

MARY

ALSO KNOWN AS: *Mary*—Madonna, Blessed Mother, the Blessed Virgin, the Virgin Mary; *St. Anthony*—St. Anthony the Abbot; *St. Theresa*—the Little Flower, Little Flower of Jesus, St. Therese, St. Therese of the Child Jesus (St. Theresa of Avila is a different saint). Also spelled St. Teresa.

DESCRIPTION: Any one of a number of Catholic saints or important biblical religious figures in traditional religious poses, made of painted (often with several layers of acrylic lacquer) or plain cast cement, stone, marble, plastic, or lead, and ranging in height from 18 to 54 inches, most commonly including the ones listed above.

Most saints are left unpainted, but are also available in full color: *Jesus* and *Mary* are more often available painted in multiple colors, and in *Bleeding Heart* or *Sacred Heart* versions; both are shown in the forms of various apparitions, such as the Infant of Prague or Lady of Lourdes. Jesus, Mary, and Joseph may often be sold as a set, usually with Jesus shown as a child, in a year-round version different from the *nativity scene,* another common item. *St. Francis* is usually shown with a few birds. *Grottos*—small parabolic shell backdrop/shelters—are sold separately, and may have a provision for electric lighting, though some gardeners still prefer to use rare clawfoot bathtubs as backdrops. Grottos are usually painted royal or sky blue on the inside and fade to white on the outside; the inside top may be plain, with a gold star, scalloped with a radiant gold star or a gold sun, or with a radiant golden cross. *Praying children* and *cherubim* are also available, with similarly small grottos or the means to be attached to them. Some religious figures appear on the market in response to a momentary fad, such as a three-foot figure of the Pope during a tour here. One such model had nozzles in the fingertips from which water flowed.

USE: Adding inspiration to a garden, to demonstrate an affinity to whatever the religious personage stands for, or to fulfill a vow, ranging from promises to build a shrine for deliverance from disease to personal accomplishment. Some religious articles are seasonal and help to celebrate a particular holiday (e.g., a fully lighted, plastic nativity set complete with three wise men and a baby Jesus, for Christmas). Choice of most displays is influenced greatly by ethnic background and geographic location. An ancient tradition.

Jesus: All aspects of faith.

Mary: Most popular figure, perhaps because of relation of women to earth, as far as gardening is concerned, as

ST. FRANCIS

one of the most popular figures to pray to, or because reputedly appears in many visions.

St. Joseph: Patron saint of workers and families. Also, sometimes buried in the front lawn of a house that is proving difficult to sell in order to find a buyer.

St. Anthony: Patron saint of lost articles—particularly helpful for those gardeners who continually lose their tools.

St. Fiacre: Patron saint of gardeners, most appropriately. Usually depicted with a spade and a small plant.

St. Francis: Universal symbol for the love of animals and wildlife. Protestant Christians as well as Catholics put a St. Francis statue in a conspicious place in their garden to show their affinity with nature. Often accompanied by tiny animals.

St. Jude: Associated with lost and impossible causes, usually those more serious than a failed garden.

St. Patrick: If you have a snake problem, this one is for you (especially if you're Irish).

St. Theresa: "Little Flower" is often shown with a small bouquet of flowers or surrounded by roses (in relation to her experience of a miraculous shower of roses). Symbolic of a simple life. *St. Theresa of Avila* was a Spanish mystic with a good sense of humor who is associated with common sense. (It is not always clearly indicated to the consumer by the manufacturer which St. Theresa is being sold, but it is more likely to be the former.)

USE TIPS: Do not mix the sacred and the profane: Disney characters do not look natural beside a nativity crèche. If you bury a statue of St. Joseph, be sure to note where it is buried so that you can retrieve it after the house is sold.

BUYING TIPS: There are so many statues and shrines on the market today that you should be able to pick and choose the one that is suited for you at a price you can afford. Mary outsells all the saints ten to one at some garden centers (indeed, some stock only Mary). Because of the lack of difference between the two St. Theresas, accepting the one you bought as the one you want requires an act of faith. Some people relate the price of the shrine to the difficulty of the task involved in the vow it fulfills: Deliverance from death would seem to deserve, for example, more than a plastic Mary.

SPECIAL PLANTERS

DESCRIPTION: Plastic or cast cement planters in the shape of wheelbarrows, swans, geese, turtles, hippos, bears, frogs, lambs, burros (with or without sombrero-clad napping figure), or other creatures. Some burros, also known as mules, are accompanied by a walking figure, commonly referred to as "Pedro." These are similar to the same objects sold as lawn ornaments, but they contain an additional receptacle for holding plants.

DONKEY PLANTER

USE: As a decorative or attention-getting planter for terraces, roof gardens, or the lawn, especially in areas where there is little soil.

USE TIP: Once you have determined where the planter is most effective from a design point of view, select plants that can grow well in the light of that particular place. For example, put impatiens or caladiums in a shady or partially shady spot.

BUYING TIP: Unless they are being used for aquatic gardening, be sure that there are drainage holes in the bottoms of the planters. If it is impossible to add holes, place plenty of gravel and charcoal in the bottom before adding soil.

SPINNING DAISY

ALSO KNOWN AS: Lawn daisy pinwheel

DESCRIPTION: Brightly colored plastic flowers about 12 inches in diameter with thick wire "stems" for staking in the ground. The petals spin on their own stems, like pinwheels, when the wind blows through them. Some are available without propellers but with reflectors for lining driveways, or as an aid to snowplows.

USE: As a pure lawn decoration and also used to mark the entrance to your driveway for gardeners who entertain many out-of-town friends.

USE TIP: For the best motion, turn daisies to face the direction that the wind blows from most frequently.

BUYING TIP: Considered a safe fallback to add color to your garden if you do not have a green thumb.

ARMILLARY SUNDIAL

SUNDIAL

DESCRIPTION: Round, flat, cast bronze or stone clock face, almost always with Roman numerals. Designed to be mounted on a pedestal or rock, or as a wall plaque. A pointer, called a *gnomon,* is attached in the center and angles up over the XII. (The 4 on clock faces is written IIII instead of IV, for some reason.) A few are manufactured with Arabic numerals for those who resist the traditional (this kind of clock has been around for twenty-two centuries—that's a lot of tradition). Usually inscribed with phrases such as "Time takes all but memories" or *"Tempus fugit"* and/or decorated with American eagles, frogs, turtles, small boys fishing, or sailboats, any of which may double as gnomons. Another version is the *sun clock,* which has a half-circle band with Arabic numerals cut out, held at an angle over a flat piece (usually a star) and with a line down its middle. The reverse shadow of the appropriate numeral falls on the line to tell the time. Still another model is the *equatorial sundial,* in which the numerals are on a curved, angled band with a line, usually an arrow, at its axis; a full-sphere model is called an *armillary sundial.*

USE: Tells time on sunny days by the fall of the shadow from the gnomon.

USE TIPS: Follow installation directions carefully for accurate readings. Mount on a large rock or pedestal, and *make sure it is perfectly level.* Align the gnomon with the North Star (not magnetic north). The word *gnomon* is especially useful for those gardeners who play Scrabble.

BUYING TIP: Get good bronze (about 88 percent copper).

TORCHES AND CANDLES

DESCRIPTION: Wicks surrounded by citronella-scented wax, either in glass jars *(low boy candles),* small galvanized buckets, or on 3-foot-long wooden stakes. *Tonga torches* hold a quart of petroleum fuel (can be citronella-scented) and come in either bronze or black metallic finishes.

USE: Dramatic source of light which also repels mosquitoes.

USE TIPS: Large wax torches drip on the ground, so do not place them near a patio that must remain pristine. Do not use torches indoors.

PUMPING GIRL WHIRLIGIG

FLYING DUCK WHIRLIGIG

WHIRLIGIG

DESCRIPTION: Wooden or plastic decoration with propellers that are either linked to wires which move a figure or else are simply placed alongside in the shape or place of legs or wings. Designs of the former include women washing clothes, churning butter, or watering plants; men sawing wood, pumping water, starting a car, or being kicked in the derrière by a donkey; also excitable scarecrows and feeding chickens. Designs of the latter type include ducks, geese, flamingos, roadrunners, airplanes, Dutch windmills, American farm-type windmills, California raisins, Maine potatoes, cartoon characters (with the blades functioning as feet, not wings), and political figures. Usually painted bright colors. Mounted on long stakes that are stuck in the ground.

USE: Adds eye-catching action to a garden. A combination wind vane and novelty item. Often sold as folk art, particularly in the Smoky Mountains and parts of Appalachia. May also scare birds away and keep you from napping in the garden, depending on the amount of noise it makes. Originally used to repel moles: The vibrations set up by a moving whirligig scare them away.

USE TIP: When these are mounted on a pole, be sure that they are level and that the moving parts are well oiled. With the models of a person working, the greatest pleasure is commonly found in watching them work at top speed in the winds that occur just before a summer thunderstorm.

BUYING TIP: If you wish to have one of these moving weather vanes as a "folk art" item, buy only those that are handcrafted in wood. They will cost a little more than the less authentic, mass-produced plastic or wooden ones. Some people find the depiction of chores linked to the traditional gender sexist.

WILD AND DOMESTIC ANIMALS

DESCRIPTION: A wide variety of animals, including skunks (with or without a flower in paw), bunnies (with or without carrots), frogs, raccoons, cats, dogs, kittens, little lambs (with Mary), alligators, armadillos (also in boot scraper version), turtles, pelicans, deer, lions, giant flapping butterflies, birds, bees, ladybugs, donkeys, dogs, pheasants, and a few imaginary creatures. Frogs are available with lipstick and bow ties, depending on the sex, and playing various musical instruments. Butterflies and some birds may come with a clothespin-type clip or other clamp for

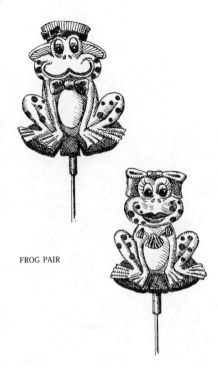

FROG PAIR

attaching to branches or parts of your house. *Flocked* models have lifelike, weatherproof fur. All are available in a range of materials, including plastic, aluminum, ½-inch-thick wooden cutouts with spikes for securing in the ground, or full-sized cast cement sculpture painted an unrealistic bronze color. Rabbits, ducks, and chipmunks are commonly available in sets as well. Certain manufacturers offer a number of wooden cutout animals with signs attached, such as "Skunk Crossing" or "Snail Trail." Others make cast brass signs with the animal and appropriate "_____ Crossing" underneath, including quail (both single and family group), flamingo, duck, bunny, frog, hummingbird, kitty, boy, and girl figures. Many dog and cat models are recognizable by breed.

USE: Often collected by people who are into collecting one type of animal—for example, there are people who collect only skunks or turtles or owls. But these animals could also be mixed and matched.

USE TIPS: Plastic and cement (painted and unpainted) in the same garden looks particularly unnatural. Stick with the same material, such as all unpainted cement. Some people like to treat their fur-covered animals with Scotchgard.

BUYING TIP: Animals with exceptionally expressive eyes tend to cost more.

WISHING WELL

DESCRIPTION: Plastic, plaster, cement, or wooden structure that resembles an old covered wellhouse above a well shaft. These replicas are often complete with bucket, chain or rope, and crank.

USE: To add a certain rustic charm to your garden, a charm that is particularly lacking in the suburbs.

USE TIP: People can't resist the urge to toss money into a wishing well, so locate yours near a heavily traveled thoroughfare and collect what you can.

BUYING TIP: Go for the larger sizes. Small ones especially tend to look more ridiculous than larger ones, almost like a child's beach toy, and should be avoided.

General Buying Guide for Bulbs, Seeds, Plants, Shrubs, and Trees

In keeping with the mandate of the title of this book—*The Complete Illustrated Guide to Everything Sold in Garden Centers (Except the Plants)*—the following is a simplified buying guide to the basic groups of live items—the "greengoods"—sold at garden centers, as opposed to the "hard lines" and "packaged goods" that are covered in the main body of this book. This appendix is not meant to be a detailed list of the items themselves (grass seed rates the detailed treatment it gets in the book because it is treated like a basic commodity and is such a common purchase). However, we couldn't resist giving just a few basic pointers on the most common groups of plants to help orient you as you walk back into the greenhouses and nurseries from the front part of the garden center.

A knowledgeable salesperson should ask you questions about your growing conditions—light, soil, and moisture—prior to selling you a plant. Seek out this kind of help.

A final note about names: You will be confronted by rows of plants labeled with Latin botanical names. While this may seem daunting, this type of labeling is much more accurate than relying exclusively on common names and gen-erally ensures that you get the plant you want, as the same common name can refer to two totally different plants. These botanical names are always made up of two components, and sometimes three. The first component is the *genus* name; the genus is the basic group that a particular plant comes from. The second component is the *species designate,* which when used with the genus denotes the species (the species is a distinct subgroup of the genus that possesses specific characteristics). In the case of *Geranium dalmaticum,* for example, *Geranium* is the genus name, while *Geranium dalmaticum* indicates the species. When a plant's name is repeated in a text such as this several times in a row, you will often find the genus name abbreviated by just its first initial after the first mention. In our example, *Geranium dalmaticum* would be shortened to *G. dalmaticum.*

Finally, our plant may be a *variety,* a variation within the species. If it is a naturally occurring variety, its name will appear in italics after the species name. If it is an artificially created variety, or *cultivar* (short for *cultivated variety),* or a *hybrid* (a cross between two different plants), its name will appear within single quotation marks in roman type, such as *Geranium dalmaticum* 'A.T. Johnson.' Keep in mind that cultivars usually can be propagated only by cuttings; they will not grow true to seed, meaning that if you harvest their seeds and plant them, the resulting plant will not possess the important characteristics (usually flower and leaf color, though it depends on what qualities it was bred for) of its parent.

BULBS

A seasonal item, most garden centers offer bulbs for sale twice a year in colorful displays. The banner announcing "The Dutch Bulbs Are Here," which goes up on garden centers in the early fall, heralds the arrival of the most popular ones, the spring-blooming bulbs whose appearance signals the end of winter. Bulbs are also well loved because they are colorful and require little care to make them bloom. Because most bulbs are not expensive, and a wide variety are stocked by most garden centers, this is a good kind of plant with which to experiment. Most bulbs are guaranteed to bloom at least once and often become "established" in the garden, rewarding the gardener with blooms for years to come. Others are easily grown indoors, even in the smallest apartment, and can be "forced," or made to bloom off-season (the most familiar of these are the popular amaryllis, commonly offered as a Christmas present in the northern parts of this country, or the paperwhite narcissus).

The basic definition of a bulb, many of which look like nothing more than an onion, is a plant that has a large storage root or stem or even an entire compressed plant which remains in the ground during a dormant season and from which the plant blooms again during its growing season.

As for quality, avoid "bargain mixes," which may be just a mix of bad or undersized leftovers. Always look for the largest bulbs of each type, too, and solid, not squishy ones. Don't buy bulbs with mold on their top crowns or basal plate (bottom). Solid plastic bags without holes are generally not good for bulbs, as they create conditions ripe for these problems—try those sold in net bags or loose.

The process by which bulbs establish themselves and multiply in a garden is called *naturalizing*. Most gardeners prefer bulbs that naturalize well—check your gardening books to find which kinds tend to naturalize. Beyond a few modest requirements, bulbs are carefree—they generally require only sunlight and good drainage to grow well. Some bulbs even grow and bloom in part shade. Although the spring-blooming bulbs are the best known, different types of bulbs bloom at all different times during the growing season. Always check the bloom time on the package and aim for a mixture of dates that suits your garden plan. Be sure to note the planting depth and the sun and water requirements. Store bulbs in a cool, dry place until you plant them. When you do plant bulbs, note that they need well-drained and aerated soil, as they may rot in overly moist soils. And do your best to wait until the right season to plant—too soon or too late will not do.

Some, such as the popular paperwhites, can be forced to bloom indoors. A little research and experimentation will show you which ones are easily grown on a dining room table in January, and stand up to various moves, including a stint in your refrigerator for rejuvenation. (If you do put them in your refrigerator to make them go dormant before forcing, make sure they are clearly marked and not confused with your shallots, or your next sauce may taste a little strange.)

A true bulb is one in which not only a plant part comprises the storage unit, but an entire plant that is compressed into an underground storage chamber. If you cut a true bulb in half, you will find a compressed basal plate or stem, roots, and even leaves. Daffodils, onions, narcissus, and lilies are true bulbs. However, not everything marketed as a bulb is a true bulb. The term *bulb* is used to describe underground storage units formed from modified roots, branches, buds, stems, or tubers.

The following are sold as bulbs:

• *Corms* are underground stems without the storage leaves that true bulbs have. If cut in half, the corm will not show the rings or layers (actually leaves and storage leaves) that you find in an onion, which is a true bulb. In corms, buds form at the top of these squat stems and produce the plant. Popular corms include gladiolus and crocus.

• *Rhizomes* are lateral underground stems. Roots develop from the underside of the rhizome and buds, called *pips,* along the top. Lilies of the valley, many iris, Chinese lotus, and ginger grow from rhizomes.

• *Tubers* are underground buds or underground stems, like the corm, that swell with stored nutrients. Tubers do not have a basal plate. Jerusalem artichoke, the white potato, and some begonias are tubers.

• *Tuberous roots* are swollen roots that store starches. A new plant will grow from the *eye,* or *bud,* found on a tuberous root. The sweet potato and the dahlia are well-known plants that grow from tuberous roots.

About Spring Bulbs

These bulbs are sold and planted in the fall to bloom in the spring. The smaller spring bulbs usually bloom first and are the jewels of the spring garden. These are followed by the daffodils and tulips. It is wise to buy a variety of bulbs to ensure bloom throughout the spring season. Hardy spring bulbs often need to go through a winter season where the temperature is near or below freezing before they will bloom in the spring. This is known as *stratification.* Hardy spring bulbs can be purchased at

any time during the fall and planted as long as the ground has not frozen. It is often best, however, to get bulbs into the ground in the early fall so that roots will begin to grow before the winter freeze sets in. The exceptions to this rule are hybrid tulips, which, if planted too early, may actually start to sprout, only to be killed in the colder weather.

Superphosphate (see pages 73–74), bulb food (pages 67–68), or bone meal (pages 59–60) can be placed with soil in the hole with the bulb as it is planted. This will help with root development and produce better bloom in the spring.

About Summer and Fall Bulbs

In much of the country where winters are harsh, summer- and fall-blooming bulbs are offered for sale in garden centers in the spring. These are planted in the spring and, depending on the local climate, removed from the garden in the fall before the first hard freeze and stored over winter in a dark, dry place, such as a paper bag or dry peat moss, to be replanted the following spring after the ground has warmed up. In milder areas of the country, many summer- and fall-flowering bulbs can be planted in the fall and left in the ground to bloom year after year.

SEEDS

Flower and vegetable seeds are easy to buy. There is plenty of reference material in magazines and books to guide you at the beginning, and there is more information on each package, including a picture of the plant. For some of us, it's like being a kid in a candy store—the stuff is right there, it looks good, and doesn't cost much. But, hard as it may be to accept, you have to grow up and accept the fact that not all seeds are for you, at least for now.

To determine what's right for you, first look

at the back of the package to find the basic information as to what kind of light is needed, when to plant, and germination time (the time it takes the seed to sprout), and to get a feel for the general ease of cultivation of the item. There is plenty of choice, so pick one that fits your depth of experience and desire for involvement.

Seeds with germinating times over twenty-one days are usually very difficult for the home gardener to grow, because of the need to maintain uniform soil conditions, temperature, and moisture levels during that entire period. Gardeners need to rely on heating sources and controls; this is generally the case when starting seeds indoors for long germination periods. Seven to ten days' germination time is the most desirable for beginning gardeners.

Many flowers and vegetables do better in the garden if they are started indoors and then transplanted as seedlings. Check the packet to see if it is labeled as such, usually with the phrase "best if started indoors." Recommendations for container gardening are usually given as well.

In addition to sowing instructions, the seed packets also have a *test date.* This usually indicates the month and year in which the seed was last tested for *percentage of germination,* or the percent of seeds that will eventually grow into plants. This date should be *in the current growing year* for best germination of the seed purchased and the germination rate should be around 90 percent. In any case, when comparing two brands of the same seed, the one with the higher germination rate is the better buy. And don't squeeze the package to see how many seeds are inside—you'll break the seed coats and ruin the embryos.

About Vegetable Seeds

The first things you should look for on the packet are the *planting* and *maturing times.* The seed packets offer information on when to plant, saying, for example, "Plant indoors in February or March, and transplant i. late April or May or when the temperature has reached a constant 70° F." However, if you are not familiar with starting seed indoors or do not have the required equipment, the same plants can be purchased as seedlings in April and May. Garden centers will offer these transplants for sale at reasonable prices when it is appropriate to plant them. Some of the vegetable plants that may be better purchased as seedlings include tomatoes, eggplants, and peppers. It is often fun, however, to try to grow these plants from seed indoors (see "Seed Starting Products," chapter 9).

If the seed packet says, "Plant directly in the garden when the soil has warmed up in late spring," it is considerably cheaper to buy the seed rather than seedlings. Some of the plants that can easily be grown from seed in late spring include cucumbers, squash, sunflowers, pole and bush beans, and corn.

Still other seed is offered that can be planted as soon as the soil can be worked in early spring. Crops that do best in the cooler temperatures of spring and fall are often referred to as *cold crops* (or *cold* or *cool weather crops).* Many plants in the cabbage family (cabbage, kohlrabi, boc choy, kale, collard greens) are cold crops. Other cold crops include lettuce, peas, radishes, and many other leafy green vegetables.

During the warmer summer season, heat-tolerant plants such as tomatoes and peppers can be planted in the same place that the cold crops grew. Cold crop seed can be sown again in early fall to extend the garden season up until hard frost time.

If you know the length of your growing season (for example, in the Northeast, the growing season is from April until October—about 210 days), you should choose seed that will produce fruit or crops well within that time span. This information is stated with a phrase such as, "Matures from 90 to 100 days." You should also know if you've had problems with certain pests or diseases in your soil, and look for seeds that have been treated or developed to be resistant to these problems. Some varieties of tomato seeds, for example, are available which are resistant to nematodes (labeled *N)* or the diseases verticillium wilt *(V)* and fusarium wilt (labeled *F,* or *F 1 & 2* if resistant to two types), or all three (labeled *VFN).* Seeds may also be treated with a fungicide to control damping-off disease and noted as such on the packet.

About Flower Seeds

Growing flowering plants from seed is not costly. Seed packets are usually sold for under two dollars, so even if the seed does not germinate, it is not a great loss. Growing flowers and other plants from seed is highly recommended, if only for the fun of it. It is also an easy way to experiment in your garden.

There are three types of flowers: *annuals, biennials,* and *perennials.* Annuals are plants that grow, bloom, and set seed in one growing season—they bloom continuously during the season and then die. Popular annuals include marigolds, zinnias, cosmos, sweet alyssum, ageratum, celosia, salvia, and petunias. These plants do not survive, or *overwinter,* in areas where the winter temperatures dip below freezing. However, annuals are the easiest flowers to grow from seed.

Biennials are plants that grow in the wild for one season without blooming and then bloom during the second season, after which they die. Once established in a garden, however, biennials often *self-seed* (seed themselves) and then grow and produce a succession of blooming plants for many years to come. For this reason they are often confused with perennials. Popular biennials include hollyhocks, sweet william, Canterbury bells, and wallflowers. The latter is a much-neglected flower that is a fine addition to almost any border.

Perennials are plants that are *winter hardy,* meaning they will survive cold winters (that is, their roots survive, while their tops die off) and grow and bloom in the garden for many years; different plants blooming at different times of the season. Perennials can be purchased as grown plants, too. Among the popular perennials are hosta, peonies, lamb's ears, daisies, and periwinkle.

PLANTS

Most garden centers don't sell just "plants"—they sell *annuals, perennials, tropicals, woody plants,* and so on. Do a little shopping research in reference books first to save yourself some time at the garden center. Definitions for some of these terms are found in the preceding section on seeds. *Bare-root stock* refers to plants sold without any soil.

You should have in mind where you plan to put these plants, and be able to describe the kind of sun—northern or southern, direct or shade—and the temperature conditions: Near a drafty door? In a greenhouse? In a house where you lower the temperature at night? The personnel at the nursery should ask you these questions. Avoid sales clerks who are more interested in pushing a particular plant than in your growing conditions. Plants can't be plunked down anywhere willy-nilly, so don't buy something just because it's on sale, no matter how tempting it is. Conditions have to be right for a plant to grow. Don't buy until you know exactly where you want to put it.

Questions you should ask the clerks include: Does it bloom? How long will it bloom? Will it rebloom within the year? Will it drop leaves? Is it fragile or durable? Is it the kind that likes to "dry out" every now and then, or not? How sensitive would it be to my own schedule of watering, dictated by my life-style? How damp should I keep the soil? Is it basically an indoor or outdoor plant?

A few rules of thumb can be applied to buying most plants, whether bought as seedlings or full grown. Look for symmetry. Consult a good illustrated gardening book to figure if the leaves should be even in height or staggered, and how thick the leaves should be. Especially with those sold in small six-pack containers, look for flowers that are *not* blooming, but are about to do so. Blooms mean that the plant has been growing in that confined space for a long time and it may be stressed out, though of course a few blooms are necessary to judge color. Don't hesitate to squeeze the pot and pull roots apart a bit to stimulate them before planting. Avoid woody, thick stems on small plants. Look for signs of disease: Yellow leaves or leaves with brown edges are typical (brown tips are natural), though one or two bad leaves may be acceptable. Avoid plants with wilted leaves, or ones that are tall and spindly—look for compact and sturdy plants. Roots should not be poking out of the holes in the bottom of the pot, and there should be no weeds growing in it. Square pots are preferable—they keep the roots from growing in circles. And don't forget, when purchasing big plants for indoors, to check your door and ceiling heights first, as well as door widths. Figure out an appropriate route for such a heavy, big, and probably dirty object. Double-check the plant's sun and shade requirements, and notice if the garden center has met them. Make sure that your garden or home can meet them as well.

When purchasing spreading plants, get yourself a "deal" by finding a larger one with several stems. You'll be getting more plant for your money. The better plant buys at local garden centers are bedding annuals and vegetable seedlings.

It is hard to beat the quality you can expect from a plant sold by its grower. Look for garden centers with their own nurseries, and you will usually get better material. Of course, if the plants have been grown under special conditions, you may have trouble keeping the plant growing just as well. Ask. Natural conditions similar to your own are a better bet. Plants purchased from a mail-order source across the country may not be suited to your growing conditions, by this reasoning. Be sure you check your reference books thoroughly before making a purchase via catalog that might not grow in your area.

Bargains are not worth the money you save if the plant dies soon after you get it home. They are only bargains if you really know what you are doing and have the resources to handle plant problems.

SHRUBS AND TREES

Much of what goes for shrubs applies to trees as well. Check to see that no weeds or grass is growing on the burlap root ball or container. Remember to remove any plastic string that is binding the ball when you plant it—only natural jute should be left on to disintegrate in the ground. Remove it from the neck of the plant.

One of the first things to look for is a shrub or tree that appears balanced. If a specimen has symmetry, you're on the right track. As for details, check for wounds and any splitting where the branches join the trunk. Research before you buy: Some trees or shrubs need lots of care or drop potentially annoying seedpods. Most shrubs want well-drained soil with some full sun. If you are interested in a tree or shrub with ornamental berries or flowers, you should check to learn whether the male and female flowers occur on the same plant or on separate plants. An example of this is the hollies, where the fruit is found only on the female plant, or the pussy willow, where the attractive bloom is only on the male plant.

Be sure to arrange for delivery at a convenient time so you can get your trees and shrubs in properly placed and sized holes without having to rearrange your whole life. Then be ready for the delivery to be late and have to be rearranged anyway. Plan the placement very carefully by determining the plant's mature size, both in height and width. You'll probably have to plant them a bit farther apart than you originally thought so they can fill in naturally and not hit the house or each other. Don't expect to be able to move them if you place them poorly. Take your time and plan very, very carefully.

Don't forget to have a good water source, the right fertilizer, and plenty of peat moss and humus on hand for the planting. Make sure that trees have no roots broken off, are delivered with proper containers or burlapped balls, and are staked sturdily once they are planted.

Of course some trees are purchased dead: Christmas trees. When buying any kind of *cut greens,* as these are called, check the branches: They should be soft and supple, not brittle. If they are brittle and many needles fall when you shake them, it is dried out, and should be avoided.

One last note: The actual distinction between trees and shrubs is not perfectly clear. Probably the most common definition is that shrubs are less than 10 or 12 feet tall and do not have real trunks.

Items of Special Interest to Gardeners with Physical Limits

Many tools are found in garden centers which are particularly comfortable to use or helpful to gardeners who have difficulty gripping, bending, kneeling, reaching, or are confined to wheelchairs. The most useful ones are noted as such throughout this book and are listed here as well.

Unfortunately, some of the specially designed tools are quite expensive. For those gardeners desiring these tools but who are on a limited budget, or just habitually frugal, passing them by should be no hardship: There are many ways to adapt regular tools for comfort and convenience. Use your creativity and lots of tape and foam rubber—and bicycle handlebar grips, Velcro, insulating pipe tape, and so on. Additional grips (many available from mail-order catalogs) can be attached partway up a long wooden handle. Lightweight interchangeable systems of heads and handles, "ladies'," "floral," and children's tools can be handled more easily from a wheelchair than regular tools. Your local botanic garden or Cooperative Extension office should be able to advise you if you cannot find suggestions in magazines and books.

Furthermore, there is such a wide range of design among the common tools that seeking out one that is particularly good for you should not be hard. For example, cultivating can be done standing up with long-handled tools instead of hand-held ones used from a kneeling position. With the right tool, weeding can be done with push-pull movement or just a pulling movement, instead of a lifting and digging movement. Read the descriptions of all these items in this book to note the differences between them.

Finally, garden design and planning have as much to do with the handicapped gardener's ability to enjoy work as anything—indeed, some consider it the most important thing. There are many theories on low-maintenance gardening and landscaping found in numerous articles and books, including specific barrier-free design elements such as wheelchair-high raised beds and built-in irrigation systems. Just putting houseplants at a convenient level or hanging them on pulleys can solve the problem in the simplest cases. Using slow-release or natural organic fertilizers generally reduces the number of times you have to apply fertilizer (see chapter 3), and proper mulching (chapter 2) helps reduce weeds. Ultimately, gadgets are only part of the solution to the challenge of making gardening something everyone can enjoy.

Items of special interest include:

Chapter 5: Digging Tools and Wheel Goods

Bulb planter (long handle)
Cultifork (scoop-headed garden fork)
Dibble (long-handled)
Garden cart
Trowel (long handle, offset, and trigger grip)

Chapter 6: Cultivating, Weeding, and Raking Tools

Back-saver rake
Dandelion digger
Garden rake (made of tubular aluminum)
Hand fork (long-handled and trigger grip models)
Heart hoe
High wheel cultivator
Spiked wheel cultivator
The original weeder
Weed slicer
Weeding hoes
Yard arm, or handy weeder (or spring-operated puller)

Chapter 7: Pruning, Cutting, and Trimming Tools

All power tools, especially cordless models
Flower gatherer
Flower shears with butterfly handles
Grass shears with trigger grip
Long-handled grass shears
Long-reach fruit and flower picker
Long-reach pole saw and lopper (pump-style pole pruner)
Pruning shears (with long reach extension and lever, and with ratchet)
String trimmer
Swing blade and grass whip
Weed hook (pull-action pruner)

Chapter 8: Maintenance Tools and Equipment

Aerator sandals
Bags and accessories (hoop to hold bags open)
Blower
Compost aerator tool
Compression sprayer (pressurized hand sprayer)
Drip irrigation system
Hanging plant waterer (pump-action)
Herbicide applicator
Hose guides
Hose reel (and hose reel cart)
House hose
Quick-connect hose system
Shutoff valve
Soaker hose
Traveling sprinkler
Trombone sprayer
Water controller
Water wand
Water wick
Watering can (long-reach style)

Chapter 9: Starting Products and Gardening Aids

Capillary waterer
Hooks, hangers, and brackets (with pulleys and swivels, pot clips)
Plant ties (from reels, made of wire)
Plastic planter (with self-watering feature)
Rigid plant trellis
Seed-planting template
Seeder (long handle as well as hand-sized devices)
Trellis net

Chapter 10: Personal and Miscellaneous Gear and Equipment

Graden scoop
Knee protectors (pads and bench)
Lawn tweezers

APPENDIX C

Information Sources

Choosing products to use in your garden involves biology and philosophy as much as it does good common sense. While garden center personnel (and this book) can help you learn to differentiate among the various products available, to determine what your basic needs and desires are and what type of solution you feel comfortable with, you may want to consult with other experts. Three areas (besides the thousands of books and magazines available) are good places to start: your local Cooperative Extension, organizations and companies devoted to consumer awareness regarding fertilizers and pesticides, and your local botanic garden.

The *Cooperative Extension* is an agency of the Department of Agriculture and functions from the land-grant university in each state. A Cooperative Extension office is located in each county in the country, and is listed in your phone book under any of a variety of titles, though it should be the college name followed by "Cooperative Extension." Keep looking if you don't find it right away—it may be listed under the county name or with the county or state government offices. Call a botanic garden

for help if need be. Each office has many helpful publications and programs.

The activities and publications of each office are tailored to its constituency: In urban areas, they may help start community vegetable gardens in abandoned lots or teach classes in home economics; in rural areas, they may specialize in that region's crop, such as fruit trees or cotton, and so are oriented to help professional growers; all are active with the 4-H clubs. Suburban ones usually have information about chemicals and insects as well as houseplants and vegetables. A few have clinics or diagnostic labs available on a fee basis. Research at the state's land-grant college is often focused on a policy on particular products or weather conditions, such as droughts. Most offices have a list of publications available that indicates which are free and those for which there is a charge. Not all are oriented to the amateur gardener— many are geared to farmers, nursery owners, or landscape architects. Because of their relationship with the land-grant colleges and the FDA experiment stations, they are your best source of current research-based information.

Nothing is more fundamental to gardening than knowing the makeup of your soil, both in terms of structure and acidity (chapter 1) and in terms of nutrients (chapter 3). Though reference books can be a big help in analyzing your soil structure, and there are plenty of test kits available for analyzing the acidity and nutrient level of your soil, it makes sense to call on experts, especially for a first time, at Cooperative Extension offices. Most offices—and some of the larger garden centers—can do an extremely thorough and accurate soil test for you. Although there is a nominal fee for a soil test, usually under $10, the results are much more accurate than those you get from a simplistic, inexpensive, off-the-shelf kit. And it's a government service.

There are a good number of places to turn to for help in learning about fertilizers and pesticides. The synthetic chemical approach is pretty thoroughly covered by the bulk of advertising and existing literature, and the EPA (see address below) has many good publications. The catalogs that specialize in natural organic products, listed in appendix D, are an easy place to start for alternatives to synthetic chemical products. Check your library for numerous books and magazines on this subject which are not normally sold in bookstores and at newsstands. Many magazine editors will handle basic questions with ease or send you back issues on the subject you ask about. You can also write:

United States Environmental Protection Agency
Office of Pesticides and Toxic Substances
401 M Street, SW
Washington, DC 20460
Attention: Chief, Document Management Section (H7502C)
Information Services Branch
703-557-4474

Many publications are free, and detailed reports on individual chemicals are available for a standard fee. Ask for a list.

NCAMP (National Coalition Against the Misuse of Pesticides)
530 7th Street, SE
Washington, DC 20003
202-543-5450

Ask for brochures or newsletters on a variety of subjects.

Bio-Integral Resource Center
P.O. Box 7414
Berkeley, CA 94707
415-524-2567

Ask for their publications catalog. Newsletter is available.

Many botanic gardens or horticultural societies are terrific sources of all kinds of information, from the purely practical to the purely theoretical. Whether or not they have an educational program, most are staffed by gardeners who may informally share information you don't readily find in traditional sources, especially during the less busy seasons. Look them up in your phone book, or try the book *American Gardens: A Traveler's Guide* (Plants and Gardens Handbook Series #111, Brooklyn Botanic Garden Record, vol. 42, no. 3, 1000 Washington Avenue, Brooklyn, NY 11225). It lists some 250 public gardens around the country.

Mail-Order Catalog Guide

While there is no doubt that garden centers generally supply whatever the gardener really needs, as well as personal service and expertise, there is an element of dream and fantasy that mail-order catalogs provide what garden centers just do not, especially off-season. Think of them as a particularly convenient browsers' heaven. In any case, it is a firmly established tradition to shop by mail for many garden items.

In keeping within the parameters of this book, all noteworthy catalogs reviewed here feature tools and supplies—the hard lines and packaged goods. There are plenty of seed and nursery catalogs, but they are not listed, though many offer both types of items.

All mail-order sources back up their products with a guarantee, though some are explicitly more flexible and reassuring than others. Be sure to note the conditions before ordering. (If you are ordering seeds, bulbs, or plants, note that most catalogs have a Plant Hardiness Zone map, which you should refer to, or else call your local Cooperative Extension office to determine your zone or to see if a particular plant is borderline for your area. Many catalogs list the acceptable zones alongside each plant.) And don't let the term *mail order* limit you to the written word: Many catalogs have real folks at an 800 number who are more than willing to chat and, of course, take orders. Some have a fax number for electronic mail convenience and efficiency—a nice new twist. Many of the catalogs have a special number for customer service or technical questions in addition to the order number shown, but those numbers are not listed here.

One general note of interest: Virtually all of the catalogs contain a personal note from the owner, usually on the inside cover. This seems to be some sort of tradition, but in any case, it highlights the warm, personal feeling most of us have about gardening—and the high competition among the catalogs in regard to service and quality.

This listing is not meant to be all-inclusive but rather a sampling of the better-known catalogs that offer a variety of merchandise. Catalogs that feature only one manufacturer's items are not included. Omission or inclusion of a catalog does not reflect or imply approval or disapproval.

The Alsto Company—"Handy Helpers"

"Practical Products for Your Home, Yard, &
   Garden"
P.O. Box 1267
Galesburg, IL 61401
800-447-0048

Though at first glance this looks like many of
the other glossy color catalogs, the pictures are
not too clear and the copy is often quite long.
Consecutive editions feature mostly the same
items, but with a different layout and new
photos and copy.

The choice of items includes many common
and some uncommon high-quality garden supplies, tools, and gift items, such as an electronic
rain gauge that measures up to 100 inches of
rain and never needs emptying, garden furniture, products for cutting, splitting, and stack-
ing firewood, gloves, tools, rubber boots, and
many nongarden gadgets. Less than half the
pages are devoted to garden items—the rest is
general home maintenance, leisure, or furniture
products.

Bird'n Hand—"Pure seed bird feed"

40 Pearl Street
Framingham, MA 01701
508-879-1552

With a formal design and conservative range
of items well-suited to its gentle subject, this
catalog specializes in gourmet food for birds,
but also carries feeders of many designs. Feeds
listed contain no fillers of any kind and are a bit
more expensive per pound, but it goes farther
(so they claim) than normal seed. Twelve types
of seed are offered so you can tailor your feedings to attract your favorite birds. The birdseed
is backed with a full money-back guarantee. (A
larger but slicker, more commercial catalog is
put out by Duncraft®, Penacook, New Hampshire 03303-9020, Tel. 603-224-0200.)

A handy feature of this catalog is an Automatic Supply Shipment which can be paid up
yearly so you don't have to continually reorder.
All prices include freight.

Brookstone—Hard-to-Find Tools

127 Vose Farm Road
Peterborough, NH 03458
603-924-9541 (24 hours a day)

Brookstone wrote the book on browser-ori-
ented catalogs, so to speak, and has done very
well since the mid-1970s. Their bright and colorful layout, with crystal-clear color photos, is
cheerful and well written, though it is quite
busy and crammed with exclamatory headlines.

Not just a garden catalog, Brookstone's section of tools and equipment for the garden and
greenhouse fills under one-third of their summer catalog. Included are such items as sundials, hose guides, spigot extenders, edgers,
weeding tools, ultrasonic bird chasers, solid
brass hose fittings, tool hangers, hose repair
kits, a faucet rethreader, earth auger bits, folding wheelbarrows, a flat hose and reel, a back-
saving wheeled rake, a lightweight scythe, and
so on—a strong emphasis on the unusual.

Clapper's Garden Catalog

1125 Washington Street
West Newton, MA 02165
617-244-7909
Fax: 617-244-5260

An interesting hybrid of an organization,
Clapper's has an institutional and professional
background that dates from 1922. The catalog's
orientation is definitely toward those with, as
they say in their introductory note, "suburban
and country properties." Thus it is no surprise
to find that the first part of the catalog is devoted to furniture and accessories that include

a $4,000 circular tree seat made of teak and a $300 faux terra-cotta planter. The color photography is regular catalog photography, but because all the tools are grouped into one photo per spread, they are more clearly visible than in most catalogs.

Items featured include carts, wooden wheelbarrows, and a full selection of reasonably priced, well-made garden tools. There is a good assortment of hand tools, plus burlap, canvas totes, Wellington boots, gloves, plant supports, watering cans, sprayers, hoses, flower arranging accessories, wind chimes, and botanical prints, as well as a small selection of gift books. Their retail store is located in one of the fanciest suburbs of Boston, but their professional equipment is well chosen and well priced.

Gardener's Eden—A Garden Catalog from Williams-Sonoma

P.O. Box 7307
San Francisco, CA 94120-7307
415-421-4242

Published three times a year, this is a catalog with a refined feel, definitely for the upscale, leisure- and convenience-minded gardener. Each catalog focuses on products appropriate for each season. Prices on selected items are often marked down 15 to 20 percent, at least in the late summer catalog.

There is a consistent style, quality, and tone to the gift-type products listed, which include French wire baskets, florist's buckets, odd ornaments like a bee skep (a woven grass beehive), English watering cans, many vases and beautiful containers, potpourri saucers, wreaths, shoe/boot brushes, wooden doormats, and garden furniture. Serious tools and practical equipment are listed in black and white on the order blank, under a category called "Simple Solutions," as though it was an afterthought.

Gardener's Supply—Innovative Gardening Solutions

128 Intervale Road
Burlington, VT 05401
802-863-1700 (24 hours, 7 days a week for credit card orders)

A pleasant, unpretentious catalog with reasonable prices and a large variety of items, with an emphasis on well-chosen selections of practical and serious equipment. Published twice a year, the spring catalog features seed starting products, while the fall catalog features chippers and shredders as well as equipment for canning fruit and vegetables. Some of the items are products that they developed themselves or helped develop in their own test gardens with the help of friends, test gardeners around the country, and the university as well as the State of Vermont. They also are active in a number of nonprofit gardening activities there and abroad, including the management of a compost pile that produces 700 tons annually. Each product description is quite informative, and the color photos feature many older people as "models," lending genuine, down-to-earth feeling to the whole production. Definitely for the serious gardener. A retail store and greenhouse/garden area are located in Burlington.

Gardener's Supply includes only organic fertilizers and safe, natural pest controls, as well as biodegradable trash bags. Standard listings are quite wide-ranging and include portable and permanent greenhouses, row covers, minimum/maximum thermometers, kneepads, boot brushes, trellises, bean poles, tomato ties, soil test kits, rotary tillers, sprayers, flower supports, garden carts, hand tools, edging, books, gloves, birdhouses and feeders, sundials, and a few pieces of modestly priced furniture. Surprisingly few everyday tools are listed—only special ones. One interesting item is Rodent Rocks, porous lava stones that have been soaked in an herbal formula containing garlic and onion. When buried, the rocks give off an odor that repels most rodents.

Gardens Alive!—Natural Gardening Research Center

Highway 48 P.O. Box 149
Sunman, IN 47041
812-623-3800

Of all the catalogs listed here, this is perhaps the least inviting to read, let alone look at. It has the smallest print and the smallest pictures of any of the catalogs reviewed, condensed into a dense layout. Furthermore, numerous "editions" are almost alike.

However, some of the copy is educational, including a nine-page section on pests complete with color photos. They have a comprehensive collection of organic, nontoxic, and biological controls for many pests, including a good selection of live insect predators like ladybugs and spined soldier bugs, as well as beneficial nematodes. Gardens Alive! also lists bird supplies (including one of the more exotic items, a birdbath heater), seed starting equipment, watering equipment, row covers, dusters and syringes for biological controls, and their own organic fertilizers or soil conditioners, all with the Alive! name. There is plenty of information found among the product listings, if you can stand looking for it.

The Growing Naturally Catalog

P.O. Box 54
149 Pine Lane
Pineville, PA 18946
215-598-7025

An attractive annual catalog, with its green print on buff-colored paper, Growing Naturally is intended for gardeners and small-scale farmers who are dedicated to organic and "low input" farming and gardening. The copy is both friendly and informative, and gives the impression that each item has been carefully chosen at the exclusion of many others—unlike some more commercial catalogs that are equally effusive about similar items. Prices are very good.

Includes mostly natural organic fertilizers, conditioners, and pest control products, with a notably large section of beneficial insects and biological controls, some natural pet-care products, and a very tight selection of basic but high-quality tools, equipment, and watering devices.

Harmony Farm Supply

P.O. Box 451
Graton, CA 95444
707-823-9125
Fax: 707-823-1734

A straightforward catalog that is dedicated to organic farming, it caters to small farmers as well as home gardeners. Almost half of the pages are dedicated to irrigation equipment, including some inexpensive drip irrigation material. Laid out clearly and simply in black and white on newsprint, most copy is extremely informative and thorough. Comes out two to three times a year. Started in 1980 by an entomologist and her irrigation engineer husband to help organic farmers—except for some noted exceptions, no materials are sold that do not meet the California Organic Foods Act, and nothing is synthetically compounded. The warehouse is open for visitors six days a week (4050 Ross Road, Sebastopol, CA).

Items include an incredible range of irrigation equipment, tools and equipment that run the gamut from kitchen utensils to power sprayers, and ten pages of books. Also lists their workshops—half a dozen during a typical summer—on ecological pest controls, pruning, and drip irrigation, for example.

Kinsman Company—Gardener's Catalog
"Special gardening items we use ourselves"

River Road
Point Pleasant, PA 18950
215-297-5613

Kinsman has an amusing range of items that are both fun and practical. Along with the top-quality English hand tools, they feature such everyday but hard-to-find items as barbecue covers and tool hooks, as well as a number of simple decorative items like weather vanes and leaded glass roundels, Victorian plant holders, and wall baskets. There is a fine assortment of watering cans, cold frames (including a portable one), pot hangers, specialized bags and aprons, a good selection of plant supports, arbors, leaf-exclusive gutters, and tool sharpeners. Prices are average and include the cost of freight. Kinsman has a warehouse store in Point Pleasant.

Langenbach—A Collection of the World's Finest Garden Tools

P.O. Box 453
38 Millbrook-Stillwater Road
Blairstown, NJ 07825
201-362-5886

Perhaps the least cluttered, easiest to read, and most focused of all the catalogs, Langenbach limits itself to a small number of imported, high-quality tools, equipment, and accessories, with an emphasis on hand tools. Very serious writing, though personal, with little comments in a number of captions. In fact, the whole enterprise is small and personal—Paul Langenbach himself might answer the phone if you call. But this is no fly-by-night family circus. The Langenbachs have a vineyard and winery in New Jersey and were on a quest for these tools for use on their property, then spent about four years putting the catalog together, getting the first one out in 1989. Superior reproduction of color photos on heavy stock.

Characteristically, they feature mirror-polished stainless steel Burgon & Ball English spades and forks on the cover and first four pages. Other high-quality items include Gardena tools and system, Felco pruners, and the Solo power system, and a stand-out selection of unusual wooden-handled English machetes and unique hoes, and a very cleverly designed British garden cart. Also includes a small collection of gift books.

Mellinger's—Garden Catalog for Year-Round Country Living

2310 West South Range Road
North Lima, OH 44452-9731
800-321-7444

Mellinger's once-yearly catalog opens up not only with the usual personal letter, but with a snapshot of at least three generations of Mellingers and in-laws who run the place, including founder Port B. Mellinger, in his eighties, who, according to the caption, "remains active at his desk every day." A traditional-looking catalog packed full of listings in columns, it is as useful to the professional grower (for whom there is a special section) as it is accessible to the home gardener. Brief copy lacks hyperbole, making it easy to read, and the range is all-inclusive (a complete index is found near the rear). Despite its "Ma and Pa" appearance, it is a very large operation with real business rules. Plants are guaranteed one year. Merchandise is "sold according to manufacturer's warranty," except sale items, and any product returned for general dissatisfaction is subject to a 10 percent handling charge.

Just under half of this catalog is devoted to hundreds of plants, while the rest lists one of the most complete selections of garden supplies, soil conditioners, tools, books, birdseed, beneficial insects, bonsai tools, and pesticides (including a special organic section) found in any consumer-oriented catalog. It has the most extensive book listing of all the catalogs, with over one hundred titles included, grouped by subject. Books may be returned and exchanged within seven days. Also includes a few pages of cooking utensils and processing accessories. Retail store at headquarters, which, a map says, is not near Lima, Ohio—*North* Lima is near Youngstown. Prices are competitive and there are many small items that can be had for just a few dollars.

The Necessary Catalogue—"From the Earth for the Earth"

Necessary Trading Company
New Castle, VA 24127
800-447-5354 (Answering machine. Open Saturdays in the spring)
Fax: 703-864-5186

Published annually since 1978, the Necessary is oriented to the serious organic gardener or small farmer, but also to the knowledgeable home gardener—it even includes pet and houseplant products. Specializing in the latest in biotechnological problem solvers that are natural, biologically safe, and nonpolluting, they claim to list only products that "fit into the natural cycle," which underlies the attitude that permeates the whole catalog. The copy is educational and interesting as well as straightforward, including details on how the products are derived, some IPM orientation, and a how-to box in most sections.

This is probably the most complete listing of natural pest control products among the catalogs. Items include slug and beetle kits, a fruit fly trap that looks like an apple, fly swatters, sticky yellow pest paper, an entire line of Bt products, dormant oil, animal traps, deer repellents, sulfur fungicides, sprayers and dusters, and a wetting agent for powders. There are

plenty of organic fertilizers and soil conditioners. Equipment includes advanced soil testing and analyzing equipment (including a $200 optical refractometer), compost turners, spreaders, and a soil thermometer. They also have green manures (cover crops planted in fall and turned under in the spring) and a good listing of books and pamphlets on subjects of interest to organic gardeners. Very orderly—there is a table of contents as well as an index. Prices are very competitive.

The Nitron Formula—Natural Products for Organic Gardening

Nitron Industries, Inc.
4605 Johnson Road
P.O. Box 1447
Fayetteville, AR 72702-0400
800-835-0123
Fax: 501-750-3008

One of the most educational catalogs to read, Nitron features few items but spends as much as a page on each. Nitron is a unique catalog for two reasons. The first pages are devoted exclusively to touting and explaining their basic product, a natural, nontoxic enzyme soil conditioner called Formula A-35, and much of their catalog is given over to explaining organic gardening. They sponsor an annual organic growers' seminar and even have a list of organic growers and suppliers as one of their products. Long testimonial letters fill one page and are scattered throughout the rest of the catalog, giving a feeling that Nitron is on some kind of mission. They put out five or six issues a year, and have been selling enzymes since 1977. Though they have a basic unconditional guarantee, it is expressed vaguely, albeit warmly: They just say to call them and talk to them about your problem.

Items made with their natural enzymes include compost starter, septic tank cleaners, jewelry cleaners, and pet deodorizers. Also listed are a few tools and gifts, a few books, water filters, soaker hoses and a good selection of organic fertilizers (including bat guano), soil builders, and conditioners such as earthworm castings and greensand. Although there is a page that explains "Enzymes and Trace Elements," it does not really define them satisfactorily. Prices are average.

Park Seed Co.—Flowers and Vegetables and Bulbs
"Park Helps You Grow"

Cokesbury Road
Greenwood, SC 29647-0001
803-223-7333
800-845-3369

Since 1868, Park Seed Co. has been family owned, and the catalog maintains an appropriate all-American, traditional tone. You actually have to hunt for the phone number—they are that traditional about "mail order." And there are pictures of cute kids chomping on corn on the cob or hovering around giant jack-o'-lanterns. But this is the largest company of its kind. The basic catalog is full of bright color photos of flowers, fruit, and vegetables for 123 pages, followed by 8 pages of seed starting and garden maintenance products. No tools are listed.

Catalogs are issued twice a year (one is just for bulbs), and products concentrate on seed propagation, of course, including seed trays, Jiffy-7 pots, seedbed mulches, pH measurers, soil heating cables, thermometers, plant supports, solar window openers, plant-light units, and growing media. A number of the products are their own inventions. It is convenient to order seed and supplies at the same time from this sensible selection.

Peaceful Valley Farm Supply

P.O. Box 2209
Grass Valley, CA 95945
916-272-GROW

This simply illustrated, straightforward catalog, printed on newsprint, has one of the most serious tones of all the catalogs. Featuring products for state-of-the-art sustainable agriculture, they include only ecologically sound growing supplies and services. They are so sincere that they offer comments on gardening techniques which would actually eliminate the need for the product being described, and offer on-site consultation by one of their staff members, classes, seminars, pest and irrigation management, comprehensive soil audits, animal feed analysis, and plant tissue analysis—all a great help for those new to organic farming. They also offer radionics testing "only to growers who are progressive, open minded and able to follow directions" *(sic)*. Very obviously oriented toward the small farmer, but large enough to have items for the home gardener as well. Open Monday through Saturday, 9:00 A.M. to 5:30 P.M.

Peaceful Valley carries animal health and pet products, books, chipper/shredders, cold frames, composting aids and equipment, seed mixes, hand tools, gourmet vegetable seeds, microbial inoculants, an extensive selection of natural pest control items, tools for monitoring pests, ladders, watering equipment, and heavy-duty farm equipment.

The Plow & Hearth—Products for Country Living

560 Main Street
Madison, VA 22727
800-527-5247

Well-printed color photos on good paper make this one of the nicer catalogs that arrive two or more times during the year, and they not only guarantee everything unconditionally, but offer a guarantee on lowest prices as well. However, the copy headlines tend to the declaratory, which wears thin after a while.

Only eight or so pages out of forty list garden tools and equipment. The rest is furniture, pet, and household gadgets and gift items. Garden items include planters, a small sundial, croquet sets, bird supplies, a bat box, several pages of Adirondack furniture (assembled and in kits), and novelty items like weather vanes and wind chimes. There is even a propane torch for burning weeds.

Ringer Lawn & Garden Products Catalog—100% Natural

"Ringer's natural products work to achieve and maintain a biologically active and balanced soil. The result is stronger, healthier plants."

> 9959 Valley View Road
> Eden Prairie, MN 55344-3585
> 800-654-1047 plus answering machine; 7 days during spring
> Fax 612-941-5036

Just to underscore the fact that organic gardening is nothing new, Ringer points out that they have been around since 1962, and they have a slick commercial image that makes their products, especially for lawns, compare directly with those from the big petrochemical companies. Their own line of fertilizing and soil-building products is substantial, and they are expanding into natural pest control items. A bright, all color, easily read catalog that comes out in spring and fall editions. Prices are average but include shipping, though a $1 handling fee is added to any order.

The catalog is filled chiefly with Ringer's own line of natural lawn and garden products. Their biologically safe, organic lawn fertilizers and conditioners differ from others in that they contain the microorganisms needed to break the material down and make it accessible to the plants; they build the soil structure and increase the biological activity. Their long-range benefits to the soil and root development make them well worth any extra cost, although they are hard to compare directly to traditional products. A small variety of supplies and products from other manufacturers include grass seed, a soil testing service (unique among the catalogs, but more expensive than the Cooperative Extension), an inexpensive hand lawn mower, biodegradable garbage bags, a soil core sampler, stump remover, pruning tools, compost bins and supplies (and compost itself, in case you can't make your own), chipper/shredders, sprayers, watering accessories, and small plastic greenhouses.

Smith & Hawken—Catalog for Gardeners, Bulb Book, Garden Furniture, Rose & Gerard Catalog

> 25 Corte Madera
> Mill Valley, CA 94941
> 415-383-2000 or 800-777-4556
> Rose & Gerard: 415-383-4050
> Fax: 415-383-7030

The Smith & Hawken Catalog sets the standard for good design, effective copy, and general polite and respectful attitude toward the consumer. They even send a confirmation letter for orders that are going out the same day. Probably the most readable catalog of all.

Smith & Hawken has become one of the more popular garden supply catalogs, making a reputation among gardeners largely because of the quality of their merchandise, the variety of the selection, and the caring and often personal service one gets when ordering from them. They also demonstrate a corporate concern for the environment, doing things like buying teak from commercial tree plantations and otherwise showing an intelligent choice of suppliers.

Their choice of items is incomplete in the tool area but does cover the basics with a tinge of the whimsical. It includes genuine Panama hats, Sussex trugs (low baskets), some special vegetable seed collections, a few helpful books, pigskin garden gloves, sprayers, praying mantis egg cases, ladybugs, and other organic pest control items (these only in the spring), garden clogs, soil blockers, nursery flats, watering devices, Reemay floating row covers, Felco pruners, children's tools (good ones—not flimsy ones), plant supports, wildflower field mixes, sheep shears and other hand tools, top-quality English shovels and spades, as well as extensive and beautiful selections of accessories and furniture very obviously oriented to the gift market. Surprisingly for an outfit that stresses quality so much, their prices are average or only a few dollars more than in other catalogs. Service is excellent.

They started another forty-page catalog just for beautiful decorative and accessory items, "the garden as idiom" in their words, called *Rose & Gerard.* Some of the furniture is found in the regular catalog, but this catalog contains no tools. It does contain incredibly lush, romantic, flower-filled photos of fine garden furniture and accessories that range so far afield that they include terra-cotta candelabras and hand-loomed place mats, as well as French olive oil soap.

plies and equipment are listed side by side. Illustrations are mostly simple line drawings though there are a good number of very, very gray photos on the plain paper. The layout is simple and clear, and there is an easy-to-read table of contents. Intended for the serious gardener as well as the gadget hound, prices are among the lowest of all the catalogs.

Tools, almost all of which are imported from Europe, include modified designs of planters, weeders, and hoes, including items like the West German hoelike tool that "cultivates ground without destroying the natural soil layers, thus preserving the subsurface microenvironment for soil bacteria. In addition, the Bio-Aerator is made of a copper alloy, and therefore, does not leave traces of iron in the soil to deplete oxygen." They also carry tools crafted specifically for gardeners with disabilities, such as a curved-handle, solid-cast trowel for people with carpal tunnel syndrome and arthritis. Other items include how-to books, a cold frame, small greenhouse equipment, and various propagation products, as well as lots of watering accessories. Despite all the practical items, it is not surprising somehow to see a listing for "gay blade" windmills, listed with the admonition, "Order a windmill and give yourself and the kids a giggle." At only $3.95, it is a nice complement to the $89.95 stainless steel spades.

Walt Nicke's Garden Talk

36 McLead Lane
P.O. Box 433
Topsfield, MA 01983
508-887-3388

Published three times a year, this simple black-and-white catalog is particularly inviting, perhaps because of its personal feel. Enthusiastic but detailed descriptions satisfy your curiosity, and common and uncommon garden sup-

Wind & Weather Catalogue

The Albion Street Watertower
P.O. Box 2320
Mendocino, CA 95460
800-922-9463

One of the few catalogs that specializes in a particular area, this one is entirely devoted to weather devices and sundials. Despite its narrow range, it is quite interesting and pleasantly readable, although it has a cluttered design with annoyingly small print. Items range from high-tech barographs to folk-art wind vanes, including humidity and rain gauges, all kinds of sundials (even a pocket model), wind chimes, books, cloud charts, calendars, and logs.

Catalogs for the Professional

Three catalogs stand out for range of choice, price, and service. However, before you call them up, please note that they cater to repeat business from professional horticulturalists, whether they be groundskeepers of institutions, growers, florists, growers, foresters, landscapers, or arborists. They do not relish handling small orders (though they all will, for a fee of a few dollars).

These three companies differ in two primary ways from the consumer-oriented catalogs listed here. First, their selection is much more extensive, with many more items than even a fully stocked garden center, in many cases without narrowing the choice for you (they may carry several lines of the same tool). Second, in place of the nice personal letter in the front, they usually have a "statement of terms of conditions of sale" in contract language, noting restrictions for returns and guarantees—quite opposed to those of the consumer catalogs. It is really quite a different ball of wax.

Good-Prod Sales, Inc.
825 Fairfield Avenue
Kenilworth, NJ 07033
201-245-5055
Fax: 201-245-6906
Tools, supplies, and ornaments (many items for resale).

A. H. Hummert Seed Co.
2746 Chouteau Avenue
St. Louis, MO 63103
800-325-3055
Fax: 314-771-5203
(Catalog costs $35)
Tools, supplies, nursery equipment, greenhouses, and greenhouse equipment Established 1934.

A. M. Leonard, Inc.
6665 Spiker Road
Piqua, OH 45356
800-543-8955
Fax: 513-773-8640
Quality tools and equipment only—no supplies. More amenable to consumer orders than the others. Two editions per year: Spring/Summer and Summer/Fall. Established 1885.

Index

Note: *Italics* indicate main item entries.